Teach
Yourself
JavaScript

in a Week

Teach Yourself
JavaScript
in a Week

Arman Danesh

201 West 103rd Street
Indianapolis, Indiana 46290

To my parents—Michele and Hossain—for instilling in me a thirst for knowledge, and to my wife—Tahirih—who inspires me to press forward.

Copyright © 1996 by Sams.net Publishing

FIRST EDITION

International Standard Book Number: 1-57521-073-8

Library of Congress Catalog Card Number: 95-72943

99 98 97 96   4 3 2 1

Interpretation of the printing code: the rightmost double-digit number is the year of the book's printing; the rightmost single-digit, the number of the book's printing. For example, a printing code of 96-1 shows that the first printing of the book occurred in 1996.

Composed in AGaramond and MCPdigital by Macmillan Computer Publishing

Printed in the United States of America

President, Sams Publishing	Richard K. Swadley
Publishing Manager	Mark Taber
Managing Editor	Cindy Morrow
Marketing Manager	John Pierce
Assistant Marketing Manager	Kristina Perry

Acquisitions Editor
Mark Taber

Development Editor
Kelly Murdock

Software Development Specialist
Merle Newlon

Production Editor
Marla Reece

Technical Reviewer
Wes Tatters

Editorial Coordinator
Bill Whitmer

Technical Edit Coordinator
Lynette Quinn

Formatter
Frank Sinclair

Editorial Assistants
Carol Ackerman
Andi Richter
Rhonda Tinch-Mize

Cover Designer
Tim Amrhein

Book Designer
Gary Adair

Copy Writer
Peter Fuller

Production Team Supervisor
Brad Chinn

Production
Mary Ann Abramson
Stephen Adams, Carol Bowers
Mona Brown, Michael Dietsch
Tim Griffin, Jason Hand
Sonja Hart, Ayanna Lacey
Clint Lahnen, Laura Robbins
Bobbi Satterfield, Laura A. Smith
Mark Walchle, Todd Wente
Colleen Williams

Overview

Contents

Acknowledgments

Writing this book has been a process that has involved many people. I particularly would like to thank the staff at Sams.net who worked with me in developing the manuscript: Kelly Murdock, Marla Reece, and Mark Taber and many others I am sure were involved.

I would also like to thank Gautam Das at the Bahá'í World Centre in Haifa, Israel, for reading sections of the book as I was writing it.

About the Author

Arman Danesh

Arman Danesh works as the Web Development Specialist at the Bahá'í World Centre in Haifa, Israel. He is also Editorial Director of Juxta Publishing Limited, based in Hong Kong. He received his Masters of Science in mass communication from Boston University in 1990. He has also worked as a technology journalist and is a regular contributor and Internet columnist for the *South China Morning Post* and *The Dataphile*. Arman lives with his wife, Tahirih, in Haifa.

Introduction

The World Wide Web has come a long way since its days as a modest hypertext system used by a few scientists to share information on the Internet.

Today the World Wide Web is the medium of information exchange for millions of people. They are sharing text, video, sound, and data, and increasingly, they are trying to make their Web pages interactive. Businesses are trying to sell their products, artists are producing new forms of interactive art, and programmers are producing program development aids—all delivered via the World Wide Web and accessed from inside everyday Web browser applications.

In many ways, we are in the midst of an information revolution with a move away from document-centric computing to a network-centric paradigm. Right at the center of this shift is Netscape Communications and its immensely popular Web browser, Netscape Navigator.

By incorporating Java from Sun Microsystems and its own JavaScript scripting language into the current version of the Netscape Navigator browser, Netscape has helped generate a flurry of movement on the World Wide Web aimed at creating interactive documents and information.

Java is a platform-independent programming language designed for distributed applications on the Internet. JavaScript presently enhances the functionality of the immensely popular Netscape Navigator Web browser, enabling Web authors and developers to produce content that changes in response to user actions—dynamic data that makes information more accessible and easier to organize and digest.

In this book we are going to take a look at JavaScript—the internal scripting language Netscape has developed and included in the Navigator browser.

JavaScript is an evolving tool, like so many tools associated with the Internet and the World Wide Web. Still, the future of JavaScript is sufficiently clear that many people have already developed sophisticated Web-based applications using the language.

Goal of this Book

As I mentioned in the Introduction, this book is designed to teach the JavaScript scripting language.

We start by taking a broad look at Netscape Navigator 2.0, the current version of the popular Web browser, which some estimates say commands more than 80 percent of the Web browser market. Following this, we take an introductory look at JavaScript and its relationship with Java and its place in the Netscape suite of Web development tools.

Once this is done, we will be ready to look at the nuts and bolts of the JavaScript language and learn how to apply them to real-world scenarios on the Web. JavaScript can be used to add a wide range of interactivity and functionality to Web pages, including the following:

- ☐ Dynamic forms that include built-in error checking
- ☐ Spread sheets and calculators
- ☐ User interaction in the form of warning messages and confirmation messages
- ☐ Dynamic changes to text and background colors
- ☐ The ability to analyze URLs and access URLs in a user's history list
- ☐ The capability to open, name, clear, and close new windows and direct output to specific frames

These types of functions already appear in numerous Web sites on the World Wide Web, and it is expected that the number will grow rapidly in early 1996, now that Navigator 2.0 has moved from a beta product to commercial release software.

Throughout the book, you will have the opportunity to develop several small scripts that you can immediately use in your own Web pages.

Finally, we close with an overview of the future of JavaScript and where it seems to be heading. We will consider Netscape's plans as well as announcements from other companies to include JavaScript in their products.

Who Should Read This Book?

The JavaScript scripting language naturally interests a diverse group of people, including Web designers and authors, programmers, and application developers.

Web Authors and Designers

This book is clearly of interest to Web developers and authors with experience using HTML and designing Web sites, including using Netscape extensions. Although basic knowledge of HTML is assumed throughout the book, any advanced or complicated HTML tags being used are introduced and described as needed.

Naturally, programming knowledge and an understanding of the Common Gateway Interface (CGI)—used for adding interactivity at the server end—is helpful in any discussion of Web development. However, it is not essential for learning JavaScript, and readers with a sound knowledge of HTML tags can follow the lessons in this book. By the end of the book, not only will you be able to write simple (and complex) JavaScript programs, but you also will have learned to use some of the newer Netscape extensions to HTML.

Others

Naturally, discussion of a programming language such as JavaScript is not solely of interest to Web authors and designers.

Programmers looking to add the latest technology to their list of credits are increasingly interested in learning JavaScript. In addition, applications developers looking at Navigator 2.0 as an engine for deploying platform-independent graphical user interface applications will quickly find that JavaScript is going to play a critical role in implementing their applications.

Preparing to Begin

In order to take full advantage of this book, you will need several tools. A copy of the latest version of Netscape 2.0 is essential to develop and test program code. In addition, a good editing program that you feel comfortable using will make the program development process easier.

Where to Obtain Navigator 2.0

Today, JavaScript capabilities can be found only in Netscape's Navigator 2.0 Web browser. Navigator 2.0 moved from beta software to actual release software in early 1996.

In order to take full advantage of the lessons in this book, it is necessary to have access to a copy of Navigator 2.0 to try the examples and exercises for yourself. Navigator 2.0 is available for most computer platforms, including all versions of Windows, Mac OS, and a wide range of UNIX variants including Sun OS, Solaris, and Linux. At the present time, there is no native OS/2 version of Netscape Navigator available.

If you need to download a copy of the current version of Navigator 2.0, you can get it from Netscape's home page at `http://home.netscape.com/` or from Netscape's numerous ftp servers or their many mirrors:

`ftp://ftp.netscape.com/`

`ftp://ftp2.netscape.com/`

`ftp://ftp3.netscape.com/`

`ftp://ftp4.netscape.com/`

`ftp://ftp5.netscape.com/`

`ftp://ftp6.netscape.com/`

```
ftp://ftp7.netscape.com/
```

`ftp://ftp.leo.chubu.ac.jp/pub/WWW/netscape/` (Japan)

`ftp://sunsite.ust.hk/pub/WWW/netscape/` (Hong Kong)

`ftp://sunsite.huji.ac.il/Netscape/` (Israel)

`ftp://ftp.adelaide.edu.au/pub/WWW/Netscape/` (Australia)

`ftp://sunsite.doc.ic.ac.uk/computing/information-systems/www/Netscape/` (United Kingdom)

`ftp://ftp.informatik.rwth-aachen.de/pub/mirror/ftp.netscape.com/` (Germany)

`ftp://wuarchive.wustl.edu/packages/www/Netscape/` (U.S.A.)

`ftp://sunsite.unc.edu/pub/packages/infosystems/WWW/clients/Netscape` (U.S.A.)

Editing and Development Tools

In addition to a copy of Navigator 2.0, a strong editor or development tool will make the task of entering, developing, and debugging JavaScript much easier.

If you already do a lot of HTML authoring or programming, you probably have your own favorite tools that will be well-suited to JavaScript development. As long as your editing software produces plain ASCII text files, you should be just fine.

However, several tools may make it easier to develop, edit, and troubleshoot your JavaScript programs. In considering editors, it would be worth looking at tools that can help you identify the current line number for debugging scripts. In addition, the ability to launch Netscape Navigator from an editor is a useful feature already found in many HTML editors. Most HTML editors are suitable to JavaScript development, although a few—including leading products such as HoTMetaL—are designed to perform validation of HTML and can't be used to develop JavaScript scripts easily.

In addition to a high quality text or programming editor, many users may want to consider Netscape's Navigator 2.0 Gold. Although Navigator Gold was only available in an early beta version (beta 1) when this book was written, Netscape has indicated that it will take the Navigator 2.0 browser and add a suite of development and editing tools that make it easy for developers to produce interactive applications deployed on Netscape technology—all in a WYSIWYG (What You See Is What You Get) environment (or as close as is possible with the Web). More information about Navigator Gold is available from the site at

`http://home.netscape.com/comprod/products/navigator/version_2.0/gold.html`

Conventions in this Book

This book uses certain conventions to aid you, the reader, in your learning process.

 A *new term* is highlighted in italics or with this icon to clarify its meaning.

 NOTE

Note boxes highlight important or explanatory information in the surrounding text.

 TIP

These helpful nuggets offer insight or shortcuts to programming puzzles.

WARNING

Pay special attention to warnings. They may just save your system!

 TYPE This icon appears next to a listing that you should enter to follow along with the author's lesson. A listing without a Type icon is for illustration or explanation only.

➥This arrow at the beginning of a line of code means that a single line of code requires multiple lines on the page. Many lines of code contain a large number of characters, which might normally wrap on your screen. However, printing limitations require a break when lines reach a maximum number of characters. Continue typing all characters after the ➥ as though they are part of the previous line.

 OUTPUT Besides on-screen output, this icon is often used, in this book, to point to a figure that results from the preceding code listing.

 ANALYSIS The author offers detailed explanations regarding the parts and purposes of the code. (**Hint:** If you think you might not understand what the code is meant to perform, skip to this section before you input the listings!)

This book also uses `monospaced fonts` to denote terms, functions, keywords, variables, and so on, that are taken from or are part of the code. `monospaced italic` refers to a place holder that should be filled in with the actual number, variable, or value represented. Typically, HTML code terms are in ALL CAPS, while JavaScript terms are in the case required.

DAY

1

Chapter 1

Where Does JavaScript Fit In?

Navigator 2.0 is the most powerful version of Netscape's Web browser. Besides bringing together a collection of useful Internet-access tools, such as a mail client, a news reader, and improved support for the developing HTML 3 standard, Navigator 2.0 adds several features that enhance the ability of Web authors to develop complete, platform-independent applications deployed and executed in the Netscape browser. Going beyond the Web browser, Navigator Gold adds editing and development tools to the package.

These capabilities include an applications programmer's interface (API) for plug-ins. *Plug-ins* are program modules that dynamically extend the capability of Navigator 2.0 to handle new types of data and information, along with JavaScript and Java, which allow the addition of flexible progammability to Web pages.

In this chapter we take a detailed look at the main features and aspects of JavaScript, as well as review the major strengths and weaknesses of the JavaScript language and its suitability to particular tasks.

We then dive deeper into objects and how they work and take a look at properties and methods—the building blocks of objects. We also look at the built-in objects in JavaScript and what they offer the programmer.

In this chapter we take a broad look at Navigator 2.0 and consider how JavaScript fits into the puzzle. You'll learn about the following topics:

- Frames: The ability to divide a window into multiple, independent sections
- Plug-ins: Third-party add-ons for Navigator 2.0 that extend the browser's ability to handle new data and information
- Java: An object-oriented programming language for distributed applications
- JavaScript: A simple, object-based programming language incorporated into Navigator 2.0 (and the subject of this book)
- The similarities and differences between Java and JavaScript
- JavaScript as a scripting language
- Objects, properties, and methods
- The Navigator Object Hierarchy and other built-in objects
- Strengths and weaknesses of JavaScript

Navigator 2.0 Is More Than a Web Browser

Although Netscape Navigator started out its life as a basic Web browser, as it has grown increasingly popular, it has become much more.

Unlike earlier browsers and today's basic Web applications, Navigator 2.0 provides authors with numerous tools to step beyond the traditional constraints of HTML. Instead of simply combining text, pictures, sound and video, authors now have finer control over document layout, fonts, and color; they are able to extend the functionality of the browser using plug-ins and Java; and they can produce interactive applications using JavaScript.

A quick look at the Netscape Web site shows that today's Navigator can do so much more than previous versions—even without special programming by Web developers. With freely available plug-ins from leading software companies, Web authors can include native CorelDRAW graphics or Microsoft Word files in their documents, as well as view VRML (Virtual Reality Modeling Language) worlds, and view documents formatted in Adobe's device-independent Acrobat format.

On top of all this, Navigator 2.0 provides several tools that Web page developers and authors can take advantage of to enhance their documents and add dynamic interaction with the information they are providing on the Internet.

Frames

Frames are the most visually noticeable extension of HTML in Navigator 2.0. Using frames, authors are able to partition the screen into multiple rectangular sections. Each section is independent of all the others, and a different URL is loaded into each frame. In addition, links in one frame can be used to update another frame, without disturbing any others.

Frames are being used today to produce fixed, bannerlike mastheads for Web Pages, for menus that always stay on the screen and don't need to be reloaded or redrawn, and for forms-based searches where the form is always available.

In addition to the obvious visual appeal of frames technology, this extension to HTML may have an added benefit in that it reduces the amount of data that may need to be requested from the server and sent to clients. On the increasingly congested World Wide Web, this may prove to make Web browsing slightly more efficient and reduce some of the load on over-burdened Web servers.

Figure 1.1 shows an example of how frames can be used to divide the screen and provide both a fixed masthead and a permanent menu next to several frames of dynamic information. In Figure 1.2, you can see how choosing a menu item updated the bottom-left section of the screen without affecting the rest of the window.

Figure 1.1.

Using frames provides fixed and dynamic elements.

Figure 1.2.
Using a menu to update one frame.

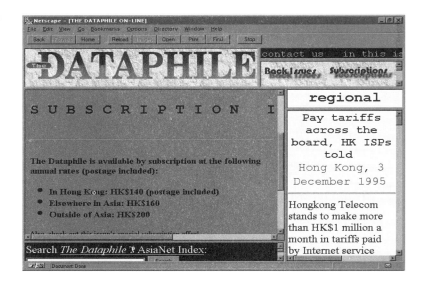

To get a better idea of the promise of frames, check Netscape's introduction to frames at the following site:

http://home.netscape.com/comprod/products/navigator/version_2.0/
frames/index.html

On this page, there are several examples of how frames can be used to improve access to information.

Plug-Ins

Another exciting feature of Navigator 2.0 is the open plug-in technology. By providing an open application programmer's interface for plug-ins, Netscape has made it possible for third-party software vendors to provide the ability to view a wide range of data and documents in the Navigator browser window. Netscape refers to objects displayed by plug-ins as *Live Objects*.

To date, a significant number of vendors including Corel, Paper Software, and Adobe have produced plug-ins for their own formats. (Figure 1.3 shows one such company.) Many of these will likely be extended to support JavaScript, enabling JavaScript programs to interact with plug-ins directly and further enhancing the power of JavaScript in future versions of Netscape Navigator. At the present time there are no tools for doing this.

 TIP The number of available plug-ins is constantly changing. Netscape provides an up-to-date list of available plug-ins at this site:

`http://home.netscape.com/comprod/products/navigator/version_2.0/plugins/index.html`

Figure 1.3.
Paper Software's WebFX™ plug-in enables Navigator 2.0 to browse VRML worlds.

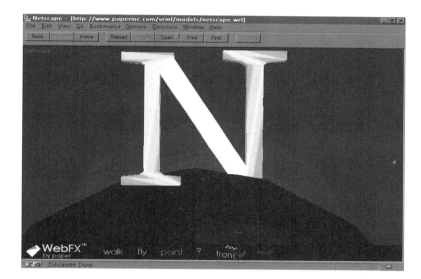

Interactivity with Java and JavaScript

Using JavaScript and Java, Web developers have come up with further enhancements to Web pages beyond the ability to load multiple documents in separate frames and view new file formats.

Some of the common Java applets available today include the following:

NEW TERM The term *applet* has come into common use since Sun Microsystems introduced Java to the Web community in 1995. Applets are small applications that are included in Web pages and downloaded on demand to be executed by the client browser. Although the term technically only refers to the type of Java programs described above, with the introduction of JavaScript, the term is now being used by some people on the Web to describe the type of integrated scripts developed with JavaScript.

☐ Scrolling text applets: Java is being used to add marquees to Web pages.

☐ Live data feeds: Current examples include a live stock ticker, such as the financial portfolio demonstration by Sun Microsystems' Jim Graham, shown in Figure 1.4.

Figure 1.4.

This Web page demo by Sun Microsystems' Jim Graham uses Java to include live data feeds.

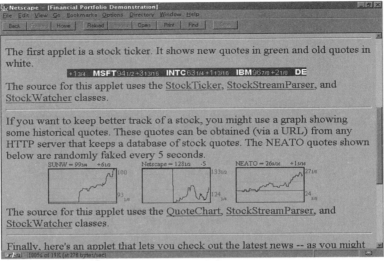

☐ Search engines: Java applets can be used to build database queries, which are then sent to remote databases.

☐ Adding protocols to Web browsers: One of the potential possibilities offered by Java is that, as protocols are developed on the Internet, Java can be used to add functionality to Web browsers on demand.

☐ New file formats: Java allows Web browsers to display new file formats by downloading applets to display the files as needed.

The widespread popularity of Java means that the range of uses will increase in the future, but today Java is being used primarily for cosmetic enhancements to Web pages.

By comparison, JavaScript is used to produce scripts designed to react to user and environment events—as well as in the future being the glue to hook Java applets more seamlessly into Web pages. The following are some examples:

☐ An interactive color picker for Web developers to test different background and text colors in their documents.

☐ Calculators: Examples on the Web include a unit conversion calculator and loan interest calculators.

☐ Dynamic output based on the current environment and the user's previous surfing history.

☐ Forms verification: JavaScript can be used to ensure that form data is entered properly before sending it to the server, rather than relying on the server to verify form content after it is submitted. Figure 1.5 illustrates the form verification.

Figure 1.5.
JavaScript prompts the user for correct information before a form is sent to a server.

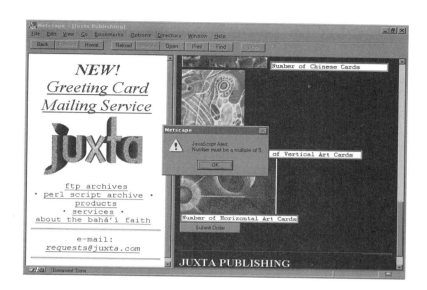

☐ Building URLs: JavaScript is used to build custom URLs based on user choices in forms.

☐ JavaScript can be used to replace many CGI scripts for client-side processing, easing bandwidth demands, and decreasing server load for busy Web servers.

JavaScript's Place in Navigator 2.0

JavaScript is one of the least-used components of Netscape's suite of interactivity tools (although that is quickly changing), but it could be the most significant. Not only does it bring interactive programming within the reach of the average Web author with no formal programming experience, it can also be used to move much of the processing away from over-burdened servers to increasingly powerful client workstations.

JavaScript Programs Are Built into Web Pages

As opposed to the independent application files used to deliver Java applets to Web browsers, the actual source code for JavaScript scripts can be included directly in Web pages. This is distinct from Java applets, which exist independently of the HTML Web pages.

JavaScript Gives Programmers Access to Browser Properties

JavaScript is integrated tightly into HTML and the Navigator 2.0 browser. Developers have available to them a wide range of tools and information to interact with the currently loaded HTML document, as well as the current browser session.

JavaScript exposes properties related to the document windows, the history list, the loaded documents, frames, forms, and links to the programmer. In addition, JavaScript can be used to trap user events, such as changing form values or pointing at links, so that appropriate programs can be developed for each event.

Java and JavaScript: Compare and Contrast

Given the tremendous popularity of Java since its introduction in 1995, it is important to take a look at the differences between Java and JavaScript. Although they are related—JavaScript borrows most of Java's syntax, for instance—they are fundamentally different and serve different purposes. They are complementary rather than competing with each other.

Using Java: A Complex, Complete Object-Oriented Programming Language

Java is much more than a language for developing Web-based applications. It is designed to compete in a market of full-fledged, general-purpose programming languages such as C, C++, Pascal, and FORTRAN. Unlike its predecessors, Java's claims to fame include the fact that it is platform-independent and that it can be used for both applications development and the development of in-line applets, or small applications, for Web pages.

Like C++ and Smalltalk, Java is object-oriented and relies heavily on the syntax and style of C++. With this comes the steep learning curve of a high-end object-oriented programming language.

A Compiled Language

Unlike most other general-purpose programming languages, Java is not compiled in the traditional sense. Instead of compiling to native machine code, the Java compiler converts source code into Java byte codes (known as architecture-neutral byte-codes)—a platform-independent representation of the Java program code—which are then run on a

machine-dependent runtime interpreter. In this way, developers only need to develop and maintain one set of source code and compile it once, and the code can then be run using the runtime interpreters for any machine.

Like all compiled languages, though, this adds the complexity of a compilation cycle to development and especially to debugging. However, to a certain degree like other compiled languages, an efficient runtime engine means that Java should offer better performance than general-purpose, interpreted scripting languages.

Fully Extensible

A fundamental feature of true object-oriented languages is that they are extensible. That is, programmers can create their own classes—or groupings of objects and data structures—to extend the basic classes that are part of the programming languages.

NEW TERM A *class* is a term used in object-oriented programming to refer to a set of related objects that share common characteristics. Classes, and the ability to create new classes, are what make object-oriented programming a powerful and flexible programming model.

Java is no exception to this rule. Java programmers routinely create their own extensions to the base set of tools or classes.

Steep Learning Curve

As mentioned before, object-oriented programming languages tend to have steep learning curves, especially for nonprogrammers. Java is not exempt from this difficulty.

The general consensus among beginning programmers is that learning Java is a formidable task, especially considering the complexity of the available on-line documentation on the Internet.

Enables Client-Server Interaction

The base set of classes that comes with the Java distribution make it ideally suited to client-server interactions. The ability to work with URLs and talk to HTTP servers already exists. The support for applets adds the ability to interact with user events in the client Web browser.

In addition, HotJava, the demonstration browser from Sun Microsystems, demonstrates how Java can become the means by which browsers dynamically learn to handle new protocols as that ability is needed.

NOTE

> Sun developed HotJava when Java was still in alpha development to demonstrate the potential of Java for distributed applications on the World Wide Web and to show how browsers could dynamically learn to handle new protocols and file types. HotJava is available for Solaris and 32-bit Windows (Windows NT and Windows 95) from the Java home page at `http://www.javasoft.com/`.

Developing Stand-Alone Applications and Applets

Java is famous because it can be used to develop applets that are delivered on the World Wide Web and executed in client Web browsers. However, Java can also be used to develop complete, platform-independent GUI applications using the Java runtime interpreter.

Offers Sophisticated Security

Because of the extremely open and public nature of the World Wide Web, security is a major issue for Java and Java applets. After all, allowing application code from unknown remote machines to be downloaded and executed on your computer system is potentially dangerous. Not only is there potential for applets to contain viruses, but they could simply be malicious applications intent on destroying your data and rendering your computer inoperable.

To address this, Sun implemented tight security features from the earliest stages of Java development. These features include verification of bytecodes (to ensure they don't violate access restrictions and more), as well as configurable network security that ranges from disabling network access to limiting access by an applet only to the host where the code originated, all the way to completely free network access.

Distinct from HTML

Even though applets are a feature of the World Wide Web and are included as in-line applets in HTML files, they are distinct and separate from HTML and HTML files. New HTML tags force a Web browser to initiate a new connection to the server and tell the browser where to display the applet's output on the Web page, but beyond that, applets are separate and distinct from HTML.

Using JavaScript: A Simple, Object-Based Scripting Language

In contrast to Java, JavaScript joins the ranks of simple, easy-to-use scripting languages. JavaScript promises an easier learning curve than Java along with powerful tools to add interactivity to Web pages with little effort.

Derived from Java

JavaScript owes a lot to Java. Its syntax and basic structure are similar to Java, even if the range of functions and the style of programming can differ greatly. JavaScript started life as Netscape's own scripting language with the name LiveScript, but in late 1995, Sun endorsed the language, and it became JavaScript.

JavaScript keeps more than just the basic syntax and structure of Java—it also borrows most of Java's flow constructs and implements some of the same security precautions, such as preventing applets from writing to the local disk.

An Interpreted Language

Unlike Java, JavaScript is an interpreted language. Whereas in Java, source code is compiled prior to runtime, in an interpreted language, source code files are executed directly at runtime in JavaScript.

Interpreted languages offer several advantages—as well as several drawbacks. Interpreted languages such as JavaScript are generally simpler than compiled languages and are easy to learn. It is often easier to develop, change, and trouble-shoot programs because the need to recompile with each change is removed.

On the negative side, the need to interpret commands as the program is run can produce a performance hit with some interpreted languages. In the case of JavaScript, this doesn't seem to be a problem.

JavaScript scripts are compiled to byte codes (similar to Java) as the script is downloaded and evaluated, and for most scripts, performance feels quite snappy.

Not Fully Extensible

Unlike Java, JavaScript is not fully extensible. The JavaScript model is one of a limited set of base objects, properties, methods, and data types, which provide enough capabilities to create client-side applications.

While users can create their own objects and write functions, this is not the same as the classes and inheritance offered in Java and other object-oriented programming languages.

Since JavaScript is an object-based scripting language, this book will be devoted to learning about the objects, properties, methods, and data types available in JavaScript.

Limited Client-Server Interaction

JavaScript in its current form is not designed for complete client-server interaction. Beyond analyzing, building, and invoking URLs, JavaScript can't talk directly to servers or talk different protocols. Essentially, JavaScript is well suited to handling client-end activity.

Still, there are indications that future versions of JavaScript will support protocols such as HTTP and ftp, but several security issues surrounding client-server interaction through JavaScript need to be addressed by Netscape before it implements these features.

In addition, JavaScript will be part of the LiveWire Web server being developed by Netscape. LiveWire is aimed at groups and organizations developing interactive Web applications. In this role, JavaScript will provide an alternative to today's CGI scripting for server-end programming.

Integrated into HTML

Where Java is only loosely tied to HTML, JavaScript is tightly integrated into HTML files. Typically, entire scripts are in the same files as the HTML that defines a page, and these scripts are downloaded at the same time as the HTML files.

The Current State of JavaScript

In undertaking the task of learning JavaScript, it is important to keep in mind the current status of the language and where its development appears to be headed.

Under Development

Both Navigator 2.0 and JavaScript are under intense development and are constantly evolving. So, JavaScript is, by definition, a language under development (as are most programming languages). In practical terms, that means that the complete language specification is not implemented yet.

In a very real way, JavaScript is a moving target. Some of the methods and properties of the current implementation may be dropped in the next version or the final release; the actual completed language specification may change; and the way in which some things are done could change as the language develops.

Supported by Sun

In late November, LiveScript became JavaScript in a joint announcement by Netscape and Sun that Sun would be supporting JavaScript as the Java-based open scripting standard for the Internet.

Given this support, there is little doubt that JavaScript will continue to resemble Java and that it will become the choice tool for gluing Java applets into Web pages, at least in the Netscape environment.

Essentially, this endorsement from Sun breathed life into a scripting language that very few people were paying attention to, but which is now the hot topic on the World Wide Web.

Endorsed by Many Companies

Sun Microsystems isn't the only company to support JavaScript. At the same time as Netscape and Sun made their announcement, more than 28 companies including America Online, Apple Computers, Oracle, Silicon Graphics, Architext, and SCO announced that they would also be endorsing JavaScript as the open scripting standard for the Internet, and many indicated they were considering licensing the technology to include in their own products.

Potential Use in Different Products

In addition to including JavaScript in its Navigator Web browser, Netscape is going to include JavaScript in its server-end products, including LiveWire, the Netscape Commerce Server, and the Netscape Communications Server.

Once this happens, it is entirely possible that the momentum for Perl and Bourne Shell as the languages of choice for CGI programming will shift toward JavaScript, producing a consistent development environment at both the client and server ends.

In addition, the endorsements from numerous companies mean that JavaScript will start to appear in products from companies other than Netscape and in products other than Web browsers and servers.

JavaScript Today: Scripting for the Netscape Web Browser

In this book, we are focusing on using JavaScript in the Navigator Web browser because this is where most JavaScript development is taking place and because this is the easiest environment in which to learn and practice JavaScript.

What is JavaScript?

By now, you probably have some idea of what JavaScript is and what it isn't, but let's look more closely at the features you'll be learning and using throughout the course of this book.

JavaScript Is a Scripting Language

Scripting languages have been in use long before the Web came around. In the UNIX environment, scripts have been used to perform repetitive system administration tasks and to automate many tasks for less computer-literate users. In addition, scripting languages are the basis of much of the CGI-BIN programming that is currently used to add a limited form of interactivity to Web pages.

Examples of scripting languages include Perl, well known in CGI programming, Awk and SED (designed for intensive text processing), and even HyperTalk which, like JavaScript, is an object-oriented scripting language.

Of course, this still doesn't tell you what the main advantages of scripting languages are. Like all scripting languages, JavaScript is interpreted, which provides an easy development process; it contains a limited and easy-to-learn command set and syntax; and it is designed for performing a well-defined set of tasks.

Designed for Simple, Small Programs

Because JavaScript is a scripting language, it is well suited to implementing simple, small programs. For instance, JavaScript would ideally be suited to developing a unit conversion calculator between miles and kilometers or pounds and kilograms. These tasks can be easily written and performed at acceptable speeds with JavaScript and would be easily integrated into a Web page. A more robust language such as Java would be far less suitable for the quick development and easy maintenance of these types of applications.

By contrast, JavaScript would not be well suited to implementing a distributed CAD document display and manipulation environment. While eventually JavaScript will be a tool for integrating this type of Java applet or plug-in into a Web page, to attempt to develop the actual applet in JavaScript would be at best, difficult and inefficient and, more likely, would be impossible.

Of course, this doesn't mean that sophisticated applications can't be—and aren't being—developed with JavaScript. Nonetheless, scripting languages are generally used for smaller tasks rather than for full, compiled programs.

Performs Repetitive Tasks

Just as JavaScript is suited to producing small programs, it is especially well designed for repetitive, event-invoked tasks. For example, JavaScript is ideal for calculating the content of one field in a form based on changes to the data in another field. Each time the data changes, the JavaScript program to handle the event is invoked, and the new data for the other field is calculated and displayed.

Designed for Programming User Events

Because of the way in which JavaScript is integrated into the browser and can interact directly with HTML pages, JavaScript makes it possible to program responses to user events such as mouse clicks and data entry in forms.

For instance, a JavaScript script could be used to implement a simple help system. Whenever the user points at a button or a link on the page, a helpful and informative message can be displayed in the status bar at the bottom of the browser window.

This adds interactivity to Web pages, makes forms dynamic, and can decrease the bandwidth requirements and server load incurred by using forms and CGI programming.

Easy Debugging and Testing

Like other scripting languages, JavaScript eases development and trouble-shooting because it is not compiled. It is easy to test program code, look at the results, make changes, and test it again without the overhead and delay of compiling.

The Java Glue

The popular phrase when referring to JavaScript is that it will "glue Java applets into Web pages." It will do this in future versions by using its capabilities to trap user events and pass relevant information, triggered by these events, to Java applets which, in many ways, are more limited in their ability to interact with the user and the browser environment.

JavaScript Is Object-Based

Object-oriented is a term that has been overused by the media and marketing arm of the computer and software industries. Nonetheless, the fact that JavaScript has a limited object-oriented model is an important distinction.

JavaScript's Object Model

In order to understand what it means for JavaScript to be *object-based*, we need to look at objects and how they work.

Fundamentally, *objects* are a way of organizing information, along with the methods for manipulating and using that information.

Objects provide a way to define specific pieces of data related to the item in question; these pieces are known as *properties*. In addition, these are supplemented by *tasks* that can be performed on or with that information, known as *methods*. Together properties and methods make up objects.

Because of the general nature of objects, specific instances can be created for each case where they are needed. For instance, a car object could then have several instances for Toyotas, Fords, and Volkswagens.

A Comparison with Procedural Languages

Defining objects in this way differs greatly from the way in which information is handled in traditional procedural programming languages such as FORTRAN and C.

In these languages, information and procedures (similar to methods) are kept separate and distinct and are not linked in the way that objects are. Also, the concept of creating instances isn't as well developed in procedural languages.

Working with Objects in JavaScript

JavaScript includes both built-in objects to work with elements of the currently loaded HTML document, as well as performing other useful tasks, such as mathematical calculations. It also offers the programmer the chance to create her own objects.

Built-In Objects

JavaScript offers a set of built-in objects that provide information about the currently loaded Web page and its contents, as well as the current session of Navigator. In addition, these objects provide methods for working with their properties.

The Navigator Object Hierarchy

Most of the built-in objects in JavaScript are part of the Navigator Object Hierarchy. The Navigator Object Hierarchy is built from a single base object called the window object, as illustrated in the following outline.

Window
    Location
    History
    Document
        Forms
        Anchors

Table 1.1 highlights the major features of these objects.

Table 1.1. Overview of the Navigator Object Hierarchy.

Object	Description
window	The `window` object provides methods and properties for dealing with the actual Navigator window, including objects for each frame.
location	The `location` object provides properties and methods for working with the currently open URL.
history	The `history` object provides information about the history list and enables limited interaction with the list.
document	The `document` object is one of the most heavily used objects in the hierarchy. It contains objects, properties, and methods for working with document elements including forms, links, anchors, and eventually, with applets.

Other Built-In Objects

In addition to the objects in the Navigator Object Hierarchy, JavaScript provides several objects that are not related to the current windows or loaded documents. Table 1.2 outlines the major features of these objects.

Table 1.2. Other built-in objects.

Object	Description
string	The `string` object enables programs to work with and manipulate strings of text, including extracting substrings and converting text to upper- or lowercase characters.
Math	The `Math` object provides methods to perform trigonometric functions, such as sine and tangent, as well as general mathematical functions, such as square roots.

continues

Table 1.2. continued

Object	Description
Date	With the Date object, programs can work with the current date or create instances for specific dates. The object includes methods for calculating the difference between two dates and working with times.

Extending JavaScript: Creating Your Own Objects

In addition to a wide range of built-in objects, as a JavaScript programmer, you can create your own objects to use in your scripts.

Properties

For example, if you need to build an object in JavaScript to represent the different types of airplanes sold by an aircraft manufacturer, you would have several pieces of information related to the airplane that you would want included in the object, including the following:

- ☐ Model
- ☐ Price
- ☐ Normal seating capacity
- ☐ Normal cargo capacity
- ☐ Maximum speed
- ☐ Fuel capacity

Properties are like variables in traditional languages, such as C and Pascal. Variables are named containers which are used to hold pieces of data, such as numbers or text. Variables are discussed in more detail in Chapter 3, "Working with Data and Information."

So, in JavaScript, if you call your object `airplane`, these properties might be referred to as:

```
airplane.model
airplane.price
airplane.seating
airplane.cargo
airplane.maxspeed
airplane.fuel
```

NOTE As you will learn later, in JavaScript, the properties of objects are referred to by the structure *object-name.property-name*.

Methods

Of course, having this information isn't worth much without ways to use the information. For instance, in this example, you want to be able to print out a nicely formatted description of the aircraft or be able to calculate the maximum distance the plane can travel based on the fuel capacity.

In object-oriented terminology, these tasks are known as methods. Like properties, your methods might be referred to as:

```
airplane.description()
airplane.distance()
```

Objects within Objects

Objects can also include other objects in much the same way as properties and methods. For instance, the airplane manufacturer may want to include an object inside his object definition to handle information about the number of planes in use worldwide, who is using them, and their safety records. This information, along with methods for working with the information, could be combined into an object called `airplane.record`. This object could then include properties and methods such as:

```
airplane.record.number_in_use
airplane.record.crashes
```

Instances

What you have created is a general description of an object that defines the information you want to work with and the ways you want to work with it. These general descriptions of objects are known as classes. In object-oriented programming, then, you can create specific instances of the class as needed.

NOTE

> In object-oriented programming, creating specific copies of classes is known as creating instances. JavaScript itself is classless, but provides mechanisms to create instance of objects (thus providing the same basic functionality). We cover the details of creating objects and instances in Chapter 4, "Functions and Objects—The Building Blocks of Programs."

For instance, in this example, the airplane manufacturer might want to create an instance of the `airplane` object for its newest aircraft, the SuperPlane. If this instance were created, then a program could assign specific values to the properties of the new instance by referring to `superplane.price`, `superplane.model`, and so on. Likewise, a description of the new plane could be printed out using `superplane.description()`.

Strengths of JavaScript

JavaScript offers several strengths to the programmer including a short development cycle, ease-of-learning, and small size scripts. These strengths mean that JavaScript can be easily and quickly used to extend HTML pages already on the Web.

Quick Development

Because JavaScript does not require time-consuming compilation, scripts can be developed in a relatively short period of time. This is enhanced by the fact that most of the interface features, such as dialog boxes, forms, and other GUI elements, are handled by the browser and HTML code. JavaScript programmers don't have to worry about creating or handling these elements of their applications.

Easy to Learn

While JavaScript may share many similarities with Java, it doesn't include the complex syntax and rules of Java. By learning just a few commands and simple rules of syntax, along with understanding the way objects are used in JavaScript, it is possible to begin creating fairly sophisticated programs.

Platform Independence

Because the World Wide Web, by its very nature, is platform-independent, JavaScript programs created for Netscape Navigator are not tied to any specific hardware platform or operating system. The same program code can be used on any platform for which Navigator 2.0 is available.

Small Overhead

JavaScript programs tend to be fairly compact and are quite small, compared to the binary applets produced by Java. This minimizes storage requirements on the server and download times for the user. In addition, because JavaScript programs usually are included in the same file as the HTML code for a page, they require fewer separate network accesses.

Weaknesses of JavaScript

As would be expected, JavaScript also has its own unique weaknesses. These include a limited set of built-in methods, the inability to protect source code from prying eyes, and the fact that JavaScript still doesn't have a mature development and debugging environment.

Limited Range of Built-In Methods

Early versions of the Navigator 2.0 beta included a version of JavaScript that was rather limited. In the final release of Navigator 2, which was the current version at the time of writing this book, the number of built-in methods had significantly increased, but still didn't include a complete set of methods to work with documents and the client windows. Still, the current version is about as complete as we will get until the next version of Navigator.

No Code Hiding

Because the source code of JavaScript script presently must be included as part of the HTML source code for a document, there is no way to protect code from being copied and reused by people who view your Web pages.

This raises concerns in the software industry about protection of intellectual property. The consensus is that JavaScript scripts are basically freeware at this point in time.

Lack of Debugging and Development Tools

Most well-developed programming environments include a suite of tools that make development easier and simplify and speed up the debugging process.

At the time of writing this book, there were no JavaScript-specific tools available for this purpose, although some people have begun developing Web-based applications (using JavaScript) to achieve some of this.

Summary

JavaScript is one of several key components in Navigator 2.0 designed to help Web developers produce interactive applications on the Internet. Other features include support for plug-ins, frames, and of course, Java.

Where Java is compiled, object-oriented, complex, and distinct from HTML, JavaScript is interpreted, object-based, simple to use and learn, and tightly integrated with HTML.

JavaScript exposes properties of the current browser session to the programmer, including elements of the currently loaded HTML pages, such as forms, frames, and links.

In this chapter we also took a look at the implications of the fact that JavaScript is a scripting language, took a close look at what objects are and how they are used in JavaScript, and took a broad look at the built-in objects in JavaScript.

You learned that, while JavaScript offers many benefits including a quick development cycle and platform independence, it still has drawbacks.

In the next chapter, you will begin taking a look at the specifics of developing JavaScript scripts and will work on your first script.

Q&A

Q I've only used visual programming tools for making Web pages. Can I learn JavaScript? How will knowing JavaScript make my home page better?

A While it's true that programming in JavaScript is more similar to programming in C than using a visual programming tool, most JavaScript programming is simple enough to make it easy for the complete beginner.

In addition, the development of interfaces to JavaScript programs almost entirely involves the use of HTML and HTML forms, which can be developed in a visual environment using several HTML development tools, including Navigator Gold from Netscape.

If you learn JavaScript, you will be able to add interactivity to Web pages. For instance, if a user enters data in a form, a result can be calculated and displayed for the user. Similarly, if the user moves the mouse over a link or button, help information can be displayed in the status bar of the Navigator window.

Q I want to add interactivity to my Web pages. Should I learn Java or JavaScript?

A Java and JavaScript are not competitors. They are complementary programming languages which both extend the functionality of Web browsers—in this case Navigator 2.0.

You will find that Java is suited to a different set of tasks than JavaScript. For instance, a viewing tool for CAD documents would need to be developed using Java applets while an interactive HTML form could only really be developed using JavaScript.

1

Chapter 2

Your First Script

In this chapter, you finally get down to the details of producing a JavaScript script.

You learn about the following topics, which will lead to your first complete JavaScript script:

- ☐ How to incorporate JavaScript into HTML
- ☐ Command and command block structure in JavaScript
- ☐ Output functions

You then learn how to use JavaScript scripts to create text output that is directed to the client window, in sequence with an HTML file, and then is interpreted just like regular HTML.

Of course, this doesn't really allow you to do anything with JavaScript that you can't already do with HTML. So, as the chapter continues, you will take the next step: generating output in dialog boxes, as opposed to putting it on the Web page itself, and generating dynamic output that can change each time the page is loaded.

We cover the following topics:

- ☐ Creating output in a dialog box using the `alert()` method
- ☐ Prompting users for input in a dialog box using the `prompt()` method
- ☐ Displaying dynamic output by combining the prompt method with `document.write()` and `document.writeln()`

Incorporating JavaScript into HTML

At the present time, all JavaScript scripts need to be included as an integral part of an HTML document. To do this, Netscape has implemented an extension to standard HTML: the `SCRIPT` tag.

The `SCRIPT` Tag

Including scripts in HTML is simple. Every script must be contained inside a `SCRIPT` container tag. In other words, an opening `<SCRIPT>` tag starts the script and a closing `</SCRIPT>` tag ends it:

```
<SCRIPT>

JavaScript program

</SCRIPT>
```

The `SCRIPT` tag takes two optional attributes which determine how the JavaScript script in question is incorporated into the HTML file. These attributes are outlined in Table 2.1.

Table 2.1. Attributes for the `SCRIPT` tag.

Attribute	Description
SRC	URL for a file containing the JavaScript source code. The file should have the extension `.js`. This attribute is not implemented in the final release version of Navigator 2.0 but is expected to make it into the next version of Navigator.
LANGUAGE	Indicates the language used in the script. In the current version of Navigator 2.0 this attribute can take only two values: `JavaScript` and `LiveScript`. `LiveScript` is provided for backward compatibility with early scripts developed when the language was called LiveScript. You should use `JavaScript` in your scripts.

NOTE

Using the SCRIPT tag and its attributes will eventually enable you to use two techniques to integrate a JavaScript program into an HTML file. Right now, programmers have only one choice—to include their JavaScript programs in their HTML files. Once the SRC attribute becomes available, developers will be able to store JavaScript code in separate files and simply load it into separate Web pages.

TIP

Although the final release of Navigator 2.0 still supports the use of LANGUAGE="LiveScript" for backward compatibility, this will likely be dropped in future versions of the browser. It is best to use LANGUAGE="JavaScript".

Including JavaScript in an HTML File

The first, and easiest, way is to include the actual source code in the HTML file, using the following syntax:

```
<SCRIPT LANGUAGE="JavaScript">

JavaScript program

</SCRIPT>
```

Hiding Scripts from Other Browsers

Of course, an immediate problem crops up with this type of SCRIPT container: Browsers that don't support JavaScript will happily attempt to display or parse the content of the script. In order to avoid this, Netscape recommends the following approach using HTML comments:

```
<SCRIPT LANGUAGE="JavaScript">
<!-- HIDE THE SCRIPT FROM OTHER BROWSERS

JavaScript program

// STOP HIDING FROM OTHER BROWSERS -->
</SCRIPT>
```

These comments (<!-- HIDE THE SCRIPT FROM OTHER BROWSERS and // STOP HIDING FROM OTHER BROWSERS -->) ensure that other Web browsers will ignore the entire script and not display it because everything between <!-- and --> should be ignored by a standard Web browser. Of course, if users were to view the source code of the document, they would still see the script.

Problems with the SCRIPT Tag

This technique of combining the SCRIPT container tag with comments isn't foolproof, however. Right now, the SCRIPT tag is not an accepted part of the HTML 2.0 standard and the HTML 3.0 specification is incomplete. For the time being, competing browser makers could use the SCRIPT tag for another purpose.

NOTE

At press time, it looked as though the SCRIPT tag, and possibly JavaScript itself, would become part of the HTML 3.0 specification because it is backed by Netscape and Sun, among others.

In fact, with Netscape Navigator 2.0, the latter problem has already occurred with the implementation of frames. Among several tags used to produce frames, Netscape uses a FRAME tag that is used by IBM's Web Explorer for another purpose.

In addition, by hiding the script from other browsers, users of these other browsers will be unaware of the script's existence. One solution to this problem could be to use the following approach:

```
<SCRIPT LANGUAGE="JavaScript">

// JavaScript Script Appears Here<BR>
// Download Netscape Navigator 2.0 to use it.

<!-- HIDING FROM OTHER BROWSERS

JavaScript Program

// STOP HIDING FROM OTHER BROWSERS -->
</SCRIPT>
```

NOTE

Unlike HTML, which creates comments with the structure <!-- Comments Here -->, JavaScript comments start with a double-slash (//) anywhere on the line and continue to the end of the line. If not contained within an HTML comment structure, a JavaScript comment will be displayed by non-Netscape browsers. As you learn later in this chapter, JavaScript also includes multiline comments.

2

Where to Put Your JavaScript Code

JavaScript scripts and programs can be included anywhere in the header or body of an HTML file. Many of the examples on Netscape's Web site, as well as elsewhere, make it a habit to include the SCRIPT container in the header of the HTML file, and this is the preferred format.

Still, other developers prefer to include the JavaScript program next to the element or section of the HTML it refers to, such as a form. Because an HTML file can contain more than one SCRIPT tag, it is possible to place JavaScript functions in logical places in a file for ease of coding and debugging.

As you will see in Chapter 4, "Functions and Objects—The Building Blocks of Programs," where we discuss functions, there are compelling reasons to put certain segments of your JavaScript code in the header of the HTML file to ensure they are evaluated before users can initiate events.

Using External Files for JavaScript Programs

While including JavaScript programs directly in HTML files can be convenient for small scripts and basic HTML pages, it can quickly get out of hand when pages require long and complex scripts.

To make development and maintenance of HTML files and JavaScript scripts easier, the JavaScript specification includes the proposed option of keeping your JavaScript scripts in separate files and using the SRC attribute of the SCRIPT tag to include the JavaScript program in an HTML file. Even though the SRC attribute is not implemented in the final release version of Navigator 2.0 currently available, it should be in the next version of Navigator. While we can't be sure that the syntax of this attribute will match the proposed specification, the following discussion is based on the current proposal.

In its simplest form, the SRC construct can be used like this:

```
<SCRIPT LANGUAGE="JavaScript" SRC="http://www.you.com/JavaScript.js">
</SCRIPT>
```

NOTE   For the SRC attribute to work, the name of the JavaScript source files should include the extension .js.

One of the benefits of this approach is that your scripts are automatically hidden from other browsers that don't support JavaScript. At the same time, though, this technique requires an additional server request and server access, which may be problematic on a slow server or across a slow connection to the Internet.

In addition, both techniques (JavaScript code in an HTML file and JavaScript code in an external file) can be used at the same time. You can do this with a single SCRIPT container or more than one:

```
<SCRIPT LANGAUGE="JavaScript" SRC="http://www.you.com/JavaScript.js">
<!-- HIDE FROM OTHER BROWSERS

More JavaScript code

// STOP HIDING FROM OTHER BROWSERS -->
</SCRIPT>
```

or

```
<SCRIPT LANGUAGE="JavaScript" SRC="http://www.you.com/JavaScript.js">
</SCRIPT>

<SCRIPT LANGUAGE="JavaScript">
<!-- HIDE FROM OTHER BROWSERS

More JavaScript code

// STOP HIDING FROM OTHER BROWSERS -->
</SCRIPT>
```

Listing 2.1 demonstrates a simple JavaScript script inside an HTML file.

TYPE **Listing 2.1. Including a program in an HTML file.**

```
<HTML>

<HEAD>
<TITLE>Listing 2.1</TITLE>
</HEAD>

<BODY>
Here's the result:

<SCRIPT LANGUAGE="JavaScript">
<!-- HIDE FROM OTHER BROWSERS

// Output "It Works!"
document.writeln("It works!<BR>");

// STOP HIDING FROM OTHER BROWSERS -->
</SCRIPT>

</BODY>

</HTML>
```

2

This HTML file produces results similar to those in Figure 2.1. By comparison, using a browser that doesn't support JavaScript (such as NCSA Mosaic), the results look like those in Figure 2.2.

Figure 2.1.

In Navigator 2.0, the output displays in source code order.

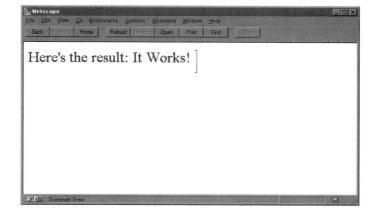

Figure 2.2.

Part of the script is hidden when JavaScript is unsupported.

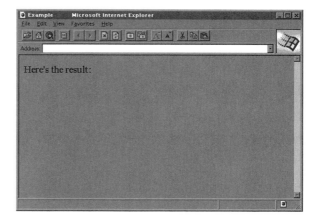

 The script in Listing 2.1 demonstrates several important points which will become clear in later chapters.

First, it is possible to generate dynamic HTML output at the time of document loading using JavaScript scripts. Second, nothing in the script is displayed on other browsers even though the rest of the HTML file loads and displays without any difficulty. To compare, delete the HTML comment lines, and the output looks like Figure 2.3. You can see that the entire JavaScript command `document.writeln("It Works!<BR>");` has been displayed, and the `<BR>` tag has been interpreted by Mosaic.

Figure 2.3.
*Without the
HTML comments,
the JavaScript code
displays.*

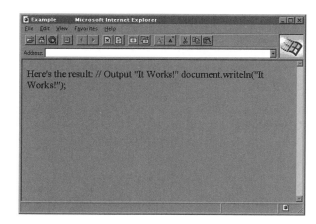

In this example, you also see how JavaScript comments work. The line that begins with two slashes,

```
// Output "It Works!"
```

is a single-line JavaScript comment similar to those used in C++. Everything after the // until the end of the line is a comment. JavaScript also supports C-style multiline comments, which start with /* and end with */:

```
/* This
   is
   a
   comment */
```

Comments are useful to help other people read your programs and understand what different commands and functions are doing. In addition, when you write long or complex programs, liberal use of meaningful comments will help you understand your own program if you come back to alter it after an extended period of time.

Basic Command Syntax

The basic syntax and structure of JavaScript looks familiar to anyone who has used C, C++, or Java. A JavaScript program is built with functions (covered in Chapter 4) and statements, operators, and expressions. The basic command unit is a one-line command or expression followed by a semicolon; for example:

```
document.writeln("It Works!<BR>");
```

This command invokes the writeln() method, which is part of the document object. The semicolon indicates the end of the command.

> **NOTE**
>
> JavaScript commands can span multiple lines. Multiple commands can also appear on a single line, as long as the semicolon is there to mark the end of each command. In fact, except where it is essential to distinguish between commands, the semicolon is optional. I use it throughout this book to make source code clearer and easier to read.

Command Blocks

Multiple commands can be combined into command blocks using curly braces ({ and }). Command blocks are used to group together sets of JavaScript commands into a single unit, which can then be used for a variety of purposes, including loops and defining functions. (These subjects will be discussed in later chapters.) A simple command block looks like this:

```
{
  document.writeln("Does it work? ");
  document.writeln("It works!<BR>");
}
```

Command blocks can be embedded, as the following lines illustrate.

```
{
  JavaScript code

  {

    More JavaScript code

  }

}
```

When you embed command blocks like this, it is important to remember that all open curly braces must be closed and that the first closing brace closes the last opened curly brace. In the following example, the first } closes the second { as shown by the ¦ markers:

```
{
¦ JavaScript code
¦
¦ {
¦ ¦
¦ ¦ More JavaScript code
¦ ¦
¦ }
¦
}
```

TIP When embedding command blocks inside each other, it is common practice to indent each successive command block so that it's easy to identify where blocks start and end when reading program code. Extra spaces and tabs don't have any effect on JavaScript programs.

In JavaScript, object, property, and method names are case sensitive, as are all keywords, operators, and variable names. You learn about operators and variables in Chapter 3, "Working with Data and Information." Case is important only in strings of text (otherwise known as *string literals* and discussed in Chapter 3). In this way, all the following commands are different (and some are illegal):

```
document.writeln("Test");
Document.Writeln("Test");
document.WriteLN("Test");
```

Outputting Text

In most programming languages, one of the basic capabilities is to output—or display—text. In JavaScript output can be directed to several places including the current document window and pop-up dialog boxes.

Output in the Client Window

In JavaScript, programmers can direct output to the client window in sequence with the HTML file. As discussed in the previous section, JavaScript that produces output is evaluated where it occurs in the HTML file, and the resulting text is interpreted as HTML for the purpose of displaying the page.

In addition to this, JavaScript allows programmers to generate alert and confirm boxes that include text and one or two buttons. Text and numbers can also be displayed in `text` and `TEXTAREA` fields in a form.

In the following sections, you look at outputting text to the document window.

The `document.write()` and `document.writeln()` Methods

The `document` object in JavaScript includes two methods designed for outputting text to the client window: `write()` and `writeln()`. In JavaScript, methods are called by combining the object name with the method name:

```
object-name.property-name
```

Data that the method needs to perform its job is provided as an argument in the parentheses; for example:

```
document.write("Test");
document.writeln('Test');
```

 Arguments are data provided to a function or a method for use in its calculations and processing. They are provided (or *passed*) to the function or method by listing them in the parentheses following the function or method name. Multiple arguments are separated by commas.

NOTE
A quick look at these examples shows you that strings of text are surrounded by double (or single) quotes and that the two methods (`document.write()` and `document.writeln()`) are invoked in the same manner. Open and close quotes must be of the same type—you cannot open with double quotes and close with single quotes or vice versa.

The `write()` method outputs text and HTML as a string of text to the current window in sequence with the current HTML file. Because the SCRIPT container does not affect the HTML structures where it occurs, any format tags or other elements in the HTML file will affect the text and HTML produced by the `write()` method. For example, Listing 2.2 produces output like Figure 2.4.

TYPE **Listing 2.2. Outputting HTML tags from JavaScript.**

```
<HTML>

<HEAD>
<TITLE>Ouputting Text</TITLE>
</HEAD>

<BODY>
This text is plain.<BR>
<B>
<SCRIPT LANGUAGE="JavaScript">
<!-- HIDE FROM OTHER BROWSERS

document.write("This text is bold.</B>");

// STOP HIDING FROM OTHER BROWSERS -->
</SCRIPT>

</BODY>

</HTML>
```

OUTPUT   Figure 2.4. shows the resulting effect:

Figure 2.4.
*HTML tags affect
output from
JavaScript scripts.*

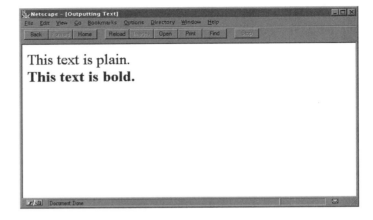

ANALYSIS   Listing 2.2 also demonstrates that HTML tags, as well as regular text, can be output
by the write() method. You will notice that the <B> and </B> tags can either be
output as part of the write() method or left outside the script. In either case, the text and
HTML is evaluated in the order it appears in the complete HTML and JavaScript source
code.

The writeln() method is the same as the write() method except that it adds a carriage return
at the end of the string that is being output. This is really only relevant inside of PRE and XMP
containers where carriage returns are interpreted in displaying the text. Listing 2.3 shows an
example of the writeln() method.

TYPE   **Listing 2.3. Using the writeln() method with the PRE tag.**

```
<PRE>
<SCRIPT LANGUAGE="JavaScript">
<!-- HIDE FROM OTHER BROWSERS

document.writeln("One,");
document.writeln("Two,");
document.write("Three ");
document.write("...");

// STOP HIDING FROM OTHER BROWSERS -->
</SCRIPT>
</PRE>
```

2

This example produces results like those in Figure 2.5.

Figure 2.5.

Output using the `writeln()` *method.*

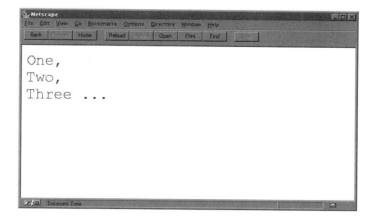

In JavaScript, strings of text, such as those used to produce output with the `write()` and `writeln()` methods, can include special keystrokes to represent characters that can't be typed, such as new lines, tabs, and carriage returns. The special characters are reviewed in Table 2.2.

Table 2.2. Special characters in strings.

Character	Description
\n	new line
\t	tab
\r	carriage return
\f	form feed
\b	backspace

For example, the following command displays the text "It Works!" followed by a new line:

```
document.write("It Works!\n");
```

All special characters start with a backslash (\). This is called *escaping* characters. Escaping a character is used in many scripting and programming languages to represent a character that cannot be typed or that has special meaning in the language and would be interpreted incorrectly if left unescaped.

A perfect example of this is the backslash itself. In order to output a backslash in JavaScript, it is necessary to escape the backslash:

```
document.write("A backslash: \\");
```

In this example, the first backslash tells JavaScript that the next character is a special character and not to treat it normally. In this case it outputs a backslash rather than treating the second backslash in the normal way (as the escape character).

Listing 2.4 is a variation on the traditional Hello World program that most students learn as their first program in a new programming language. Instead of simply outputting "Hello World!" to the display windows, you are going to produce the entire output using JavaScript and include a GIF image along with the phrase "Welcome to Netscape Navigator 2!" The GIF is included with the source code on the enclosed CD-ROM.

TYPE   **Listing 2.4. Welcome to Netscape Navigator 2!**

```
<HTML>

<HEAD>
<TITLE>Example 2.4</TITLE>
</HEAD>

<BODY>
<SCRIPT LANGUAGE="JavaScript">
<!-- HIDE FROM OTHER BROWSERS

document.write('<IMG SRC="welcome.gif">');
document.write("<BR><H1>Welcome to Netscape Navigator 2!</H1>");

// STOP HIDING FROM OTHER BROWSERS -->
</SCRIPT>
</BODY>

</HTML>
```

OUTPUT   This script produces output like that in Figure 2.6.

Figure 2.6.
JavaScript can be used to generate complete HTML output.

ANALYSIS In this example, you can see how both text and HTML tags can be output to the current HTML windows using the `write()` method. Notice the use of both single quotes and double quotes to delimit the start and end of the text strings. In the first call to the `write()` method, you use the single quotes so that the text string can contain the double quotes required by the `IMG` tag.

Stepping Beyond the Document Window

One of the restrictions of HTML has always been that Web site developers have been limited to a single client window. Even with the appearance of frames and the `TARGET` tag in Navigator 2.0, authors are still constrained to displaying HTML files in complete browser windows and are unable to direct small messages to the user through another window without having the message become part of an HTML page.

Working with Dialog Boxes

JavaScript provides the ability for programmers to generate output in small dialog boxes— the content of the dialog box is independent of the HTML page containing the JavaScript script and doesn't affect the appearance or content of the page.

The simplest way to direct output to a dialog box is to use the `alert()` method. To use the `alert()` method, you just need to provide a single string of text as you did with `document.write()` and `document.writeln()` in the previous section:

```
alert("Click OK to continue.");
```

NOTE You will notice that the `alert()` method doesn't have an object name in front of it. This is because the `alert()` method is part of the `window` object. As the top-level object in the Navigator Object Hierarchy, the `window` object is assumed when it isn't specified.

The preceding command generates output similar to Figure 2.7. The alert dialog box displays the message passed to it in parentheses, as well as an OK button. The script and HTML holding the script will not continue evaluating or executing until the user clicks the OK button.

Figure 2.7.

Alert dialog boxes display a message along with an OK button to continue.

Generally, the alert() method is used for exactly that—to warn the user or alert him or her to something. Examples of this type of use include:

☐ Incorrect information in a form

☐ An invalid result from a calculation

☐ A warning that a service is not available on a given date

Nonetheless, the alert() method can still be used for friendlier messages.

NOTE

Notice that JavaScript alert boxes include the phrase "JavaScript Alert" at the start of the message. All dialog boxes generated by scripts have similar headings in order to distinguish them from those generated by the operating system or the browser. This is done for security reasons so that malicious programs cannot trick users into doing things they don't want to do. Netscape designers have indicated that they may make dialog boxes generated by scripts visually different in future versions.

Next, take the preceding example, Listing 2.4, the "Welcome to Netscape Navigator 2!" example, and have the message display in an alert box.

To do this, you need to make only a small change in your original script, as shown in Listing 2.5:

TYPE **Listing 2.5. Displaying a message in an alert box.**

```
<HTML>

<HEAD>
<TITLE>Example 2.5</TITLE>
</HEAD>

<BODY>
<SCRIPT LANGUAGE="JavaScript">
<!-- HIDE FROM OTHER BROWSERS

alert("Welcome to Netscape Navigator 2!");
document.write('<IMG SRC="welcome.gif">');
```

```
// STOP HIDING FROM OTHER BROWSERS -->
</SCRIPT>
</BODY>

</HTML>
```

 Figures 2.8 and 2.9 show the progression of events with this script.

Figure 2.8.
The alert dialog box is displayed first.

Figure 2.9.
After OK is clicked, the rest of the script executes.

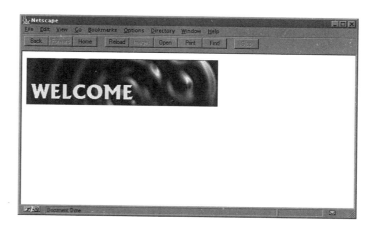

 Notice in this example, you have reversed the order of the message and the graphic. This way, the user will see the message in a dialog box and the graphic will not load until OK has been clicked.

As with document.write(), you can use special characters, such as \n, in the alert message to control the formatting of the text displayed in the dialog box. The following command would generate an alert box similar to the one in Figure 2.10:

```
alert("Welcome!\n\n\tYou are using Netscape Navigator 2!");
```

Figure 2.10.
By using special characters, you can format text in dialog boxes.

Interacting with the User

The alert() method still doesn't enable you to interact with the user. The addition of the OK button provides you with some control over the timing of events, but it still cannot be used to generate any dynamic output or customize output based on user input.

The simplest way to interact with the user is with the prompt() method. Like alert(), prompt() creates a dialog box with the message you specify, but it also provides a single entry field with a default entry. The user needs to fill in the field and then click OK. An example of the prompt() method is the following line, which generates a dialog box like the one in Figure 2.11:

```
prompt("Enter Your favourite color:","Blue");
```

Figure 2.11.

The prompt dialog box includes a message and an entry field along with an OK button and a Cancel button.

You will immediately notice a difference with the way you used the alert() method: You are providing two strings to the method in the parentheses. The prompt() method requires two pieces of information: The first is text to be displayed, and the second is the default data in the entry field.

NEW TERM The pieces of information provided in parentheses to a method or function are known as *arguments*. In JavaScript, when a method requires more than one argument, they are separated by commas.

You might have noticed that if used by itself, the prompt() method accepts input from the user, but the information is essentially lost. This is solved by realizing that methods and functions can return results, as mentioned in the previous chapter. That means that the prompt() method will return the user's input as its result.

The result returned by a method can be stored in a variable (which you will learn about in the next chapter) or can be used as an argument to another method:

```
document.write("Your favorite color is: ");
document.writeln(prompt("Enter your favorite color:","Blue"));
```

In the second line of this code segment, the document.writeln() method displays the results returned by the prompt() method as illustrated by Figures 2.12 and 2.13.

Figure 2.12.
The prompt()
*method can be used
to ask the user
questions.*

Figure 2.13.
*Based on the
answers, dynamic
content can be
created.*

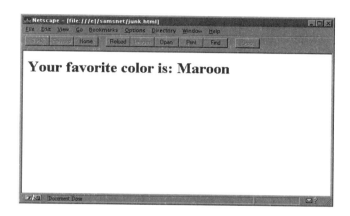

Using the prompt() method, you are now in a position to generate a personalized version of the "Welcome to Netscape Navigator 2!" example you have been working with. Listing 2.6 shows the new program.

TYPE **Listing 2.6. The revised welcome program.**

```
<HTML>

<HEAD>
<TITLE>Example 2.6</TITLE>
</HEAD>

<BODY>
<SCRIPT LANGUAGE="JavaScript">
<!-- HIDE FROM OTHER BROWSERS

document.write('<IMG SRC="welcome.gif">');
document.write("<H1>Greetings, ");
document.write(prompt("Enter Your Name:","Name"));
document.write(". Welcome to Netscape Navigator 2.0!</H1>");

// STOP HIDING FROM OTHER BROWSERS -->
</SCRIPT>
</BODY>

</HTML>
```

OUTPUT This script first displays the welcome graphic and the word "Greetings" in the Navigator window. Then, a prompt dialog box asks for the user's name and once this is entered the sentence is completed and displayed with the user's name following "Greetings."

ANALYSIS In this example, you have used the `prompt()` method to construct a personalized welcome greeting. However, notice that the process was somewhat cumbersome, requiring four `document.write()` commands to display what could easily be two short lines in HTML.

This can be made a little easier by combining multiple strings of text into a single string of text using what is known as concatenation.

NEW TERM *Concatenation* is discussed in more depth in Chapter 3. Using concatenation, multiple strings are combined into a single string and are treated as a single string by JavaScript.

In order to do this, you can combine the various pieces of your welcome message into a single `document.write()` command using a simple plus sign (+):

```
document.write('<IMG SRC="welcome.gif">');
document.write("<H1>Greetings, " + prompt("<BR>Enter Your Name:","Name") +
  ". Welcome to Netscape Navigator 2.0!</H1>");
```

Summary

In this chapter you learned how to combine JavaScript scripts into HTML files using the `SCRIPT` tag. The `SCRIPT` tag can also be used to include JavaScript code kept in separate external files. Multiple `SCRIPT` containers can be used in a single HTML file. You also learned the basic structure of JavaScript commands and how to use curly braces to build blocks of multiple commands.

We also took a look at how to use the `write()` and `writeln()` methods which are part of the `document` object, as well as reviewed the special characters which can be used when outputting text. In addition, you learned the syntax of JavaScript comments.

In this chapter you also moved beyond static output limited to the current client window.

Using the `alert()` method, it is possible to direct output from a JavaScript script to a dialog box. This can be taken a step further with the `prompt()` method.

The `prompt()` method enables you to ask the user to enter a single item of data in an entry field in a dialog box. The data the user enters is returned by the `prompt()` method and can be output using `document.write()` or `document.writeln()`. This is one way you can generate dynamic, custom output in a Web page.

Commands and Extensions Review

Command/Extension	Type	Description
SCRIPT	HTML tag	Container for JavaScript scripts.
SRC	SCRIPT attribute	Holds the URL of an external JavaScript file. External files must have the extension .js. (Not yet implemented; optional.)
LANGUAGE	SCRIPT attribute	Specifies the language of the script. Currently, the only valid values for this attribute are LiveScript and JavaScript; (optional).
//	JavaScript comment	Start of a single-line comment. Comment starts with // and ends at the end of the line.
/* ... */	JavaScript comment	JavaScript multiline comments start with /* and end with */.
document.write()	JavaScript method	Outputs string to the current window in sequence with HTML file containing the script.
document.writeln()	JavaScript method	Outputs string to current document followed by a carriage return.
alert()	JavaScript method	Displays a message in a dialog box.
prompt()	JavaScript method	Displays a message in a dialog box and provides a single input field for the user to enter a response to the message.

Exercises

1. Change Listing 2.4 so that it produces output in preformatted text (using HTML's PRE tag) with "Welcome to" and "Netscape Navigator 2.0!" on separate lines.

2. How would you rewrite the example from exercise question 1 using only one `write()` or `writeln()` command?

3. How would you customize the output in Listing 2.5 to include the user's name?

4. Try entering the following in the prompt dialog box generated by the script from Listing 2.6 and see what happens:

☐ Press Cancel instead of OK.

☐ Enter text that includes some simple HTML tags, such as **John
Doe**.

☐ Enter text that contains special characters such as **John\nDoe**.

What do you learn from the results?

Answers

1. The following code uses the `writeln()` method to produce the desired result:

```
<HTML>

<HEAD>
<TITLE>Welcome to Netscape Navigator 2.0!</TITLE>
</HEAD>

<BODY>

<SCRIPT LANGUAGE="JavaScript">
<!-- HIDE FROM OTHER BROWSERS

document.write('<IMG SRC="welcome.gif">');
document.writeln("<BR><PRE>Welcome to");
document.write("Netscape Navigator 2.0!</PRE>");

// STOP HIDING FROM OTHER BROWSERS -->
</SCRIPT>

</BODY>

</HTML>
```

2. Using the \n special character, it is possible to produce the same results as the previous exercise question using only one call to the `write()` method:

```
<HTML>

<HEAD>
<TITLE>Welcome to Netscape Navigator 2.0!</TITLE>
</HEAD>

<BODY>

<SCRIPT LANGUAGE="JavaScript">
<!-- HIDE FROM OTHER BROWSERS
```

```
document.write('<IMG SRC="welcome.gif"><BR><PRE>Welcome to\nNetscape
➥ Navigator 2!</PRE>');
// STOP HIDING FROM OTHER BROWSERS -->
</SCRIPT>

</BODY>

</HTML>
```

3. The following example customizes the script from Listing 2.5 to include the user's name:

```
<HTML>

<HEAD>
<TITLE>Exercise 2.3</TITLE>
</HEAD>

<BODY>
<SCRIPT LANGUAGE="JavaScript">
<!-- HIDE FROM OTHER BROWSERS

alert("Greetings, " + prompt("Enter Your Name:","Name") + ".\nWelcome to
➥ Netscape Navigator 2.0!");
document.write('<IMG SRC="welcome.gif">');

// STOP HIDING FROM OTHER BROWSERS -->
</SCRIPT>
</BODY>

</HTML>
```

4. You learn several things from the tests in this exercise:

☐ Clicking on Cancel returns a value of null. You learn about the null value in Chapter 3.

☐ Special characters entered in a string returned by the prompt() method are not evaluated but are just displayed as plain text. In this way, if the user types \n, it will be displayed as \n rather than being evaluated to a new line.

☐ HTML tags entered by the user are interpreted by the Web browser before displaying the text on the page.

DAY 2

Chapter 3

Working with Data and Information

In order to move beyond outputting text and very basic user interaction, it is necessary to work with data and information—both when it is generated by the user and by calculations in a script.

JavaScript provides four basic data types that can be used to work with numbers and text. Variables offer containers to hold information and work with it in useful and sophisticated ways by using expressions.

To help you master variables and expressions, this chapter covers the following topics:

- ☐ Data types in JavaScript
- ☐ Using and declaring variables
- ☐ Assignment expressions
- ☐ Operators
- ☐ Comparison with `if ... else`
- ☐ Extending user interaction with the `confirm()` method

Data Types in JavaScript

JavaScript uses four data types—numbers, strings, boolean values, and a null value—to represent all the information the language can handle. Compared with most languages, this is a small number of data types, but it is sufficient to intelligently handle most data used in everything except the most complex programs.

The four data types in JavaScript are outlined in Table 3.1.

Table 3.1. JavaScript's data types.

Type	Example
Numbers	Any number, such as 17, 21.5, or 54e7
Strings	`"Greetings!"` or `'Fun!'`
Boolean	Either `true` or `false`
Null	A special keyword for exactly that—the `null` value (that is, nothing)

Literals

The term *literals* refers to the way in which each of the four data types are represented. Literals are fixed values which literally provide a value in a program. For example, `11` is a literal number, `"hello"` is a string literal, and `true` is a boolean literal.

You have already seen literals in use in the previous chapters when you gave arguments to different methods in the form of text strings such as `"Welcome to Netscape Navigator 2.0!"` and `"Enter Your Name:"`.

For each data type, there are different ways of specifying literals.

Numbers

The JavaScript number type encompasses what would be several types in languages such as Java. Using the numbers, it is possible to express both integers and floating point values.

Integers

Integers are numbers without any portion following the decimal point; that is, they are whole numbers—no fractions. Integers can be either positive or negative numbers. The maximum integer size is dependent on the platform running the JavaScript application.

3

In JavaScript, you can express integers in three different bases: base 10 (*decimal*—what you normally use in everyday situations), base 8 (known as *octal*), and base 16 (*hexadecimal*).

NOTE

> Base 8 numbers can have digits only up to 7 so that a decimal value of 18 would be an octal value of 22. Similarly, hexadecimal allows digits up to F, where A is equivalent to decimal 10 and F is 15. So, a decimal value of 18 would be 12 in hexadecimal notation.

In order to distinguish between these three bases, JavaScript uses the notations outlined in Table 3.2 to specify the different bases.

Table 3.2. Specifying bases in JavaScript.

Number System	Notation
Decimal (base 10)	A normal integer without a leading 0 (zero) (e.g., 752)
Octal (base 8)	An integer with a leading 0 (zero) (e.g., 056)
Hexadecimal (base 16)	An integer with a leading 0x or 0X (e.g., 0x5F or 0XC72)

Floating Point Values

Floating point values can include a fractional component. A floating point literal can include a decimal integer plus either a decimal point and a fraction expressed as another decimal number or an exponent indicator and a type suffix, as shown in the following examples:

- 7.2945
- –34.2
- 2E3

Floating point literals must, at a minimum, include a decimal integer and either the decimal point or the exponent indicator ("e" or "E"). As with integers, floating point values can be positive or negative.

NOTE

> It should be noted that JavaScript's handling of floating point numbers can introduce inaccuracy into some calculations. You should keep this in mind for your programs.

Strings

You have already encountered string literals in Chapter 2, "Your First Script," where you used them as arguments for several methods.

Technically, a string literal contains zero or more characters enclosed, as you know, in single or double quotes:

- [ ] `"Hello!"`
- [ ] `'245'`
- [ ] `""`

 The last example is called the *empty string*. It is important to note that the empty string is distinct from the `null` value in JavaScript.

Boolean

A boolean literal can take two values: either `true` or `false`. This type of literal comes in handy when comparing data and making decisions, as you will see later in this chapter.

 NOTE Unlike Java, C, and other languages, in JavaScript boolean values can only be represented with `true` and `false`. Values of 1 and 0 are not considered boolean values in JavaScript.

The `null` Value

The `null` value is a special value in JavaScript. The `null` value represents just that—nothing. If you try to reference a variable that isn't defined and therefore has no value, the value returned is the `null` value. Likewise, in a prompt dialog box, if the user selects the Cancel button, a `null` value is returned.

This is distinct from a value of zero or an empty string where this is an actual value.

The `null` value is indicated in JavaScript by the term `null`.

Casting

JavaScript is what is called a *loosely typed* programming language. In loosely typed languages, the type of a literal or variable (which we discuss in the next section) is not defined when a variable is created and can, at times, change based on the context. By comparison, Java and C are not loosely typed.

In its earliest forms, LiveScript and JavaScript allowed programmers to combine two literals of different types, with the result being a literal value of the same type as the first literal in the expression. For instance, combining the string `"Count to "` with the integer literal `10` results in a string with the value `"Count to 10"`.

By contrast, adding together the numeric literal `3.5` and the string `"10"` results in the floating point numeric literal `13.5`.

NEW TERM   This process is known as *casting*. The first example casts the number `10` into a string, and the second casts the string `10` into a number.

However, as JavaScript and Java have been brought closer together, this has begun to change. In the version of JavaScript currently available, it is no longer possible to cast a string into a number by using a form such as `0 + "1"`. JavaScript has added the `parseInt()` and `parseFloat()` functions, which convert strings into integers or floating point numbers. For instance, `parseInt("13")` returns the integer `13` and `parseFloat("45.2")` returns the floating point number `45.2`.

It is still possible to cast a number into a string as in `"Count to " + 10` evaluating to a string with the value `"Count to 10"`.

Creating Variables

In order to make working with data types useful, you need ways to store values for later use. This is where variables come in.

In JavaScript you can create variables that can contain any type of data. Variables have names, and after assigning values to a variable, you can refer to the value by name. If you subsequently assign a new value to the variable, you can continue referring to that new value by the name of the variable.

Declaring Variables

In order to use a variable, it is good programming style to declare it. Declaring a variable tells JavaScript that a variable of a given name exists so that the JavaScript interpreter can understand references to that variable name throughout the rest of the script.

Although it is possible to declare variables by simply using them, declaring variables helps to ensure that programs are well organized and helps to keep track of the scope of variables (discussed in Chapter 4, "Functions and Objects—The Building Blocks of Programs").

3

You can declare a variable using the var command:

```
var example;
```

In this line, you have defined a variable named example, which currently has no value. It is also possible to assign value to a variable when you declare it:

```
var example = "An Example";
```

Here you have declared the variable named example and assigned a string value of "An Example" to it. Because JavaScript allows variables to also be declared on first use, the command example = "An Example" would also achieve the same result.

 The equal sign (=) used in assigning a value to a variable is known as an *assignment operator*. Assignment operators are discussed later in this chapter.

To better understand how to declare, assign, and use variables, the following code segment produces output similar to Figure 3.1.

```
var example="An Example";
document.write(example);
```

Figure 3.1.

Variables can hold string literals, numbers, or boolean values.

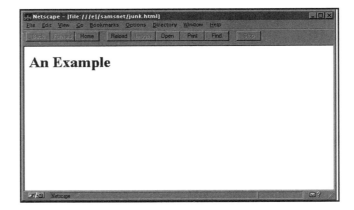

Valid Variable Names

Like property and method names in JavaScript, variable names are case sensitive. In addition, variable names must start with a letter or an underscore (_). After that, the remaining characters can also include numbers.

Incorporating Variables in a Script

Using variables, you can simplify the personalized "Welcome to Netscape Navigator 2!" script from the previous chapters. In Listing 3.1, you want to ask for the user's name prior to using `document.write()` and store the value in a variable.

TYPE **Listing 3.1. Using variables in the welcome program.**

```
<HTML>

<HEAD>

<TITLE>Example 3.1</TITLE>

<SCRIPT LANGUAGE="JavaScript">
<!--HIDE FROM OTHER BROWSERS

var name=prompt("Enter Your Name:","Name");

// STOP HIDING FROM OTHER BROWSERS -->
</SCRIPT>

</HEAD>

<BODY>
<SCRIPT LANGUAGE="JavaScript">
<!-- HIDE FROM OTHER BROWSERS

document.write('<IMG SRC="welcome.gif">');
document.write("<H1>Greetings, " + name + ". Welcome to Netscape
➥Navigator 2!</H1>");

// STOP HIDING FROM OTHER BROWSERS -->
</SCRIPT>
</BODY>

</HTML>
```

ANALYSIS There are several things to note in this script. First, the part of the script that needs to execute before things are displayed is in the header of the script. This helps ensure that nothing else can be loaded and evaluated until after the user provides a name.

Second, you have assigned the result returned by the `prompt()` method to the variable `name` in the same way you previously assigned a literal value to a variable. This works because the `prompt()` method is returning a string value, which can be assigned to a variable.

This script also demonstrates how using variables can make scripts easier to read because the names of variables can be carefully selected to impart meaning to someone reading the source code of a script.

You can now take using variables a step further and look at how you can assign values to them in succession. In Listing 3.2, you ask for two names in a row.

TYPE **Listing 3.2. Assigning a new value to the variable.**

```
<HTML>

<HEAD>

<TITLE>Example 3.2</TITLE>

<SCRIPT LANGUAGE="JavaScript">
<!--HIDE FROM OTHER BROWSERS

var name=prompt("Enter Your Name:","Name");
alert("Greetings " + name + ".");
name=prompt("Enter Your Friend's Name:","Friend's Name");

// STOP HIDING FROM OTHER BROWSERS -->
</SCRIPT>

</HEAD>

<BODY>
<SCRIPT LANGUAGE="JavaScript">
<!-- HIDE FROM OTHER BROWSERS

document.write('<IMG SRC="welcome.gif">');
document.write("<H1>Greetings, " + name + ". Welcome to Netscape
➥Navigator 2!</H1>");

// STOP HIDING FROM OTHER BROWSERS -->
</SCRIPT>
</BODY>

</HTML>
```

OUTPUT This script produces a sequence of results similar to Figures 3.2, 3.3, and 3.4.

Figure 3.2.
Store the first name in
name.

Figure 3.3.
The second name can
then also be assigned to
name.

Figure 3.4.

The final value of name *is the second name.*

 In this example, you see how assigning a new value to a variable completely replaces the previous value. Rather than combining the user's name with the friend's name, the final value of name is just the friend's name.

In addition, assigning subsequent values to variables works much the same way as assigning values when declaring a variable, except that the var command is not used.

By using two variables you can provide a final greeting to both users.

You will notice that the alert dialog box with the first name seems small. If you use a longer name, the size of the box is adjusted to accommodate the longer name.

Working with Variables—Expressions

In order to make variables useful, you need to be able to manipulate variables and evaluate them in different contexts.

This ability is provided by expressions. At its most basic, an expression is nothing more than a collection of variables, operators, and other expressions—all of which evaluate to a single value.

In practical terms, that means there are two types of expressions: those that simply have a value and those that assign a value to a variable. You have seen simple examples of both: example = "An Example" is an expression that assigns a value to the variable, example, while "The Number is " + "10" is an example of an expression that simply has value.

As with data types, JavaScript has several kinds of expressions:

☐ Assignment: Assigns a value to a variable
☐ Arithmetic: Evaluates to a number
☐ String: Evaluates to a string
☐ Logical: Evaluates to a boolean value

Assignment Expressions

Assignment expressions use assignment operators to assign value to a variable. The typical structure of an assignment expression is:

```
variable operator expression
```

In other words, the operator assigns a value to the variable by performing some type of operation on the expression. Table 3.3 outlines the assignment operators in JavaScript.

NEW TERM   Technically, the element to the left of the operator is called the *left operand* and the element to the right is called the *right operand*.

Table 3.3. Assignment operators in JavaScript.

Operator	Description
=	Assigns value of right operand to the left operand
+=	Adds the left and right operands and assigns the result to the left operand
-=	Subtracts the right operand from the left operand and assigns the result to the left operand
*=	Multiplies the two operands and assigns the result to the left operand
/=	Divides the left operand by the right operand and assigns the value to the left operand
%=	Divides the left operand by the right operand and assigns the remainder to the left operand

NOTE   The %= operand assigns the modulus to the left operand. That is, x %= y is the same as x = x % y. The modulus is the remainder when two numbers are divided.

3

For example, if x = 10 and y = 5, then x += y sets x to 15, x *= y sets x to 50, x /= y sets x to 2, and x %= y sets x to zero because the remainder of 10 divided by 5 is zero.

NOTE There are other assignment operators known as *bitwise assignment operators*, such as <<=, >>=, and ^=, but these are advanced and require an understanding of binary (base 2) numbers.

Other Operators

Besides the assignment operators we have already discussed, JavaScript also has operators for expressions that simply evaluate to a value. These are the arithmetic operators, string operators, and logical operators, as well as the bitwise operators, which are beyond the scope of this book.

As you will see in the following examples, these operators include both operators that require two operands and those that require a single operand.

NEW TERM An operator requiring a single operand is referred to as a *unary* operator, and one that requires two operands is a *binary* operator.

In addition, all the operators under discussion here can take expressions as their operands. In these cases, the expressions that act as operands are evaluated before evaluating the final expression. For example, in the next section, you will learn about simple arithmetic expressions such as 15 + 3. Because operators can take other expressions as their operands, you could write an expression such as x += 15 + 3. This adds 15 and 3, then adds the result (18) to the value of x, and assigns the final result to x.

Arithmetic Operators

The standard binary arithmetic operators are the same as those on a basic calculator: addition (+), subtraction (-), multiplication (*), and division (/). In addition to these basic operators is the modulus (%) operator, which, as mentioned before, calculates the remainder of dividing its operands. The following are examples of valid expressions using these:

```
8 + 5

32.5 - 72.3

12 % 5
```

In addition to these binary operators, there are three unary arithmetic operators that are quite useful: increment (++), decrement (--) and unary negation (-).

Both the increment and decrement operators can be used in two different ways: before the operand or after. For example, ++x increments x by one and returns the result, while x++ returns x and then increments the value of x. Similarly, --x decreases the value of x by one before returning a result, while x-- returns the value of x before decreasing its value by one.

For example:

```
x = 5;
y = ++x;
z = x++;
```

In these lines of code, x is first assigned the value of 5, then it is increased to 6 and assigned to y. Then, the new value of 6 is assigned to z and the value of x is increased to 7. So, at the end, x is 7, y is 6, and z is 6.

Unary negation works a little differently. The operator must precede its single operand, and the result is the negation of the operand. Typically, the usage of this operand looks like this:

```
x = -x;
```

Here, if the value of x is 5, then it becomes -5. Likewise, if x were -4, it would become 4.

Logical Operators

Logical operators include both binary and unary operators. They take boolean values as operands and return boolean values, as outlined in Table 3.4.

Table 3.4. Logical operators in JavaScript.

Operator	Description
&&	Logical "and"—returns true when both operands are true; otherwise it returns false.
||	Logical "or"—returns true if either operand is true. It only returns false when both operands are false.
!	Logical "not"—returns true if the operand is false and false if the operand is true. This is a unary operator and precedes the operand.

In discussing logical operators and expressions, it is necessary to discuss *short-circuit evaluation*. With short-circuit evaluation, JavaScript will finish evaluating an expression after evaluating the first (left) operand, if the first operand provides sufficient information to evaluate the expression. Short-circuit evaluation uses the following rules:

☐ false && anything is always false.

☐ true || anything is always true.

For example, if x equals 10 and y equals 20, then the expression (x > y) && (x < y) would immediately evaluate to false once the first part of the expression (x > y) is evaluated to false. Likewise, (y > x) ¦¦ (x > y) is evaluated to true simply because the first part of the expression (y > x) is true. These examples use comparison operators, which are discussed in the next section.

Because the logical "not" operator (!) takes a single operator, there is no short-circuit evaluation for it.

Comparison Operators

Comparison operators are similar to logical operators in that they return boolean values. Unlike logical operators, they don't require that their operands be boolean values.

Comparison operators are used to compare the value of the operands for equality as well as for a number of other conditions. Table 3.5 lists the comparison operators available in JavaScript.

Table 3.5. Comparison operators in JavaScript.

Operator	Description
==	Returns true if the operands are equal
!=	Returns true if the operands are not equal
>	Returns true if the left operand is greater than the right operand
<	Returns true if the left operand is less than the right operand
>=	Returns true if the left operand is greater than or equal to the right operand
<=	Returns true if the left operand is less than or equal to the right operand

In JavaScript, all comparison operators are binary operators.

Comparison operators can be used to compare numbers as well as strings; for instance:

```
1 == 1 returns true.
3 < 1 returns false.
5 >= 4 returns true.
"the" != "he" returns true.
4 == "4" returns true.
```

NOTE

When comparing string and numeric values, if the string value begins with nonnumeric characters, JavaScript will generate an error.

Conditional Operators

Conditional expressions are a little different than the others you have seen so far because a conditional expression can evaluate to one of two different values based on a condition. The structure of a conditional expression is:

```
(condition) ? val1 : val2
```

The way a conditional expression works is that the `condition`, which is any expression that can be evaluated to a boolean value, is evaluated; based on the result, the whole expression evaluates to either `val1` (true condition) or `val2` (false condition).

The expression

```
(day == "Saturday") ? "Weekend!" : "Not Saturday!"
```

evaluates to `"Weekend!"` when `day` is `"Saturday"`. Otherwise, the expression evaluates to `"Not Saturday!"`.

String Operators

In Chapter 2, you learned to use the concatenation operator (+). Concatenation returns the union of two strings so that

```
"Welcome to " + "Netscape Navigator 2.0!"
```

evaluates to a single string with the value "Welcome to Netscape Navigator 2.0!" As with numbers, this can be done with a short cut concatenation operator. For example, if the variable `welcome` has the value "Welcome to ", then

```
welcome += "Netscape Navigator 2.0!";
```

would assign the string "Welcome to Netscape Navigator 2.0!" to the variable `welcome`.

Operator Precedence

Because expressions can be the operands for other expressions, it is necessary to understand operator precedence. Operator precedence is the set of rules that determines the order in which these compound expressions are evaluated.

The operators that you have learned are evaluated in the following order (from lowest precedence to highest):

> Assignment operators (= += -= *= /= %=)
> Conditional (?:)
> Logical or (¦¦)
> Logical and (&&)
> Equality (== !=)
> Relational (< <= > >=)
> Addition/subtraction (+ -)
> Multiply/divide/modulus (* / %)
> Parentheses (())

Based on these rules, the expression

```
5 + 3 * 2
```

evaluates to

```
5 + 6
```

which evaluates to 11. Without these rules, the addition operator would be evaluated before the multiplication operator and the result would be 16. Likewise, the expression

```
false ¦¦ true && false
```

evaluates to

```
false
```

because the `&&` expression is evaluated to `false` first, and then the `¦¦` expression (which becomes `false ¦¦ false`) evaluates to `false`.

The rules of operator precedence can be overridden by the use of parentheses. Expressions in parentheses evaluate before those outside the parentheses, so that the expression

```
(5 + 3) * 2
```

would evaluate to 16, instead of 11 without the parentheses.

Testing a User's Response

In this example, you go beyond the "Welcome to Netscape Navigator 2!" scripts you have been working on to something a little different. In Listing 3.3, you will pose a test question to the user and based on the answer, display a different result for the user in the form of one of two different GIF images.

The question will be presented in a prompt dialog box, and the result displayed by outputting to the client window.

TYPE **Listing 3.3. Using conditional operators to test input.**

```html
<HTML>

<HEAD>
<TITLE>Example 3.3</TITLE>

<SCRIPT LANGUAGE="JavaScript">
<!-- HIDE FROM OTHER BROWSERS

// DEFINE VARIABLES FOR REST OF SCRIPT
var question="What is 10+10?";
var answer=20;
var correct='<IMG SRC="correct.gif">';
var incorrect='<IMG SRC="incorrect.gif">';

// ASK THE QUESTION
var response = prompt(question,"0");

// CHECK THE ANSWER
var output = (response == answer) ? correct : incorrect;

// STOP HIDING FROM OTHER BROWSERS -->
</SCRIPT>

</HEAD>

<BODY>

<SCRIPT LANGUAGE="JavaScript">
<!-- HIDE FROM OTHER BROWSERS

// OUTPUT RESULT
document.write(output);

// STOP HIDING FROM OTHER BROWSERS -->
</SCRIPT>

</BODY>

</HTML>
```

OUTPUT The results of this script would look like Figures 3.5 and 3.6.

3

Figure 3.5.
The prompt dialog box is used to test the user.

Figure 3.6.
Conditional operators determine the final Web page.

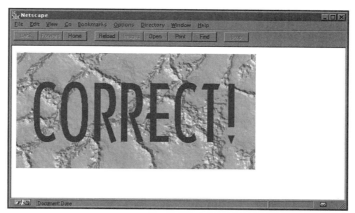

ANALYSIS In this example, you can see the use of several of the concepts learned earlier in this chapter and in earlier sections.

The first part of the script appears in the header because this is the advisable style, except where the script must generate output in sequence with the HTML file. For this reason, all the variable declarations—asking the question and checking the answer—take place in the header. The script in the body of the HTML document outputs only the final results.

Notice the extensive use of variables, both strings and numbers, all declared with the `var` command. Every important item in the script is assigned to a variable. This makes the script easier to read and easier to change. By changing the `question` and `answer` variables, you can change the test, and by changing the `correct` and `incorrect` variables, you can change the response given to the user.

In addition, you see a practical example of conditional expressions (`(response == answer) ? correct : incorrect`) and how the value of a conditional expression can be assigned to a variable.

Applying Comparison: `if-else` Constructs

Now that you know how to create expressions and, more importantly, how to create comparison expressions and logical expressions, you are ready to apply them.

In the preceding section you saw how an expression, such as a comparison, could be the condition in a conditional expression. The conditional operator gives you a simple way to make a decision: evaluate to one value when the condition is true and to another when the condition is false.

Still, by using conditional expressions, you cannot break beyond the bounds of a linear program flow. That is, every line of the script is evaluated and executed in order—you still can't alter the order.

Using the if-else construct, combined with expressions, you can alter the flow of a program—to determine which sections of program code run based on a condition.

At its most simple structure, the if statement is used as follows:

```
if condition
  command;
```

That is, if the condition is true, execute the command. Otherwise, don't execute it and skip to the next command or condition following. As you learned in Chapter 2, however, commands can be grouped together in command blocks using curly braces. The if statement can be used with command blocks as well:

```
if condition {
  several lines of JavaScript code
}
```

For example, these lines

```
if (day == "Saturday") {
  document.writeln("It's the weekend!");
  alert("It's the weekend!");
}
```

will write "It's the weekend!" to both the document window and an alert dialog box only if the variable day has the value "Saturday". If day has any other value, neither line is executed.

By using this you can have a different message for both Saturday and every other day of the week:

```
if (day == "Saturday") {
  document.writeln("It's the weekend!");
}
if (day != "Saturday") {
  document.writeln("It's not Saturday.");
}
```

The if-else construct provides an easier way to do this by using else:

```
if (day == "Saturday") {
  document.writeln("It's the weekend!");
} else {
  document.writeln("It's not Saturday.");
}
```

The else construct allows the creation of a command block to execute when the condition in the associated if statement is false.

Also, note that if-else constructs can be embedded:

```
if condition1 {
  JavaScript commands
  if condition2 {
    JavaScript commands
  } else {
    Other commands
  }
  More JavaScript commands
} else {
  Other commands
}
```

Using if for Repetition

Using the if statement, you are going to extend Listing 3.3 one step—you are going to enable the user to indicate if she wants a second chance to answer the question correctly, as shown in Listing 3.4.

What you want to do is ask the question and check the result. If the result is incorrect, you will ask the user if she wishes to try again. If she does, you ask one more time.

In order to make this easier, you will use the confirm() method, which is similar to the alert() and prompt() methods that you already know how to use. The confirm() method takes a single string as an argument. It displays the string in a dialog box with OK and Cancel buttons and returns a value of true if the user selects OK or false if Cancel is selected.

TYPE   **Listing 3.4. The confirm() method with the if statement.**

```
<HTML>

<HEAD>
<TITLE>Example 3.4</TITLE>

<SCRIPT LANGUAGE="JavaScript">
<!-- HIDE FROM OTHER BROWSERS

// DEFINE VARIABLES FOR REST OF SCRIPT
var question="What is 10+10?";
var answer=20;
var correct='<IMG SRC="correct.gif">';
var incorrect='<IMG SRC="incorrect.gif">';

// ASK THE QUESTION
var response = prompt(question,"0");
```

continues

Listing 3.4. continued

```
// CHECK THE ANSWER THE FIRST TIME
if (response != answer) {
  // THE ANSWER WAS WRONG: OFFER A SECOND CHANCE
  if (confirm("Wrong! Press OK for a second chance."))
    response = prompt(question,"0");
}

// CHECK THE ANSWER
var output = (response == answer) ? correct : incorrect;

// STOP HIDING FROM OTHER BROWSERS -->
</SCRIPT>

</HEAD>

<BODY>

<SCRIPT LANGUAGE="JavaScript">
<!-- HIDE FROM OTHER BROWSERS

// OUTPUT RESULT
document.write(output);

// STOP HIDING FROM OTHER BROWSERS -->
</SCRIPT>

</BODY>

</HTML>
```

ANALYSIS   In order to add the second chance, you have to add only two embedded if statements. In order to grasp how this works, let's look at the program line by line starting with the first prompt() method.

```
var response = prompt(question,"0");
```

In this line, you declare the variable response, ask the user to answer the question and assign the user's answer to response.

```
if (response != answer)
```

Here, you compare the user's response to the correct answer. If the answer is incorrect, then the next line is executed. If the answer is correct, the program skips down to output the result.

```
if (confirm("Wrong! Press OK for a second chance."))
```

The user has made an incorrect response. Now you check whether the user wants a second chance with the confirm() method, which returns a boolean value, which is evaluated by the if statement.

```
response = prompt(question,"0");
```

If the user selects OK in the confirm dialog box, the confirm() method returns true, and this line executes. With this command, the user is again asked the question, and the second response is stored in the response variable, replacing the previous answer.

Summary

JavaScript has four basic data types: numeric (both integer and floating point), string, boolean, and the null value. Literals, which literally express a value, can be of either numeric, string, or boolean type, and specific rules govern the format of these literals.

Variables, which are named containers to hold data and information in a program, are declared using the var statement. Because JavaScript is a loosely typed language, the type of literals and variables change dynamically depending on what actions are performed on them or with them.

Expressions provide a means to analyze and work with variables and literals. There are several types of expressions, including assignment expressions, arithmetic expressions, logical expressions, comparison expressions, string expressions, and conditional expressions. Expressions are made up of a series of operands and operators that evaluate to a single value.

The rules of operator precedence tell you the order in which compound expressions will be evaluated. Parentheses can be used to override operator precedence.

The if-else construct enables you to decide which program code will be executed based on the value of variables, literals, or expressions.

In Chapter 4, we will look at functions and objects as the building blocks for most programs.

Commands and Extensions Review

Command/Extension	Type	Description
var	JavaScript command	Declares a variable
=	Assignment operator	Assigns the value of the right operand to the left operand
+=	Assignment operator	Adds together the operands and assigns the result to the left operand
-=	Assignment operator	Subtracts the right from left operand and assigns the result to the left operand

continues

Command/Extension	Type	Description
*=	Assignment operator	Multiplies the operands and assigns the result to the left operand
/=	Assignment operator	Divides the left by the right operand and assigns the result to the left operand
%=	Assignment operator	Divides the left by the right operand and assigns the remainder to the left operand
+	Arithmetic operator	Adds the operands
-	Arithmetic operator	Subtracts the right from the left operand
*	Arithmetic operator	Multiplies the operands
/	Arithmetic operator	Divides the left by the right operand
%	Arithmetic operator	Divides the left by the right operand and calculates the remainder
&&	Logical operator	Evaluates to true when both operands are true
¦¦	Logical operator	Evaluates to true when either operand is true
!	Logical operator	Evaluates to true if the operand is false and to false if the operand is true
==	Comparison operator	Evaluates to true if the operands are equal
!=	Comparison operator	Evaluates to true if the operands are not equal
>	Comparison operator	Evaluates to true if the left operand is greater than the right operand
<	Comparison operator	Evaluates to true if the left operand is less than the right operand

3

Command/Extension	Type	Description
>=	Comparison operator	Evaluates to true if the left operand is greater than or equal to the right operand
<=	Comparison operator	Evaluates to true if the left operand is less than or equal to the right operand
+	String operator	Combines the operands into a single string
if	JavaScript command	Executes a command or command block if a condition is true
else	JavaScript command	Executes a command or command block if the condition of an associated if statement is false
parseInt()	JavaScript function	Converts a string to an integer number
parseFloat()	JavaScript function	Converts a string to a floating point number
confirm()	JavaScript method	Displays a message in a dialog box with OK and Cancel buttons.

Exercises

1. Evaluate each of the following expressions:

   a. `7 + 5`

   b. `"7" + "5"`

   c. `7 == 7`

   d. `7 >= 5`

   e. `7 <= 7`

   f. `(7 < 5) ? 7 : 5`

   g. `(7 >= 5) && (5 > 5)`

   h. `(7 >= 5) || (5 > 5)`

2. Write the segment of a script that would ask the user if he wants a greeting message and, if he does, display a GIF file called `welcome.gif` and display `"Welcome to Netscape Navigator 2.0!"` in the document window following the GIF.

3. Extend Listing 3.4 so that if users answer correctly, they have the choice to answer a second question, but they get only one chance to answer the second question.

Answers

1. The expressions evaluate as follows:

    a. `12`

    b. `"75"`

    c. `true`

    d. `true`

    e. `true`

    f. `5`

    g. `false`

    h. `true`

2. The following code uses the `confirm()` method and an `if` statement to complete the task:

```
if (confirm("Click OK to see a welcome message")) {
    document.write('<IMG SRC="welcome.gif">');
    document.write("<BR><H1>Welcome to Netscape Navigator 2.0!</H1>");
}
```

3. In order to add this functionality, use an `if-else` construct:

```
<HTML>

<HEAD>
<TITLE>Exercise 3.3</TITLE>

<SCRIPT LANGUAGE="JavaScript">
<!-- HIDE FROM OTHER BROWSERS

// DEFINE VARIABLES FOR REST OF SCRIPT
var question="What is 10+10?";
var answer=20;
var correct='<IMG SRC="correct.gif">';
var incorrect='<IMG SRC="incorrect.gif">';

// ASK THE QUESTION
var response = prompt(question,"0");
```

```
// CHECK THE ANSWER THE FIRST TIME
if (response != answer) {
  // THE ANSWER WAS WRONG: OFFER A SECOND CHANCE
  if (confirm("Wrong! Press OK for a second chance."))
    response = prompt(question,"0");
} else {
  // THE ANSWER WAS RIGHT: OFFER A SECOND QUESTION
  if (confirm("Correct! Press OK for a second question.")) {
    question = "What is 10*10?";
    answer = 100;
    response = prompt (question,"0");
  }
}

// CHECK THE ANSWER
var output = (response == answer) ? correct : incorrect;

// STOP HIDING FROM OTHER BROWSERS -->
</SCRIPT>

</HEAD>

<BODY>

<SCRIPT LANGUAGE="JavaScript">
<!-- HIDE FROM OTHER BROWSERS

// OUTPUT RESULT
document.write(output);

// STOP HIDING FROM OTHER BROWSERS -->
</SCRIPT>

</BODY>

</HTML>
```

Chapter 4

Functions and Objects—The Building Blocks of Programs

Once you start to write more complex programs, you will quickly find the need to perform some tasks and actions more than once during the course of a program.

This need is addressed by functions, which are similar to methods but are not attached to any particular object. As a programmer, you can create numerous functions in your programs—this helps organize the structure of your applications and makes maintaining and changing your program code easier.

In addition, functions are particularly useful in working with events and event handlers as you will learn in Chapter 5, "Events in JavaScript."

You can also use functions as the basis for creating your own objects to supplement those available to you in JavaScript.

In this chapter we will cover these topics:

- [ ] The nature of functions
- [ ] Built-in functions versus programmer-created functions
- [ ] How to define and use functions
- [ ] How to create new objects, properties, and methods
- [ ] How to use associative arrays

What Are Functions?

Functions offer the ability for programmers to group together program code that performs a specific task—or function—into a single unit that can be used repeatedly throughout a program.

Like the methods you have seen in earlier chapters, a function is defined by name and is invoked by using its name.

Also, like some of the methods you have seen before (such as `prompt()` and `confirm()`), functions can accept information in the form of arguments and can return results.

JavaScript includes several built-in functions as well as methods of base objects. You have already seen these when you used `alert()`, `document.write()`, `parseInt()`, or any of the other methods and functions you have been working with. The flexibility of JavaScript, though, lies in the ability for programmers to create their own functions to supplement those available in the JavaScript specification.

Using Functions

In order to make use of functions, you need to know how to define them, pass arguments to them, and return the results of their calculations. It is also important to understand the concept of variable scope, which governs whether a variable is available in an entire script or just within a specific function.

Defining Functions

Functions are defined using the `function` statement. The `function` statement requires a name for the function, a list of parameters—or arguments—that will be passed to the function, and a command block that defines what the function does:

```
function function_name(parameters, arguments) {
  command block
}
```

As you will notice, the naming of functions follows basically the same rules as variables: They are case sensitive, can include underscores (_), and start with a letter. The list of arguments passed to the function appears in parentheses and is separated by commas.

It is important to realize that defining a function does not execute the commands that make up the function. It is only when the function is called by name somewhere else in the script that the function is executed.

Passing Parameters

In the following function, you can see that printName() accepts one argument called name:

```
function printName(name) {
  document.write("<HR>Your Name is <B><I>");
  document.write(name);
  document.write("</B></I><HR>");
}
```

Within the function, references to name refer to the value passed to the function.

There are several points here to note:

☐ Both variables and literals can be passed as arguments when calling a function.

☐ If a variable is passed to the function, changing the value of the parameter within the function does not change the value of the variable passed to the function.

☐ Parameters exist only for the life of the function—if you call the function several times, the parameters are created afresh each time you call the function, and values they held when the function last ended are not retained.

For example, if you call printName() with the command:

```
printName("Bob");
```

then, when printName() executes, the value of name is "Bob". If you call printName() by using a variable for an argument:

```
var user = "John";
printName(user);
```

then name has the value "John". If you were to add a line to printName() changing the value of name:

```
name = "Mr. " + name;
```

name would change, but the variable user, which was sent as an argument, would not change.

NOTE

When passing arguments to a function, two properties that can be useful in working with the arguments are created: `functionname.arguments` and `function.arguments.length`. `functionname.arguments` is an array with an entry for each argument and `functionname.argument.length` is an integer variable indicating the number of variables passed to the function. You can use these properties to produce functions that accept a variable number of arguments.

Variable Scope

This leads to a discussion of variable scope. Variable scope refers to where a variable exists.

For instance, in the example `printName()`, `name` exists only within the function `printName()`—it cannot be referred to or manipulated outside the function. It comes into existence when the function is called and ceases to exist when the function ends. If the function is called again, a new instance of `name` is created.

In addition, any variable declared using the `var` command within the function will have a scope limited to the function.

If a variable is declared outside the body of a function, it is available throughout a script—inside all functions and elsewhere.

NEW TERM   Variables declared within a function are known as *local variables*. Variables declared outside functions and available throughout the script are known as *global variables*.

If you declare a local variable inside a function that has the same name as an existing global variable, then *inside* the function, that variable name refers to the new local variable and *not* the global variable. If you change the value of the variable inside the function, it does not affect the value of the global variable.

Returning Results

As mentioned in the previous section, functions can return results. Results are returned using the `return` statement. The `return` statement can be used to return any valid expression that evaluates to a single value. For example, in the function `cube()`,

```
function cube(number) {
  var cube = number * number * number;
  return cube;
}
```

4

the `return` statement will return the value of the variable `cube`. This function could just as easily have been written like this:

```
function cube(number) {
  return number * number * number;
}
```

This works because the expression `number * number * number` evaluates to a single value.

Functions in the File Header

As was mentioned in Chapter 3, "Working with Data and Information," there are compelling reasons to include function definitions inside the HEAD tags of the HTML file.

This ensures that all functions have been *parsed* before it is possible for user events to invoke a function. This is especially relevant once you begin working with event handlers where incorrect placement of a function definition can mean an event can lead to a function call when the function has not been evaluated and Navigator doesn't know it exists. When this happens, it causes an error message to be displayed.

NEW TERM The term *parsed* refers to the process by which the JavaScript interpreter evaluates each line of script code and converts it into a pseudo-compiled Byte Code (much like Java), before attempting to execute it. At this time, syntax errors and other programming mistakes that would prevent the script from running may be caught and reported to the user or programmer.

Putting Functions to Work

To demonstrate the use of functions, you are going to rewrite the simple test question example you used in Listing 3.3. In order to do this, you are going to create a function that receives a question as an argument, poses the question, checks the answer, and returns an output string based on the accuracy of the user's response.

In order to do this, you need to learn the `eval()` method, which evaluates a string to a numeric value; for instance,

```
eval("10*10")
```

returns a numeric value of `100`.

Listing 4.1. Evaluating an expression with the `eval()` function.

```
<HTML>

<HEAD>
<TITLE>Example 4.1</TITLE>

<SCRIPT LANGUAGE="JavaScript">
<!-- HIDE FROM OTHER BROWSERS

//DEFINE FUNCTION testQuestion()
function testQuestion(question) {
  //DEFINE LOCAL VARIABLES FOR THE FUNCTION
  var answer=eval(question);
  var output="What is " + question + "?";
  var correct='<IMG SRC="correct.gif">';
  var incorrect='<IMG SRC="incorrect.gif">';

  //ASK THE QUESTION
  var response=prompt(output,"0");

  //CHECK THE RESULT
  return (response == answer) ? correct : incorrect;
}

// STOP HIDING FROM OTHER BROWSERS -->
</SCRIPT>

</HEAD<

<BODY>

<SCRIPT LANGUAGE="JavaScript">
<!-- HIDE FROM OTHER BROWSERS

//ASK QUESTION AND OUTPUT RESULTS
var result=testQuestion("10 + 10");
document.write(result);

//STOP HIDING FROM OTHER BROWSERS -->
</SCRIPT>

</BODY>

</HTML>
```

At first glance, this script may seem a little more complicated than the version used in Listing 3.3. In reality, though, it simply separates the work into logical blocks and moves most of the work into the function testQuestion().

To understand the function, let's analyze the key lines.

```
function testQuestion(question) {
```

In this line, you define the function testQuestion() and indicate that it receives one argument, which is referred to as question within the function. In the case of this function, it is expected that question will be a string containing an arithmetic expression.

```
var answer=eval(question);
```

The first thing you do after entering the function is to declare the variable answer and assign to it the numeric value of the arithmetic expression contained in the string question. This is achieved using the eval() function.

```
var output="What is " + question + "?";
var correct='<IMG SRC="correct.gif">';
var incorrect='<IMG SRC="incorrect.gif">';
```

In these lines you declare several more variables. The variable output contains the actual question to display, which is created using the concatenation operator.

```
var response=prompt(output,"0");
```

Here you ask the question and assign the user's response to the variable response.

```
return (response == answer) ? correct : incorrect;
```

In this line you use the conditional operator to check the user's response. The resulting value is returned by the return command.

Now that you understand the function, it should be clear how you are invoking it later in the body of the HTML file. The line

```
var result=testQuestion("10 + 10");
```

calls testQuestion() and passes a string to it containing an arithmetic expression. The function returns a result, which is stored in the variable result. Then you are able to output the result using document.write().

These two lines could be condensed into a single line:

```
document.write(testQuestion("10 + 10"));
```

Recursive Functions

Now that you have seen an example of how functions work, let's take a look at an application of functions called recursion.

 Recursion refers to situations in which functions call themselves. These types of functions are known as *recursive functions*.

For instance, the following is an example of a recursive function that calculates a factorial:

> **NOTE**
>
> A factorial is a mathematical function. For example, factorial 5 (written 5!) is equal to 5×4×3×2×1 and 7! = 7×6×5×4×3×2×1.

```
function factorial(number) {
  if (number > 1) {
    return number * factorial(number - 1);
  } else {
    return number;
  }
}
```

At first glance, this function may seem strange. This function relies on the fact that the factorial of a number is equal to the number multiplied by the factorial of one less than the number. Expressed mathematically, this could be written:

```
x! = x * (x-1)!
```

In order to apply this formula, you have created a recursive function called `factorial()`. The function receives a number as an argument. Using the following `if-else` construct:

```
if (number > 1) {
  return number * factorial(number - 1);
} else {
  return number;
}
```

the function either returns a value of 1 if the argument is equal to 1, or applies the formula and returns the number multiplied by the factorial of one less than the number.

In order to do this, it must call the function `factorial()` from within the function `factorial()`. This is where the concept of variable scope becomes extremely important. It is important to realize that when the function calls `factorial()`, a new instance of the function is being invoked, which means that a new instance of `number` is created. This continues to occur until the expression `number-1` has a value of 1.

WARNING

Recursive functions are powerful, but they can be dangerous if you don't watch out for infinite recursion. *Infinite recursion* occurs when the function is designed in such a way as to call itself forever without stopping.

At a practical level, in JavaScript, infinite recursion isn't likely to happen because of the way in which JavaScript handles some of its memory allocation. This means that deep recursions, even if they aren't infinite, may cause Navigator to crash.

It is important to note that the function `factorial()` prevents infinite recursion because the `if-else` construct ensures that eventually the function will stop calling itself once the number passed to it is equal to one. In addition, if the function is initially called with a value less than two, the function will immediately return without any recursion.

Using recursive functions, it is possible to extend the program used in Listing 4.1 so that it continues to ask the question until the user provides the correct answer, as shown in Listing 4.2.

4

TYPE **Listing 4.2. Using a recursive function to repeat input.**

```
<HTML>

<HEAD>
<TITLE>Example 4.2</TITLE>

<SCRIPT LANGUAGE="JavaScript">
<!-- HIDE FROM OTHER BROWSERS

//DEFINE FUNCTION testQuestion()
function testQuestion(question) {
  //DEFINE LOCAL VARIABLES FOR THE FUNCTION
  var answer=eval(question);
  var output="What is " + question + "?";
  var correct='<IMG SRC="correct.gif">';
  var incorrect='<IMG SRC="incorrect.gif">';

  //ASK THE QUESTION
  var response=prompt(output,"0");

  //CHECK THE RESULT
  return (response == answer) ? correct : testQuestion(question);
}
```

continues

Listing 4.2. continued

```
// STOP HIDING FROM OTHER BROWSERS -->
</SCRIPT>

</HEAD<

<BODY>

<SCRIPT LANGUAGE="JavaScript">
<!-- HIDE FROM OTHER BROWSERS

//ASK QUESTION AND OUTPUT RESULTS
var result=testQuestion("10 + 10");
document.write(result);

//STOP HIDING FROM OTHER BROWSERS -->
</SCRIPT>

</BODY>

</HTML>
```

ANALYSIS Notice that you have made only a single change to the conditional expression:

```
return (response == answer) ? correct : testQuestion(question);
```

Where you originally returned the value of the variable `incorrect` when the user provided an incorrect response, you are now returning the result of asking the question again (by calling `testQuestion()` again).

It is important to realize that this example could cause JavaScript to crash because of its memory handling problems if the user never provides the correct answer. This can be remedied by adding a counter to keep track of the number of chances the user has to provide a correct answer:

```
<HTML>

<HEAD>
<TITLE>Example 4.2</TITLE>

<SCRIPT LANGUAGE="JavaScript">
<!-- HIDE FROM OTHER BROWSERS

//DEFINE FUNCTION testQuestion()
function testQuestion(question,chances) {
  //DEFINE LOCAL VARIABLES FOR THE FUNCTION
  var answer=eval(question);
  var output="What is " + question + "?";
  var correct='<IMG SRC="correct.gif">';
  var incorrect='<IMG SRC="incorrect.gif">';
```

4

```
//ASK THE QUESTION
var response=prompt(output,"0");

//CHECK THE RESULT
if (chances > 1) {
  return (response == answer) ? correct : testQuestion(question,chances-1);
} else {
  return (response == answer) ? correct : incorrect;
}
}

// STOP HIDING FROM OTHER BROWSERS -->
</SCRIPT>

</HEAD<

<BODY>

<SCRIPT LANGUAGE="JavaScript">
<!-- HIDE FROM OTHER BROWSERS

//ASK QUESTION AND OUTPUT RESULTS
var result=testQuestion("10 + 10",3);
document.write(result);

//STOP HIDING FROM OTHER BROWSERS -->
</SCRIPT>

</BODY>

</HTML>
```

By adding the if-else construct when you check the user's answer, you are ensuring that you cannot enter an infinite recursion. The if-else construct could be replaced by a conditional expression:

```
return (response == answer) ? correct : ((chances > 1) ?
➥testQuestion(question,chances-1) : incorrect);
```

What this expression says is if the user's response is correct (response==answer evaluates to true), then return the value of correct. Otherwise, if there are chances left (chances > 1 evaluates to true), ask the question again and return the result. If there are no chances left and the answer is incorrect, return the value of the variable incorrect.

Building Objects in JavaScript

As you learned earlier, it is possible to use functions to build custom objects in JavaScript. In order to do this, you must be able to define an object's properties, to create new instances of objects, and to add methods to objects.

Defining an Object's Properties

Before creating a new object, it is necessary to define that object by outlining its properties. This is done by using a function that defines the name and properties of the function. This type of function is known as a *constructor function*.

If you want to create an object type for students in a class, you could create an object named student with properties for name, age, and grade. This could be done with the function:

```
function student(name,age, grade) {
  this.name = name;
  this.age = age;
  this.grade = grade;
}
```

NOTE

Notice the use of the special keyword this. this plays a special role in JavaScript and refers to the current object. You will learn more about this in Chapter 5, when we begin discussing event handlers.

Using this function, it is now possible to create an object using the new statement:

```
student1 = new student("Bob",10,75);
```

This line of JavaScript code creates an object called student1 with three properties: student1.name, student1.age, and student1.grade. This is known as an *instance* of the object student. By creating a new object student2 using the new statement,

```
student2 = new student("Jane",9,82);
```

you would be creating a new instance of the object that is independent from student1.

It is also possible to add properties to objects once they are created simply by assigning values to a new property. For instance, if you want to add a property containing Bob's mother's name, you could use the structure

```
student1.mother = "Susan";
```

This would add the property to student1 but would have no effect on student2 or future instances of the student object. To add the property mother to all instances of student, it would be necessary to add the property to the object definition before creating instances of the object:

```
function student(name, age, grade, mother) {
  this.name = name;
  this.age = age;
```

```
    this.grade = grade;
    this.mother = mother;
}
```

Objects as Properties of Objects

You can also use objects as properties of other objects. For instance, if you were to create an object called grade

```
function grade (math, english, science) {
  this.math = math;
  this.english = english;
  this.science = science;
}
```

you could then create two instances of the grade object for the two students:

```
bobGrade = new grade(75,80,77);
janeGrade = new grade(82,88,75);
```

NOTE
The order of arguments is important in JavaScript. In the preceding example, if Jane hasn't taken English, you would need to pass a place-holder to the function, such as zero or a string value, such as "N/A" or the empty string. The function would then need to be written to handle this eventuality.

4

Using these objects, you could then create the student objects like this:

```
student1 = new student("Bob",10,bobGrade);
student2 = new student("Jane",9,janeGrade);
```

You could then refer to Bob's math grade as student1.grade.math or Jane's science grade as student2.grade.science.

Adding Methods to Objects

In addition to adding properties to object definitions, you can also add a method to an object definition. Because methods are essentially functions associated with an object, first you need to create a function that defines the method you want to add to your object definition.

For instance, if you want to add a method to the student object to print the student's name, age, and grades to the document window, you could create a function called displayProfile():

```
function displayProfile() {
  document.write("Name: " + this.name + "<BR>");
  document.write("Age: " + this.age + "<BR>");
```

```
        document.write("Mother's Name: " + this.mother + "<BR>");
        document.write("Math Grade: " + this.grade.math + "<BR>");
        document.write("English Grade: " + this.grade.english + "<BR>");
        document.write("Science Grade: " + this.grade.science + "<BR>");
      }
```

NOTE Here again, you use this to refer to the object that is invoking the method. If you call a method as object1.method, then this refers to object1.

Having defined the method, you now need to change the object definition to include the method:

```
function student(name,age, grade) {
  this.name = name;
  this.age = age;
  this.grade = grade;
  this.mother = mother;
  this.displayProfile = displayProfile;
}
```

Then, you could output Bob's student profile by using the command:

```
student1.displayProfile();
```

This would produce results similar to those in Figure 4.1.

Figure 4.1.

The display-Profile() *method displays the profile for any instance of the* student *object.*

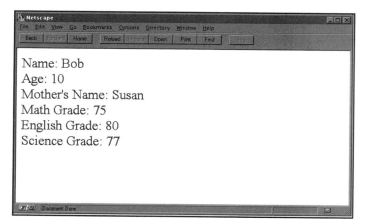

Name: Bob
Age: 10
Mother's Name: Susan
Math Grade: 75
English Grade: 80
Science Grade: 77

Defining Your Own Objects

To further demonstrate the application of objects and defining your own objects, Listing 4.3 is a program that asks the user for personnel information of an employee and then formats it for display on the screen.

In order to do this, you need to define an employee object, as well as a method for displaying the employee information.

TYPE **Listing 4.3. Creating an employee profile.**

```
<HTML>

<HEAD>
<TITLE>Example 4.3</TITLE>

<SCRIPT LANGUAGE="JavaScript">
<!-- HIDE FROM OTHER BROWSERS

//DEFINE METHOD
function displayInfo() {
  document.write("<H1>Employee Profile: " + this.name + "</H1><HR><PRE>");
  document.writeln("Employee Number: " + this.number);
  document.writeln("Social Security Number: " + this.socsec);
  document.writeln("Annual Salary: " + this.salary);
  document.write("</PRE>");
}

//DEFINE OBJECT
function employee() {
  this.name=prompt("Enter Employee's Name","Name");
  this.number=prompt("Enter Employee Number for " + this.name,"000-000");
  this.socsec=prompt("Enter Social Security Number for " +
➥this.name,"000-00-0000");
  this.salary=prompt("Enter Annual Salary for " + this.name,"$00,000");
  this.displayInfo=displayInfo;
}

newEmployee=new employee();

// STOP HIDING  FROM OTHER BROWSERS -->
</SCRIPT>

</HEAD>

<BODY>
<SCRIPT LANGUAGE="JavaScript">
<!-- HIDE FROM OTHER BROWSERS

newEmployee.displayInfo();
```

continues

Listing 4.3. continued

```
// STOP HIDING FROM OTHER BROWSERS -->
</SCRIPT>

</BODY>

</HTML>
```

OUTPUT This script produces results similar to those in Figure 4.2 and 4.3.

Figure 4.2.
The program prompts the user for the employee information.

Figure 4.3.
The method you defined displays the formatted data.

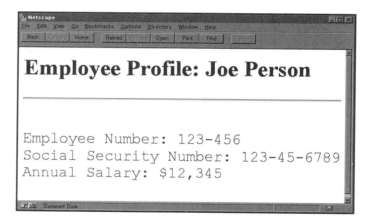

ANALYSIS In this example, the most noticeable variation on what you have learned is that you don't pass any arguments to the object definition function, `employee()`.

Instead, this object definition is more of a dynamic object definition in that when a new instance of the object is created, the user is prompted for all the relevant data for the properties.

Associative Arrays

Anyone who has programmed in other structured languages has probably encountered arrays of one sort or another and will be wondering where JavaScript's arrays are.

Arrays are ordered collections of values referred to by a single variable name. For instance, if you have an array named `student`, you might have the following ordered values:

```
student[0] = "Bob"
student[1] = 10
student[2] = 75
```

NOTE

Array elements are referred to by their indexes—the numbers in brackets. In JavaScript, arrays start with index `0`, so the fifth element in an array is actually `array_name[4]`.

Although JavaScript doesn't have a unique data type for arrays, properties and arrays are closely tied in JavaScript. In fact, arrays and properties are different ways of accessing the same information. In the example of the `student` object in the preceding section, you can refer to the properties of the `student2` object as:

```
student2["name"]
student2["age"]
```

and so on, or by index numbers, where

```
student2[0] = "Jane"
student2[1] = 9
```

and so on.

This capability to interchangeably treat object properties as an array will become particularly useful later when you learn about the `for ... in` loop structure in Chapter 7, "Loops."

NOTE

The type of array available in JavaScript is known as an *associative array* because each index element is associated with a string value that can also be used to reference the array element (and which is also the property name).

To demonstrate how referring to object properties as an array can be useful, Listing 4.4 builds on the personnel information example in the Listing 4.3.

In this example, you do not have the user enter the personnel information for the new employee in the same way. You present a list of information you want. The users select a number for the information they want to enter. When they are done, they select "0."

After a user finishes entering the information, then the script displays the formatted employee profile.

TYPE Listing 4.4. Creating a user menu.

```html
<HTML>

<HEAD>
<TITLE>Example 4.4</TITLE>

<SCRIPT LANGUAGE="JavaScript">
<!-- HIDE FROM OTHER BROWSERS

//DEFINE METHOD
function displayInfo() {
  document.write("<H1>Employee Profile: " + this.name + "</H1><HR><PRE>");
  document.writeln("Employee Number: " + this.number);
  document.writeln("Social Security Number: " + this.socsec);
  document.writeln("Annual Salary: " + this.salary);
  document.write("</PRE>");
}

//DEFINE METHOD TO GET EMPLOYEE INFORMATION
function getInfo() {
  var menu="0-Exit/1-Name/2-Emp. #/3-Soc. Sec. #/4-Salary";
  var choice=prompt(menu,"0");
  if (choice != null) {
    if ((choice < 0) || (choice > 4)) {
      alert ("Invalid choice");
      this.getInfo();
    } else {
      if (choice != "0") {
        this[choice-1]=prompt("Enter Information","");
        this.getInfo();
      }
    }
  }
}

//DEFINE OBJECT
function employee() {
  this.name="";
  this.number=0;
  this.socsec=0;
  this.salary=0;
  this.displayInfo=displayInfo;
  this.getInfo=getInfo;
}

newEmployee=new employee();

// STOP HIDING FROM OTHER BROWSERS -->
</SCRIPT>

</HEAD>

<BODY>
```

4

```
<SCRIPT LANGUAGE="JavaScript">
<!-- HIDE FROM OTHER BROWSERS

newEmployee.getInfo();
newEmployee.displayInfo();

// STOP HIDING FROM OTHER BROWSERS -->
</SCRIPT>

</BODY>

</HTML>
```

OUTPUT This script produces a series of results similar to those in Figures 4.4, 4.5, and 4.6.

Figure 4.4.
A menu in a prompt box.

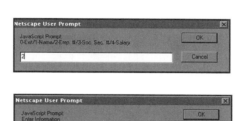

Figure 4.5.
Prompting for input.

Figure 4.6.
The final result.

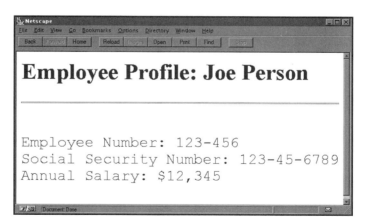

ANALYSIS In this example, you can see several of the concepts you have learned in action here, including recursion and associative arrays.

The method getInfo() needs some explanation:

```
var menu="0-Exit/1-Name/2-Emp. #/3-Soc. Sec. #/4-Salary";
```

The menu variable contains the string that presents the choices to the user. Notice the use of the \n special character to create a multiline menu in a single text string.

```
var choice = prompt(menu,"0");
```

Here you present the menu to the user and ask for a choice, which is stored in the variable choice.

```
if (choice != null) {
  if ((choice < 0) || (choice > 4)) {
    alert ("Invalid choice");
    this.getInfo();
  } else {
    if (choice != "0") {
      this[choice-1]=prompt("Enter Information","");
      this.getInfo();
    }
  }
}
```

This set of if statements is where the real work of the getInfo() method is done. The first if statement checks whether the user has selected Cancel. If not, then the user's choice is checked to make sure it is in range (from zero to four). If the choice is out of range, then the user is alerted, and the getInfo() method is called again. If the user's choice is in range, it is checked to see if the user has chosen 0 for exit. If the user doesn't select 0, the user is prompted to enter the data he has indicated. Then the getInfo() method is called again to present the menu again.

You will notice the use of the this keyword to refer to the current object and the use of this[choice-1] to refer to the array element (or property) selected by the user. Use choice-1 because the menu presents choices from 1 to 4 to the user, but array indexes start from 0 and, in this case, the index goes up to 3.

Summary

Functions provide a means to define segments of code that can be used more than once in a program. Like methods, which are part of objects, functions are defined by names, can be passed arguments, and can return results.

4

Variable scope, whether a variable exists locally to a function or globally for the entire program, is an important concept in dealing with functions.

Recursive functions are functions that call themselves one or more times. Recursion is a powerful tool, but it needs to be used carefully to avoid infinite recursion, which occurs when a function repeatedly calls itself without ever ending. With the current implementation of JavaScript, infinite recursion can't really happen because memory handling shortcomings mean that Navigator will crash when recursion gets too deep.

Functions are also used to define the properties and objects that make up user-defined methods. Using the new keyword, it is possible to create multiple instances of an object which all exist independently.

Associative arrays are another way of referring to properties in an object.

If you have made it to the end of this chapter, you are making progress because both recursion and functions and objects are advanced topics.

In Chapter 5, you begin to work with events and event handlers which will allow you to design programs that interact with the user in a sophisticated way.

Commands and Extensions Review

Command/Extension	Type	Description
function	JavaScript keyword	Declares a function
new	JavaScript keyword	Creates a new instance of an object
eval()	JavaScript method	Evaluates a string to a numeric value
this	JavaScript keyword	Refers to the current object

Exercises

1. Write the object definition for an object called car with four properties: model, make, year, and price.

2. If you have an object defined as follows
   ```
   function house(address,rooms,owner) {
     this.address = address;
     this.rooms = rooms;
     this.owner = owner;
   }
   ```
   and you create two instances of the house object

```
house1 = new house("10 Maple St.",10,"John");
house2 = new house("15 Sugar Rd.",12,"Mary");
```

then, what would be the value of the following:

   a. house1.rooms

   b. house2[3]

   c. house2["owner"]

   d. house1[0]

3. Create a function that calculates the value of x to the power of y. For instance, if you have a function called power() and you issue the command

```
value = power(10,4);
```

then power() should return the value of 10 to the power of 4, or 10 * 10 * 10 * 10.

NOTE

> If the notation x^y refers to x to the power of y, then it will be helpful in writing this function to realize that x^y = x * x^(y-1).

Answers

1. The object definition would look like this:
```
function car(model, make, year, price) {
  this.model = model;
  this.make = make;
  this.year = year;
  this.price = price;
}
```

2. The values are as follows:

   a. 10

   b. house2[3] has the null value because the house2 object has only three properties which would be referred to by the array elements house2[0], house2[1], and house2[2].

   c. "Mary"

   d. "10 Maple St."

3. The power() function could be written using recursion:
```
function power(number, exponent) {
  if (exponent > 1) {
    return number * power(number, exponent - 1);
  } else {
    return 1;
```

4

```
  }
}
```

This function makes use of a similar principle as the factorial example earlier in the chapter. This function uses the fact that x to the power of y equals x multiplied by x to the power of y-1.

While this function works, it is important to note that it isn't perfect. Although negative exponents are mathematically legal, this function will not calculate the result correctly for this type of exponent.

Remembering that x to the power of -y is the same as 1 divided by x to the power of y, you could fix the problem with negative exponents by making the following change to the function:

```javascript
function power(number, exponent) {

  // CHECK IF WE HAVE A NEGATIVE EXPONENT
  var negative = (exponent < 0) ? true : false;

  // DECLARE WORKING VARIABLE
  var value=0;

  // CALCULATE number TO THE POWER OF exponent
  if (exponent > 1) {
    value = number * power(number, exponent - 1);
  } else {
    value = 1;
  }

  // IF THE EXPONENT WAS NEGATIVE, TAKE THE RECIPROCAL
  if (negative)
    value = 1 / value;

  return value;
}
```

NOTE

JavaScript includes a method that performs the same thing as your power() function. The Math.pow() method is part of the Math object and is discussed in Chapter 10, "Strings, Math, and the History List."

From the Web:

Dave Eisenberg's Calendar

Dave Eisenberg's calendar (`http://www.best.com/~nessus/js-today.html`) is a good example of the use of expressions and variables, as well as functions and objects. The program generates a dynamic Web page that includes a greeting suited to the time of day (such as "Good Evening!"), the time of day, and the current month's calendar with the current date highlighted.

In addition, the page includes an image suited to the current time of day.

In doing this, Eisenberg makes use of several techniques that we haven't seen yet. His script uses the `Date` object, as well as several new methods including `Math.floor()` from the `Math` object and others from the `Date` object.

The source code for the page is in Listing W1.1.

Listing W1.1. Dave Eisenberg's calendar.

```
<HTML>
<HEAD>
<TITLE>Greetings from Dave Eisenberg</TITLE>
</HEAD>

<BODY>

<SCRIPT LANGUAGE="JavaScript">
<!-- to hide script contents from old browsers

function greeting()
{
   var today = new Date();
   var hrs = today.getHours();

   document.writeln("<CENTER>");
   if ((hrs >=6) && (hrs <=18))
   {
      document.writeln("<IMG SRC=\"daypix/day");
      document.write(Math.floor(hrs / 10));
      document.write(Math.floor(hrs % 10));
      document.write("00.gif\">");
   }
   else
      document.write("<IMG SRC=\"daypix/night1.gif\">");

   document.writeln("<BR>");
   document.write("<H1>Good ");
   if (hrs < 6)
      document.write("(Early) Morning");
   else if (hrs < 12)
      document.write("Morning");
   else if (hrs <= 18)
      document.write("Afternoon");
   else
      document.write("Evening");
   document.writeln("!</H1>");
   document.write("You entered this page at ");
   dayStr = today.toLocaleString();
   i = dayStr.indexOf(' ');
   n = dayStr.length;
   document.write(dayStr.substring(i+1, n));
   document.writeln("</CENTER>");
}

function montharr(m0, m1, m2, m3, m4, m5, m6, m7, m8, m9, m10, m11)
{
   this[0] = m0;
   this[1] = m1;
   this[2] = m2;
   this[3] = m3;
   this[4] = m4;
   this[5] = m5;
   this[6] = m6;
```

```
      this[7] = m7;
      this[8] = m8;
      this[9] = m9;
      this[10] = m10;
      this[11] = m11;
}

function calendar()
{
      var monthNames = "JanFebMarAprMayJunJulAugSepOctNovDec";
      var today = new Date();
      var thisDay;
      var monthDays = new montharr(31, 28, 31, 30, 31, 30, 31, 31, 30,
         31, 30, 31);

      year = today.getYear() + 1900;
      thisDay = today.getDate();

      // do the classic leap year calculation
      if (((year % 4 == 0) && (year % 100 != 0)) || (year % 400 == 0))
         monthDays[1] = 29;

      // figure out how many days this month will have...
      nDays = monthDays[today.getMonth()];

      // and go back to the first day of the month...
      firstDay = today;
      firstDay.setDate(1);
      // and figure out which day of the week it hits...
      startDay = firstDay.getDay();

      document.writeln("<CENTER>");
      document.write("<TABLE BORDER>");
      document.write("<TR><TH COLSPAN=7>");
      document.write(monthNames.substring(today.getMonth() * 3,
         (today.getMonth() + 1) * 3));
      document.write(". ");
      document.write(year);
      document.write("<TR><TH>Sun<TH>Mon<TH>Tue<TH>Wed<TH>Thu<TH>Fri<TH>Sat");

      // now write the blanks at the beginning of the calendar
      document.write("<TR>");
      column = 0;
      for (i=0; i<startDay; i++)
      {
         document.write("<TD>");
         column++;
      }

      for (i=1; i<=nDays; i++)
      {
         document.write("<TD>");
         if (i == thisDay)
            document.write("<FONT COLOR=\"#FF0000\">")
         document.write(i);
         if (i == thisDay)
```

continues

Listing W1.1. continued

```
        document.write("</FONT>")
    column++;
    if (column == 7)
    {
        document.write("<TR>"); // start a new row
        column = 0;
    }
}
document.write("</TABLE>");
document.writeln("</CENTER>");
}
document.write(greeting());
document.write("<HR>");
document.write(calendar());
document.write("<HR>");
document.write("<A HREF=\"http://www.best.com/~nessus\">");
document.write("Back to Dave Eisenberg's resume<\A>");

<!-- end hiding contents from old browsers  -->
</SCRIPT>

</BODY>
</HTML>
```

OUTPUT The code produces results like those in Figures W1.1 and W1.2.

Figure W1.1.
During the day-time, the user gets one of several images depicting the time of day.

Figure W1.2.

Using the Date *object, the program builds a calendar for the current month.*

ANALYSIS The first thing you notice about this script is that it is not placed inside the header of the HTML file. The author does this because there is no chance of events triggering calls to functions which have not yet been defined.

In addition, all HTML code is dynamically generated by the script.

The calendar program uses three functions. The calls are made in sequence by the main body of the script:

```
document.write(greeting());
document.write("<HR>");
document.write(calendar());
document.write("<HR>");
document.write("<A HREF=\"http://www.best.com/~nessus\">");
document.write("Back to Dave Eisenberg's resume<\A>");
```

At the top of the script, two global declarations (today and hrs) occur. The command var today = new Date(); creates an instance of the system's Date object in much the same way you could create an instance of any object you defined yourself.

The Date object enables programmers to create an object that contains information about a particular date and provides a set of methods to work with that information.

In order to create an instance of the Date object, you use the form: *variable* = new Date(*parameters*) where the parameters can be any of the following:

- Empty to create today's date and the current time
- A string of the form "*Month day, year hours:minutes:seconds*" (for example "May 11, 1979 8:00:00")
- Integer values for the current year, month, and day as in Date(79,5,11)
- Integer values for the current year, month, day, and time as in Date(79,5,11,8,0,0)

NOTE In JavaScript, it is not possible to create dates before 1 January 1970. 1 January 1970 at 00:00:00 is known as the epoch.

The Date object provides the methods outlined in Table 4.1.

Table 4.1. Methods of the Date object.

Name	Description
getDate	Returns the day of the month as an integer from 1 to 31
getDay	Returns the day of the week as an integer where zero is Sunday and one is Monday
getHours	Returns the hour as an integer between 0 and 23
getMinutes	Returns the minutes as an integer from 0 to 59
getMonth	Returns the month as an integer from 0 to 11 where zero is January and 11 is December
getSeconds	Returns the seconds as an integer between 0 and 59
getTime	Returns the number of milliseconds since 1 January 1970 at 00:00:00
getTimezoneOffset	Returns the difference between the local time and Greenwich Mean Time in minutes
getYear	Returns the year as a two-digit integer
parse	Returns the number of milliseconds since 1 January 1970 at 00:00:00 for the date string passed to it
setDate	Sets the day of the month based on an integer argument from 1 to 31
setHours	Sets the hour based on an argument from 0 to 23
setMinutes	Sets the minutes based on an argument from 0 to 59
setMonth	Sets the month based on an argument from 0 to 11
setSeconds	Sets the seconds based on an argument between 0 and 59
setTime	Sets the time based on an argument representing the number of milliseconds since 1 January 1970 at 00:00:00
setYear	Sets the year based on a four-digit integer greater than 1900
toString	Returns the current date as a string
toGMTString	Returns the current date and time using the Internet GMT conventions (i.e. in the form "Mon, 18 Dec 1995 17:28:35 GMT")
toLocaleString	Returns the date as a string in the form "*MM/DD/YY HH:MM:SS*"
UTC	Takes a comma delimited date and returns the number of milliseconds since 1 January 1970 at 00:00:00 GMT time

Based on this information, the variable declaration var hrs = today=getHours() will contain the current hour when the user loads the page.

The first function the script calls is greeting(), which displays the appropriate image and welcome message along with the current time:

```
function greeting()
{
   var today = new Date();
   var hrs = today.getHours();

   document.writeln("<CENTER>");
   if ((hrs >=6) && (hrs <=18))
   {
      document.writeln("<IMG SRC=\"daypix/day");
      document.write(Math.floor(hrs / 10));
      document.write(Math.floor(hrs % 10));
      document.write("00.gif\">");
   }
   else
      document.write("<IMG SRC=\"daypix/night1.gif\">");

   document.writeln("<BR>");
   document.write("<H1>Good ");
   if (hrs < 6)
      document.write("(Early) Morning");
   else if (hrs < 12)
      document.write("Morning");
   else if (hrs <= 18)
      document.write("Afternoon");
   else
      document.write("Evening");
   document.writeln("!</H1>");
   document.write("You entered this page at ");
   dayStr = today.toLocaleString();
   i = dayStr.indexOf(' ');
   n = dayStr.length;
   document.write(dayStr.substring(i+1, n));
   document.writeln("</CENTER>");
}
```

The function determines that it is daytime if hrs is between 6 and 18 and then builds an image tag. The filename includes a number built out of the hrs variable using Math.floor(). This method returns the closest integer less than the argument. In that way, if hrs is 12, the image's filename would be day1200.gif.

TIP

Math.ceil() is similar to Math.floor() except it returns the nearest integer greater than the value of the argument.

The current time, which is output at the end of the function, is obtained from the string returned by the Date.toLocaleString() method. This string contains the date and time separated by a single space. The function uses the indexOf() method of the string object to locate the index of the space in the string. The length property of the string object is used to determine the index of the last character in the string.

The substring() method then returns the portion of the string after the index up to the end of the string. The string object, and in particular the substring() method, are discussed in more detail in later chapters. The string object is covered in depth in Chapter 10, "Strings, Math, and the History List."

The next function to be called is the calendar() function, which does the more complex job of building the calendar. The calendar is designed using HTML tables, which are discussed further in Chapter 7, "Loops."

```
function calendar()
{
    var monthNames = "JanFebMarAprMayJunJulAugSepOctNovDec";
    var today = new Date();
    var thisDay;
    var monthDays = new montharr(31, 28, 31, 30, 31, 30, 31, 31, 30,
        31, 30, 31);

    year = today.getYear() + 1900;
    thisDay = today.getDate();

    // do the classic leap year calculation
    if (((year % 4 == 0) && (year % 100 != 0)) || (year % 400 == 0))
        monthDays[1] = 29;

    // figure out how many days this month will have...
    nDays = monthDays[today.getMonth()];

    // and go back to the first day of the month...
    firstDay = today;
    firstDay.setDate(1);
    // and figure out which day of the week it hits...
    startDay = firstDay.getDay();

    document.writeln("<CENTER>");
    document.write("<TABLE BORDER>");
    document.write("<TR><TH COLSPAN=7>");
    document.write(monthNames.substring(today.getMonth() * 3,
        (today.getMonth() + 1) * 3));
    document.write(". ");
    document.write(year);
    document.write("<TR><TH>Sun<TH>Mon<TH>Tue<TH>Wed<TH>Thu<TH>Fri<TH>Sat");

    // now write the blanks at the beginning of the calendar
    document.write("<TR>");
    column = 0;
    for (i=0; i<startDay; i++)
    {
```

```
      document.write("<TD>");
      column++;
   }

   for (i=1; i<=nDays; i++)
   {
      document.write("<TD>");
      if (i == thisDay)
         document.write("<FONT COLOR=\"#FF0000\">")
      document.write(i);
      if (i == thisDay)
         document.write("</FONT>")
      column++;
      if (column == 7)
      {
         document.write("<TR>"); // start a new row
         column = 0;
      }
   }
   document.write("</TABLE>");
   document.writeln("</CENTER>");
}
```

The function starts by defining variables that will be used later in the function, as well as defining an instance of the Date object called today and an instance of the montharr object (defined by the montharr() function), which contains 12 properties with the number of days in each month of the year.

The first step is to determine whether it is a leap year so that the value of monthDays[1] (for February) can be adjusted. This is done by using today.getYear() to get the current year and then using the following if statement to check whether the year is a leap year:

```
if (((year % 4 == 0) && (year % 100 != 0)) || (year % 400 == 0))
    monthDays[1] = 29;
```

Next, the variable nDays is assigned the number of days in the current month. The index used in monthDays is the value returned by today.getMonth() because it returns an integer that corresponds to the indexes of the monthDays object.

A copy of today, called firstDay, is created, and the date is set to the first of the month using firstDay.setDate(1), in order to figure out the day of the week using startDay = firstDay.getDay(). You could have used today.setDate(1) and today.getDay(), but that would have made the script harder to read and understand.

The function then outputs the opening tags of the table and writes out the current month by using the substring() method on the variable monthNames. This is followed by writing the number of blank calendar spaces needed in the first row, using a for loop, which is covered in Chapter 7.

Next, another for loop is used to write out the dates of the month in sequence. The if statements with the condition (i== thisDay) are used to determine whether the text color should be changed for the current table cell.

The variable column is incremented throughout both for loops to keep track of which column of the seven-column table the current date is written into. If the date has been written into the seventh column, then the last if statement in the second loop starts a table row with the TR tag and resets column to zero.

Finally, the function writes out all the closing HTML for the table.

DAY 3

Chapter 5

Events in JavaScript

Now that you know how to organize programs using functions and build your own objects, you are ready to take a look at events.

Events provide the basis of interacting with the Navigator window and the currently loaded document. Events are triggered in the browser primarily by user actions, including finishing loading a page, entering data in a form, and clicking on form buttons.

Using event handlers built into JavaScript, you can write functions to perform specific actions based on the occurrence of selected events.

In this chapter, we will cover:

- [ ] What events are
- [ ] What event handlers are
- [ ] How to use event handlers
- [ ] How to emulate events
- [ ] The load and unload events and the onLoad and onUnload event handlers
- [ ] The basics of using events to interact with forms

What Are Events?

Events are signals generated when specific actions occur. JavaScript is aware of these signals, and scripts can be built to react to these events.

Examples of events include when a user clicks on a hypertext link, changes data in a form entry field, or when a page finishes loading. A complete list of the events available in JavaScript appears in Table 5.1.

Table 5.1. Events in JavaScript.

Event	Description
blur	Occurs when input focus is removed from a form element (when the user clicks outside a field)
click	Occurs when the user clicks on a link or form element
change	Occurs when the value of a form field is changed by the user
focus	Occurs when input focus is given to a form element
load	Occurs when a page is loaded into Navigator
mouseover	Occurs when the user moves the pointer over a hypertext link
select	Occurs when the user selects a form element's field
submit	Occurs when a form is submitted (i.e., when the user clicks on a submit button)
unload	Occurs when the user leaves a page

NEW TERM   *Input focus* refers to the act of clicking on or in a form element or field. This can be done by clicking in a text field or by tabbing between text fields.

What Are Event Handlers?

In order to take advantage of events in JavaScript, it is necessary to use event handlers. Event handlers are scripts, in the form of attributes of specific HTML tags, which you as the programmer can write.

The event handlers you write are executed when the specified events occur. The basic format of an event handler is:

```
<HTML_TAG OTHER_ATTRIBUTES eventHandler="JavaScript Program">
```

While any JavaScript statements, methods, or functions can appear inside the quotation marks of an event handler, typically, the JavaScript script that makes up the event handler is actually a call to a function defined in the header of the document or a single JavaScript command. Essentially, though, anything that appears inside a command block (inside curly braces ({}) can appear between the quotation marks).

For instance, if you have a form with a text field and want to call the function `checkField()` whenever the value of the text field changes, you could define your text field as follows:

```
<INPUT TYPE="text" onChange="checkField(this)">
```

NOTE

> The onChange event handler is one of many event handlers available in JavaScript. onChange and other event handlers are discussed in more depth later in this chapter.

Nonetheless, the entire code for the function could appear in quotation marks rather than a function call:

```
<INPUT TYPE="text" onChange="
  if (parseInt(this.value) <= 5) {
    alert('Please enter a number greater than 5.');
  }
">
```

To separate multiple commands in an event handler, use semicolons, as shown in the following lines:

```
<INPUT TYPE="text" onChange="
  alert('Thanks for the entry.');
  confirm('Do you want to continue?');
">
```

The advantage of using functions as event handlers, however, is that you can use the same event handler code for multiple items in your document and, (as you saw earlier in Chapter 4, "Functions and Objects—The Building Blocks of Programs"), functions make your code easier to read and understand.

For instance, you may have a form with several text entry fields and in each, the user can only enter numbers. You could use an event handler to check the value of any field if the content changes. By having a single function to check the value of a field, you don't have to write the complete code in the event handler for each text field.

this **Keyword**

Notice in the examples in the preceding section that you used the this keyword which you first encountered when you learned to build your own objects in Chapter 4.

The this keyword refers to the current object. In the case of

```
<INPUT TYPE="text" onChange="checkField(this)">
```

this refers to the current field object. In JavaScript, forms are objects and, as you'll learn in Chapter 6, "Creating Interactive Forms," they have objects for each element as properties. These form elements include text fields, checkboxes, radio buttons, buttons, and selection lists.

Which Event Handlers Can Be Used?

The names of event handlers are directly connected to the events introduced earlier in the chapter. For instance, the click event is associated with the onClick event handler, and the load event with the onLoad event handler.

Table 5.2 outlines which window and form elements have event handlers available to them. All of these elements are dealt with later in this book when we cover forms, the document object, and the window object (see Chapter 8, "Frames, Documents, and Windows").

Table 5.2. Event handlers in JavaScript.

Object	Event Handlers Available
Selection list	onBlur, onChange, onFocus
Text element	onBlur, onChange, onFocus, onSelect
Textarea element	onBlur, onChange, onFocus, onSelect
Button element	onClick
Checkbox	onClick
Radio button	onClick
Hypertext link	onClick, onMouseOver
Reset button	onClick
Submit button	onClick
Document	onLoad, onUnload
Window	onLoad, onUnload
Form	onSubmit

Emulating Events

In addition to event handlers, it is possible to emulate events. This can prove particularly useful to submit a form without requiring the user to click on a submit button or to force the input focus into a particular form field based on user actions.

For instance, if a clothing company has on its Web site an on-line order form for ordering designer clothes and it wants to ensure that the users provide a name, address, phone number, and fax number before sending the order to the company's server for processing, then using event emulation could be useful.

When a user fills in the form and clicks on the Order button, a JavaScript script could then check if the form is correctly filled out. If it is, then it could emulate a submit event to cause the content of the form to be sent to the company's server.

On the other hand, if there is a missing piece of information, the script could alert the user and then emulate a focus event to put input focus into the text field in question.

The following list outlines the event methods available in JavaScript.

- ☐ blur()
- ☐ click()
- ☐ focus()
- ☐ select()
- ☐ submit()

WARNING

The select(), focus(), and blur() methods display inconsistent behavior on different platforms. For instance, on Windows 95, blur() removes focus from a field but will leave the cursor displayed in the field even though users won't be able to enter information into the text field.

It is important to note that events generated with these methods do invoke their corresponding event handlers. This can lead to infinite loops, as illustrated in the following script:

WARNING

Don't try to run this code! It is for illustration purposes *only*.

5

```
<HTML>

<HEAD>
<TITLE>Events</TITLE>

<SCRIPT>
<!-- HIDE FROM OTHER BROWSERS

function react(field) {

  alert("Please Enter a Value");
  field.focus();

}

// STOP HIDING FROM OTHER BROWSERS -->
</SCRIPT>

</HEAD>

<BODY>

<FORM METHOD=POST>
<INPUT TYPE=text NAME=stuff onFocus="react(this);">

</FORM>

</BODY>

</HTML>
```

You can see that because `field.focus()` invokes the `onFocus` event handler, you face a situation of infinite recursion with `react()` being continually called until it caused Navigator 2 to crash.

Using the `onLoad` and `onUnload` Event Handlers

The first events you will learn to work with are load and unload. The load event is generated when a page has completed loading. Likewise, the unload event occurs when the user exits a page.

The `onLoad` and `onUnload` event handlers enable you to script JavaScript program code to execute at these times. The `onLoad` event handler, for instance, enables you to be sure a page, including associated graphics, has loaded completely before executing the event handler.

This ability to control the timing of certain actions is important. For instance, if you want an alert message to appear after a page has loaded, it would be simple to place a script at the end of the HTML file. However, it is still possible for the alert box to appear before the page, particularly in-line graphics, has completely loaded and been displayed on the screen.

The onLoad event solves that problem. Similarly, onUnload enables a script to be executed before a new page loads.

The onLoad and onUnload events are used as an attribute of the BODY HTML tag. For instance, in this line:

```
<BODY onLoad="hello()" onUnload="goodbye()">
```

the function hello() is executed after the page is loaded and goodbye() is called when the page is exited.

In Listing 5.1, you simply generate a welcome message after a page has loaded and generate a farewell message when the user decides to move on to another page.

 Listing 5.1. Using the onLoad and onUnload event handlers.

```
<HTML>

<HEAD>
<TITLE>Example 5.1</TITLE>
</HEAD>

<BODY onLoad="alert('Welcome to my page!');"
  onUnload="alert('Goodbye! Sorry to see you go!');">

<IMG SRC="title.gif">

</BODY>

</HTML>
```

OUTPUT This script produces results similar to Figure 5.1.

Figure 5.1.
The onLoad *event handler generates this alert box.*

ANALYSIS   This script provides a simple example of how event handlers are used.

Once the page has completed loading, the onLoad event handler causes the welcome alert dialog box to be displayed. Then, when the user leaves the page, such as by opening another URL, the good-bye dialog box is displayed by the onUnload event handler.

You could expand and personalize this script as you did in using the prompt() method in the "Welcome to Netscape Navigator 2!" examples earlier:

```
<HTML>

<HEAD>
<TITLE>Example 5.1</TITLE>

<SCRIPT LANGUAGE="JavaScript">
<!-- HIDE FROM OTHER BROWSERS

var name = "";

// STOP HIDING FROM OTHER BROWSERS -->
</SCRIPT>

</HEAD>

<BODY onLoad="
         name = prompt('Enter Your Name:','Name');
         alert('Greetings ' + name + ', welcome to my page!');"
      onUnload=" alert(Goodbye  ' + name + ', sorry to see you go!');">

<IMG SRC="title.gif">

</BODY>

</HTML>
```

Likewise, you could use functions for this script to make it easier to read:

```
<HTML>

<HEAD>
<TITLE>Example 5.1</TITLE>

<SCRIPT LANGUAGE="JavaScript">
<!-- HIDE FROM OTHER BROWSERS

// DEFINE GLOBAL VARIABLE
var name = "";

function hello() {
  name = prompt('Enter Your Name:','Name');
  alert('Greetings ' + name + ', welcome to my page!');
}
```

```
function goodbye() {
  alert(Goodbye ' + name + ', sorry to see you go!');

}

// STOP HIDING FROM OTHER BROWSERS -->
</SCRIPT>

</HEAD>

<BODY onLoad="hello();"  onUnload="goodbye();">

<IMG SRC="title.gif">

</BODY>

</HTML>
```

Web-Hopping with `window.open()`

In this example, you take a closer look at using the onLoad event handler for a more complex task. You are going to produce a random page. That is, when the user comes to the page, a "Please Wait…Selecting Destination" message is displayed and shortly after that, a randomly selected site from the Internet is loaded in a new window. In Listing 5.2, the program chooses from a list of five possible sites to jump to.

In order to achieve this, you need to use a new method: `window.open()`. The `window.open()` method takes two required arguments:

```
window.open("URL","window name")
```

The `window.open()` method is covered in more detail in Chapter 8 where we also discuss a third argument available for the `window.open()` method. For this example, you need to ensure that the window you open the URL in, is the same one your message appeared in. Because you don't know how many windows are currently open when the user opens your Web page, you will open both the message and the subsequent URL in a new window by using `window.open("URL","new_window_name")`.

TYPE **Listing 5.2. A random page selector.**

```
<HTML>

<HEAD>
<TITLE>Example 5.2</TITLE>
```

continues

Listing 5.2. continued

```
<SCRIPT LANGUAGE="JavaScript">
<!-- HIDE FROM OTHER BROWSERS

function urlList(a,b,c,d,e) {
  // DEFINE FIVE-ELEMENT OBJECT
  this[0] = a;
  this[1] = b;
  this[2] = c;
  this[3] = d;
  this[4] = e;
}

function selectPage(list) {
  // SELECT RANDOM PAGE
  var today = new Date();
  var page = today.getSeconds() % 5;

  // MAKE page AN INTEGER (GET RID OF THE STUFF AFTER THE DECIMAL POINT)

  // OPEN PAGE
  window.open(list[page],"Random_Page");

}

// DEFINE SELECTION LIST
choices = new urlList("http://www.yahoo.com",
                      "http://www.cnn.com",
                      "http://www.dataphile.com.hk",
                      "http://home.netscape.com",
                      "http://www.landegg.org/landegg");

// STOP HIDING FROM OTHER BROWSERS -->
</SCRIPT>

</HEAD>

<BODY onLoad = "selectPage(choices);">
<H1>
<HR>
Please Wait ... Selecting Page.
<HR>
</H1>
</BODY>

</HTML>
```

ANALYSIS   In this example you learn several useful techniques. The script is built out of two functions and a main body of JavaScript code. The function urlList() is an object constructor used to build an array of five URL strings. It takes five arguments and builds a five-element array.

You will notice that you don't use any property names in defining the object, but instead use numeric indexes to reference each of the five properties. This is done because you will only be using numeric references throughout the script to access the URLs in the array.

The `selectPage()` function is a little more complex. The function generates a pseudo-random number by calculating the number of seconds modulo five. This produces an integer in the range of zero to four:

```
var today = new Date();
var page = today.getSeconds() % 5;
```

This number is then used in the command `window.open(list[page],"Random_Page")` to open the selected page in a new window called `Random_Page`.

Following the two functions, you define the five sites you have to choose from and store them in an array called `choices`. You use the constructor function `urlList()` to create the array.

Finally, the script contains a good example of using the `onLoad` event handler. The message `Please Wait... Selecting Page.` is displayed in the original browser window and then `selectPage()` is called from the event handler. For users on slower dial-up connections, the message may display for a few seconds, and users on fast direct connections may barely have time to see the message.

Events and Forms

Now that you understand the basics of events, let's take a look at working with forms.

Today, most JavaScript programmers are using forms and event handlers to produce complex applications. The events generated by forms provide a fairly complete set of tools for reacting to user actions in forms.

Common Form Events

The most common events used for processing forms are the `focus`, `blur`, and `change` events with their corresponding event handlers `onFocus`, `onBlur`, and `onChange`. Using these events, it is possible for a program to keep track of when a user moves between fields in a form and when he or she changes the value of an input field.

Other Form Events

There are other events available in forms, which we will cover in Chapter 6 when we take a detailed look at working with forms. These include `click` and `submit` with their corresponding `onClick` and `onSubmit` event handlers.

Using Event Handlers with Form Tags

Event handlers are included as attributes of form and field tags. For instance, the following tag defines a text input field with three event handlers.

```
<INPUT TYPE=text NAME="test" VALUE="test"

        onBlur="alert('Thank You!');"
        onChange="check(this);">
```

When the user moves the focus out of the field by clicking anywhere outside the field (or using the tab button where there are multiple text fields in a form), an alert dialog box with the message Thank You! is displayed.

When the value of the field is changed, the function check() is called. This function would be defined elsewhere in the HTML page—probably in the header. Note the use of the this keyword to pass the current field object to the function.

You first saw the this keyword in Chapter 4, when you learned to build constructor functions. The this keyword refers to the current object. In the case of an event handler, this refers to the object the event handler applies to. For instance, in a form field definition, this refers to the object for the form element (which we discuss in Chapter 6 in detail). You can then refer to properties and methods for the current object as this.methodName() or this.propertyName.

An Interactive Calculator

In this example, you will use event handlers and text input fields to produce a simple calculator. You will use a form that consists of two fields: one for the user to enter a mathematical expression and another for the results to be displayed.

If the user moves the focus into the results field, a prompt dialog box is displayed asking the user for a mathematical expression which is then displayed in the entry field with the evaluated result in the results field.

You already have learned all the methods, properties, and event handlers necessary to produce the script in Listing 5.3.

Listing 5.3. Using event handlers to create a JavaScript calculator.

```
<HTML>

<HEAD>
<TITLE>Example 5.3</TITLE>
```

```
<SCRIPT LANGUAGE="JavaScript">
<!-- HIDE FROM OTHER BROWSERS

function calculate(form) {

  form.results.value = eval(form.entry.value);

}

function getExpression(form) {

  form.entry.blur();
  form.entry.value = prompt("Please enter a JavaScript mathematical
➥expression","");
  calculate(form);

}


// STOP HIDING FROM OTHER BROWSERS -->
</SCRIPT>

</HEAD>

<BODY>

<FORM METHOD=POST>
Enter a JavaScript mathematical expression:
<INPUT TYPE=text NAME="entry" VALUE=""
      onFocus="getExpression(this.form);">
<BR>
The result of this expression is:
<INPUT TYPE=text NAME="results" VALUE=""
      onFocus="this.blur();">

</FORM>

</BODY>

</HTML>
```

OUTPUT   This script produces results similar to Figure 5.2.

Figure 5.2.

When a user enters an expression, the result is calculated and displayed.

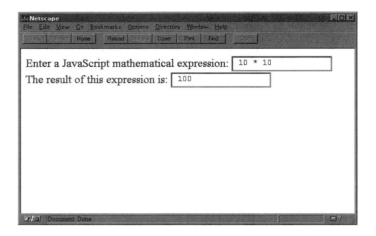

ANALYSIS There are several techniques employed in this script that are worth noting. In the HTML form, you have two fields, each with a single event handler. The entry field has an onFocus event handler which calls the function getExpression(), which handles the input of the expression. Notice that the function is passed this.form as an argument. Where this refers to the object for the current field in the HTML form, this.form refers to the object for the form containing the current field.

The second field's onFocus event handler calls this.blur() which immediately removes focus so that the user cannot alter the contents of the field. Remember that on some platforms, the cursor will actually appear in the field, but the user will be unable to enter information.

The getExpression() function takes a single form object as an argument. The first thing it does is remove focus from the entry field. You do this so you don't get into an infinite loop with the prompt dialog box. If you don't, then focus is removed from the field when the dialog box appears and returns to the field when the dialog box closes. This triggers another focus event and would invoke the event handler again.

After you remove focus from the entry field, you prompt the user for an expression and store the results in the entry field to display them. Then you call the function calculate() and pass it the form object.

The calculate() function uses the eval() function to calculate the result of the expression in the entry field and displays the result in the appropriate field in the form.

Throughout both functions, you will notice that you can refer to particular fields in a form as properties of the form object:

formObjectName.fieldname

5

Likewise, you can directly address, and change, the value of a field by using its value property (remember that while fields are properties of the `form` object, they are objects in their own right with properties of their own):

```
formObjectName.fieldname.value
```

It is also important to realize that with JavaScript, authors often want to create forms that actually do not submit any data back to the server with the `ACTION` attribute of the `FORM` tag. For instance, a JavaScript application may implement a simple currency calculator that uses HTML forms for its interface. All calculations and displaying of the results are done by a JavaScript script, and the contents of the forms never need to be sent to the server.

To accommodate this use of forms, it is sufficient to have no attributes in the `FORM` tag or to simply have the `METHOD=POST` attribute without an `ACTION` attribute in the `FORM` tag.

Summary

In this chapter, you have made a big step toward being able to write the type of interactive Web pages and scripts that JavaScript is widely used for today.

You learned about events and event handlers. Event handlers react to actions by the user or events generated by the browser. Scripts can also emulate many events such as the `click()` method and `submit()` method.

In particular, you used the `onLoad` and `onUnload` event handlers to react to the loading of the page and the user's opening another URL. You also began to look at events in relationship to HTML forms and learned to use `onFocus`, `onBlur`, and `onChange`.

In Chapter 6, you look at the `form` object in more detail and work more with the events and event handlers in relationship to forms.

5

Commands and Extensions Review

Command/Extension	Type	Description
`blur()`	JavaScript method	Removes focus from a specified object
`click()`	JavaScript method	Emulates a mouse click on an object
`focus()`	JavaScript method	Emulates the user focusing on a particular form field

continues

Command/Extension	Type	Description
submit()	JavaScript method	Emulates a click on the submit button of a form
select()	JavaScript method	Selects the input area of a particular form field
onLoad	Event handler	Specifies JavaScript code to execute when a page finishes loading
onUnload	Event handler	Specifies JavaScript code to execute when the user opens a new URL
Math.random()	JavaScript method	Generates a random number between 0 and 1
Math.sqrt()	JavaScript method	Calculates the square root of a number
window.open()	JavaScript method	Opens a URL in a named window or frame
Math.round()	JavaScript method	Rounds a floating-point value to the closest integer
onFocus	Event handler	Specifies JavaScript code to execute when the user gives focus to a form field
onBlur	Event handler	Specifies JavaScript code to execute when the user removes focus from a form field
onChange	Event handler	Specifies JavaScript code to execute when the user changes the value of a form field

Q&A

Q Can I ensure my page elements, including large graphics and tables, have been displayed before the onLoad script is executed?

A Yes. onLoad is executed when all elements of the page have been loaded and displayed.

5

Q You used `getSeconds()` to simulate a random number. I have seen a random number method in other languages such as Perl. Does JavaScript have one?

A Yes and No. According to the specifications of JavaScript, the `Math` object will include a `random()` method. However, in the release of Navigator 2.0 currently available, the method is implemented only on the UNIX platforms.

Exercises

1. Which of the following are legitimate uses of event handlers?

    a. `<BODY onClick="doSomething();">`

    b. `<INPUT TYPE=text onFocus="doSomething();">`

    c. `<INPUT TYPE=textarea onLoad="doSomething();">`

    d. `<BODY onUnload="doSomething();">`

    e. `<FORM onLoad="doSomething();">`

    f. `<FORM onSubmit="doSomething();">`

2. What happens with the following script?

```
<HTML>

<HEAD>
<TITLE>Exercise 5.2</TITLE>

<SCRIPT LANGUAGE="JavaScript">
<!-- HIDE FROM OTHER BROWSERS

var name = "";

function welcome() {

  name = prompt("Welcome to my page! What's Your Name?","name");

}

function farewell() {

  alert("Goodbye " + name + ". Thanks for visiting my page.");

}

// STOP HIDING FROM OTHER BROWSERS -->
</SCRIPT>

</HEAD>

<BODY onLoad="welcome();" onUnload="farewell();";>

<IMG SRC="welcome.gif">
```

5

```
</BODY>

</HTML>
```

3. Create an HTML page and JavaScript script that includes a form with three input fields. The relationship of the value of the fields is that the second field is twice the value of the first field, and the third field is the square of the first field.

   If a user enters a value in the second or third field, the script should calculate the appropriate value in the other fields.

TIP

To make this script easier, you will probably want to use the Math.sqrt() method, which returns the square root of the argument passed to it.

Answers

1. Lines b, d, and f are valid according to Table 5.2. Choices a, c, and e all use event handlers which are not available for the particular objects in question.

2. The script welcomes the user and asks for a name after the page (and graphic) have loaded. When the user moves on to another URL, a good-bye message is displayed in an alert dialog box. Results would be similar to Figures 5.3 and 5.4.

Figure 5.3.

The prompt dialog box is displayed only after the page has finished loading.

Figure 5.4.

Loading another Web page triggers the farewell() *function and this alert box.*

3. The following script would achieve the desired results:

```
<HTML>

<HEAD>
<TITLE>Exercise 5.3</TITLE>
```

```
<SCRIPT>
<!-- HIDE FROM OTHER BROWSERS

function calculate(form) {

  form.twice.value = form.entry.value * 2;
  form.square.value = form.entry.value * form.entry.value;

}

// STOP HIDING FROM OTHER BROWSERS -->
</SCRIPT>

</HEAD>

<BODY>

<FORM METHOD=POST>

Value: <INPUT TYPE=text NAME="entry" VALUE=0
               onChange="calculate(this.form);">
<BR>
Double: <INPUT TYPE=text NAME="twice" VALUE=0
               onChange="this.form.entry.value = this.value / 2;
➥calculate(this.form);">
<BR>
Square: <INPUT TYPE=text NAME="square" VALUE=0
               onChange="this.form.entry.value = Math.sqrt(this.value);
➥calculate(this.form);">

</FORM>

</BODY>

</HTML>
```

This script page produces results similar to those in Figure 5.5.

Figure 5.5.

The onChange *event handler calculates and updates fields.*

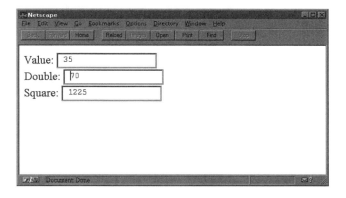

5

Notice the use of the this.form argument again in the calls to the calculate() function. In addition, the onChange event handlers for both the double and square fields have multiline scripts for their event handlers. The semicolons separate the lines of the script, even though the script appears on a single physical line.

The onChange event handlers in both the double and square fields first calculate the value of the entry field and then call calculate() which calculates the value of both double and square based on the value of the entry field. While this technique works, it has a couple of problems.

First, you end up replacing the value the user has entered in the double or square field with a new value calculated when you call calculate(). This is an extra, unnecessary step.

Second, due to limitations in floating-point calculations, it is possible that if a user enters a value in the square field, for example, the result of calculating the square root and then recalculating the value of the square field may produce a result slightly different from the original value the user entered.

This can be remedied with the following script. At first glance, these changes make the script seem more complex, but they stop the script from calculating the value the user has just entered, preventing both these problems.

```
<HTML>

<HEAD>
<TITLE>Exercise 5.3</TITLE>

<SCRIPT>
<!-- HIDE FROM OTHER BROWSERS

function calculate(form,currentField) {

  if (currentField == "square") {
    form.entry.value = Math.sqrt(form.square.value);
    form.twice.value = form.entry.value * 2;
  } else if (currentField == "twice") {
    form.entry.value = form.twice.value / 2;
    form.square.value = form.entry.value * form.entry.value;
  } else {
    form.twice.value = form.entry.value * 2;
    form.square.value = form.entry.value * form.entry.value;
  }

}

// STOP HIDING FROM OTHER BROWSERS -->
</SCRIPT>

</HEAD>

<BODY>
```

5

```
<FORM METHOD=POST>

Value: <INPUT TYPE=text NAME="entry" VALUE=0
              onChange="calculate(this.form,'entry');">
Double: <INPUT TYPE=text NAME="twice" VALUE=0
              onChange="calculate(this.form,'twice');">
Square: <INPUT TYPE=text NAME="square" VALUE=0
              onChange="calculate(this.form,'square');">

</FORM>

</BODY>

</HTML>
```

Here you see that you have added a second argument passing an indicator of which field's event handler called the `calculate()` function. The function uses this in a complex `if ... else` construct to do only the necessary calculations and not rewrite the values just entered by the users.

The `if ... else` construct used in the `calculate()` function shows how it is possible to have more than one alternative:

```
if (condition1) {
  JavaScript commands
} else if (condition2) {
  JavaScript commands
} else if (condition3) {
  JavaScript commands
} else {
  JavaScript commands
}
```

This example can be extended to any number of conditions.

The script can be made easier to use and more general purpose by using the `name` property of the `text` field object. For instance, you can pass `this.name` to the function in all three event handlers (because the current object in each case is a text field):

```
<FORM METHOD=POST>

Value: <INPUT TYPE=text NAME="entry" VALUE=0
              onChange="calculate(this.form,this.name);">
Double: <INPUT TYPE=text NAME="twice" VALUE=0
              onChange="calculate(this.form,this.name);">
Square: <INPUT TYPE=text NAME="square" VALUE=0
              onChange="calculate(this.form,this.name);">

</FORM>
```

5

Chapter **6**

Creating Interactive Forms

Working with forms is the cornerstone of many of the JavaScript programs currently available on the World Wide Web. From simple spreadsheets to conversion calculators and color-pickers, many scripts use forms and their associated properties, methods, and event handlers to produce sophisticated interactive programs.

In order to effectively use forms in JavaScript, you need to understand the `form` object and its properties and methods and to have a firm command of the events generated by different form elements.

In this chapter, you will learn this through the following topics:

- ☐ The `form` object, its properties, and methods
- ☐ Event handlers for form elements
- ☐ More about the `Math` object
- ☐ The `forms[]` array
- ☐ The `elements[]` array
- ☐ Limitations of event handlers

The form Object

The form object is one of the most heavily used objects in JavaScript scripts written for Navigator 2.0. As a programmer, by using the form object, you have at your disposal information about the elements in a form and their values and can alter many of these values as needed.

A separate instance of the form object is created for each form in a document. As you learn later in the section about the forms[] array, forms all have a numeric index. They can also be referred to by name.

Properties of the form Object

Table 6.1 outlines the properties available with the form object.

Table 6.1. Properties of the form object.

Property	Description
action	String containing the value of the ACTION attribute of the FORM tag
elements	Array containing an entry for each element in the form (such as checkboxes, text fields, and selection lists)
encoding	String containing the MIME type used for encoding the form contents sent to the server. Reflects the ENCTYPE attribute of the FORM tag.
name	String containing the value of the NAME attribute of the FORM tag
target	String containing the name of the window targeted by a form submission

As you learn later in the section on the elements[] array, each of the elements of the form is itself an object with associated properties and methods. Elements can be referred to by name, as well as through their numeric index in the elements[] array.

The action Property

With this property, you can ascertain the action specified in the form definition. For instance, in a form defined with the following

```
<FORM METHOD=POST ACTION="/cgi-bin/test.pl">
```

the action property has a value of "/cgi-bin/test.pl".

The `elements` **Property**

This property is covered in more depth later in the section about the `elements[]` array.

The `encoding` **Property**

The `encoding` property reflects the MIME type, which is used to encode the data submitted from a form to the server. In practical terms, this means that the property reflects the ENCTYPE attribute of the FORM tag, and you can set the encoding of a form by changing the value of this property.

This is useful when you want to upload a file to be processed by a CGI script on the server. More details about form-based file upload is available in the *Internet Engineering Task Force's Request for Comments* document number 1867 at the following site:

```
http://www.ics.uci.edu/pub/ietf/html/rfc1867.txt
```

The `name` **Property**

This property provides the programmer with the name specified in the form definition. In a form defined with the tag

```
<FORM METHOD=POST ACTION="/cgi-bin/test.pl" NAME="thisform">
```

the `name` property has a value of `"thisform"`.

NOTE   Using named forms is especially useful in documents with multiple forms where the JavaScript scripts must work with all the forms in the document.

The `target` **Property**

The `target` property is similar to the `action` and `name` properties and makes the content of the TARGET attribute available to the programmer. In the FORM definition

```
<FORM METHOD=POST ACTION="/cgi-bin/test.pl" NAME="thisform" TARGET="thatframe">
```

the `target` property has a value of `"thatframe"`.

NOTE   The TARGET attribute is particularly useful in the context of frames, which we discuss in Chapter 8, "Frames, Documents, and Windows."

Methods of the form **Object**

There is only one method available with the form object: submit(). As mentioned in Chapter 5, "Events in JavaScript," this method emulates a click on the submit button of a form without invoking the onSubmit event handler.

For instance, in the following script, the form has no submit button and can be submitted when the user enters the correct value in the text field. The onSubmit event handler, which returns false, ensures that the form is not submitted if the user hits return in the text entry field.

```
<HTML>

<HEAD>
<TITLE>submit() Example</TITLE>

<SCRIPT LANGUAGE="JavaScript">
<!-- HIDE FROM OTHER BROWSERS

function checkValue(form) {

  if (form.answer.value == "100")
    form.submit();
  else
    form.answer.value = "";

}

// STOP HIDING FROM OTHER BROWSERS -->
</SCRIPT>

</HEAD>

<BODY>

<FORM METHOD=POST ACTION="/cgi-bin/correct.pl" onSubmit="return false;">
What is 10 * 10? <INPUT TYPE="text" NAME="answer"
➥onChange="checkValue(this.form);">
</FORM>

</BODY>

</HTML>
```

Event Handlers for the form **Object**

Just as it has only one method, the form object has only a single event handler associated with it: onSubmit. This event handler is invoked when the user submits a form. For instance, in the following script, when the user submits the form, she is thanked for doing so.

6

```
<HTML>

<HEAD>
<TITLE>onSubmit Example</TITLE>
</HEAD>

<BODY>
<FORM METHOD=POST ACTION="/cgi-bin/test.pl"
➥onSubmit="alert('Thanks for taking the test.');">
What is 10 * 10? <INPUT TYPE="text" NAME="answer">
<BR>

<INPUT TYPE="submit">
</FORM>
</BODY>

</HTML>
```

Working with Form Elements

Forms are made up of a variety of elements that enable users to provide information. Traditionally, the content (or value) of these elements is passed to programs on the server through an interface known as the Common Gateway Interface, or CGI for short.

Using JavaScript, though, you can write scripts into your HTML documents to work with form elements and their values. You already saw a basic example of this in Chapter 5, in Listing 5.3 where you produced an extremely simple calculator that calculated the value of a JavaScript expression and displayed the result.

In this section, you will take a look at each type of form element in detail and see what properties and methods and event handlers are available for each.

Table 6.2 outlines the elements that make up forms. Each element has a corresponding object.

Table 6.2. Form elements.

6

Form Element	Description
button	A new element that provides a button other than a submit or reset button (`<INPUT TYPE="button">`)
checkbox	A checkbox (`<INPUT TYPE="checkbox">`)
hidden	A hidden field (`<INPUT TYPE="hidden">`)
password	A password text field in which each keystroke appears as an asterisk (*) (`<INPUT TYPE="password">`)
radio	A radio button (`<INPUT TYPE="radio">`)

continues

Table 6.2. continued

Form Element	Description
reset	A reset button (`<INPUT TYPE="reset">`)
select	A selection list (`<SELECT><OPTION>option1</OPTION><OPTIONoption2</OPTION></SELECT>`)
submit	A submit button (`<INPUT TYPE="submit">`)
text	A text field (`<INPUT TYPE="text">`)
textArea	A multiline text entry field (`<TEXTAREA>default text</TEXTAREA>`)

Each of these elements can be named and referred to by name in a JavaScript script. Each also has properties and methods associated with it.

The button Element

In standard HTML forms, only two buttons are available—submit and reset—because the data contained in a form must be sent to some URL (usually a CGI-BIN script) for processing or storage.

A button element is specified using the INPUT tag:

```
<INPUT TYPE="button" NAME="name" VALUE="buttonName">
```

In the above INPUT tag, a button named name is created. The VALUE attribute contains the text that the Navigator browser displays in the button.

The button element has two properties: name (as specified in the INPUT tag) and value, which is also specified in the INPUT tag.

There is a single event handler for the button element: onClick. Associated with this is a single method: click().

The addition of the button element enables JavaScript programmers to write JavaScript code to be executed for additional buttons in a script.

For instance, in Listing 5.3, instead of using the onChange element, you could alter the script as shown in Listing 6.1 to evaluate the supplied expression when a button is pressed.

6

Listing 6.1. Evaluating a form using the button element.

```
<HTML>

<HEAD>
<TITLE>button Example</TITLE>

<SCRIPT LANGUAGE="JavaScript">
<!-- HIDE FROM OTHER BROWSERS

function calculate(form) {

  form.results.value = eval(form.entry.value);

}


// STOP HIDING FROM OTHER BROWSERS -->
</SCRIPT>

</HEAD>

<BODY>

<FORM METHOD=POST>
Enter a JavaScript mathematical expression:
<INPUT TYPE="text" NAME="entry" VALUE="">
<BR>
The result of this expression is:
<INPUT TYPE=text NAME="results"
       onFocus="this.blur();">
<BR>
<INPUT TYPE="button" VALUE="Calculate" onClick="calculate(this.form);">
</FORM>

</BODY>

</HTML>
```

The checkbox **Element**

Checkboxes are toggle switches in an HTML form. They are used to select or deselect information. Checkboxes have more properties and methods available than buttons do, as outlined in Table 6.3.

Table 6.3. Properties and methods for the `checkbox` element.

Method or Property	Description
checked	Indicates the current status of the checkbox element (property)
defaultChecked	Indicates the default status of the element (property)
name	Indicates the name of the element as specified in the INPUT tag (property)
value	Indicates the current value of the element as specified in the INPUT tag (property)
click()	Emulates a click in the checkbox (method)

As you might expect, there is a single event handler for checkboxes: onClick.

For example, you can use checkboxes to produce an alternative to the double and square exercise (Exercise 3) from Chapter 5. Instead of three fields, you can have an entry text field, a checkbox to indicate squaring (doubling will be the default action) and a results text field.

The resulting script would look like Listing 6.2.

TYPE   **Listing 6.2. Doubling and squaring with checkboxes.**

```
<HTML>

<HEAD>
<TITLE>checkbox Example</TITLE>

<SCRIPT>
<!-- HIDE FROM OTHER BROWSERS

function calculate(form,callingField) {

  if (callingField == "result") {
    if (form.square.checked) {
      form.entry.value = Math.sqrt(form.result.value);
    } else {
      form.entry.value = form.result.value / 2;
    }
  } else {
    if (form.square.checked) {
      form.result.value = form.entry.value * form.entry.value;
    } else {
      form.result.value = form.entry.value * 2;
    }
  }

}
```

6

```
// STOP HIDING FROM OTHER BROWSERS -->
</SCRIPT>

</HEAD>

<BODY>

<FORM METHOD=POST>

Value: <INPUT TYPE="text" NAME="entry" VALUE=0
                onChange="calculate(this.form,this.name);">
<BR>
Action (default double): <INPUT TYPE=checkbox NAME=square
➥onClick="calculate(this.form,this.name);">
Square
<BR>
Result: <INPUT TYPE="text" NAME="result" VALUE=0
                onChange="calculate(this.form,this.name);">

</FORM>

</BODY>

</HTML>
```

ANALYSIS In this script, you see an example of how to use the onClick event handler as well as how the checked property is a boolean value that can be used as the condition for an if ... else statement.

You have added a checkbox named square to the form. If the checkbox is checked, the program will square the value. If it isn't, then the default action will be to double the value. The onClick event handler in the checkbox definition (<INPUT TYPE=checkbox NAME=square onClick="calculate(this.form,this.name);">) ensures that when the user changes the desired action, the form recalculates (as well as if the user changes the value of the entry field).

To take advantage of the checkbox, you also changed the calculate() function, as follows:

```
function calculate(form,callingField) {

  if (callingField == "result") {
    if (form.square.checked) {
      form.entry.value = Math.sqrt(form.result.value);
    } else {
      form.entry.value = form.result.value / 2;
    }
  } else {
    if (form.square.checked) {
      form.result.value = form.entry.value * form.entry.value;
    } else {
      form.result.value = form.entry.value * 2;
    }
  }

}
```

6

In this function, you use the boolean property `checked` to determine the correct action. If `form.square.checked` is `true`, then you should be squaring; if the value is `false`, you should be doubling the value in the entry field.

The `hidden` Element

The `hidden` element is unique among all the form elements in that it is not displayed by the Web browser. Hidden fields can be used to store values that need to be sent to the server along with a form submission but that shouldn't be displayed in the page. They can also be used in JavaScript to store values used throughout a script and for calculations within a form.

The `hidden` object has only two properties associated with it: `name` and `value`, both of which are string values like other objects. There are no methods or event handlers for the `hidden` object.

The `password` Element

The `password` element is a unique type of text entry field in that any keystrokes are displayed as an asterisk (*). This makes the `password` element ideal for accepting input of confidential information, such as account passwords or bank account personal identification numbers (PINs).

The `password` object has three properties, similar to text fields: `defaultValue`, `name`, and `value`. Unlike the previous two elements, the password fields include more methods (`focus()`, `blur()`, and `select()`) and the corresponding event handlers: `onFocus`, `onBlur`, and `onSelect`.

We will discuss these methods and event handlers in more detail in the section on the text element.

The `radio` Element

The `radio` element is similar to toggle checkboxes, except that several radio buttons are combined into a group and only a single button can be selected at any given time. For instance, the following lines produce a group of three radio buttons named `test`, similar to those in Figure 6.1.

```
<INPUT TYPE="radio" NAME="test" VALUE="1" CHECKED>1<BR>
<INPUT TYPE="radio" NAME="test" VALUE="2">2<BR>
<INPUT TYPE="radio" NAME="test" VALUE="3">3<BR>
```

The group of radio buttons is formed by using a consistent name in all the `INPUT` tags.

Figure 6.1.
With a group of radio buttons, only one element can be selected at any given time.

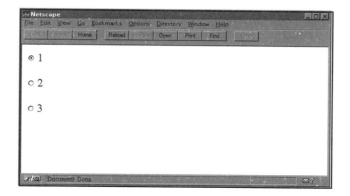

The radio element is accessible in JavaScript through the radio object, which has several properties for checking the current status of a radio button group. Table 6.4 outlines the properties and methods available with the radio object.

Table 6.4. Properties and methods for the radio object.

Method or Property	Description
checked	Indicates the current status of the radio element (property)
defaultChecked	Indicates the default status of the element (property)
index	Indicates the index of the currently selected radio button in the group
length	Indicates the number of radio buttons in a group
name	Indicates the name of the element as specified in the INPUT tag (property)
value	Indicates the current value of the element as specified in the INPUT tag (property)
click()	Emulates a click in the radio button (method)

As with checkboxes, the single event handler, onClick, is available for radio buttons.

The index and length properties haven't appeared in any of the form elements we have looked at so far in this chapter. Because a radio button group contains multiple elements, the radio object maintains an array of the radio buttons with indexes starting at zero. In the example of a radio button group named "test" above, if the group were part of a form named "testform", you could reference the second radio button as testform.test[1], and you could check the current status of the button with testform.test[1].checked.

To illustrate usage of the radio object, you can rewrite Listing 6.2, used to demonstrate checkboxes, using radio buttons instead.

TYPE **Listing 6.3. Doubling and squaring with radio buttons.**

```
<HTML>

<HEAD>
<TITLE>radio button Example</TITLE>

<SCRIPT>
<!-- HIDE FROM OTHER BROWSERS

function calculate(form,callingField) {

  if (callingField == "result") {
    if (form.action[1].checked) {
      form.entry.value = Math.sqrt(form.result.value);
    } else {
      form.entry.value = form.result.value / 2;
    }
  } else {
    if (form.action[1].checked) {
      form.result.value = form.entry.value * form.entry.value;
    } else {
      form.result.value = form.entry.value * 2;
    }
  }

}

// STOP HIDING FROM OTHER BROWSERS -->
</SCRIPT>

</HEAD>

<BODY>

<FORM METHOD=POST>
Value: <INPUT TYPE="text" NAME="entry" VALUE=0
               onChange="calculate(this.form,this.name);">
<BR>
Action:<BR>
<INPUT TYPE="radio" NAME="action" VALUE="twice"
➡onClick="calculate(this.form,this.name);"> Double<BR>
<INPUT TYPE="radio" NAME="action" VALUE="square"
➡onClick="calculate(this.form,this.name);"> Square <BR>
Result: <INPUT TYPE=text NAME="result" VALUE=0
               onChange="calculate(this.form,this.name);">

</FORM>

</BODY>

</HTML>
```

6

In this example, the changes from the checkbox version are subtle. Instead of one checkbox, you now have a pair of radio buttons with different values: double and square.

You know that the individual radio buttons are accessible through an array so that the double button is action[0] and the square button is action[1]. In this way, you need to change only the references in the calculate() function from form.square.checked to form.action[1].checked.

The reset Element

Using the reset object in JavaScript, you can react to clicks on the Reset button. Like the button object, the reset object has two properties (name and value) and one method (click()). The onClick event handler is also available.

NOTE

> A bug in the current version of Navigator results in odd behavior with the Reset button: When text fields are cleared by the Reset button, this isn't reflected into the corresponding element until the field is given focus.

Although most programmers do not find a need to use the onClick event handler for reset buttons or need to check the value of the button, the reset object can be used to clear the form to some value other than the default.

Listing 6.4. demonstrates how the Reset button can be used to clear a form to values other than the default.

TYPE   **Listing 6.4. Clearing a form to new values with Reset.**

```
<HTML>

<HEAD>
<TITLE>reset Example</TITLE>

<SCRIPT LANGUAGE="JavaScript">
<!-- HIDE FROM OTHER BROWSERS

function clearForm(form) {

  form.value1.value = "Form";
  form.value2.value = "Cleared";

}
```

continues

6

Listing 6.4. continued

```
// STOP HIDING FROM OTHER BROWSERS -->
</SCRIPT>

</HEAD>

<BODY>

<FORM METHOD=POST>
<INPUT TYPE="text" NAME="value1"><BR>
<INPUT TYPE="text" NAME="value2"><BR>
<INPUT TYPE="reset" VALUE="Clear Form" onClick="clearForm(this.form);">

</FORM>

</BODY>

</HTML>
```

ANALYSIS This script is fairly simple. You have created a form with two text fields and a Reset button. The Reset button has an onClick event handler, which calls clearForm() when the button is clicked.

The clearForm() function takes the form object as an argument and proceeds to place two new values in the two text fields of the form.

The select Element

Selection lists in HTML forms appear as drop-down menus or scrollable lists of selectable items. Lists are built using two tags: SELECT and OPTION. For instance, the following code snippet

```
<SELECT NAME="test">
<OPTION SELECTED>1
<OPTION>2
<OPTION>3
</SELECT>
```

creates a three-item, drop-down menu with the choices 1, 2, and 3. Using the SIZE attribute you can create a scrollable list with the number of elements visible at one time indicated by the value of the SIZE attribute. To turn your drop-down menu into a scrollable menu with two visible items you could use the following:

```
<SELECT NAME="test" SIZE=2>
<OPTION SELECTED>1
<OPTION>2
<OPTION>3
</SELECT>
```

In both of these examples, the user can make only one choice. Using the MULTIPLE attribute, you can enable the user to select more than one choice in a scrollable selection list:

```
<SELECT NAME="test" SIZE=2 MULTIPLE>
<OPTION SELECTED>1
<OPTION>2
<OPTION>3
</SELECT>
```

Selection lists are accessible in JavaScript through the select object. This object bears some similarity to both the buttons you have seen, as well as with radio buttons.

As with radio buttons, the list of options is maintained as an array with indexes starting at zero. In this case, the array is a property of the select object called options.

Both selection option and the individual option elements have properties. In addition to the options array, the select object has the selectedIndex property, which contains the index number of the currently selected option.

Each option in a selection list also has several properties. defaultSelected indicates whether the option is selected by default in the OPTION tag. The index property contains the index value of the current option in the options array. Again, as you might expect, selected indicates the current status of the option, text contains the value of the text displayed in the menu for the specific option, and value contains any value indicated in the OPTION tag.

The select object has no available methods. However, the select object has three event handlers that don't correspond to the available event emulating method. These are onBlur, onFocus, and onChange—the same as for the text object.

NOTE

> In the current version of JavaScript (in Navigator 2.0), the onChange event handler is not invoked immediately after the user changes his selection. Rather, once the user leaves the selection list (that is, removes focus from the list), then the onChange event handler works.

6

For example, if you have the following selection list:

```
<SELECT NAME="example" onFocus="react();">
<OPTION SELECTED VALUE="Number One">1
<OPTION VALUE="The Second">2
<OPTION VALUE="Three is It">3
</SELECT>
```

then when the list is first displayed, you would have access to the following information:

```
example.options[1].value = "The Second"

example.options[2].text = "3"

example.selectedIndex = 0
```

```
example.options[0].defaultSelected = true

example.options[1].selected = false
```

If the user then clicks on the menu and selects the second option, the onFocus event handler would execute (the react() function would be called), and then the values of these same properties would be as follows:

```
example.options[1].value = "The Second"

example.options[2].text = "3"

example.selectedIndex = 1

example.options[0].defaultSelected = true

example.options[1].selected = true
```

The submit Element

The Submit button is another special-purpose button like the Reset button. This button submits the current information from each field of the form to the URL specified in the ACTION attribute of the FORM tag using the METHOD indicated in the FORM tag.

Like with the button object and the reset object, you have name and value properties available to you, along with a click() method and an onClick event handler.

The text Element

text elements are among the most common entry fields used in HTML forms. Similar to the password field you looked at earlier, text fields enable a single line of text entry, but unlike the password element, the text is displayed as normal type rather than as asterisks.

The text object has three properties: defaultValue, name, and value. Three methods emulate user events: focus(), blur(), and select() (which selects the text in the entry field). Four event handlers are available: onBlur, onFocus, onChange, and onSelect (for when the user selects some of the text in the field).

Table 6.5 outlines the properties and methods for the text element.

Table 6.5. Properties and methods for the text object.

Method or Property	Description
defaultValue	Indicates the default value of the element as specified in INPUT tag (property)
name	Indicates the name of the element as specified in the INPUT tag (property)

Method or Property	Description
value	Indicates the current value of the element (property)
focus()	Emulates giving focus to the text field (method)
blur()	Emulates removing focus from the text field (method)
select()	Emulates selecting text in the text field (method)

It is important to note that the content of a text field can be changed by assigning values to the value property. Thus, in the following example, whatever text is entered in the first field is echoed in the second field, and any text entered in the second field is echoed in the first field. By itself, this has little value, but the ability to use data from a text field and to dynamically update and change data in a text field is a powerful feature of JavaScript as shown in Listing 6.5.

TYPE **Listing 6.5. Dynamically updating text fields.**

```
<HTML>

<HEAD>
<TITLE>text Example</TITLE>

<SCRIPT LANGUAGE="JavaScript">
<!-- HIDE FROM OTHER BROWSERS

function echo(form,currentField) {

  if (currentField == "first")
    form.second.value = form.first.value;
  else
    form.first.value = form.second.value;

}

// STOP HIDING FROM OTHER BROWSERS -->

</SCRIPT>

</HEAD>

<BODY>

<FORM>
<INPUT TYPE=text NAME="first" onChange="echo(this.form,this.name);">
<INPUT TYPE=text NAME="second" onChange="echo(this.form,this.name);">
</FORM>

</BODY>

</HTML>
```

NOTE

In current versions of Navigator 2.0, the onChange event handler is not invoked as soon as the user types a change. Rather, it is invoked when focus leaves the field and the text has changed.

The textarea **Element**

The TEXTAREA tag provides a custom size multiple-line text entry field defined by a container. The example in this code

```
<TEXTAREA NAME="fieldName" ROWS=10 COLS=25>
Default Text Here
</TEXTAREA>
```

creates a text entry field of 10 rows with 25 characters on each line. The words Default Text Here would appear in the field when it is first displayed.

Like the text element, JavaScript provides you with the defaultValue, name, and value properties, the focus(), blur(), and select() methods and the onBlur, onFocus, onChange, and onSelect event handlers.

Using Tables to Create a Calculator

Now that we have taken a detailed look at the form object, its elements, properties, and methods, you are ready to use this information to build a somewhat more complicated script.

In this example, you will build a simple mathematical calculator using forms. That is, each number and the four mathematical functions (addition, subtraction, multiplication, and division) will each be a button. You will also have two other buttons: one to clear the running total and the other to clear the current entry.

In order to make your calculator appear more organized, you will make use of HTML tables. For those without experience using tables, tables are contained in the TABLE container tag and consist of rows contained in the TR tag and column elements contained in the TD tag. In addition, the COLSPAN attribute causes a cell to cover two columns. Similarly, ROWSPAN makes a cell two rows deep.

NOTE

A more detailed discussion of HTML tables is available at Netscape's Web site at the URL:

`http://home.netscape.com/assist/net_sites/tables.html.`

For instance, the HTML code in Listing 6.6 produces a simple table.

TYPE **Listing 6.6. A simple table.**

```
<TABLE BORDER=1>
<TR>
<TD COLSPAN=2>This is a table</TD>
</TR>
<TR>
<TD>One</TD>
<TD>Two</TD>
</TR>
<TR>
<TD>Three</TD>
<TD>Four</TD>
</TR>
</TABLE>
```

OUTPUT The output from Listing 6.6 looks like the one in Figure 6.2.

Figure 6.2.
HTML tables contain rows and columns of cells.

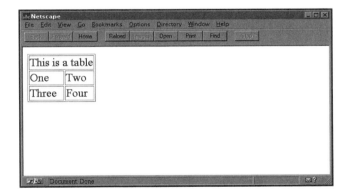

Using tables, then, you are ready to work on developing your calculator.

In terms of behavior, your calculator should work the way a simple electronic calculator does: When a user enters a number, it is immediately displayed to the right of previously entered digits. Mathematical functions are executed in the order entered (no precedence here), and the effects of operations are cumulative until the clear button is pressed. Listing 6.7 is the source code for this calculator.

6

TYPE **Listing 6.7. Creating a calculator with tables.**

```html
<HTML>

<HEAD>
<TITLE>Example 6.7</TITLE>

<SCRIPT>
<!-- HIDE FROM OTHER BROWSERS

var total = 0;
var lastOperation = "+";
var newnumber = true;

function enterNumber(digit) {

  var form = digit.form;

  if (newnumber) {
    clearNumber(form);
    newnumber = false;
  }

  form.display.value = form.display.value + digit.name;

}

function clear(form) {

  total = 0;
  lastOperation = "+";
  form.display.value = "";

}

function clearNumber(form) {

  form.display.value = "";

}

function calculate(operation) {

  var form = operation.form;

  var expression = total + lastOperation + form.display.value;

  lastOperation = operation.value;
  total = eval(expression);
  form.display.value = total;
  newnumber = true;

}

// STOP HIDING FROM OTHER BROWSERS -->
</SCRIPT>
```

6

```
</HEAD>

<BODY>

<FORM>

<TABLE BORDER=1>

<TR>
<TD COLSPAN=4>
<INPUT TYPE=text NAME=display VALUE="" onFocus="this.blur();">
</TD>
</TR>

<TR>
<TD>
<INPUT TYPE=button NAME="7" VALUE=" 7 " onClick="enterNumber(this);">
</TD>
<TD>
<INPUT TYPE=button NAME="8" VALUE=" 8 " onClick="enterNumber(this);">
</TD>
<TD>
<INPUT TYPE=button NAME="9" VALUE=" 9 " onClick="enterNumber(this);">
</TD>
<TD>
<INPUT TYPE=button NAME="+" VALUE=" + " onClick="calculate(this);">
</TD>
</TR>

<TR>
<TD>
<INPUT TYPE=button NAME="4" VALUE=" 4 " onClick="enterNumber(this);">
</TD>
<TD>
<INPUT TYPE=button NAME="5" VALUE=" 5 " onClick="enterNumber(this);">
</TD>
<TD>
<INPUT TYPE=button NAME="6" VALUE=" 6 " onClick="enterNumber(this);">
</TD>
<TD>
<INPUT TYPE=button NAME="-" VALUE="  -  " onClick="calculate(this);">
</TD>
</TR>

<TR>
<TD>
<INPUT TYPE=button NAME="1" VALUE=" 1 " onClick="enterNumber(this);">
</TD>
<TD>
<INPUT TYPE=button NAME="2" VALUE=" 2 " onClick="enterNumber(this);">
</TD>
<TD>
<INPUT TYPE=button NAME="3" VALUE=" 3 " onClick="enterNumber(this);">
</TD>
<TD>
<INPUT TYPE=button NAME="*" VALUE=" * " onClick="calculate(this);">
</TD>
```

continues

Listing 6.7. continued

```
</TR>

<TR>
<TD>
<INPUT TYPE=button NAME="0" VALUE=" 0 " onClick="enterNumber(this);">
</TD>
<TD>
<INPUT TYPE=button NAME="C" VALUE=" C " onClick="clear(this.form);">
</TD>
<TD>
<INPUT TYPE=button NAME="CE" VALUE="CE" onClick="clearNumber(this.form);">
</TD>
<TD>
<INPUT TYPE=button NAME="/" VALUE="  /  " onClick="calculate(this);">
</TD>
</TR>

</TABLE>

</FORM>

</BODY>

</HTML>
```

OUTPUT   This script produces results like those in Figure 6.3.

Figure 6.3.
Tables make the calculator look appealing, and JavaScript makes it work.

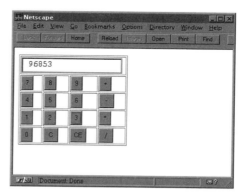

ANALYSIS   Several interesting techniques are used in this script. Let's take a look at selected parts of the script sequentially from the start.

```
var total = 0;
var lastOperation = "+";
var newnumber = true;
```

Here you declare the global variables to keep track of information. The `total` variable contains the current running total of the user's calculations. This is the same as the last displayed value before the user began entering a new number. `lastOperation` is used to keep track of the operation last entered by the user to be performed on the running total and the newly entered number. `newnumber` is used to keep track of when user input should be treated as a new number or part of the currently displayed number.

The initial values of these variables require some explanation. Obviously, `total` starts with a zero value. However, as you will see later in the `calculate()` function, you need a `lastOperation` value to perform on every number entered. By assigning the value `"+"` to `lastOperation`, the first number entered by the user will be added to the initial total of zero.

```
function enterNumber(digit) {

  var form = digit.form;

  if (newnumber) {
    clearNumber(form);
    newnumber = false;
  }

  form.display.value = form.display.value + digit;



}
```

You pass the currently clicked button object to `enterNumber()` as the argument `digit`. The line `var form = digit.form;` provides you with reference to the form containing the current button in much the same way as when you pass `this.form` to a function.

Because each new digit is added to the right side of the number, you can treat the digits as strings to concatenate.

```
function calulate(operation) {

  var form = operation.form;

  var expression = total + lastOperation + form.display.value;

  lastOperation = operation.value;
  total = eval(expression);
  form.display.value = total;
  newnumber = true;

}
```

The `calculate()` function is where the real work of the calculator script is done. The function is invoked when the user clicks on one of the operator buttons. When this happens, the line `var expression = total + lastOperation + form.display.value;` builds an expression in the form of a string.

You then use the `eval()` function to evaluate the expression you have just built. This value becomes the new value of `total`, is displayed in the text field, and the operation the user has just clicked is assigned to `lastOperation`.

One component of this calculator that is lacking is an equal (=) button. To implement it would require changing the logic of the `calculate()` function.

The `elements[]` Array

As mentioned in the section on the properties of the `form` object, all the elements in a form can also be referenced by the `elements[]` array. For instance, you could create the following form:

```
<FORM METHOD=POST NAME=testform>
<INPUT TYPE="text" NAME="one">
<INPUT TYPE="text" NAME="two">
<INPUT TYPE="text" NAME="three">
</FORM>
```

You can refer to the three elements as `document.testform.elements[0]`, `document.testform.elements[1]`, and `document.testform.elements[2]` in addition to the obvious `document.testform.one`, `document.testform.two`, `document.testform.three`.

This can be useful in situations where the sequential relationship of form elements is more important than their names.

Building a Multiplication Table

In this example, you will take advantage of the `elements[]` array to build a simple dynamic multiplication table. The form will have 11 elements. The user fills in the first field to specify which multiplication table to calculate, and the rest of the fields provide the one to ten multiplication table for that number.

Listing 6.8. Using the `elements[]` array in a multiplication table.

`TYPE`

```
<HTML>

<HEAD>
<TITLE>Example 6.8</TITLE>

<SCRIPT LANGUAGE="JavaScript">
<!-- HIDE FROM OTHER BROWSERS

function calculate(form) {
```

6

```
      var num=1;
      var number=form.number.value;
      form.elements[num].value = number * num++;
      form.elements[num].value = number * num++;
      form.elements[num].value = number * num++;
      form.elements[num].value = number * num++;
      form.elements[num].value = number * num++;
      form.elements[num].value = number * num++;
      form.elements[num].value = number * num++;
      form.elements[num].value = number * num++;
      form.elements[num].value = number * num++;
      form.elements[num].value = number * num++;

}

// STOP HIDING FROM OTHER BROWSERS -->
</SCRIPT>

</HEAD>

<BODY>

<FORM METHOD=POST>
Number: <INPUT TYPE=text NAME="number" VALUE=1
➥onChange="calculate(this.form);"><BR>
x 1: <INPUT TYPE=text NAME="1" VALUE=1 onFocus="blur();"><BR>
x 2: <INPUT TYPE=text NAME="2" VALUE=2 onFocus="blur();"><BR>
x 3: <INPUT TYPE=text NAME="3" VALUE=3 onFocus="blur();"><BR>
x 4: <INPUT TYPE=text NAME="4" VALUE=4 onFocus="blur();"><BR>
x 5: <INPUT TYPE=text NAME="5" VALUE=5 onFocus="blur();"><BR>
x 6: <INPUT TYPE=text NAME="6" VALUE=6 onFocus="blur();"><BR>
x 7: <INPUT TYPE=text NAME="7" VALUE=7 onFocus="blur();"><BR>
x 8: <INPUT TYPE=text NAME="8" VALUE=8 onFocus="blur();"><BR>
x 9: <INPUT TYPE=text NAME="9" VALUE=9 onFocus="blur();"><BR>
x 10: <INPUT TYPE=text NAME="10" VALUE=10 onFocus="this.blur();"><BR>
<ITEM TYPE=button NAME="calculcate" VALUE="Calculate"
➥onClick="calculate(this.form);">
</FORM>


</BODY>

</HTML>
```

OUTPUT Listing 6.8 produces results similar to those in Figure 6.4.

Figure 6.4.

Using the
`elements[]`
array, you can
reference each field
in order.

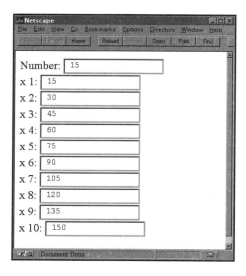

ANALYSIS   Notice in this script that you can refer to form elements by number. Because the
            `elements[]` array starts with an index of zero, you have made the first element (index
zero) the entry field and have started the multiplication table with element two (which has
an index value of one).

In the function `calculate()`, you use the variable `num` as a counter which starts at one. You
use the following command 10 times to build the multiplication table:

```
form.elements[num].value = number * num++;
```

What this line tells you to do is assign the value of `number * num` to the current element and
then increase `num` by one. This provides an excellent example of how to use the unary
increment operator (`++`) to return the value of an expression and then increase it by one.

Typically, you would not write the `calculate()` function the way you have here. Instead, you
would use a `for` loop:

```
function calculate(form) {

  var number=form.number.value;
  for(num = 1; num <= 10; num++) {
    form.elements[num].value = number * num;
  }

}
```

`for` loops are covered in Chapter 7, "Loops."

The `forms[]` Array

While event handlers are generally designed to work with individual forms or fields, at times, it is useful to be able to reference forms in relationship to other forms on a page.

This is where the `document.forms[]` array comes into play. It would be possible to have multiple identical forms on the same page and have information in a single field match in all three forms. This could be more easily achieved using the `document.forms[]` array than with form names. In this script, you have two text entry fields in separate forms. Using the `forms[]` array, you keep the value of the fields in each form the same when the user changes a value in one form.

```
<HTML>

<HEAD>
<TITLE>forms[] Example</TITLE>
</HEAD>

<BODY>

<FORM METHOD=POST>
<INPUT TYPE=text onChange="document.forms[1].elements[0].value = this.value;">
</FORM>

<FORM METHOD=POST>
<INPUT TYPE=text onChange="document.forms[0].elements[0].value = this.value;">
</FORM>

</BODY>

</HTML>
```

In addition to referring to forms numerically in the `forms[]` array, they can also be refereed to by name. Using the NAME attribute of the FORM tag, you can assign a name to a form:

```
<FORM METHOD=POST NAME="name">
```

Then, this form can be referred to as `document.forms["name"]` or as `document.name`.

Prompting with Text Fields

Now you are going to put together some of the skills you have learned in this chapter in a different type of interactive form.

Usually, text entry forms consist of field names followed by fields. What you want to do is produce forms where the field name (that is, the prompt for the field) is the initial value of the field. This should look like the example in Figure 6.5.

Figure 6.5.

*Prompt informa-
tion as a field's
default value looks
less cluttered on
Landegg Academy's
home page.*

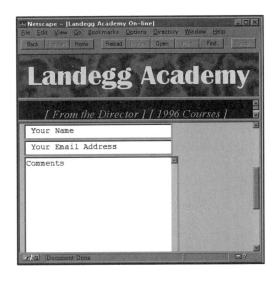

If the user clicks in an unchanged field, the field clears and the user enters information. If he
moves the focus out of the field and hasn't entered any information, the original content
reappears.

At the same time, if the user clicks in a field that contains data entered by the user, the field
is not cleared.

This can be done by developing a general-purpose set of functions, such as those in Listing 6.9.

TYPE   **Listing 6.9. An interactive entry form.**

```
<HTML>

<HEAD>
<TITLE>Listing 6.9</TITLE>

<SCRIPT LANGUAGE="JavaScript">
<!-- HIDE FROM OTHER BROWSERS

function clearField(field) {

  // Check if field contains the default value
  if (field.value == field.defaultValue) {

    // It does, so clear the field
    field.value = "";
  }
```

```
    }

    function checkField(field) {

      // Check if user has entered information in the field
      if (field.value == "") {

        // User has not entered anything
        field.value = field.defaultValue;
      }

    }

    // STOP HIDING FROM OTHER BROWSERS -->
    </SCRIPT>

    </HEAD>

    <BODY>

    <FORM METHOD=POST>
    <INPUT TYPE=text NAME="name" VALUE="Name"
          onFocus="clearField(this);"
          onBlur="checkField(this);">
    <BR>
    <INPUT TYPE=text NAME="email" VALUE="E-mail Address"
          onFocus="clearField(this);"
          onBlur="checkField(this);">
    <BR>
    <INPUT TYPE=text NAME="phone" VALUE="Phone Number"
          onFocus="clearField(this);"
          onBlur="checkField(this);">
    </FORM>

    </BODY>

    </HTML>
```

OUTPUT This script produces a form with three text entry fields that looks like Figure 6.6. If a user clicks in the "E-mail" field, the result is similar to Figure 6.7.

Figure 6.6.

A form with prompt information as the default value for each field.

Figure 6.7.

The
`clearField()`
function clears the
content of a field if
needed.

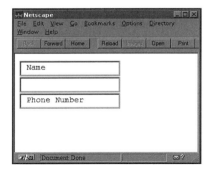

 In Listing 6.9, you highlight the use of the `defaultValue` property. By using this, you are able to build two simple functions, `clearField()` and `checkField()`, to handle all the work.

`clearField()` is called when the user places focus in a field. By comparing the current value of the field with the default value, the function decides whether it should clear the field before the user starts entering information.

Similarly, `checkField()` is called when the focus leaves a field. If the content of the field is blank, then the default value is reassigned to the field.

Summary

In this chapter, you have taken the major step from simple scripts to complex, interactive Web page development using JavaScript.

By working with form elements and event handlers, you can write scripts that enable sophisticated user interaction. For instance, you can develop simple spreadsheets, complex calculators, and can perform error checking before sending forms to a server for processing by CGI scripts.

Event handlers are specified HTML tags. Event handlers take as their values JavaScript code, usually in the form of a function call.

In order to step beyond the bounds of the simple sort of processes you have been scripting up to this point, in Chapter 7, you will take a detailed look at loops, which provide you with increased control over the flow of a program.

Commands and Extensions Review

Command/Extension	Type	Description
`blur()`	JavaScript method	Emulates removing focus from a form element
`form.action`	JavaScript property	String containing the value of the ACTION attribute of the FORM tag
`form.elements`	JavaScript property	Array containing an entry for each element in the form (such as checkboxes, text fields, and selection lists)
`form.encoding`	JavaScript property	String containing the MIME type used when submitting form data to the server
`form.name`	JavaScript property	String containing the value of the NAME attribute of the FORM tag
`form.target`	JavaScript property	String containing the name of the window targeted by a form submission
`form.submit()`	JavaScript method	Emulates the submission of an HTML form
`onSubmit`	Event handler	Event handler for the submission of an HTML form
`button`	HTML attribute	Type attribute for HTML buttons (<INPUT TYPE=button>)
`checkbox`	HTML attribute	Type attribute for checkbox toggle switches (<INPUT TYPE=checkbox>)
`password`	HTML attribute	Type attribute for password text entry fields (<INPUT TYPE=password>)
`radio`	HTML attribute	Type attribute for radio button toggle switches in forms (<INPUT TYPE=radio>)

continues

Command/Extension	Type	Description
reset	HTML attribute	Type attribute for reset buttons (`<INPUT TYPE=reset>`)
SELECT	HTML tag	Container tag for selection lists
OPTION	HTML tag	Indicates options in a selection list (`<SELECT><OPTION>Option 1<OPTION>Option 2</SELECT>`)
submit	HTML attribute	Type attribute for submit buttons (`<INPUT TYPE=submit>`)
text	HTML attribute	Type attribute for text fields in forms (`<INPUT TYPE=text>`)
TEXTAREA	HTML tag	Container tag for multiline text entry field (`<TEXTAREA>default text</TEXTAREA>`)
name	JavaScript property	String containing the name of an HTML element (button, checkbox, password, radio button, reset, submit, text, text area)
value	JavaScript property	String containing the current value of an HTML element (button, checkbox, password, radio button, reset, selection list, submit, text, text area)
click()	JavaScript method	Emulates clicking on a form element (button, checkbox, radio button, reset, selection list, submit)
onClick	JavaScript property	Event handler for a click event (button, checkbox, radio button, reset, submit)
checked	JavaScript property	Boolean value indicating if a choice is checked (checkbox, radio button)
defaultChecked	JavaScript property	Boolean value indicating if a choice is checked by default (checkbox, radio button)

6

Command/Extension	Type	Description
defaultvalue	JavaScript property	String containing the default value of an HTML element (password, text, text area)
focus()	JavaScript method	Emulates giving focus to an element (password, text, text area)
blur()	JavaScript method	Emulates removing focus from an element (password, text, text area)
select()	JavaScript method	Emulates selecting text in a field (password, text, text area)
onFocus	Event handler	Event handler for a focus event (password, selection list, text, text area)
onBlur	Event handler	Event handler for a blur event (password, selection list, text, text area)
onChange	Event handler	Event handler for when the value of a field changes (password, selection list, text, text area)
onSelect	Event handler	Event handler for when the user selects text in a field (password, text, text area)
index	JavaScript property	Integer indicating the current choice from a group of choices (radio button, selection list)
length	JavaScript property	Integer indicating the number of choices in a group of choices (radio button)
defaultSelected	JavaScript property	Boolean value indicating if a choice is selected by default (selection list)
options	JavaScript property	Array of options in a selection list
text	JavaScript property	Text displayed for a menu item in a selection list

6

continues

Command/Extension	Type	Description
TABLE	HTML tag	Container tag for HTML tables
TR	HTML tag	Container tag for rows of an HTML table
TD	HTML tag	Container tag for cells of an HTML table
COLSPAN	HTML attribute	Attribute of the TD tag to indicate if a cell spans multiple columns
ROWSPAN	HTML attribute	Attribute of the TD tag to indicate if a cell spans multiple rows
BORDER	HTML attribute	Attribute of the TABLE tag to indicate the width of the borders in a table
document.forms[]	JavaScript property	Array of form objects with an entry for each form in a document
string.substring()	JavaScript method	Returns a portion of the string based on being passed the indexes of the first and last character as arguments
Math.floor()	JavaScript method	Returns the next integer value less than the argument
string.length	JavaScript property	Integer value indicating the index of the last character in a string

NOTE

The Math.floor() and string.substring() methods will be used in the exercises later in this chapter. More details about the use of these methods will be discussed at that time.

Q&A

Q **Can I dynamically change the text in a button or on a drop-down SELECT list by assigning values to properties such as button.value?**

A No. Once a page has been rendered, its appearance (outside of text fields and a few other exceptions) cannot be altered at all.

NOTE This capability is expected to be included in the next release of Netscape Navigator.

Q Is it possible to have an event handler, maybe onChange, invoked with each keystroke as a user enters data in a text field?

A No; the onChange event handler is invoked only when focus leaves the field. Currently, there is no way to trap and react to individual keystrokes.

NOTE This capability is expected to be included in the next release of Netscape Navigator.

Exercises

1. Which of these HTML tags are valid?

   a. `<FORM METHOD=POST onClick="go();">`

   b. `<BODY onLOAD="go();">`

   c. `<INPUT TYPE=text onChange="go();">`

   d. `<INPUT TYPE=checkbox onChange="go();">`

   e. `<BODY onUnload="go();">`

   f. `<INPUT TYPE=text onClick="go();">`

2. Take the script from Listing 6.7 (the calculator program) and extend it to add the following:

   ☐ A positive/negative toggle button (that is, click on the button and the currently entered number changes sign).

   ☐ A decimal point button so that the user can enter floating point numbers.

   ☐ Check for errors as the user performs actions; specifically: check that the user is not trying to divide by zero and the user does not enter two decimal points. (If the user divides by zero, display a warning, and don't perform the action; if the user enters a second decimal point, ignore it.)

3. Extend the functionality of Listing 6.9 to check optionally whether entered information is in a specific numeric range and, if not, to warn the user.

Answers

1. The following are valid: (c) and (e). Example (a) is not valid because onClick is not a valid event handler for the BODY tag; (b) is wrong because JavaScript is case sensitive and the correct form is onLoad; (d) is incorrect because checkboxes have the onClick event handler only; and (f) is incorrect because the onClick event handler is not available for text fields.

2. In the following script, you can add three functions to implement the additional features:

TYPE **Listing 6.10. Adding features to the calculator.**

```
<HTML>

<HEAD>
<TITLE>Exercise 6.2</TITLE>

<SCRIPT>
<!-- HIDE FROM OTHER BROWSERS

var total = 0;
var lastOperation = "+";
var newnumber = true;

function enterNumber(digit) {

  var form = digit.form;

  if (newnumber) {
    clearNumber(form);
    newnumber = false;
  }

  form.display.value = form.display.value + digit.name;

}

function clear(form) {

  total = 0;
  lastOperation = "+";
  form.display.value = 0;

}

function clearNumber(form) {

  form.display.value = 0;

}
```

```
function calculate(operation) {

  var form = operation.form;

  if (checkErrors(form)) {

    var expression = total + lastOperation + form.display.value;

    lastOperation = operation.value;
    total = eval(expression);
    form.display.value = total;
    newnumber = true;
  } else {
    alert("You cannot divide by zero!");
    form.display.value = "";
  }

}

function changeSign(form) {

  var num = eval(form.display.value);
  form.display.value = -num;
  if (newnumber)
    total = -num;

}

function decimalPoint(form) {

  if (Math.floor(form.display.value) == form.display.value) {
    form.display.value += ".";
  }

}

function checkErrors(form) {

  noErrors = true;

  if ((lastOperation == "/") && (form.display.value == 0))
    noErrors = false;

  return noErrors;

}


// STOP HIDING FROM OTHER BROWSERS -->
</SCRIPT>

</HEAD>

<BODY>

<FORM>
```

continues

Listing 6.10. continued

```
<TABLE BORDER = 1>

<TR>
<TD COLSPAN=4>
<INPUT TYPE=text NAME=display VALUE="0" >
</TD>
</TR>

<TR>
<TD>
<INPUT TYPE=button NAME="7" VALUE=" 7 " onClick="enterNumber(this);">
</TD>
<TD>
<INPUT TYPE=button NAME="8" VALUE=" 8 " onClick="enterNumber(this);">
</TD>
<TD>
<INPUT TYPE=button NAME="9" VALUE=" 9 " onClick="enterNumber(this);">
</TD>
<TD>
<INPUT TYPE=button NAME="+" VALUE=" + " onClick="calculate(this);">
</TD>
</TR>

<TR>
<TD>
<INPUT TYPE=button NAME="4" VALUE=" 4 " onClick="enterNumber(this);">
</TD>
<TD>
<INPUT TYPE=button NAME="5" VALUE=" 5 " onClick="enterNumber(this);">
</TD>
<TD>
<INPUT TYPE=button NAME="6" VALUE=" 6 " onClick="enterNumber(this);">
</TD>
<TD>
<INPUT TYPE=button NAME="-" VALUE="  -  " onClick="calculate(this);">
</TD>
</TR>

<TR>
<TD>
<INPUT TYPE=button NAME="1" VALUE=" 1 " onClick="enterNumber(this);">
</TD>
<TD>
<INPUT TYPE=button NAME="2" VALUE=" 2 " onClick="enterNumber(this);">
</TD>
<TD>
<INPUT TYPE=button NAME="3" VALUE=" 3 " onClick="enterNumber(this);">
</TD>
<TD>
<INPUT TYPE=button NAME="*" VALUE=" * " onClick="calculate(this);">
</TD>
</TR>

<TR>
<TD>
<INPUT TYPE=button NAME="0" VALUE=" 0 " onClick="enterNumber(this);">
```

```
</TD>
<TD>
<INPUT TYPE=button NAME="C" VALUE=" C " onClick="clear(this.form);">
</TD>
<TD>
<INPUT TYPE=button NAME="CE" VALUE="CE" onClick="clearNumber(this.form);">
</TD>
<TD>
<INPUT TYPE=button NAME="/" VALUE="  /  " onClick="calculate(this);">
</TD>
</TR>

<TR>
<TD>
<INPUT TYPE=button NAME="sign" VALUE="+/-"
➡onClick="changeSign(this.form);">
</TD>
<TD>
</TD>
<TD>
<INPUT TYPE=button NAME="decimal" VALUE="  .  "
➡onClick="decimalPoint(this.form);">
</TD>
<TD>
</TD>
</TR>

</TABLE>

</FORM>

</BODY>

</HTML>
```

OUTPUT This script produces a calculator that looks like the one in Figure 6.8.

Figure 6.8.
Two buttons and three functions added to the calculator.

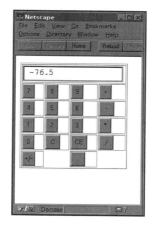

ANALYSIS There are several points worth noting in this new version of the calculator program. First, you make use of the unary negation operation (-) in the `changeSign()` function.

In the `decimalPoint()` function, you check whether the number is currently a floating point value by using the `Math.floor()` method. Only an integer evaluates to itself using `Math.floor()` and only integers lack a decimal point (in this particular case). It is important to note that this method isn't foolproof. A user could still enter two decimal points in a row.

You can handle this by using the `substring()` method of the `string` object to check if the last character of the display field is already a decimal point. The `substring()` method takes two arguments as follows:

```
stringname.substring(firstCharacter,lastCharacter)
```

where *firstCharacter* and *lastCharacter* are the numeric offset of the desired characters from the start of a string. The numeric offset is calculated based on the first character being number zero. So, if you have a variable called `testString` with the value `"JavaScript"`, then `testString.substring(1,4)` returns a value of `"avaS"`.

Of course, in this example, you don't know the numeric offset of the last character in `form.display.value`. You can find this out by using the `string.length` property. Now you can test whether the last character is a decimal point using the expression:

```
(form.display.value.substring(form.display.value.length,
➥form.display.value.length) == ".")
```

Then, the `decimalPoint()` function would look like this:

```
function decimalPoint(form) {

  var lastChar = form.display.value.length;
  var display = form.display.value;

  if ((Math.floor(form.display.value) == form.display.value) ||
      (display.substring(lastChar,lastChar) == ".")) {
    form.display.value += ".";
  }

}
```

The last function you added to your script is `checkErrors()`. In this script you simply check whether the last operation is divide and the current value is zero, and then you alert the user and disallow the operation.

3. In order to extend the functionality to include the optional range checking and alert, you need to add an additional function:

```
function checkRange(field,low,high,message) {

  if (field.value != "") {
    if ((field.value < low) || (field.value > high)) {
      alert(message);
```

```
      field.value="";
      field.focus();
    }
  } else {
    checkField(field);
  }

}
```

This function first checks whether the user has entered information. If she has, it checks the range; if the information is outside the range, the function alerts the user, clears the field, and returns focus to the field.

If there is no data entered, the function calls `checkField()`, which displays the default value in the field.

6

From the Web:

Ashley Cheng's Ideal Weight Calculator

Hong Kong's Dr. Ashley Cheng has produced a JavaScript page that contains an example of how JavaScript and forms can be combined to create special-purpose calculators and mini-spreadsheets. It's located at this site:

`http://www.iohk.com/UserPages/acheng/javascript.html`

Cheng's example is a calculator that, given a user's height and weight, calculates the individual's Body Mass Index and then makes a comment (usually light-hearted) about the implications of the calculated index. The comments range from "Umm...You are obese, want some liposuction?" to "You are starving. Go find some food!"

The interface is simple: a form with four fields—the user fills in the height and weight fields and the remaining two fields are filled in by the script with the user's BMI and the relevant comment. Two buttons are provided. One calculates the results and displays them in the appropriate fields, and the other enables the user to reset the form.

In addition, Dr. Cheng has added basic form checking to the script so that if either of the user's entry fields is empty, an appropriate alert is displayed. In addition, the script checks whether the height and weight values are totally illogical. For instance, if the weight value is less than zero kilograms or more than 500 kilograms, the program assumes that the user has made a mistake.

 NOTE   This script uses kilograms and centimeters for the user's weight and height. One kilogram is roughly equal to 2.2 pounds and 100 centimeters is roughly the same as 3.3 feet.

The source code for the program is in Listing W2.1.

Listing W2.1. Source code for Dr. Cheng's Ideal Weight Calculator.

```
<HTML>

<HEAD>
<TITLE>Ashley's JavaScript(tm) Examples</TITLE>

<SCRIPT LANGUAGE="JAVASCRIPT">
<!-- hide this script tag's contents from old browsers

function ClearForm(form){

    form.weight.value = "";
    form.height.value = "";
    form.bmi.value = "";
    form.my_comment.value = "";

}

function bmi(weight, height) {

        bmindx=weight/eval(height*height);
        return bmindx;
}

function checkform(form) {

        if (form.weight.value==null||form.weight.value.length==0 ||
➡form.height.value==null||form.height.value.length==0){
            alert("\nPlease complete the form first");
            return false;
        }

        else if (parseFloat(form.height.value) <= 0||
                parseFloat(form.height.value) >=500||
                parseFloat(form.weight.value) <= 0||
                parseFloat(form.weight.value) >=500){
```

```
                alert("\nReally know what you're doing? \nPlease enter values
again.
➥\nWeight in kilos and \nheight in cm");
                ClearForm(form);
                return false;
        }
        return true;

}

function computeform(form) {

        if (checkform(form)) {

        yourbmi=Math.round(bmi(form.weight.value, form.height.value/100));
        form.bmi.value=yourbmi;

        if (yourbmi >40) {
            form.my_comment.value="You are grossly obese,
➥consult your physician!";
        }

        else if (yourbmi >30 && yourbmi <=40) {
            form.my_comment.value="Umm... You are obese, want some liposuction?";
        }

        else if (yourbmi >27 && yourbmi <=30) {
            form.my_comment.value="You are very fat,
➥do something before it's too late";
        }

        else if (yourbmi >22 && yourbmi <=27) {
            form.my_comment.value="You are fat, need dieting and exercise";
        }

        else if (yourbmi >=21 && yourbmi <=22) {
            form.my_comment.value="I envy you. Keep it up!!";
        }

        else if (yourbmi >=18 && yourbmi <21) {
            form.my_comment.value="You are thin, eat more.";
        }

        else if (yourbmi >=16 && yourbmi <18) {
            form.my_comment.value="You are starving. Go Find some food!";
        }

        else if (yourbmi <16) {
            form.my_comment.value="You're grossly undernourished,
➥need hospitalization ";
        }

        }
        return;
}
// -- done hiding from old browsers -->
</SCRIPT>
```

continues

Listing W2.1. continued

```
</HEAD>


<BODY BACKGROUND="background.gif">
<CENTER>

<H1>Ashley's JavaScript(tm) Examples:</H1>
<HR SIZE=3>

<UL>
<LI><A HREF="#HK1997">Hong Kong and 1997</A>
<LI><A HREF="#Calc">Want to know whether your weight is ideal?</A>
</UL>


<A NAME="HK1997">
<HR>


<P>
<SCRIPT LANGUAGE="JAVASCRIPT">

<!-- hide this script tag's contents from old browsers

document.write('<IMG SRC="hkf.jpg"> <P>');

today = new Date();

document.write("Today is <B>"+today+"</B><P>");
BigDay = new Date("July 1, 1997")
msPerDay = 24 * 60 * 60 * 1000 ;
timeLeft = (BigDay.getTime() - today.getTime());
e_daysLeft = timeLeft / msPerDay;
daysLeft = Math.floor(e_daysLeft);
e_hrsLeft = (e_daysLeft - daysLeft)*24;
hrsLeft = Math.floor(e_hrsLeft);
minsLeft = Math.floor((e_hrsLeft - hrsLeft)*60);
document.write("There are only<BR> <H3>" + daysLeft + " days "
➥+ hrsLeft +" hours and " + minsLeft + " minutes left
➥</H3><BR> before Hong Kong revert from British to Chinese
➥rule <BR> on the <B>1st of July 1997!</B><P>");

 // -- done hiding from old browsers -->
</SCRIPT>

<FORM>
<input type=button name="Refresh"  value="Refresh"
onclick="window.location='http://www.iohk.com/UserPages
➥/acheng/javascript.html'">
</FORM>
</A>

<HR>
<A NAME="Calc">
```

```
<H2><IMG SRC="scale.jpg" ALIGN=MIDDLE> Do you have an ideal weight??</H2>
Enter your weight in kilograms and your height in centimeters<BR>
in the form below and press the "Let's see" button<BR>
(Please read disclaimer below before using this form)<BR>

<FORM NAME="BMI" method=POST>
<TABLE border=1>
<TR>
<TD><DIV ALIGN=CENTER>Your Weight (kg)</DIV></TD>
<TD><DIV ALIGN=CENTER>Your Height (cm)</DIV></TD>
<TD><DIV ALIGN=CENTER>Your BMI</DIV></TD>
<TD><DIV ALIGN=CENTER>My Comment</DIV></TD>
</TR>

<TR>
<TD><INPUT TYPE=TEXT NAME=weight  SIZE=10
➥onfocus="this.form.weight.value=''"></TD>
<TD><INPUT TYPE=TEXT NAME=height  SIZE=10
➥onfocus="this.form.height.value=''"></TD>
<TD><INPUT TYPE=TEXT NAME=bmi      SIZE=8 ></TD>
<TD><INPUT TYPE=TEXT NAME=my_comment  SIZE=35 ></TD>
</TABLE>

<P>
<INPUT TYPE="button" VALUE="Let's see" onclick="computeform(this.form)">
<INPUT TYPE="reset"  VALUE="Reset" onclick="ClearForm(this.form)">
</FORM>

</A>

<HR>


</CENTER>

<B>Disclaimer</B>: This form is based on the calculation of
<A HREF="http://www.iohk.com/UserPages/acheng/bmi.html">
➥<I>"Body Mass Index"</I></A>
and is only meant to be a demonstration of how Javascript(tm) could be used
on a Web Page. Information it contains may not be accurate and is not designed
or intended to serve as medical advice. You should not act in accordance to the
"comment" provided in this form and I shall not be liable for any physical or
psychological damages suffered as a result of using this form or script.
```

```
<HR>
Access: <IMG SRC="http://www.iohk.com/cgi-bin/nph-count?
➥link=ashleycheng&width=6"> <P>
<IMG SRC="cheng3.gif" ALIGN="LEFT" HSPACE=15><BR>
Author: Ashley Cheng (<A HREF="mailto:ackcheng@ha.org.hk">
➥ackcheng@ha.org.hk</A>) Jan 1996<BR>
Go back to <A HREF="http://www.iohk.com/UserPages/acheng">
➥my Home-Page</A> or see
➥<A HREF="http://www.wahyan.edu.hk/ashleyticker.html">
➥Java(tm) applets written by me</A>. <P>


</BODY>
</HTML>
```

OUTPUT   The script produces results similar to those in Figures W2.1 and W2.2.

Figure W2.1.
Calculators and mini spreadsheets can be created using JavaScript.

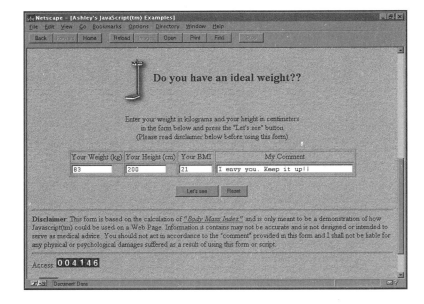

Figure W2.2.
Dr. Cheng uses simple error checking to ensure data is valid.

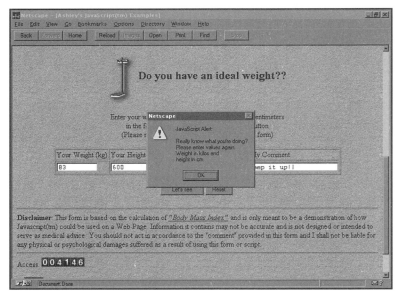

ANALYSIS Dr. Cheng's page has two JavaScript applications on it: a countdown to China's take-over of Hong Kong and the weight calculator in which we are interested.

Cheng places all the functions for the weight calculator in the header, but because the countdown application involves dynamic HTML content based on the date and time, that script is contained in the body of the HTML document.

The weight calculator is built out of four functions: ClearForm(), bmi(), checkform(), and computeform().

Before looking at each function and how it works, we need to understand the HTML form that provides the interface to the script:

```
<FORM NAME="BMI" method=POST>
<TABLE border=1>
<TR>
<TD><DIV ALIGN=CENTER>Your Weight (kg)</DIV></TD>
<TD><DIV ALIGN=CENTER>Your Height (cm)</DIV></TD>
<TD><DIV ALIGN=CENTER>Your BMI</DIV></TD>
<TD><DIV ALIGN=CENTER>My Comment</DIV></TD>
</TR>

<TR>
<TD><INPUT TYPE=TEXT NAME=weight  SIZE=10
➥onfocus="this.form.weight.value=''"></TD>
<TD><INPUT TYPE=TEXT NAME=height  SIZE=10
➥onfocus="this.form.height.value=''"></TD>
<TD><INPUT TYPE=TEXT NAME=bmi     SIZE=8 ></TD>
<TD><INPUT TYPE=TEXT NAME=my_comment  SIZE=35 ></TD>
</TABLE>

<P>
<INPUT TYPE="button" VALUE="Let's see" onclick="computeform(this.form)">
<INPUT TYPE="reset"  VALUE="Reset" onclick="ClearForm(this.form)">
</FORM>
```

For appearance, Dr. Cheng has put the four text fields into a table. He uses the <DIV ALIGN=CENTER> ... </DIV> structure to center text inside the table cells. <DIV ALIGN=CENTER> is the HTML 3 method for centering text and is supported by Navigator 2.0 along with Netscape's own methods, such as the CENTER tag.

The form contains four text fields: weight, height, bmi, and my_comment. The two that the user uses—weight and height—are cleared when the user clicks in them simply by setting the value of the field to an empty string in the onFocus event handler:

```
onfocus="this.form.height.value=''"
```

The Let's See button uses the onClick event handler to call computeform() and passes it the form object as an argument using this.form. The Reset button calls the ClearForm() function.

The next four sections elaborate on the `ClearForm()`, `bmi()`, `checkform()`, and `computeform()` functions.

The `ClearForm()` Function

This function simply sets the values of the four fields in the form to the empty string.

The `bmi()` Function

The `bmi()` function is used to calculate the Body Mass Index using the formula bmi = weight/ (height×height) where the weight is in kilograms and the height is in meters (not centimeters). The function accepts `weight` and `height` as arguments and then simply calculates the BMI and returns it.

The `checkform()` Function

`checkform()` accepts the `form` object as an argument and performs two error checks on the data. The function is called from the `computeform()` function.

First, the function checks whether either the `weight` or `height` field in the form contains a `null` value or an empty string:

```
if (form.weight.value==null||form.weight.value.length==0 ||
➡form.height.value==null||form.height.value.length==0){
          alert("\nPlease complete the form first");
          return false;
   }
```

If either field is not filled in, then an alert is displayed and the function returns a `false` value.

If both fields are filled in, the function then checks to see if the values make sense. If they seem out of a reasonable range, then an alert is displayed, and the function returns a `false` value. Notice the use of `\n` in the alert message to perform basic formatting of the text:

```
        else if (parseFloat(form.height.value) <= 0||
                parseFloat(form.height.value) >=500||
                parseFloat(form.weight.value) <= 0||
                parseFloat(form.weight.value) >=500){
                alert("\nReally know what you're doing? \nPlease enter values
                ➡again.\nWeight in kilos and \nheight in cm"); ClearForm(form);
                return false;
        }
```

If the data is acceptable following both these checks, then the function simply returns a `true` value.

The `computeform()` Function

The `computeform()` function is where the primary work of the script is done. This function is called when the user clicks on the Let's See button, and it accepts the `form` object as an argument.

The script starts by calling `checkform()` to be sure the data is valid. If the data passes muster in the `checkform()` function, the `ComputeForm()`function proceeds to make the necessary calculations:

```
yourbmi=Math.round(bmi(form.weight.value, form.height.value/100));
form.bmi.value=yourbmi;
```

The program first calls `bmi()` and passes the weight and height entered by the user. The height is divided by 100 because the `bmi()` function expects the height in meters, and there are 100 centimeters in a meter. `Math.round()` is used to round the results to the nearest integer and then the value is assigned to `yourbmi`.

Notice that `yourbmi` is not defined using the `var` statement. As you learned in Chapter 4, "Functions and Objects—The Building Blocks of Programs," JavaScript is perfectly happy to define variables when they are first used, without the `var` statement.

```
if (yourbmi >40) {
   form.my_comment.value="You are grossly obese,
➥consult your physician!";
}       else if (yourbmi >30 && yourbmi <=40) {
   form.my_comment.value="Umm... You are obese, want some liposuction?";
}

else if (yourbmi >27 && yourbmi <=30) {
   form.my_comment.value="You are very fat,
➥do something before it's too late";
}

else if (yourbmi >22 && yourbmi <=27) {
   form.my_comment.value="You are fat, need dieting and exercise";
}

else if (yourbmi >=21 && yourbmi <=22) {
   form.my_comment.value="I envy you. Keep it up!!";
}

else if (yourbmi >=18 && yourbmi <21) {
   form.my_comment.value="You are thin, eat more.";
}

else if (yourbmi >=16 && yourbmi <18) {
   form.my_comment.value="You are starving. Go Find some food!";
}
```

```
else if (yourbmi <16) {
   form.my_comment.value="You're grossly undernourished,
➥need hospitalization ";
}

}
```

The rest of the function simply consists of a long if ...else if ... else construct that checks the value of yourbmi against different ranges and places the appropriate message in the my_comment field in the form.

DAY

4

Chapter 7

Loops

Up to this point in the book, you have learned to produce fairly linear programs. That is, each line of a script gets one chance to execute (an if ... else construct can mean certain lines don't execute), and in the case of functions, each line of the function gets only one chance to execute each time the function is called.

Most programming relies on the capability to repeat a number of lines of program code based on a condition or a counter. This is achieved by using loops.

The for loop enables you to count through a list and perform the specified command block for each entry in the list. The while loop enables you to test for a condition and repeat the command block until the condition is false.

In this chapter, we take a detailed look at loops and their applications, including the following:

- [ ] Basic concepts of loops
- [ ] The for and for ... in loop
- [ ] The while loop
- [ ] The break and continue statements
- [ ] More about arrays

Loops—Basic Concepts

Loops enable script writers to repeat sections of program code or command blocks, based on a set of criteria.

For example, a loop can be used to repeat a series of actions on each number between 1 and 10 or to continue gathering information from the user until the user indicates she has finished entering all her information.

The two main types of loops are those that are conditional (`while` loops continue until a condition is met or fails to be met) and those that iterate over a set range (the `for` and `for ... in` loops).

The `for` and `for ... in` Loops

The `for` loop is the most basic type of loop and resembles similarly named loops in other programming languages including Perl, C, and BASIC.

In its most basic form, the `for` loop is used to count. For instance, in Listing 6.8 in Chapter 6, "Creating Interactive Forms," you needed to repeat a single calculation for each number between 1 and 10. This was easily achieved using a `for` loop:

```
function calculate(form) {

  var number=form.number.value;
  for(var num = 1; num <= 10; num++) {

    form.elements[num].value = number * num;
  }

}
```

What this loop says is to use the variable `num` as a counter. Start with `num` at `1`, perform the command block and increment `num` as long as `num` is less than or equal to `10`. In other words, count from 1 to 10 and for each number, perform the command.

In its general form, the `for` command looks like this:

```
for(initial value; condition; update expression)
```

The `initial value` sets up the counter variable and assigns the initial value. The initial value expression can declare a new variable using `var`. The expression is also optional.

The `condition` is evaluated at the start of each pass through the loop, so in this loop:

```
for(i=8; i<5; i++) {
  commands
}
```

the command block would never be executed because 8 < 5 evaluates to `false`. Like the initial value expression, the condition is optional, and when omitted, evaluates to `true` by default.

NOTE

If the condition always evaluates to `true`, it is possible to face an infinite loop, which means the script can never end. In situations where you omit the condition on the `for` loop, it is important to provide some alternate means to exit the loop, such as with the `break` statement, which we will look at later in this chapter.

TIP

It is traditional programming to use the variables `i`, `j`, `k`, `l`, and so on. as counters for loops. This is generally the practice unless a specific variable name adds clarity to the program code. Often, though, programs use general purpose counters, and these variable names are easily recognizable as counters to experienced programmers.

The third part of the `for` statement is the *update expression*. This expression is executed at the end of the command block before testing the condition again. This is generally used to update the counter. This expression is optional, and the counter updating can be done in the body of the command block, if needed.

To highlight the application of loops, the following script generates dynamic output to the display window. It asks the user for his name, followed by his 10 favorite foods for a JavaScript "top ten" list.

TYPE   **Listing 7.1. Creating a Top Ten list with `for` loops.**

```
<HTML>

<HEAD>
<TITLE>for Loop Example</TITLE>
</HEAD>

<BODY>

<SCRIPT LANGUAGE="JavaScript">
<!-- HIDE FROM OTHER BROWSERS

var name = prompt("What is your name?","name");
var query = "";
```

continues

Listing 7.1. continued

```
document.write("<H1>" + name + "'s 10 favorite foods</H1>");

for (var i=1; i<=10; i++) {
  document.write(i + ". " + prompt('Enter food number ' + i,'food') + '<BR>');
}

// STOP HIDING FROM OTHER BROWSERS -->
</SCRIPT>

</BODY>

</HTML>
```

OUTPUT This script produces results similar to those in Figure 7.1.

Figure 7.1.

Using loops, you can repeatedly ask users for their 10 favorite foods.

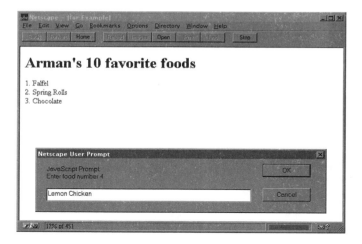

ANALYSIS In this example, you use the for loop to count from 1 (i=1) to 10 (i<=10) by increments of one (i++). For each turn through the loop, you prompt the user for a food and write the food out to the window preceded by the current number using the document.write() method.

for loops are not only used for counting in increments of one. They can be used for counting in larger quantities. The following line

```
for(j=2; j<=20; j+=2)
```

counts from 2 to 20 by twos. Likewise, for loops can be used to count backward (decrement); the following line counts down from 10 to 1:

```
for(k=10; k>=1; k--)
```

At the same time, simple addition and subtraction are not the only operations allowed in the update expression. The command

```
for(i=1; i<=256; i*=2)
```

will start with i equal to 1 and then proceed to double it until the value is more than 256. Similarly,

```
for(j=3; j<=81; j*=j)
```

repeatedly squares the counter.

The for ... in Loop

Where the for loop is a general-purpose loop, JavaScript also has the for ... in loop for more specific applications. The for ... in loop is used to automatically step through all the properties of an object. In order to understand this, remember that each property in an object can be referred to by a number—its index. For instance, this loop

```
for (j in testObject) {
  commands
}
```

increments j from 0 until the index of the last property in the object testObject.

This is useful where the number of properties is not known or not consistent, as in a general-purpose function for an event handler.

For instance, you may want to create a simple slot machine application. The slot machine can display numbers from 0 to 9—each in a separate text field in a form. If the form is named slotForm, then the loop

```
for (k in slotForm) {
  code to display number
}
```

could be the basis for displaying the results of spinning the slot machine. With this type of loop, you could easily change the number of items on the slot machine so that instead of three text fields, you could have five fields, two fields, or nine fields.

Using Loops to Check for Numbers

In this example you write a single function to check whether or not the information the user has entered in a field is a number.

In order to do this, you use the substring() method learned in Chapter 6, and you assume that numbers contain only the digits zero through nine plus a decimal point and a negative sign. The presence of any other character in a field indicates that the value is not numeric.

This type of function could then be used, for example, in checking form input. For instance, in Exercise 5.3 (the doubling and squaring form), you could add the function to the script, as shown in Listing 7.2.

TYPE **Listing 7.2. Checking input with the `isNum()` function.**

```
<HTML>

<HEAD>
<TITLE>for ... in Example</TITLE>

<SCRIPT>
<!-- HIDE FROM OTHER BROWSERS

function checkNum(toCheck) {
  var isNum = true;

  if ((toCheck == null) || (toCheck == "")) {
    isNum = false;
    return isNum;
  }

  for (j = 0; j < toCheck.length; j++) {
    if ((toCheck.substring(j,j+1) != "0") &&
        (toCheck.substring(j,j+1) != "1") &&
        (toCheck.substring(j,j+1) != "2") &&
        (toCheck.substring(j,j+1) != "3") &&
        (toCheck.substring(j,j+1) != "4") &&
        (toCheck.substring(j,j+1) != "5") &&
        (toCheck.substring(j,j+1) != "6") &&
        (toCheck.substring(j,j+1) != "7") &&
        (toCheck.substring(j,j+1) != "8") &&
        (toCheck.substring(j,j+1) != "9") &&
        (toCheck.substring(j,j+1) != ".") &&
        (toCheck.substring(j,j+1) != "-")) {
      isNum = false;
    }
  }

  return isNum;

}
function calculate(form,currentField) {

  var isNum = true;
  var thisFieldNum = true;

  for var field = 0; field < form.length; field ++) {
    thisFieldNum = checkNum(field.value);
    if (!thisFieldNum)
      isNum = false;
  }
```

```
    if (isNum) {
      if (currentField == "square") {
        form.entry.value = Math.sqrt(form.square.value);
        form.twice.value = form.entry.value * 2;
      } else if (currentField == "twice") {
        form.entry.value = form.twice.value / 2;
        form.square.value = form.entry.value * form.entry.value;
      } else {
        form.twice.value = form.entry.value * 2;
        form.square.value = form.entry.value * form.entry.value;
      }
    } else {
      alert("Please Enter only Numbers!");
    }

}

// STOP HIDING FROM OTHER BROWSERS -->
</SCRIPT>

</HEAD>

<BODY>

<FORM METHOD=POST>

Value: <INPUT TYPE=text NAME="entry" VALUE=0
              onChange="calculate(this.form,this.name);">
Double: <INPUT TYPE=text NAME="twice" VALUE=0
               onChange="calculate(this.form,this.name);">
Square: <INPUT TYPE=text NAME="square" VALUE=0
               onChange="calculate(this.form,this.name);">

</FORM>

</BODY>

</HTML>
```

ANALYSIS All the number checking takes place in the checkNum() function:

```
function checkNum(toCheck) {
  var isNum = true;

  if ((toCheck == null) || (toCheck == "")) {
    isNum = false;
    return isNum;
  }

  for (j = 0; j < toCheck.length; j++) {
    if ((toCheck.substring(j,j+1) != "0") &&
        (toCheck.substring(j,j+1) != "1") &&
        (toCheck.substring(j,j+1) != "2") &&
```

7

```
                (toCheck.substring(j,j+1) != "3") &&
                (toCheck.substring(j,j+1) != "4") &&
                (toCheck.substring(j,j+1) != "5") &&
                (toCheck.substring(j,j+1) != "6") &&
                (toCheck.substring(j,j+1) != "7") &&
                (toCheck.substring(j,j+1) != "8") &&
                (toCheck.substring(j,j+1) != "9") &&

                (toCheck.substring(j,j+1) != ".") &&
                (toCheck.substring(j,j+1) != "-")) {
            isNum = false;
        }
    }

    return isNum;

}
```

You make simple use of the for statement in this example. You start by assuming that the value is a number (var isNum = true;). First you check to make sure the value passed to the function is not the empty string or the null value, and then you use the loop to move from the first character in the field value to the last, and each time, check whether the given character is a numeric value. If not, you set isNum to false. After the loop, you return the value of isNum.

You check each character to see whether it is a number by using one if statement with multiple conditions. Remembering that && is the symbol for logical "and," we are saying if the character doesn't match any number from 0 to 9 or the decimal point or negative sign, then the entry is not a number.

An alternative approach to comparing the number to each possible number from 0 to 9 is to use the structure (toCheck.substring(j,j+1) <= "0" && toCheck.substring(j,j+1) >= "9" which would check if the digit is a numeral:

```
    if ((toCheck.substring(j,j+1) <= "0") &&
        (toCheck.substring(j,j+1) >= "9") &&
        (toCheck.substring(j,j+1) != ".") &&
        (toCheck.substring(j,j+1) != "-")) {
      isNum = false;
    }
```

The while Loop

In addition to the for loop, the while loop provides a different, but similar, function. The basic structure of a while loop is

```
while (condition) {
  JavaScript commands
}
```

where the `condition` is any valid JavaScript expression that evaluates to a boolean value. The command block executes as long as the condition is `true`. For instance, the following loop counts until the value of num is 11:

```
var num = 1;

while (num <= 10) {
  document.writeln(num);
  num++;
}
```

A while loop could easily be used in a testing situation where the user must answer a question correctly to continue:

```
var answer = "";
var correct = 100;
var question = "What is 10 * 10?";
while (answer != correct) {
  answer = prompt(question,"0");
}
```

In this example, you simply set answer to an empty string, so that at the start of the while loop, the condition would evaluate to true and the question would be asked at least once.

Now that you have learned both the for loop and the while loop, you are ready to build a more complex program.

As an educational tool for children, you are going to build a calculator to solve the typical problems children get on tests: If a leaves b at speed c and d leaves e at speed f and they travel in a straight line toward each other, when will they meet?

The student simply enters the required information into the form and then either selects the Calculate button to see the correct answer or a Test button to be tested on the problem. Listing 7.3 contains the code for this program.

TYPE **Listing 7.3. Travel problem tester.**

```
<HTML>

<HEAD>
<TITLE>Listing 7.3</TITLE>

<SCRIPT LANGUAGE="JavaScript">

function checkNum(toCheck) {
  var isNum = true;

  if ((toCheck == nul) || (toCheck == "")) {
    isNum = false;
    return isNum;
  }
```

7

continues

Listing 7.3. continued

```
        for (j = 0; j < toCheck.length; j++) {
          if ((toCheck.substring(j,j+1) != "0") &&
              (toCheck.substring(j,j+1) != "1") &&
              (toCheck.substring(j,j+1) != "2") &&
              (toCheck.substring(j,j+1) != "3") &&
              (toCheck.substring(j,j+1) != "4") &&
              (toCheck.substring(j,j+1) != "5") &&
              (toCheck.substring(j,j+1) != "6") &&
              (toCheck.substring(j,j+1) != "7") &&
              (toCheck.substring(j,j+1) != "8") &&
              (toCheck.substring(j,j+1) != "9") &&
              (toCheck.substring(j,j+1) != ".") &&
              (toCheck.substring(j,j+1) != "-")) {
            isNum = false;
          }
        }

        return isNum;

      }

      function checkFieldNum(field) {

        if (!checkNum(field.value)) {

          alert("Please enter a number in this field!");

        }

      }

      function checkFormNum(form) {

        var isNum = true;

        for (field = 0; field <=2; field ++) {
          if (!checkNum(form.elements[field].value)) {
            isNum = false;
          }
        }

        if (!isNum) {
          alert("All Fields Must Be Numbers!");
        }

        return isNum;

      }

      function calculate(form) {

        if (checkFormNum(form)) {
          with (form) {
            var time = distance.value / (eval(speedA.value) + eval(speedB.value));
```

```
      result.value = "" + time + " hour(s)";
    }
  }
}

function test(form) {

  if (checkFormNum(form)) {
    with (form) {
      var time = distance.value / (eval(speedA.value) + eval(speedB.value));
      var answer = "";
      while (eval(answer) != time) {
        answer = prompt("What is the answer to the problem?","0");
      }
      result.value = "" + time + " hour(s)";
    }
  }

}

// STOP HIDING FROM OTHER BROWSERS -->
</SCRIPT>

</HEAD>

<BODY>

<FORM METHOD=POST>
Distance: <INPUT TYPE=text NAME="distance" onChange="checkFieldNum(this);"><BR>
Speed of Person A: <INPUT TYPE=text NAME="speedA"
➥onChange="checkFieldNum(this);"><BR>
Speed of Person B: <INPUT TYPE=text NAME="speedB"
➥onChange="checkFieldNum(this);"><BR>
<INPUT TYPE=button Name="Calculate" VALUE="Calculate"
➥onClick="calculate(this.form);">
<INPUT TYPE=button Name="Test" VALUE="Test" onClick="test(this.form);"><BR>
Results: <INPUT TYPE=text NAME=result onFocus="this.blur();">
</FORM>

</BODY>

</HTML>
```

OUTPUT This script produces results like those in Figures 7.2 and 7.3.

7

Figure 7.2.

Using the for *loop, you can test the form entries before calculating the result.*

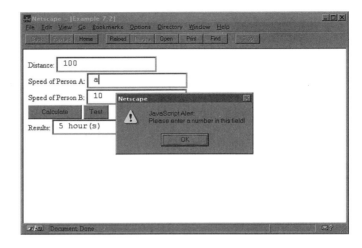

Figure 7.3.

The while *loop enables you to continually test the user for the correct answer.*

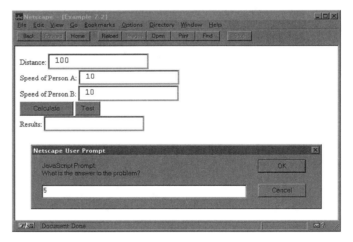

ANALYSIS You make several different uses of loops in this example.

In the checkFormNum() function, you use the for loop to cycle through all the first three form elements:

```
for (field = 0; field <=2; field ++) {
  if ((!checkNum(form.elements[field].value)) {
    isNum = false;
  }
}
```

You can then simply check whether the field contains a numeric.

You also use a while loop in the test() function to perform the testing of the student. In both the test() and calculate() functions, you also use a new statement: with. This command is used where numerous references to an object are made in a block of code to make the code shorter and easier to read. For instance, in this script, you refer to the form object. By using with (form), you can then write a block of code without the form prefix on all the properties and method calls.

To illustrate, if you have a function that assigned values to five fields in a form, you could write it two different ways:

```
function assign(form) {
  form.one.value = 1;
  form.two.value = 2;
  form.three.value = 3;
  form.four.value = 4;
  form.five.value = 5;
}
```

or

```
function assign(form) {
  with (form) {
    one.value = 1;
    two.value = 2;
    three.value = 3;
    four.value = 4;
    five.value = 5;
  }
}
```

You could even make this function easier by adding a for or for ... in loop:

```
function assign(form) {
  with (form) {
    for (j = 0; j < length; j++) {
      elements[j].value = j;
    }
  }
}
```

Here the loop cycles from 0 to one less than the value of the property form.length. form.length contains the number of elements in the form. The indexes of these elements in the elements[] array are from zero to length-1.

The break and continue Statements

To add even more utility to the for and while loops, JavaScript includes the break and continue statements. These statements can be used to alter the behavior of the loops beyond a simple repetition of the related command block.

7

The break command does what the name implies—it breaks out of the loop completely, even if the loop isn't complete. For instance, if you want to give students three chances to get a test question correct, you could use the break statement:

```
var answer = "";
var correct = "100";
var question = "What is 10 * 10?";
for (k = 1; k <= 3; k++) {
  answer = prompt(question,"0");
  if (answer == correct) {
    alert ("Correct!");
    break;
  }
}
```

In this loop, the command block gets performed three times only if the first two answers are incorrect. A correct answer simply ends the loop prematurely.

The continue statement is slightly different. It is used to jump to the next repetition of the command block without completing the current pass through the command block. For instance, if you want to total three numbers input with a prompt statement but want to simply ignore a value if it is not a number, you might use the following structure (you are assuming the existence of a similar checkNum() function to the one you used before):

```
var total = 0;
var newNumber = 0;
for (i=1; i <=3; i++) {
  newNumber = prompt ("Enter a number","0");
  if (!checkNum(newNumber))
    continue;
  total = eval(total) + eval(newNumber);
  alert ("You entered " + newNumber + " and the total is " +
         total + ".");
}
```

This loop could be extended to add numbers until the user enters 0 as the new value. You do this by using a while loop instead of a for loop:

```
var total = 0;
var newNumber = "";
while ((newNumber = prompt ("Enter a numer","0")) != 0) {
  if (!checkNum(newNumber))
    continue;
  total = eval(total) + eval(newNumber);
  alert ("You entered " + newNumber + " and the total is " +
         total + ".");
}
```

The reason you use the prompt in the while loop's condition is related to *when* the condition is tested. In this way, if the user enters 0 at the first prompt, the alert dialog box is never displayed.

7

Creating a Game of Tic-Tac-Toe

In this example, you write a script to play a simple game of tic-tac-toe.

In order to do this, you use nine text entry fields in a single form to contain the nine spaces of the tic-tac-toe board.

The basic approach is as follows: The user plays first. After each play by the user, the relevant rows, columns, and diagonals are checked for a win. If there is no win, you scan each row, column, and diagonal to see if the computer can win. Then you check all rows, columns, and diagonals to see if there is a chance for the user to win. Failing both these scenarios, the computer simply takes any available space.

In order to easily implement the game, you use a standard naming system for the fields, such as 11 for the top left corner, 13 for the top right corner and 33 for the bottom right corner. In this way, you will be able to use loops to quickly scan the board for combinations.

TIP

> If you find the task a bit overwhelming, skip ahead to the analysis section following the source code to get a better feel of what's being done.

TYPE | **Listing 7.4. Tic-tac-toe with `for` loops.**

```
<HTML>

<HEAD>
<TITLE>Listing 7.4</TITLE>

<SCRIPT LANGUAGE="JavaScript">
<!-- HIDE FROM OTHER BROWSERS

var row = 0;
var col = 0;
var playerSymbol = "X";
var computerSymbol = "O";
board = new createArray(3,3);

function createArray(row,col) {

  var index = 0;
  this.length = (row * 10) + col;
  for (var x = 1; x <= row; x ++) {
    for (var y = 1; y <= col; y++) {
      index = (x*10) + y;
      this[index] = "";
```

7

continues

Listing 7.4. continued

```
        }
      }

    }

    function buildBoard(form) {

      var index = 0;
      for (var field = 0; field <= 8; field ++) {
        index = eval(form.elements[field].name);
        form.elements[field].value = board[index];
      }

    }

    function clear(form) {

      var index = 0;
      for (var field = 0; field <= 8; field ++) {
        form.elements[field].value = "";
        index = eval(form.elements[field].name);
        board[index] = "";
      }

    }

    function win(index) {

      var win = false;

      // CHECK ROWS
      if ((board[index] == board[(index < 30) ? index + 10 : index - 20]) &&
          (board[index] == board[(index >  11) ? index - 10 : index + 20])) {
        win = true;
      }

      // CHECK COLUMNS
      if ((board[index] == board[(index%10 < 3) ? index + 1 : index - 2]) &&
          (board[index] == board[(index%10 > 1) ? index - 1 : index + 2])) {
        win = true;
      }

      // CHECK DIAGONALS
      if (Math.round(index/10) == index%10) {
        if ((board[index] == board[(index < 30) ? index + 11 : index - 22]) &&
            (board[index] == board[(index >  11) ? index - 11 : index + 22])) {
          win = true;
        }
        if (index == 22) {
          if ((board[index] == board[13]) && (board[index] == board[31])) {
            win = true;
          }
        }
      }
```

```
   if ((index == 31) || (index == 13)) {
     if ((board[index] == board[(index < 30) ? index + 9 : index - 18]) &&
         (board[index] == board[(index >  11) ? index - 9 : index + 18])) {
       win = true;
     }
   }

   // RETURN THE RESULTS
   return win;

}

function play(form,field) {

   var index = eval(field.name);
   var playIndex = 0;
   var winIndex = 0;
   var done = false;
   field.value = playerSymbol;
   board[index] = playerSymbol;

   //CHECK FOR PLAYER WIN
 if (win(index)) {
     // PLAYER WON
     alert("Good Play! You Win!");
     clear(form);
   } else {
     // PLAYER LOST, CHECK FOR WINNING POSITION
     for (row = 1; row <= 3; row++) {
       for (col = 1; col <= 3; col++) {
         index = (row*10) + col;
         if (board[index] == "") {
           board[index] = computerSymbol;
           if(win(index)) {
             playIndex = index;
             done = true;
             board[index] = "";
             break;
           }
           board[index] = "";
         }
       }
       if (done)
         break;
     }
     // CHECK IF COMPUTER CAN WIN
     if (done) {
       board[playIndex] = computerSymbol;
       buildBoard(form);
       alert("Computer Just Won!");
       clear(form);
     } else {
       // CAN'T WIN, CHECK IF NEED TO STOP A WIN
       for (row = 1; row <=3; row++) {
         for (col = 1; col <= 3; col++) {
           index = (row*10) + col;
```

continues

Listing 7.4. continued

```
            if (board[index] == "") {
              board[index] = playerSymbol;
              if (win(index)) {
                playIndex = index;
                done = true;
                board[index] = "";
                break;
              }
              board[index] = "";
            }
          }
          if (done)
            break;
        }
        // CHECK IF DONE
        if (done) {
          board[playIndex] = computerSymbol;
          buildBoard(form);
        } else {
          // NOT DONE, CHECK FOR FIRST EMPTY SPACE
          for (row = 1; row <= 3; row ++) {
            for (col = 1; col <= 3; col ++) {
              index = (row*10) + col;
              if (board[index] == "") {
                playIndex = index;
                done = true;
                break;
              }
            }
            if (done)
              break;
          }
          board[playIndex] = computerSymbol;
          buildBoard(form);
        }
      }
    }
  }

// STOP HIDING HERE -->
</SCRIPT>

</HEAD>

<BODY>

<FORM METHOD = POST>

<TABLE>

<TR>
<TD>
```

```
<INPUT TYPE=text SIZE=3 NAME="11"
       onFocus="if (this.value != '') {blur();}"
       onChange="play(this.form,this);">
</TD>
<TD>
<INPUT TYPE=text SIZE=3 NAME="12"
       onFocus="if (this.value != '') {blur();}"
       onChange="play(this.form,this);">
</TD>
<TD>
<INPUT TYPE=text SIZE=3 NAME="13"
       onFocus="if (this.value != '') {blur();}"
       onChange="play(this.form,this);">
</TD>
</TR>

<TR>
<TD>
<INPUT TYPE=text SIZE=3 NAME="21"
       onFocus="if (this.value != '') {blur();}"
       onChange="play(this.form,this);">
</TD>
<TD>
<INPUT TYPE=text SIZE=3 NAME="22"
       onFocus="if (this.value != '') {blur();}"
       onChange="play(this.form,this);">
</TD>
<TD>
<INPUT TYPE=text SIZE=3 NAME="23"
       onFocus="if (this.value != '') {blur();}"
       onChange="play(this.form,this);">
</TD>
</TR>

<TR>
<TD>
<INPUT TYPE=text SIZE=3 NAME="31"
       onFocus="if (this.value != '') {blur();}"
       onChange="play(this.form,this);">
</TD>
<TD>
<INPUT TYPE=text SIZE=3 NAME="32"
       onFocus="if (this.value != '') {blur();}"
       onChange="play(this.form,this);">
</TD>
<TD>
<INPUT TYPE=text SIZE=3 NAME="33"
       onFocus="if (this.value != '') {blur();}"
       onChange="play(this.form,this);">
</TD>
</TR>

</TABLE>
```

continues

Listing 7.4. continued

```
<INPUT TYPE=button VALUE="I'm Done-Your Go">
<INPUT TYPE=button VALUE="Start Over" onClick="clear(this.form);">

</FORM>

</BODY>

</HTML>
```

OUTPUT This script produces results similar to those in Figure 7.4.

Figure 7.4.

*This tic-tac-toe
game makes
extensive use of
loops.*

ANALYSIS This is the most complex example you have worked on. You combine what you have learned about objects as arrays, loops, and expressions to produce a functional tic-tac-toe game.

To better understand exactly what the script does, let's take a look at each section in turn.

```
var row = 0;
var col = 0;
var playerSymbol = "X";
var computerSymbol = "O";
board = new createArray(3,3);
```

Here you declare the global variables and the array object that you use throughout the script. The `board` object is an instance of the `createArray` object, which you define using a function later in the script.

You use the `board` array to hold an image of the values displayed in the form because it is easier to work with indexes of an array than the sequential order of elements in a form.

```
function createArray(row,col) {

  var index = 0;
  this.length = (row*10) + col
  for (var x = 1; x <= row; x ++) {
```

```
      for (var y = 1; y <= col; y++) {
        index = (x*10) + y;
        this[index] = "";
      }
    }
}
```

The createArray() function defines the array object you use in this script. Notice the use of for loops to define the object. This type of array definition will be discussed in further detail later in this chapter. It is important to notice how you are building the two-digit numeric indexes by multiplying the row number by 10 and adding it to the column number to produce indexes such as 11, 12, 13, 21, 22, 23, 31, 32, and 33.

```
function buildBoard(form) {

  var index = 0;
  for (var field = 0; field <= 8; field ++) {
    index = eval(form.elements[field].name);
    form.elements[field].value = board[index];
  }

}
```

buildBoard() displays the values in the board object in the form. By cycling through all the elements in the form using a for loop, you can get the relevant index from the field.name using the eval() function, which converts the name (a string) into a numeric value.

```
function win(index) {

var win = false;

  // CHECK ROWS
  if ((board[index] == board[(index < 30) ? index + 10 : index - 20]) &&
      (board[index] == board[(index >  11) ? index - 10 : index + 20])) {
    win = true;
  }

  // CHECK COLUMNS
  if ((board[index] == board[(index%10 < 3) ? index + 1 : index - 2]) &&
      (board[index] == board[(index%10 > 1) ? index - 1 : index + 2])) {
    win = true;
  }

  // CHECK DIAGONALS
  if (Math.round(index/10) == index%10) {
    if ((board[index] == board[(index < 30) ? index + 11 : index - 22]) &&
        (board[index] == board[(index >  11) ? index - 11 : index + 22])) {
      win = true;
    }
    if (index == 22) {
      if ((board[index] == board[13]) && (board[index] == board[31])) {
        win = true;
      }
```

7

```
    }
  }
  if ((index == 31) || (index == 13)) {
    if ((board[index] == board[(index < 30) ? index + 9 : index - 18]) &&
        (board[index] == board[(index >  11) ? index - 9 : index + 18])) {
      win = true;
    }
  }

  // RETURN THE RESULTS
  return win;

}
```

The win() function requires more explanation. The function is designed to check all rows, columns, and diagonals crossing the space indicated by index to see if there is a win.

For instance, to check the row that index is in, you need to compare the value of board[index] with the value to its immediate right and to its immediate left. At first, it would seem that you could use a statement such as

```
if ((board[index] == board[index+10]) && (board[index] == board[index-10]))
```

to do this. The problem with this is that if the index passed to the function is the third space in a row, you will be attempting to look at a fourth, non-existent space in the first condition. Similarly, if index represents the first space in a row, the second condition will try looking at board[index-10], which doesn't exist.

You remedy this situation through the use of conditional expressions. For instance board[(index < 30) ? index + 10 : index - 20] evaluates to board[31] if index is 21 but evaluates to board[12] if index is 32.

The testing of diagonals also requires some explanation. You start by checking whether index represents any space on the diagonal from the top left to the bottom right. If it does, you check that diagonal, and then if the space is the middle space on the board, you also check the diagonal from the top right to bottom left. You finish by checking whether the top right or bottom left corner is represented by index; if it is, you check the second diagonal.

The play() function, which comes next, is somewhat more complex and also requires more detailed explanation.

```
function play(form,field) {

  var index = eval(field.name);
  var playIndex = 0;
  var winIndex = 0;
  var done = false;
  field.value = playerSymbol;
  board[index] = playerSymbol;
```

You start by declaring global variables and assigning the correct symbol to the appropriate field form and property of the board object. You do this so that the user can type any character in the field she wants to mark for her play.

After this, you use the win() function to check if the play makes the user a winner.

```
//CHECK FOR PLAYER WIN
if (win(index)) {
    // PLAYER WON
    alert("Good Play! You Win!");
    clear(form);
  } else {
```

If the user has not won, you need to start checking for the best move by the computer. The first thing to do is to look for a position that lets the computer win. You do this with a pair of embedded for loops. These loops enable you to cycle through each position on the playing board. For each position, if the value is an empty string (meaning no play has been made there), you temporarily play the computer's symbol there and check if that produces a win. If it does, you set the appropriate variables and break out of the inside for loop.

Because the break statement breaks out of the innermost loop only, you end the outer loop with an if statement to break out of the outer loop if you have found the winning play.

At the end of the inner loop, you assign the empty string back to the current position because it did not produce a win, and you are not going to play there at this point.

```
// PLAYER LOST, CHECK FOR WINNING POSITION
for (row = 1; row <= 3; row++) {
  for (col = 1; col <= 3; col++) {
    index = (row*10) + col;
    if (board[index] == "") {
      board[index] = computerSymbol;
      if(win(index)) {
        playIndex = index;
        done = true;
        board[index] = "";
        break;
      }
      board[index] = "";
    }
  }
  if (done)
    break;
}
```

If you have found a winning position, you simply display the play with buildBoard() and then inform the user that the computer won.

```
// CHECK IF COMPUTER CAN WIN
if (done) {
  board[playIndex] = computerSymbol;
  buildBoard(form);
  alert("Computer Just Won!");
```

```
        clear(form);
    } else {
```

Next, having failed to find a winning position, it is necessary to look for potential wins by the user in the form of complete rows, columns, or diagonals missing only one play by the user. This is achieved in exactly the same way you looked for a winning computer play, except this time, you check for plays that would generate a winning play by the user.

```
// CAN'T WIN, CHECK IF NEED TO STOP A WIN
for (row = 1; row <=3; row++) {
  for (col = 1; col <= 3; col++) {
    index = (row*10) + col;
    if (board[index] == "") {
      board[index] = playerSymbol;
      if (win(index)) {
        board[index] = computerSymbol;
        playIndex = index;
        done = true;
        board[index] = "";
        break;
      }
      board[index] = "";
    }
  }
  if (done)
    break;
}
// CHECK IF DONE
if (done) {
  board[playIndex] = computerSymbol;
  buildBoard(form);
} else {
```

Having failed to find a winning play for the computer or identified a potential win on the part of the user, you simply proceed to find the first empty position and play there. You do this with another set of embedded for loops and break out of the loops once you have found the first empty space.

```
// NOT DONE, CHECK FOR FIRST EMPTY SPACE
for (row = 1; row <= 3; row ++) {
  for (col = 1; col <= 3; col ++) {
    index = (row*10) + col;
    if (board[index] == "") {
      playIndex = index;
      done = true;
      break;
    }
  }
  if (done)
    break;
}
board[playIndex] = computerSymbol;
buildBoard(form};
}
```

```
      }
    }
  }
```

Now that you've studied the functions that drive the game, let's take a look at how you use event handlers in the form. The form consists of nine identical fields (except for their names), named according to the scheme of 11, 12, 13, 21, 22, 23, and so on.

Each INPUT tag contains the same two event handlers:

```
<INPUT TYPE=text SIZE=3 NAME="31"
       onFocus="if (this.value != '') {blur();}"
       onChange="play(this.form,this);">
```

In the onFocus event handler, you are simply checking whether the field the user has selected is empty. If not, you remove the focus immediately so that the user is free to play in empty fields only and cannot alter the content of used spaces.

The onChange event handler simply calls the play() function, which records the user's play, checks if the user has won, and if necessary, chooses a play for the computer.

Creating Arrays with for Loops

Now that you have a firm grasp on the concept of loops, you can look at how for loops can create the equivalent of one-dimensional arrays in JavaScript.

As you saw in Chapter 4, "Functions and Objects—The Building Blocks of Programs," JavaScript has provisions for associative arrays in that object properties can be referred to as a numeric index of the object. However, programmers who have studied C, Perl, or Pascal are aware of the value of arrays of the same type.

That is, you need to be able to define an array as an ordered set of elements of the same type where the number of elements can vary each time the array is defined. You can do this using objects by defining the object function using a for loop.

NOTE   JavaScript provides a pre-built constructor object called Array which does just this. However, in order to understand how this is done, you will build your own here.

7

For instance, to define a numeric array of an unknown number of elements, you might write the object definition function createArray() like this:

```
function createArray(num) {
```

```
this.length = num;
for (var j = 0; j < num; j++) {
  this[j] = 0;
}

}
```

This function creates an array starting with index 0 and assigns all values of the new array to 0. Using this object, you could then use newArray = new createArray(4) to create an array of four elements called newArray. You would refer to the elements in the array as newArray[0], newArray[1], and so on.

Summary

In this chapter you have learned how to use loops to achieve sophisticated control over the flow of a function or script. Using for loops, you can repeat a command block several times, based on a range and an expression to move through the range. The for ... in loop enables you to cycle through all the properties in an object. The while loop works differently in that the associated command block is executed if a condition is true; otherwise the loop finishes. The break and continue statements enable you to alter the flow of a loop by either breaking out of the loop completely, or prematurely moving on to the next cycle through the loop. You also learned that loops can be used to create array objects.

In Chapter 8, "Frames, Documents, and Windows," you will take a close look at the document window, the methods it offers, and how to manipulate it. You will also learn to use frames and take a detailed look at the frames object.

Commands and Extensions Review

Command/Extension	Type	Description
for	Statement	Loops based on an initial value, a condition, and an expression
for ... in	Statement	Loops through all the properties in an object, returning the index of the property
while	Statement	Loops based on a condition; continues until the condition is false
with	Statement	Enables a command block to omit an object prefix

7

Command/Extension	Type	Description
break	Statement	Breaks out of the current loop
continue	Statement	Jumps to the next iteration of the current loop

Q&A

Q Can I use the same variable as the counter for more than one loop?

A Yes. As long as the loops are not embedded, you can reuse counter variables. If loops are embedded, using the same name for both loops results in scripts that don't work as expected.

Q I've seen a repeat ... until loop in some other programming languages. Does JavaScript have one?

A No. The repeat ... until loop is similar to the while loop except that it tests its condition at the end of the loop. JavaScript doesn't have this type of loop.

Exercises

1. Write while loops to emulate each of these for loops:

    a.
    ```
    for (j = 4; j > 0; j --) {
        document.writeln(j + "<BR>");
    }
    ```

    b.
    ```
    for (k = 1; k <= 99; k = k*2) {
        k = k/1.5;
    }
    ```

    c.
    ```
    for (num = 0; num <= 10; num ++) {
        if (num == 8)
          break;
    }
    ```

2. In Chapter 4 you learned about recursion and how to use it for a variety of purposes, including calculating factorials and exponents. With loops, it is possible to make the same calculations. Write a function that doesn't use recursion to calculate factorials.

7

3. In Listing 7.4, the `play()` function works but is not too intelligent. Specifically, if the computer has no obvious winning play and does not immediately need to prevent the user from winning, no strategy is applied to the computer's selection.

   Rewrite the `play()` function so that in this situation, the computer first tries to find a space so that playing there creates a row or column with two of the computer's symbols and an empty space.

Answers

1. `while` loops can be used in all three cases:

   a.
   ```
   j = 5;
   while (--j > 0) {
     document.writeln(j + "<BR>");
   }
   ```

   b.
   ```
   k = 1;
   while (k <= 99) {
     k = k * 2 / 1.5;
   }
   ```

   c.
   ```
   num = 0;
   while (num <= 10) {
     if (num++ == 8)
       break;
   }
   ```

2. A factorial function can easily be written using a single `for` loop:
   ```
   function factorial(num) {
     var factorial = 1;
     for (var i=2; i<=num; i++) {
       factorial *= i;
     }
     return factorial;
   }
   ```

3. In order to improve the computer's strategy used at the end of the `play()` function, you need to build some complex `if` statements into a pair of embedded `for` loops. The following is the complete replacement for the `play()` function in Listing 7.4:
   ```
   function play(form,field) {

     var index = eval(field.name);
     var playIndex = 0;
     var winIndex = 0;
     var done = false;
     field.value = playerSymbol;
     board[index] = playerSymbol;
   ```

7

```
//CHECK FOR PLAYER WIN
if (win(index)) {
  // PLAYER WON
  alert("Good Play! You Win!");
  clear(form);
} else {
  // PLAYER LOST, CHECK FOR WINNING POSITION
  for (row = 1; row <= 3; row++) {
    for (col = 1; col <= 3; col++) {
      index = (row*10) + col;
      if (board[index] == "") {
        board[index] = computerSymbol;
        if(win(index)) {
          playIndex = index;
          done = true;
          break;
        }
        board[index] = "";
      }
    }
    if (done)
      break;
  }
  // CHECK IF COMPUTER CAN WIN
  if (done) {
    board[playIndex] = computerSymbol;
    buildBoard(form);
    alert("Computer Just Won!");
    clear(form);
  } else {
    // CAN'T WIN, CHECK IF NEED TO STOP A WIN
    for (row = 1; row <=3; row++) {
      for (col = 1; col <= 3; col++) {
        index = (row*10) + col;
        if (board[index] == "") {
          board[index] = playerSymbol;
          if (win(index)) {
            playIndex = index;
            done = true;
            board[index] = "";
            break;
          }
          board[index] = "";
        }
      }
      if (done)
        break;
    }
    // CHECK IF DONE
    if (done) {
      board[playIndex] = computerSymbol;
      buildBoard(form);
    } else {
      // NOT DONE, CHECK FOR FIRST EMPTY SPACE
      for (row = 1; row <= 3; row ++) {
        for (col = 1; col <= 3; col ++) {
```

continues

```
                     index = (row*10) + col;
                     if (board[index] == "") {
                       //CHECK ROW
                       if (
                          ((board[index] == board[(index < 30)?index+10:index-20])
                          ➥&&
                           (board[(index>9)?index-10:index+20] == "")) ¦¦
                          ((board[index] == board[(index>9)?index-10:index+20]) &&
                           (board[(index<30)?index+10:index-20]))
                          ) {
                       playIndex = index;
                       done = true;
                       break;
                       }
                       // CHECK COLUMNS
                       if (
                          ((board[index] == board[(index%10<3)?index+1:index-2]) &&
                           (board[(index%10>1)?index-1:index+2] == "")) ¦¦
                          ((board[index] == board[(index%10>1)?index-1:index+2]) &&
                           (board[(index%10<3)?index+1:index-2]))
                          ) {
                       playIndex = index;
                       done = true;
                       break;
                       }

                     }
                   }
                   if (done)
                     break;
                 }
                 if (done) {
                   board[playIndex] = computerSymbol;
                   buildBoard(form);
                 } else {
                   // NOT DONE, CHECK FOR FIRST EMPTY SPACE
                   for (row = 1; row <= 3; row ++) {
                     for (col = 1; col <= 3; col ++) {
                       index = (row*10) + col;
                       if (board[index] == "") {
                         playIndex = index;
                         done = true;
                         break;
                       }
                     }
                     if (done)
                       break;
                   }
                   board[playIndex] = computerSymbol;
                   buildBoard(form);
                 }
               }
             }
           }

         }
```

7

Note that this function checks only rows and columns for possible good moves before going on the check for any empty space. A good exercise would be to extend this function to also check for diagonal moves before opting for the first available blank space.

Chapter 8

Frames, Documents, and Windows

Now that you have learned the basics of JavaScript and how to work with forms, you are ready to look at another advanced feature of JavaScript: frames.

Frames provide the ability to divide a document window into distinct sections, each of which contains different HTML files that can also be manipulated using JavaScript.

Besides the capability to manipulate frames, JavaScript also provides the document object, which provides properties and methods for dealing with anchors, links and colors, and the window object—the top level object of a web document window.

In this chapter we cover these topics:

- ☐ An introduction to frames
- ☐ Working with frames in JavaScript
- ☐ The document object
- ☐ The window object

☐ Working with the status bar

☐ Controlling the timing of scripts with setTimeout()

An Introduction to Frames

Frames are one of the most widely used new features of Navigator 2.0.

By using a few simple extensions to the HTML standard, Web authors are able to achieve sophisticated control over the layout of information in the Web browser window by dividing the window into rectangular sections and loading separate HTML files into each section of the window.

In addition, links in one frame can update another frame, and the result of processing form data in a CGI script on a server can be targeted at another frame.

Even without the addition of JavaScript, frames have enabled the addition of a type of interactivity that wasn't possible before, using regular HTML. For instance, sites now feature fixed tool bars and permanent search forms such as the one in Figure 8.1.

Figure 8.1.

Using frames, The Dataphile On-line *in Hong Kong has permanent search forms at its site.*

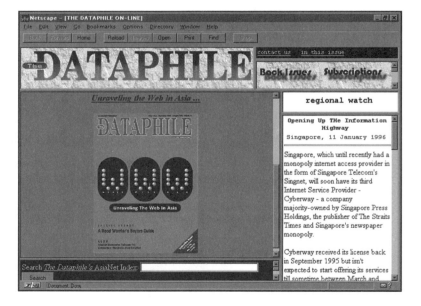

The FRAMESET Tag

A page is divided into frames using the FRAMESET tag. The tag is used in the top-level document defining a window containing frames and is used to specify how to divide the document window.

NEW TERM Because windows divided into frames are created from multiple HTML files, it is important to keep the hierarchical relationship of documents in mind. In a document window divided into frames, the *top-level document* is the HTML document that defines the frames and files that will load into those frames.

The FRAMESET container tag takes several attributes. The two basic ones are ROWS and COLS. A FRAMESET tag takes either one of these or both to divide a document into a set of rows or columns. For instance,

```
<FRAMESET COLS="25,*,25">
```

would define three columns. The two outer columns would each be 25 pixels wide, and the middle column would take the remaining space depending on the size of the window. In this example the asterisk (*) represents the remaining available space after the space is allocated for the other frames.

In addition to specifying the size of frames in pixels, the size of columns and rows can be defined using percentages relative to the space available to the document:

```
<FRAMESET ROWS="35%,*">
```

 TIP

> The use of percentages to define the size of frames is useful when you consider that different users will have different size monitors running at different resolutions. If you normally use a very high resolution, you may feel it is okay to define the width of a column as 700 pixels, but to a user running at standard 640×480 VGA resolution, this frame would be wider than his display allows.

The preceding FRAMESET tag would divide the display into two rows. The top row would be 35 percent of the height of the display area, and the bottom row would fill the remaining space (using the asterisk again).

 NOTE

> The FRAMESET tag replaces the BODY tag in a file. Files with FRAMESET containers are not used to directly display HTML data in Navigator 2.0.

The FRAME Tag

Inside a FRAMESET container, the FRAME tag is used to specify which files should be displayed in each frame. The URLs of the files—which can be relative or absolute—should be specified using the SRC attribute in the same way as the IMG tag is used to include images in an HTML document.

NEW TERM The terms *relative* and *absolute* refer to two different ways of indicating the location of files in HTML. In absolute URLs, the complete protocol (the part before the colon), domain name, and path of a file are provided. For instance,

```
http://www.juxta.com/juxta/docs/prod.htm
```

is an absolute URL.

In relative URLs, the protocol, domain name, and complete path are not indicated. Instead, the location of the file relative to the current file is indicated. If the file indicated the URL is in the same directory, then just the filename is needed. If the file is in a subdirectory, then the path from the current directory is needed.

For example, the following creates a document with two rows.

```
<FRAMESET ROWS="35%,*">
  <FRAME SRC="menu.html">
  <FRAME SRC="welcome.html">
</FRAMESET>
```

The top is 35 percent of the available space, and the bottom takes up the remaining 65 percent. The file menu.html is loaded into the top frame, and the file welcome.html is displayed in the lower frame.

In addition to the SRC attribute, the FRAME tag can take several other attributes as outlined in Table 8.1.

Table 8.1. Attributes for the FRAME tag.

Attribute	Description
SRC	Specifies the URL of the HTML file to be displayed in the frame.
NAME	Specifies the name of the frame so that it can be referenced by HTML tags and JavaScript scripts.
NORESIZE	Specifies that the size of a frame is fixed and cannot be changed by the user.
SCROLLING	Specifies whether scroll bars are available to the user. This can take a value of YES, NO, or AUTO.
MARGINHEIGHT	Specifies the vertical offset in pixels from the border of the frame.
MARGINWIDTH	Specifies the horizontal offset in pixels from the border of the frame.

8

To illustrate these attributes, look at the earlier example. The user can resize the frames by dragging on the border between the frames. By adding NORESIZE to either of the frames, this is prevented:

```
<FRAMESET ROWS="35%,*">
  <FRAME SRC="menu.html" NORESIZE>
  <FRAME SRC="welcome.html">
</FRAMESET>
```

or

```
<FRAMESET ROWS="35%,*">
  <FRAME SRC="menu.html">
  <FRAME SRC="welcome.html" NORESIZE>
</FRAMESET>
```

Typically, if a document fills more space than the frame it is assigned to, Navigator 2.0 will add scroll bars to the frame. If you don't want scroll bars to appear, regardless of the size of the frame, you can use SCROLLING=NO to prevent them from being used:

```
<FRAMESET ROWS="35%,*">
  <FRAME SRC="menu.html">
  <FRAME SRC="welcome.html" SCROLLING=NO>
</FRAMESET>
```

As you can see in Figure 8.2, by using SCROLLING=NO, no scroll bars appear in the lower frame, even though the graphic is larger than the frame.

Figure 8.2.
Preventing scroll bars in a frame, even when the document is larger than the frame.

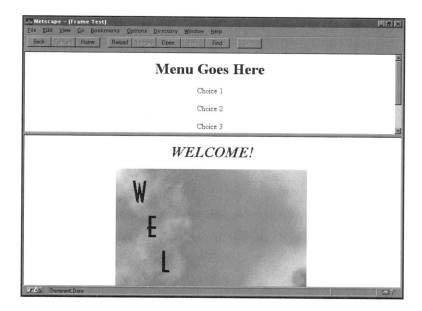

Nesting Frames

Looking at examples of frames on the Web, it quickly becomes obvious that many sites have more complex layouts than simply dividing the window into rows or columns. For instance, in Figure 8.1 you saw an example of a site that has rows and columns combined to produce a very complex layout.

This is achieved by nesting, or embedding, FRAMESET containers within each other. For instance, if you want to produce a document with three frames where you have two rows and the bottom row is further divided in two columns (to produce three frames), you could use a structure like this:

```
<FRAMESET ROWS="30%,*">
  <FRAME SRC="menu.html">
  <FRAMESET COLS="50%,50%">
    <FRAME SRC="welcome.html">
    <FRAME SRC="pic.html" SCROLLING=AUTO>
  </FRAMESET>
</FRAMESET>
```

A similar result can be achieved by using separate files. For instance, if the first file contains

```
<FRAMESET ROWS="30%,*">
  <FRAME SRC="menu.html">
  <FRAME SRC="bottom.html">
</FRAMESET>
```

and the file bottom.html contains

```
<FRAMESET COLS="50%,50%">
  <FRAME SRC="welcome.html">
  <FRAME SRC="pic.html" SCROLLING=AUTO>
</FRAMESET>
```

then you would get the same result as the previous example where both FRAMESET containers appeared in the same file.

To get a better idea of how this works, you can look at the source code for *The Dataphile On-line* which you saw in Figure 8.1. The following source code in Listing 8.1 combines the nested framesets from multiple files into a single file:

Listing 8.1. The source code for *The Dataphile On-line* frames.

```
<FRAMESET ROWS="100,*">
  <FRAMESET COLS="500,*">
    <FRAME SRC="banner.htm" NORESIZE MARGINHEIGHT=0
➡MARGINWIDTH=0 SCROLLING="no">
    <FRAMESET ROWS="30,*">
      <FRAME SRC="constant.htm" NORESIZE MARGINHEIGHT=0
➡MARGINWIDTH=0 SCROLLING="no">
      <FRAME SRC="menu.htm" NORESIZE MARGINHEIGHT=0
```

8

```
➥MARGINWIDTH=0 SCROLLING="auto">
    </FRAMESET>
  </FRAMESET>
  <FRAMESET COLS="*,250">
    <FRAMESET ROWS="*,50">
      <FRAME SRC="welcome.htm" NAME="middle" SCROLLING="auto">
      <FRAME SRC="search.htm" MARGINHEIGHT=2 MARGINWIDTH=2 SCROLLING="auto">
    </FRAMESET>
    <FRAMESET ROWS="50,*">

      <FRAME SRC="newshead.htm" SCROLLING="no" MARGINHEIGHT=0 MARGINWIDTH=0>
      <FRAME SRC="newstory.htm" SCROLLING="auto" MARGINGHEIGHT=2 MARGINWIDTH=2>
    </FRAMESET>
  </FRAMESET>
</FRAMESET>
```

ANALYSIS   You start by dividing the window into two rows. The top row is divided into two columns, and the right column is further divided into two rows. Likewise, the bottom row is divided into two columns. The left column is divided into two rows, as is the right column.

The NOFRAMES Tag

You may have noticed that the one problem with files containing FRAMESET containers is that they will go undisplayed on a non-Netscape browser because other browsers don't support this extension to HTML.

This is addressed by the NOFRAMES container tag. Any HTML code contained between the NOFRAMES tags is ignored by the Navigator 2.0 browser but will be displayed by any other browser.

For instance, this code

```
<HTML>

<HEAD>
<TITLE>NOFRAMES Example</TITLE>
</HEAD>

<FRAMESET ATTRIBUTES>
  <FRAME SRC="filename">
  <FRAME SRC="filename">
</FRAMESET>

<NOFRAMES>
  HTML code for other browsers
</NOFRAMES>

</HTML>
```

could be used to produce output like Figure 8.3 in Navigator 2.0 but like Figure 8.4 in another browser.

Figure 8.3.
*Only Navigator
2.0 recognizes the
FRAMESET tag.*

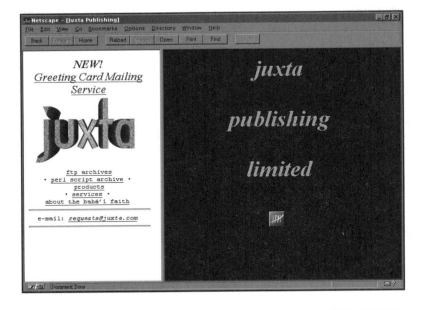

Figure 8.4.
*The NOFRAMES tag
provides an
alternative page for
users of other
browsers.*

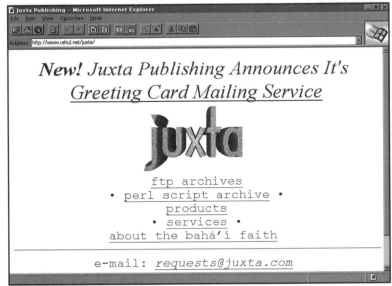

8

Naming Frames

In order to place (or target) the result of links or form submissions in specific frames, you can name frames using the NAME attribute of the FRAME tag. For instance,

```
<FRAMESET COLS="50%,*">
  <FRAME SRC="menu.html" NAME="menu">
  <FRAME SRC="welcome.html" NAME="main">
</FRAMESET>
```

would create two named frames called menu and main. In the file menu.html, you could have hypertext references target the main frame using the TARGET attribute:

```
<A HREF="choice1.html" TARGET="main">
```

Likewise, the result of a form submission could be targeted the same way:

```
<FORM METHOD=POST ACTION="/cgi-bin/test.pl" TARGET="main">
```

The TARGET attribute can also be used in the BASE tag to set a global target for all links in a document. For instance, if an HTML document has this BASE tag in its header

```
<BASE TARGET="main">
```

then all hypertext and results of form processing will appear in the FRAME named "main". This global targeting is overridden by using a TARGET attribute in an A tag or FORM tag in the body of the HTML document.

NOTE

Naming and targeting are not only relevant to frames. Windows can also be named and targeted as you learn later in this chapter, in the section about the window object.

In addition to targeting named frames, there are several special terms which can be used in the TARGET attributes. These are outlined in Table 8.2.

Table 8.2. Special values for the TARGET attribute.

Value	Description
_blank	Causes a link to load in a new, unnamed window.
_self	Causes a link to load in the same window the anchor was clicked in. (This can be used to override a target specified in a BASE tag.)
_parent	Causes a link to load in the immediate FRAMESET parent.
_top	Causes a link to load in the full body of the window regardless of the number of nested FRAMESET tags.

Working with Frames in JavaScript

JavaScript provides the `frames` property of the `window` object for working with different frames from a script.

The `frames` property is an array of objects with an entry for each child frame in a parent frameset. The number of frames is provided by the `length` property.

For instance, in a given window or frameset with two frames, you could reference the frames as `parent.frames[0]` and `parent.frames[1]`. The index of the last frame could be `parent.frames.length`.

By using the `frames` array, you can access the functions and variables in another frame, as well as objects, such as forms and links, contained in another frame. This is useful when building an application that spans multiple frames but that also must be able to communicate between the frames.

 NOTE

> Each frame has a different `document`, `location`, and `history` object associated with it. This is because each frame contains a separate HTML document and has a separate history list. You will learn about the `document` object later in this chapter and about the `history` object in Chapter 10, "Strings, Math, and the History List."

For example, if you have two frames, you could create a form in the first frame to provide the user with a field to enter an expression. Then you could display the results in a form in the other frame.

This cross-frame communication is achieved by referencing the `document` object's `forms[]` array in the second frame with `parent.frames[1].document.forms[0]`. In Listing 8.2 you build a simple calculator to evaluate expressions entered by users and use frames to display the output.

TYPE   **Listing 8.2. Cross-frame communication.**

```
<!-- HTML CODE FOR PARENT FRAMESET (this is a separate file) -->

<HTML>
<HEAD>
<TITLE>Listing 8.2</TITLE>
</HEAD>

<FRAMESET COLS="50%,*">
```

```
    <FRAME SRC="input.html">
    <FRAME SRC="output.html">
</FRAMESET>

</HTML>

<!-- HTML FOR INPUT FRAME (this is a separate file called input.html-->
<HTML>

<HEAD>
<SCRIPT LANGUAGE="JavaScript">
<!-- HIDE FROM OTHER BROWSERS
function update(field) {
  var result = field.value;
  var output = "" + result + " = " + eval(result);


  parent.frames[1].document.forms[0].result.value = output;
}
// STOP HIDING FROM OTHER BROWSERS -->
</SCRIPT>
</HEAD>

<BODY>
<FORM METHOD=POST>
<INPUT TYPE=text NAME="input" onChange="update(this);">
</FORM>
</BODY>

</HTML>

<HTML>

<!-- HTML FOR OUTPUT FRAME (this is a separate file called output.html)-->

<BODY>
<FORM METHOD=POST>
<TEXTAREA NAME=result ROWS=2 COLS=20 WRAP=SOFT></TEXTAREA>


</FORM>
</BODY>

</HTML>
```

In this example, it is important to note two things in the update() function. First, the eval() function used to evaluate the expression provided by the user doesn't work properly on the Windows 3.11 version of Navigator 2.0. Second, when you evaluate the expression and store the result in the variable output

```
var output = "" + result + " = " + eval(result);
```

you start the expression with "" to ensure a string value is assigned to the variable output.

In addition to specifying frames using the frames array, if you name the frames, you can specify certain frames using the form parent.framename. In the example you just saw, if you name the frames input and output, you could rewrite the update() function:

```
function update(field) {
  var result = field.value;
  var output = "" + result + " = " + eval(result);
  parent.output.form[0].result.value = output;
}
```

The frameset in this example would look like

```
<FRAMESET COLS="50%,*">
  <FRAME SRC="input.html" NAME="input">
  <FRAME SRC="output.html" NAME="output">
</FRAMESET>
```

The naming of elements can be taken one step further, and the forms can be named. For instance, if you name the forms inputForm and outputForm, then the files input.html and output.html can look like this:

```
<!-- HTML FOR INPUT FRAME (this is a separate file called input.html-->
<HTML>

<HEAD>
<SCRIPT LANGUAGE="JavaScript">
<!-- HIDE FROM OTHER BROWSERS
function update(field) {
  var result = field.value;
  var output = "" + result + " = " + eval(result);

  parent.output.document.outputForm.result.value = output;
}
// STOP HIDING FROM OTHER BROWSERS -->
</SCRIPT>
</HEAD>

<BODY>
<FORM METHOD=POST NAME="inputForm">
<INPUT TYPE=text NAME="input" onChange="update(this);">
</FORM>
</BODY>

</HTML>

<HTML>

<!-- HTML FOR OUTPUT FRAME (this is a separate file called output.html)-->

<BODY>
<FORM METHOD=POST NAME="outputForm">
<TEXTAREA NAME=result ROWS=2 COLS=20 WRAP=SOFT></TEXTAREA>
</FORM>
</BODY>

</HTML>
```

8

Notice, then, how the output field can be referred to with `parent.output.document.-outputForm. result`.

Nested Frames in JavaScript

With nested frames, cross-frame communication gets a little bit more complicated.

When building nested framesets, you can use subdocuments for each frameset. When you do this, the *parent will only refer back to the document containing the parent frameset and not the top-level frameset.*

For example, referring to the previous expression evaluation example, if you want to divide the display into four equal quarters (as shown in Figure 8.5) and then use only two of them, you would have to change the FRAMESET to be something like this:

```
<FRAMESET ROWS="50%,*">
  <FRAME SRC="top.html">
  <FRAME SRC="bottom.html">
</FRAMESET>
```

Where `top.html` and `bottom.html` contain further nested framesets:

```
<!-- HTML FOR top.html -->

<FRAMESET COLS="50%,*">
    <FRAME SRC="input.html" NAME="input">
    <FRAME SRC="logo.html">
  </FRAMESET>

<!-- HTML FOR bottom.html -->

  <FRAMESET COLS="50%,*">
    <FRAME SRC="about.html">
    <FRAME SRC="output.html" NAME="output">
  </FRAMESET>
```

Figure 8.5.

Using nested framesets produces complex screen layouts.

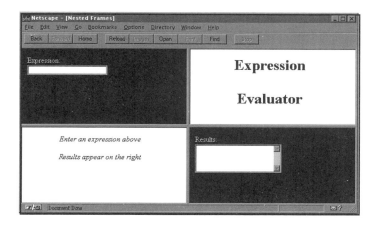

If input.html and output.html are still the files where the work is being done (logo.html and about.html are cosmetic), then you can't use the update() function you were using, because parent.frame[1] in the script will be referring to the frame containing logo.html—the parent of the input frame is the first nested frameset. You want to reference the frame containing output.html, which is in the second nested frameset. To reference this document, you need to go up two parent levels and then down two frames to reach output.html:

```
parent.parent.frame[1].frame[1]
```

With the named frame, this would become parent.parent.frame[1].output.

In addition to referring to variables and objects in other frames, the same technique can be used to invoke functions in other frames. For instance, you could add a function to output.html to handle displaying the results in the appropriate text field. Then, in input.html you could simply call the function and pass it the value of the variable output:

```
<!-- HTML FOR INPUT FRAME (this is a separate file called input.html-->
<HTML>

<HEAD>
<SCRIPT LANGUAGE="JavaScript">
<!-- HIDE FROM OTHER BROWSERS
function update(field) {
  var result = field.value;
  var output = "" + result + " = " + eval(result);

  parent.output.displayResult(output);
}
// STOP HIDING FROM OTHER BROWSERS -->
</SCRIPT>
</HEAD>

<BODY>
<FORM METHOD=POST NAME="inputForm">
<INPUT TYPE=text NAME="input" onChange="update(this);">
</FORM>
</BODY>

</HTML>

<HTML>

<!-- HTML FOR OUTPUT FRAME (this is a separate file called output.html)-->

<HEAD>
<SCRIPT LANGUAGE="JavaScript">
<!-- HIDE FROM OTHER BROWSERS

function displayResult(output) {

  document.ouputForm.result.value = output;

}
```

```
// STOP HIDING -->
</SCRIPT>
</HEAD>

<BODY>
<FORM METHOD=POST NAME="outputForm">
<TEXTAREA NAME=result ROWS=2 COLS=20 WRAP=SOFT></TEXTAREA>
</FORM>
</BODY>

</HTML>
```

Bill Dortch's hIdaho Frameset.

It quickly becomes obvious that any program can get tangled up in deeply nested frames, all of which must interact with each other to produce an interactive application.

This can quickly lead to confusing references to

```
parent.parent.frameA.frameB.frameC.form1.fieldA.value
```

or

```
parent.frameD.frameE.functionA()
```

To make this easier, Bill Dortch has produced the hIdaho Frameset. This is a set of freely available JavaScript functions to make dealing with functions in nested framesets easier. Dortch has made the hIdaho Frameset available for others to use in their scripts. Full information about the Frameset is on-line at

```
http://www.hidaho.com/frameset/
```

Using the Frameset, it is possible to register functions in a table and then call them from anywhere in a nested frameset without needing to know which frames they are defined in and without needing to use a long, and often confusing, sequence of objects and properties to refer to them. In addition, frames and framesets can be easily moved without having to recode each call to the affected functions across all your documents.

The hIdaho Frameset also provides a means of managing the timing of functions so you can ensure that a function has been loaded and registered before attempting to call it. This is especially useful during window and frame refreshes, when documents are reevaluated.

The source code is reproduced on the CD-ROM:

```
<script language="JavaScript">
<!-- begin script
//****************************************************************
// The hIdaho Frameset. Copyright (C) 1996 Bill Dortch, hIdaho Design
// Permission is granted to use and modify the hIdaho Frameset code,
// provided this notice is retained.
//****************************************************************
var debug = false;
var amTopFrameset = false;
→// set this to true for the topmost frameset
var thisFrame = (amTopFrameset) ? null : self.name;
var maxFuncs = 32;
function makeArray (size) {
  this.length = size;
  for (var i = 1; i <= size; i++)
    this[i] = null;
  return this;
}
var funcs = new makeArray ((amTopFrameset) ? maxFuncs : 0);
function makeFunc (frame, func) {
  this.frame = frame;
  this.func = func;
  return this;
}
function addFunction (frame, func) {
  for (var i = 1; i <= funcs.length; i++)
    if (funcs[i] == null) {
      funcs[i] = new makeFunc (frame, func);
      return true;
    }
  return false;
}
function findFunction (func) {
  for (var i = 1; i <= funcs.length; i++)
    if (funcs[i] != null)
      if (funcs[i].func == func)
        return funcs[i];
  return null;
}
function Register (frame, func) {
  if (debug) alert (thisFrame + ":
→Register(" + frame + "," + func + ")");
  if (Register.arguments.length < 2)
    return false;
  if (!amTopFrameset)
    return parent.Register (thisFrame + "." + frame, func);
  if (findFunction (func) != null)
    return false;
  return addFunction (frame, func);
}
function UnRegister (func) {
  if (debug) alert (thisFrame + ": UnRegister(" + func + ")");
  if (UnRegister.arguments.length == 0)
    return false;
```

```
      if (!amTopFrameset)
        return parent.UnRegister (func);
      for (var i = 1; i <= funcs.length; i++)
        if (funcs[i] != null)
          if (funcs[i].func == func) {
            funcs[i] = null;
            return true;
          }
      return false;
    }
    function UnRegisterFrame (frame) {
      if (debug) alert (thisFrame + ": UnRegisterFrame(" + frame + ")");
      if (UnRegisterFrame.arguments.length == 0)
        return false;
      if (!amTopFrameset)
        return parent.UnRegisterFrame (thisFrame + "." + frame);
      for (var i = 1; i <= funcs.length; i++)
        if (funcs[i] != null)
          if (funcs[i].frame == frame) {
            funcs[i] = null;
          }
      return true;
    }
    function IsRegistered (func) {
      if (debug) alert (thisFrame + ": IsRegistered(" + func + ")");
      if (IsRegistered.arguments.length == 0)
        return false;
      if (!amTopFrameset)
        return parent.IsRegistered (func);
      if (findFunction (func) == null)
        return false;
      return true;
    }
    function Exec (func) {
      if (debug) alert (thisFrame + ": Exec(" + func + ")");
      var argv = Exec.arguments;
      if (argv.length == 0)
        return null;
      var arglist = new makeArray(argv.length);
      for (var i = 0; i < argv.length; i++)
        arglist[i+1] = argv[i];
      var argstr = "";
      for (i = ((amTopFrameset) ? 2 : 1); i <= argv.length; i++)
        argstr += "arglist[" + i + "]" + ((i < argv.length) ? "," : "");
      if (!amTopFrameset)
        return eval ("parent.Exec(" + argstr + ")");
      var funcobj = findFunction (func);
      if (funcobj == null)
        return null;
      return eval ("self." + ((funcobj.frame == null) ? "" :
➡(funcobj.frame + "."))+ funcobj.func + "(" + argstr + ")");
    }
    //*****************************************************************
    // End of hIdaho Frameset code.
```

```
//******************************************************************
// end script -->
</script>
```

The source code should be included in each frameset document in your hierarchy of nested framesets. The only important distinction is that the `amTopFrameset` variable should be set to `false` for all framesets except the top.

Each of the functions is used for a different purpose.

The `Register()` function.

The `Register()` function is used to register functions in the function table. It is called from the function's frame by referring to the function in the immediate parent frameset as follows: `parent.Register(self.name,"functionName")`.

 NOTE `self` refers to the currently opened frame or window. You learn more about it later in this chapter.

The function will return `true` if there is room in the function table and the name is not currently registered. Otherwise, it will return `false`.

The `UnRegister()` function.

This function does exactly what its name suggests: It removes a specific function from the registration table. It takes a single argument: `UnRegister("functionName")`.

The `UnRegisterFrame()` function.

This function unregisters all functions registered for a specified frame. It takes the frame name as a single argument.

The `IsRegistered()` function.

A call to `IsRegistered("frameName")` returns `true` if the function is registered and `false` if it isn't.

The `Exec()` function.

The `Exec()` function is used to call a specific function. It takes at least one argument—the name of the function—but can take more in the form of parameters to pass to the called function as arguments. For instance, if you want to call the function `functionA` and pass two arguments, `arg1` and `arg2`, you could call

```
parent.Exec("functionA",arg1,arg2);
```

The Exec() function returns the value returned by the specified function.

It is not considered harmful to call an unregistered function using Exec(). If you do, a null value is returned. This can cause confusion, of course, if a legitimate value returned by the specified function could be the null value. This can happen when the frame containing the desired function has not finished loading when another frame's script tries to call it.

One way that Dortch suggests dealing with this timing problem is to use the IsRegsistered() function to ensure a function exists before calling it:

```
function intialize() {
  if (!parent.IsRegistered("functionA")) {
    setTimeout("initialize()",250);
    return;
  }
  JavaScript code
  parent.Exec("functionA",arg1,arg2);
  JavaScript code
}
```

In this example, the function initialize() will not get past the first if statement unless the function functionA has been registered. The function uses the setTimeout() method to cause a pause for 250 milliseconds after which initialize() is to be called again.

NOTE

> setTimeout() is a method of the window object that enables a pause to be specified before executing a command or evaluating an expression. We will look at the setTimeout() method, and the related clearTimeout() method, later in this chapter when we cover the window object.

The initialize() function is a recursive function that will continue to call itself every quarter second until the desired function is registered.

As indicated on the hIdaho Frameset Web page, Dortch has purposely not written functions to provide access to variables and other objects and properties in other frames because he feels that well-designed, multi-frame applications should use function calls to access information in other frames. Look for an updated version coming soon to his Web page.

Putting Nested Framesets to Work

Now that you know how to work with frames, you are going to produce a testing tool that teachers can use to easily produce a test in any given subject.

To do this, you will use nested framesets. The top-level frameset will produce three rows: one for the title, one for the work area, and one for a level selector.

The middle row, the work area, will be split into two equal columns. The left side will contain a form for the student to enter his answer as well as a field to display the current score. The right column will be used to display the questions and the result of a student's answer.

For these purposes, you only need to look at the source code for the student entry form and the level selection tool in the bottom frame. You will use Bill Dortch's hIdaho Frameset to make working with the nested framesets easier.

The frameset is defined by two files: the top-level `test.htm` (Listing 8.3) and `work.htm` (Listing 8.4) which defines the workspace in the middle row. `work.htm` contains the nested frameset referred to in `test.htm` (`<FRAME SRC="work.htm" NAME="work">`):

TYPE **Listing 8.3. Top-level frameset (`test.htm`).**

```
<!-- FRAMESET FROM test.htm -->
<FRAMESET ROWS="20%,*,20%">
  <FRAME SRC="title.htm">
  <FRAME SRC="work.htm" NAME="work">
  <FRAME SRC="level.htm" NAME="level">
</FRAMESET>
```

TYPE **Listing 8.4. The nested frameset (`work.htm`).**

```
<!-- FRAMESET FROM work.htm -->
<FRAMESET COLS="50%,*">
  <FRAME SRC="form.htm" NAME="form">
  <FRAME SRC="output.htm" NAME="output">
</FRAMESET>
```

Both `test.htm` and `work.htm` would include the source code of the hIdaho Frameset so that the programs can easily call functions in other frames. In the file `test.htm`, `amTopFrameset` should be set to `true` with the statement `amTopFrameset = true`.

All of the functions and information are kept in the file `form.htm` (Listing 8.5). `form.htm` is one of the frames in the nested frameset.

8

Listing 8.5. The entry form (`form.htm`).

```
<!-- SOURCE CODE OF form.htm -->
<HTML>

<HEAD>
<SCRIPT LANGUAGE="JavaScript">
<!-- HIDE FROM OTHER BROWSERS

var currentLevel=1;
var currentQuestion=1;
var toOutput = "";

// DEFINE LEVEL ONE
q1 = new question("1 + 3",4);
q2 = new question("4 + 5",9);
q3 = new question("5 - 4",1);
q4 = new question("7 + 3",10);
q5 = new question("4 + 4",8);
q6 = new question("3 - 3",0);
q7 = new question("9 - 5",4);
q8 = new question("8 + 1",9);
q9 = new question("5 - 3",2);
q10 = new question("8 - 3",5);
levelOne = new level(q1,q2,q3,q4,q5,q6,q7,q8,q9,q10);

// DEFINE LEVEL TWO
q1 = new question("15 + 23",38);
q2 = new question("65 - 32",33);
q3 = new question("99 + 45",134);
q4 = new question("34 - 57",-23);
q5 = new question("-34 - 57",-91);
q6 = new question("23 + 77",100);
q7 = new question("64 + 32",96);
q8 = new question("64 - 32",32);
q9 = new question("12 + 34",46);
q10 = new question("77 + 77",154);
levelTwo = new level(q1,q2,q3,q4,q5,q6,q7,q8,q9,q10);

// DEFINE LEVEL THREE
q1 = new question("10 * 7",70);
q2 = new question("15 / 3",5);
q3 = new question("34 * 3",102);
q4 = new question("33 / 2",16.5);
q5 = new question("100 / 4",25);
q6 = new question("99 / 6",16.5);
q7 = new question("32 * 3",96);
q8 = new question("48 / 4",12);
q9 = new question("31 * 0",0);
q10 = new question("45 / 1",45);
levelThree = new level(q1,q2,q3,q4,q5,q6,q7,q8,q9,q10);

// DEFINE TEST
test = new newTest(levelOne,levelTwo,levelThree);
```

continues

Listing 8.5. continued

```
function newTest(levelOne,levelTwo,levelThree) {
  this[1] = levelOne;
  this[2] = levelTwo;
  this[3] = levelThree;
}

function level(q1,q2,q3,q4,q5,q6,q7,q8,q9,q10) {
  this[1] = q1;
  this[2] = q2;
  this[3] = q3;
  this[4] = q4;
  this[5] = q5;
  this[6] = q6;
  this[7] = q7;
  this[8] = q8;
  this[9] = q9;
  this[10] = q10;
}

function question(question,answer) {
  this.question = question;
  this.answer = answer;
}

parent.Register(self.name,"startTest");
function startTest(newLevel) {
  currentLevel=newLevel;
  currentQuestion=1;
  document.forms[0].answer.value="";
  document.forms[0].score.value=0;
  displayQuestion();
}

function displayQuestion() {
  ask = test[currentLevel][currentQuestion].question;
  answer = test[currentLevel][currentQuestion].answer;
  toOutput = "" + currentQuestion + ". What is " + ask + "?";
  document.forms[0].answer.value = "";
  window.open("display.htm","output");
}

parent.Register(self.name,"output");
function output() {
  return toOutput;
}

function checkAnswer(form) {

  answer = form.answer.value;

  if (answer == "" || answer == null) {
    alert("Please enter an answer.");
    return;
  }
```

8

```
      correctAnswer = test[currentLevel][currentQuestion].answer;
      ask = test[currentLevel][currentQuestion].question;
      score = form.score.value;
      if (eval(answer) == correctAnswer) {
        toOutput = "Correct!";
        score ++;
        form.score.value = score;
      } else {
        toOutput = "Sorry! " + ask + " is " + correctAnswer + ".";
      }
      window.open("display.htm","output");
      if (currentQuestion < 10) {
        currentQuestion ++;
        setTimeout("displayQuestion()",3000);
      } else {
        toOutput = "You're Done!<BR>You're score is " + score + " out of 10.";
        setTimeout("window.open('display.htm','output')",3000);
        form.answer.value="";
        form.score.value="0";
      }
    }

    function welcome() {
      toOutput = "Welcome!";
      window.open("display.htm","output");
    }

    // STOP HIDING FROM OTHER BROWSERS -->
    </SCRIPT>

    </HEAD>

    <BODY BGCOLOR="#FFFFFF" TEXT="#0000FF" onLoad="welcome();">

    <FORM METHOD=POST>
    <CENTER>
    <STRONG>Type You're Answer Here:</STRONG><BR>
    <INPUT TYPE=text NAME=answer SIZE=30><P>
    <INPUT TYPE=button NAME=done VALUE="Check Answer"
    ➥onClick="checkAnswer(this.form);"><P>
    Correct Answers So Far:<BR>
    <INPUT TYPE=text NAME=score VALUE="0" SIZE=10>
    </FORM>

    </BODY>

    </HTML>
```

The file level.htm (Listing 8.6) provides users with three buttons to select different levels. level.htm is the bottom frame in the parent frameset:

TYPE **Listing 8.6. Level selection controls.**

```html
<!-- SOURCE CODE OF level.htm -->
<HTML>

<BODY BGCOLOR="#000000" TEXT="#FFFFFF">
<CENTER>
<STRONG>
Select a level here:
<FORM METHOD=POST>
<INPUT TYPE=button NAME="one" VALUE="Level One"
➥onClick="parent.Exec('startTest',1);">
<INPUT TYPE=button NAME="two" VALUE="Level Two"
➥onClick="parent.Exec('startTest',2);">
<INPUT TYPE=button NAME="three" VALUE="Level Three"
➥onClick="parent.Exec('startTest',3);">
</FORM>
</STRONG>
</CENTER>
</BODY>

</HTML>
```

All display in the frame named output is done by reloading the file display.htm (Listing 8.7):

TYPE **Listing 8.7. display.htm is reloaded to update the output.**

```html
<!-- SOURCE CODE OF display.htm -->
<HTML>

<BODY BGCOLOR="#0000FF" TEXT="#FFFFFF">
<H1>
<SCRIPT LANGUAGE="JavaScript">
<!-- HIDE FROM OTHER BROWSERS

document.write(parent.Exec("output"));

// STOP HIDING FROM OTHER BROWSERS -->
</SCRIPT>
</H1>
</BODY>

</HTML>
```

Finally, title.htm (Listing 8.8) contains the information displayed in the top frame of the parent frameset:

8

Listing 8.8. The title frame.

```
<!-- SOURCE CODE OF title.htm -->
<HTML>

<BODY BGCOLOR="#000000" TEXT="#00FFFF">
<CENTER>
<H1>
<STRONG>
The Math Test
</STRONG>
</H1>
</CENTER>
</BODY>

</HTML>
```

OUTPUT The final product would look something like Figure 8.6.

Figure 8.6.

Using nested framesets to produce a multi-level math test.

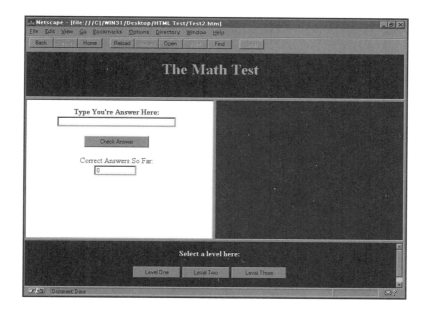

ANALYSIS As you can see in the source code listings, the file form.htm (Listing 8.5) is the centerpiece of the entire application. It is in this file that all the work of checking answers, displaying questions and results, and resetting the test is done.

Let's look at the document section by section.

```
var currentLevel=1;
var currentQuestion=1;
var toOutput = "";
```

These are the key global variables in the script which are used to keep track of the current level being tested, the current question being tested, and what should next be displayed in the output frame.

Next the questions and answers for the three levels are defined:

```
// DEFINE LEVEL ONE
q1 = new question("1 + 3",4);
q2 = new question("4 + 5",9);
q3 = new question("5 - 4",1);
q4 = new question("7 + 3",10);
q5 = new question("4 + 4",8);
q6 = new question("3 - 3",0);
q7 = new question("9 - 5",4);
q8 = new question("8 + 1",9);
q9 = new question("5 - 3",2);
q10 = new question("8 - 3",5);
levelOne = new level(q1,q2,q3,q4,q5,q6,q7,q8,q9,q10);

// DEFINE LEVEL TWO
q1 = new question("15 + 23",38);
q2 = new question("65 - 32",33);
q3 = new question("99 + 45",134);
q4 = new question("34 - 57",-23);
q5 = new question("-34 - 57",-91);
q6 = new question("23 + 77",100);
q7 = new question("64 + 32",96);
q8 = new question("64 - 32",32);
q9 = new question("12 + 34",46);
q10 = new question("77 + 77",154);
levelTwo = new level(q1,q2,q3,q4,q5,q6,q7,q8,q9,q10);

// DEFINE LEVEL THREE
q1 = new question("10 * 7",70);
q2 = new question("15 / 3",5);
q3 = new question("34 * 3",102);
q4 = new question("33 / 2",16.5);
q5 = new question("100 / 4",25);
q6 = new question("99 / 6",16.5);
q7 = new question("32 * 3",96);
q8 = new question("48 / 4",12);
q9 = new question("31 * 0",0);
q10 = new question("45 / 1",45);
levelThree = new level(q1,q2,q3,q4,q5,q6,q7,q8,q9,q10);

// DEFINE TEST
test = new newTest(levelOne,levelTwo,levelThree);

function newTest(levelOne,levelTwo,levelThree) {
  this[1] = levelOne;
  this[2] = levelTwo;
  this[3] = levelThree;
}
```

```
function level(q1,q2,q3,q4,q5,q6,q7,q8,q9,q10) {
  this[1] = q1;
  this[2] = q2;
  this[3] = q3;
  this[4] = q4;
  this[5] = q5;
  this[6] = q6;
  this[7] = q7;
  this[8] = q8;
  this[9] = q9;
  this[10] = q10;
}


function question(question,answer) {
  this.question = question;
  this.answer = answer;
}
```

The test consists of three levels with 10 questions each. You store all this information in a series of objects. The question object has two properties: question and answer. The level object consists of 10 questions as properties. The test object has three properties—each level of the test.

Notice that you only name the properties in the question object. This is because you will want to access the level and particular question using numeric indexes rather than names. For instance, you could refer to level one as test[1] and question three of level one as test[1][3] (notice the use of two indexes next to each other) and the answer to question 3 of level one as test[1][3].answer.

The structure described here is known as a *nested object construct*. In this example, test is an object. It has a set of properties (all objects in this case) which can be referred to by their numerical index. So, test[1] is a property of test and an object in its own right. Because test[1] is an object, it can also have properties, in this case, referred to by numerical index. So, test[1][3] is a property of test[1] and, again, this property is itself an object. Once again, as an object, test[1][3] can have properties—in this case, answer, referenced by name as test[1][3].answer.

The next function in Listing 8.5 is the startTest() function:

```
parent.Register(self.name,"startTest");
function startTest(newLevel) {
  currentLevel=newLevel;
  currentQuestion=1;
  document.forms[0].answer.value="";
  document.forms[0].score.value=0;
  displayQuestion();
}
```

The startTest() function is one of the functions you register with the parent.Register() function from the hIdaho Frameset. You do this because you want to be able to call the function from the level frame.

The function accepts a single argument—the level of the new test— and sets currentLevel and currentQuestion appropriately as well as clearing the fields of the form. Then the function calls displayQuestion() to start the test.

```
function displayQuestion() {
  ask = test[currentLevel][currentQuestion].question;
  answer = test[currentLevel][currentQuestion].answer;
  toOutput = "" + currentQuestion + ". What is " + ask + "?";
  document.forms[0].answer.value = "";
  window.open("display.htm","output");
}
```

This function is used to display each successive question. It takes no arguments but gets its information from the global variables currentLevel and currentQuestion. In this way, it can get the current text of the question by using test[currentLevel][currentQuestion].question.

The function then stores the complete output in toOutput and uses the method window.open() to open display.htm in the frame named output. As you will learn later in the section on the window object, open() can be used to open files in named frames and windows.

```
parent.Register(self.name,"output");
function output() {
  return toOutput;
}
```

Like the startTest() function, you register the output() function with parent.Register(). The function simply returns the value of toOutput and is used to update the display in the output frame, as you will see when you look at the source code of the file display.htm.

```
function checkAnswer(form) {
  answer = form.answer.value;

  if (answer == "" || answer == null) {
    alert("Please enter an answer.");
      return;
  }

  correctAnswer = test[currentLevel][currentQuestion].answer;
  ask = test[currentLevel][currentQuestion].question;
  score = form.score.value;
  if (eval(answer) == correctAnswer) {
    toOutput = "Correct!";
    score ++;
    form.score.value = score;
  } else {
    toOutput = "Sorry! " + ask + " is " + correctAnswer + ".";
  }
```

8

```
window.open("display.htm","output");
if (currentQuestion < 10) {
  currentQuestion ++;
  setTimeout("displayQuestion()",3000);
} else {
  toOutput = "You're Done!<BR>You're score is " + score + " out of 10.";
  setTimeout("window.open('display.htm','output')",3000);
  form.answer.value="";
  form.score.value="0";
}
}
```

checkAnswer() is where the bulk of the work is done in the script.

Because checkAnswer() is called from the form, it takes a single argument for the form object. The function compares the student's answer stored in the field form.answer with the correct answer taken from the test object.

If the student answered correctly, an appropriate message is stored in toOutput, and the score is incremented and displayed. If the answer is wrong, an appropriate message is stored in toOutput, but the score is left untouched. Once the answer is checked, the message is displayed using window.open() to open display.htm in the output frame.

The function then uses the condition currentQuestion < 10 to check if the question just answered is the last question in the test. If it is not the last question, then the currentQuestion variable is increased by one to go to the next question and setTimeout() is used to wait three seconds (3000 milliseconds) before displaying the new question with displayQuestion().

Otherwise, the function stores the results of the test in toOutput, displays them with a similar three-second delay using setTimeout(), and then clears the answer and score fields of the form.

```
function welcome() {
  toOutput = "Welcome!";
  window.open("display.htm","output");
}
```

The function welcome() stores a welcome message in toOutput and then displays it by loading display.htm into the output frame.

```
<BODY BGCOLOR="#FFFFFF" TEXT="#0000FF" onLoad="welcome();">
```

After the document finishes loading, the welcome() function is called using the onLoad event handler.

NOTE

> In the preceding segment of the BODY tag, you will notice the use of RGB triplets to define color for the background and text in the document. The RGB triplets (such as FFFFFF and 00FFFF) define colors as combinations of red, blue, and green. The six hexadecimal digits

> consist of three pairs of the form: RRGGBB. The use of colors in docu-
> ments is discussed in more detail later in this chapter in the section
> about the document object.

```
<FORM METHOD=POST>
<CENTER>
<STRONG>Type You're Answer Here:</STRONG><BR>
<INPUT TYPE=text NAME=answer SIZE=30><P>
<INPUT TYPE=button NAME=done VALUE="Check Answer"
➥onClick="checkAnswer(this.form);"><P>
Correct Answers So Far:<BR>
<INPUT TYPE=text NAME=score VALUE="0" SIZE=10 onFocus="this.blur();">
</FORM>
```

This form is where most user interaction takes place—with the exception of the level frame.
It has a text entry field named answer where users type their answers to each question, a button
they click on to check their answers, and a text field to display the current score.

Only two event handlers are used: onClick="checkAnswer(this.form);" to check the users'
answer and onFocus="this.blur;" to ensure users don't try to cheat by changing their own
scores.

The file level.htm (Listing 8.6) contains a simple three button form to start a new test at any
of the three levels:

```
<FORM METHOD=POST>
<INPUT TYPE=button NAME="one" VALUE="Level One"
➥onClick="parent.Exec('startTest',1);">
<INPUT TYPE=button NAME="two" VALUE="Level Two"
➥onClick="parent.Exec('startTest',2);">
<INPUT TYPE=button NAME="three" VALUE="Level Three"
➥onClick="parent.Exec('startTest',3);">
</FORM>
```

Each button has a similar onClick event handler which uses parent.Exec() to call the
startTest() function from the form frame and pass it a single integer argument for the level.

The only other file involving JavaScript scripting is display.htm which sets up the body of
the document and then uses document.write() to display the result returned by output()
from the form frame. The function is called using parent.Exec(). In this way, every time the
main script in form.htm reloads display.htm, the current value of toOutput is returned by
output() and displayed as the body text for display.htm.

NOTE

> You could have written the output directly to the output frame using
> document.write(). You will see an example of this later in the chapter.

8

The document Object

In any given window or frame, one of the primary objects is the document object. The document object provides the properties and methods to work with numerous aspects of the current document, including information about anchors, forms, links, the title, the current location and URL, and the current colors.

You already have been introduced to some of the features of the document object in the form of the document.write() and document.writeln() methods, as well as the form object and all of its properties and methods.

The document object is defined when the BODY tag is evaluated in an HTML page and the object remains in existence as long as the page is loaded. Because many of the properties of the document object are reflections of attributes of the BODY tag, you should have a complete grasp of all the attributes available in the BODY tag in Navigator 2.0.

The BODY Tag

The BODY tag defines the main body of an HTML document. Its attributes enable the HTML author to define colors for text and links, as well as background colors or patterns for the document.

In addition, as you have already learned, there are two event handlers, onLoad and onUnload, that can be used in the BODY tag.

The following is a list of available attributes for the BODY tag:

- [ ] BACKGROUND—Specifies the URL of a background image.
- [ ] BGCOLOR—Specifies a background color for the document as a hexadecimal RGB triplet or a color name. Color names available in Navigator 2.0 are listed at the end of the chapter.
- [ ] FGCOLOR—Specifies the foreground (and text) color as a hexadecimal triplet.
- [ ] LINK—Specifies the color for links as a hexadecimal triplet.
- [ ] ALINK—Specifies the color for an active link (when the user has the mouse clicked on a link until the user releases the mouse button) as a hexadecimal triplet.
- [ ] VLINK—Specifies the color for a followed link as a hexadecimal triplet.

Properties of the document Object

Table 8.3 outlines the properties of the document object.

Table 8.3. Properties of the `document` object.

Property	Description
alinkColor	The RGB value for the color of activated links expressed as a hexadecimal triplet.
anchors	Array of objects corresponding to each named anchor in a document.
bgColor	The RGB value of the background color as a hexadecimal triplet.
cookie	Contains the value of the cookies for the current document. Cookies are discussed in depth in Chapter 9.
fgColor	The RGB value of the foreground color as a hexadecimal triplet.
forms	Array of objects corresponding to each form in a document.
lastModified	A string containing the last date the document was modified.
linkColor	The RGB value of links as a hexadecimal triplet.
links	An array of objects corresponding to each link in a document.
location	An object defining the full URL of the document.
referrer	Contains the URL of the document that called the current document.
title	A string containing the title of the document.
vlinkColor	The RGB value of followed links as a hexadecimal triplet.

Some of these properties are obvious. For instance, in a document containing the tag

```
<BODY BGCOLOR="#FFFFFF" FGCOLOR="#000000" LINK="#0000FF">
```

document.bgColor would have a value of "#FFFFFF", document.fgColor would equal "#000000", and document.linkColor would be "#0000FF".

In addition, you have already learned to use the forms array.

However, the anchors and links arrays, along with the location object deserve a closer look.

The anchors **Array**

While the <A> tag in HTML is usually used to define hypertext links to other documents, it can also be used to define named anchors in a document so that links within a document can jump to other places in the document.

8

For instance, in the HTML page

```
<HTML>

<HEAD>
<TITLE>Anchors Example</TITLE>
</HEAD>

<BODY>
<A NAME="one">Anchor one is here
HTML Code
<A NAME="two">Anchor two is here
More HTML Code
<A HREF="#one">Go back to Anchor One</A><BR>
<A HREF="#two">GO back to Anchor Two</A>
</BODY>

</HTML>
```

two anchors are defined using <A NAME="*anchorName*"> (<A NAME="one"> and <A NAME="two">), and links to those anchors are created using <A HREF="#*anchorName*"> (<A HREF="#one"> and <A HREF="#two">).

JavaScript provides the anchors array as a means to access information and methods related to anchors in the current document. Each element in the array is an anchor object, and like all arrays, the array has a length property.

The order of anchors in the array follows the order of appearance of the anchors in the HTML document.

Therefore, in the example, document.anchors.length would have a value of 1 (since the anchors array, like the forms array and frames array starts with a zero index) and document.anchors[0] would refer to the anchor named one.

The links **Array**

Just as the anchors array provides a sequential list of all the anchors in a document, the links array offers an entry for each hypertext link defined by <A HREF="*URL*"> in an HTML document.

Also like the anchors array, each element in the links array is a link object, and the array has a length property.

The link object has a single property, target, which contains a string with the name of the window or frame indicated in the link's TARGET attribute in the HTML file. For instance, in the following simple HTML file, document.links[0].target would have a value of "test":

```
<HTML>

<HEAD>
<TITLE>Links Example</TITLE>
```

```
</HEAD>

<BODY>
<A HREF="URL" TARGET="test">Just Testing</A>
</BODY>

</HTML>
```

The location **Object**

The location object provides several properties and methods for working with the location of the current object.

Table 8.4 outlines these properties and methods.

Table 8.4. Properties and methods of the location object.

Name	Description
hash	The anchor name (the text following a # symbol in an HREF attribute)
host	The hostname and port of the URL
hostname	The hostname of the URL
href	The entire URL as a string
pathname	The file path (the portion of the URL following the third slash)
port	The port number of the URL (if there is no port number, then the empty string)
protocol	The protocol part of the URL (such as http:, gopher: or ftp:— including the colon)
search	The form data or query following the question mark (?) in the URL
assign()	Sets location.href
toString()	Returns location.href as a string

Methods of the document **Object**

In addition to the write() and writeln() methods which you have been using throughout the book, the document object provides three other methods: open(), close(), and clear().

The open() method is used to open the document window for writing a MIME type. It takes a single argument: the MIME type (such as text/html). You can also use the window.open() method to open a window or frame for writing a document, as you will see in the section on the window object.

8

NEW TERM MIME stands for Multi-purpose Internet Mail Extensions. MIME provides a way to exchange files in any format between computers using Internet mail standards. MIME supports pre-defined file types, allows the creation of custom types. MIME types are specified using two-part codes, such as `text/html` for HTML files and `image/gif` for GIF bitmap graphics.

Further more, `close()` closes the document window for writing, and the `clear()` method clears the current document window. Document output is not actually rendered (displayed) until `document.close()` is called.

Using the Document Object in a Color Tester

For this example, you are going to build a simple utility to demonstrate what different combinations of text, link, and background colors look like.

The application will use two frames: the top frame contains five text entry fields for the background color, text color, link color, active link color, and followed link color, plus a button to enable users to test their color combinations.

When users press the button, the script loads a simple document, using the specified colors, into the lower frame. The users should be able to specify colors by hexadecimal triplets or by name.

To do this, you don't need to use the hIdaho Frameset you used in Listings 8.3 through 8.8 because you won't be using nested framesets or making cross-frame function calls.

The parent frameset is defined in Listings 8.9 and 8.10.

TYPE **Listing 8.9. The parent frameset for the color tester.**

```
<HTML>

<HEAD>
<TITLE>Example 8.9</TITLE>
</HEAD>

<FRAMESET ROWS="45%,*">
  <FRAME SRC="pick.htm">
  <FRAME SRC="blank.htm" NAME="output">
</FRAMESET>

</HTML>
```

The source code for the file pick.htm, where all the processing occurs, is in Listing 8.10.

TYPE   **Listing 8.10. The pick.htm file.**

```
<HTML>

<HEAD>

<SCRIPT LANGUAGE="JavaScript">
<!-- HIDE FORM OTHER BROWSERS

function display(form) {
  doc = open("","output");
  doc.document.write ('<BODY BGCOLOR="' + form.bg.value);
  doc.document.write ('" TEXT="' + form.fg.value);
  doc.document.write ('" LINK="' + form.link.value);
  doc.document.write ('" ALINK="' + form.alink.value);
  doc.document.write ('" VLINK="' + form.vlink.value);
  doc.document.writeln ('">');
  doc.document.write("<H1>This is a test</H1>");
  doc.document.write("You have selected these colors.<BR>");
  doc.document.write('<A
➥HREF="#">
➥    This is a test link</A>');
  doc.document.write("</BODY>");
  doc.document.close();
}

// STOP HIDING SCRIPT -->
</SCRIPT>

</HEAD>

<BODY>

<CENTER>

<SCRIPT LANGUAGE="JavaScript">
<!-- HIDE FROM OTHER BROWSERS

document.write('<H1>The Colour Picker</H1>');
document.write('<FORM METHOD=POST>');
document.write('Enter Colors:<BR>');

document.write('Background: <INPUT TYPE=text NAME="bg"
➥VALUE="' + document.bgColor + '"> ... ');
document.write('Text: <INPUT TYPE=text NAME="fg"
➥VALUE="' + document.fgColor + '"><BR>');
document.write('Link: <INPUT TYPE=text NAME="link"
➥VALUE ="' + document.linkColor + '"> ...');
document.write('Active Link: <INPUT TYPE=text NAME="alink"
➥VALUE="' + document.alinkColor + '"><BR>');
document.write('Followed Link: <INPUT TYPE="text" NAME="vlink"
➥VALUE ="' + document.vlinkColor + '"><BR>');
```

8

```
document.write('<INPUT TYPE=button VALUE="TEST"
➥onClick="display(this.form);">');

document.write('</FORM>');

display(document.forms[0]);

// STOP HIDING FROM OTHER BROWSERS -->
</SCRIPT>

</CENTER>

</BODY>

</HTML>
```

OUTPUT   The program produces results like those in Figure 8.7.

Figure 8.7.
With JavaScript, you can dynamically test color combinations.

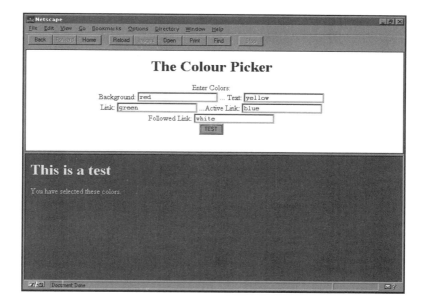

ANALYSIS   As you can see in this example, all the work is being done in the top frame, which contains the document `pick.htm`.

The file has two main components: a JavaScript function and the body of the document, which is almost entirely generated by another JavaScript script using the `document.write()` and `document.writeln()` methods.

The interface consists of a single form containing five fields for each of the color values, plus a button that calls the function display().

```
function display(form) {
  doc = open("","output");
  doc.document.write ('<BODY BGCOLOR="' + form.bg.value);
  doc.document.write ('" TEXT="' + form.fg.value);
  doc.document.write ('" LINK="' + form.link.value);
  doc.document.write ('" ALINK="' + form.alink.value);
  doc.document.write ('" VLINK="' + form.vlink.value);
  doc.document.writeln ('">');
  doc.document.write("<H1>This is a test</H1>");
  doc.document.write("You have selected these colors.<BR>");
  doc.document.write('<A
➥HREF="#">
➥    This is a test link</A>');

  doc.document.write("</BODY>");
  doc.document.close();
}
```

The function is fairly simple: An empty document is opened in the output frame using the window.open() method, and the name doc is assigned for JavaScript to refer to that window (frame).

The commands doc.document.write() and doc.document.writeln() can then be used to write HTML to the newly opened window. The values of the five form fields are then used to build a custom BODY tag that defines all the colors for the document. After the text has been output, the method doc.document.close() is used to close the open document and finish displaying it in the frame.

With this single function, you can build a simple form in the body of the document. The form is built by a JavaScript script that assigns initial values to the five fields using properties of the document object to set the values to the current browser defaults. Then the script calls display() so that an initial sample is displayed in the lower frame.

As with many programs, there is more than one way to achieve a desired effect. For instance, the display() function could be rewritten to change the colors dynamically—without rewriting the content of the frame—by using the color properties of the document object:

```
function display(form) {
  parent.output.document.bgColor = form.bg.value;
  parent.output.document.fgColor = form.fg.value;
  parent.output.document.linkClor = form.link.value;
  parent.output.document.alinkColor = form.alink.value;
  parent.output.document.vlinkColor = form.vlink.value;
}
```

Then you simply can remove the call to display() in the body of the HTML document, make the content of the output frame a separate HTML document, and load the sample document into the lower frame in the parent frameset.

The window **Object**

As you learned in Chapter 1, "Where Does JavaScript Fit In?" when you were first introduced to the Navigator Object Hierarchy, the window object is the parent object of each loaded document.

Because the window object is the parent object for loaded documents, you usually do not explicitly refer to the window object when referring to its properties or invoking its methods. For this reason, window.alert() can be called by using alert().

Table 8.5 outlines the properties and methods of the window object. You have seen many of these, including the frames array and the parent object, as well as the alert(), confirm(), open(), prompt(), and setTimeout() methods.

Table 8.5. Properties and methods of the window object.

Name	Description
frames	Array of objects containing an entry for each child frame in a frameset document.
parent	The FRAMESET in a FRAMESET-FRAME relationship.
self	The current window—use this to distinguish between windows and forms of the same name.
top	The top-most parent window.
status	The value of the text displayed in the window's status bar. This can be used to display status messages to the user.
defaultStatus	The default value displayed in the status bar.
alert()	Displays a message in a dialog box with an OK button.
confirm()	Displays a message in a dialog box with OK and Cancel buttons. This returns true when the user clicks on OK, false otherwise.
close()	Closes the current window.
open()	Opens a new window with a specified document or opens the document in the specified named window.
prompt()	Displays a message in a dialog box along with a text entry field.
setTimeout()	Sets a timer for a specified number of milliseconds and then evaluates an expression when the timer has finished counting. Program operation continues while the timer is counting down.
clearTimeout()	Cancels a previously set timeout.

Working with the Status Bar

Using the status bar—the strip at the bottom of the Navigator window where you are told about the current status of document transfers and connections to remote sites—can be used by JavaScript programs to display custom messages to the user.

This is primarily done using the onMouseOver event handler, which is invoked when the user points at a hypertext link. By setting the value of self.status to a string, you can assign a value to the status bar (you could also use window.status or status here). In the program

```
<HTML>

<HEAD>
<TITLE>Status Example</TITLE>
</HEAD>

<BODY>
<A HREF="home.html" onMouseOver="self.status='Go Home!'; return true;">Home</A>
<A HREF="next.html" onMouseOver="self.status='Go to the next Page!';
➥return true;">Next</A>
</BODY>

</HTML>
```

two different messages are displayed when the user points the mouse at the links. This can be more informative than the URLs that Navigator normally displays when a user points at a link.

NOTE Notice that both of the onMouseOver event handlers in the script return a true value after setting the status bar to a new value. This is necessary to display a new value in the status bar using the onMouseOver event handler.

Opening and Closing Windows

By using the open() and close() methods, you have control over what windows are open and which documents they contain.

The open() method is the more complex of the two. It takes two required arguments and an optional feature list in the following form:

```
open("URL", "windowName", "featureList");
```

Here the *featureList* is a comma-separated list containing any of the entries in Table 8.6.

8

Table 8.6. Windows features used in the `open()` method.

Name	Description
toolbar	Creates the standard toolbar
location	Creates the location entry field
directories	Creates the standard directory buttons
status	Creates the status bar
menubar	Creates the menu at the top of the window
scrollbars	Creates scroll bars when the document grows beyond the current window
resizable	Enables resizing of the window by the user
width	Specifies the window width in pixels
height	Specifies the window height in pixels

NOTE With the exception of `width` and `height`, which take integer values, all of these features can be set to `true` with a value of `yes` or `1` or set to `false` with a value of `no` or `0`.

For example, to open a document called `new.html` in a new window named `newWindow` and to make the window 200 pixels by 200 pixels with all window features available except `resizable`, you could use the command

```
window.open("new.html","newWindow","toolbar=yes,
➥location=1,directories=yes,status=yes,menubar=1,
➥scrollbars=yes,resizable=0,copyhistory=1,width=200,height=200");
```

which would produce a window like the one in Figure 8.8.

Note that you can open a window and then write HTML into that window using `document.writeln()` and `document.write()`. You saw an example of this in Listings 8.6. through 8.8.

For instance, the function `newwindow()` opens a new window and writes several lines of HTML into it.

```
function newwindow() {
  newWindow = open("","New_Window");

  newWindow.document.write("<H1>Testing ...</H1>");
  newWindow.document.writeln("1... 2... 3...");
  newWindow.document.close();
}
```

Figure 8.8.

You control the size of new windows, as well as which elements to display.

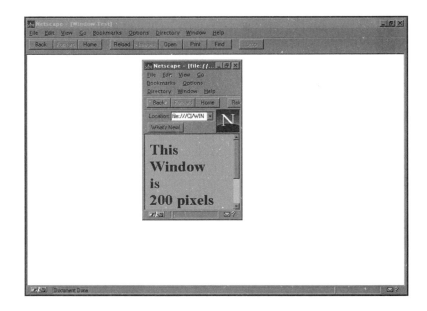

 NOTE

Notice the command newWindow = open("",:New Window"); which opens an instance of the window object and names it newWindow so that you can then use commands such as newWindow.document.write().

The close() method is simpler to use:

```
window.close();
```

simply closes the current window.

Pausing with Timeouts

You already saw an example of using setTimeout() in Bill Dortch's hIdaho Frameset earlier in this chapter where he suggests using a setTimeout() call to make sure a function is registered before trying to call the function.

The setTimeout() method takes the form

ID=setTimeout("*expression*",*milliseconds*)

where *expression* is any string expression, including a call to a function, *milliseconds* is the number of milliseconds—expressed as an integer—to wait before evaluating the expression, and *ID* is an identifier that can be used to cancel the setTimeout() before the expression is evaluated.

8

clearTimeout() is passed a single argument: the identifier of the timeout setting to be canceled.

For instance, if you want to create a page that displays a welcome message to the user and then automatically goes to a new page five seconds later if the user hasn't clicked on the appropriate button, you could write a script like Listing 8.11.

Type **Listing 8.11. Creating an automatic pause.**

```
<HTML>

<HEAD>
<TITLE>Timeout Example</TITLE>

<SCRIPT LANGUAGE="JavaScript">
<!-- HIDE FROM OTHER BROWSERS

function go() {
  open("new.html","newWindow");
}

// STOP HIDING FROM OTHER BROWSERS -->
</SCRIPT>

</HEAD>

<BODY onLoad="timeout = setTimeout('go()',5000);">
<IMG SRC="welcome.gif">
<H1>Click on the button or wait five seconds to continue ...</H1>
<FORM METHOD=POST>
<INPUT TYPE=button VALUE="Continue ..." onClick="clearTimeout(timeout); go();">
</FORM>
</BODY>

</HTML>
```

Creating a Status Bar Message Handler

In this example, you produce a simple function to implement status bar help in any HTML document. The function can be called from any event handler and will display a message in the status bar.

```
function help(message) {
  self.status = message;
  return true;
}
```

With this function, you can then implement full on-line pointers and help systems. For instance, if you use this in the math test from Listings 8.3 through 8.8, you can add help messages with only slight modifications to both form.htm and level.htm. See Listing 8.12 for the new version.

TYPE **Listing 8.12. Updating the math test program.**

```
<!-- SOURCE CODE OF form.htm -->
<HTML>

<HEAD>
<SCRIPT LANGUAGE="JavaScript">
<!-- HIDE FROM OTHER BROWSERS

var currentLevel=1;
var currentQuestion=1;
var toOutput = "";

// DEFINE LEVEL ONE
q1 = new question("1 + 3",4);
q2 = new question("4 + 5",9);
q3 = new question("5 - 4",1);
q4 = new question("7 + 3",10);
q5 = new question("4 + 4",8);
q6 = new question("3 - 3",0);
q7 = new question("9 - 5",4);
q8 = new question("8 + 1",9);
q9 = new question("5 - 3",2);
q10 = new question("8 - 3",5);
levelOne = new level(q1,q2,q3,q4,q5,q6,q7,q8,q9,q10);

// DEFINE LEVEL TWO
q1 = new question("15 + 23",38);
q2 = new question("65 - 32",33);
q3 = new question("99 + 45",134);
q4 = new question("34 - 57",-23);
q5 = new question("-34 - 57",-91);
q6 = new question("23 + 77",100);
q7 = new question("64 + 32",96);
q8 = new question("64 - 32",32);
q9 = new question("12 + 34",46);
q10 = new question("77 + 77",154);
levelTwo = new level(q1,q2,q3,q4,q5,q6,q7,q8,q9,q10);

// DEFINE LEVEL THREE
q1 = new question("10 * 7",70);
q2 = new question("15 / 3",5);
q3 = new question("34 * 3",102);
q4 = new question("33 / 2",16.5);
q5 = new question("100 / 4",25);
q6 = new question("99 / 6",16.5);
q7 = new question("32 * 3",96);
q8 = new question("48 / 4",12);
q9 = new question("31 * 0",0);
q10 = new question("45 / 1",45);
```

8

```
levelThree = new level(q1,q2,q3,q4,q5,q6,q7,q8,q9,q10);

// DEFINE TEST
test = new newTest(levelOne,levelTwo,levelThree);

function newTest(levelOne,levelTwo,levelThree) {
  this[1] = levelOne;
  this[2] = levelTwo;
  this[3] = levelThree;
}

function level(q1,q2,q3,q4,q5,q6,q7,q8,q9,q10) {
  this[1] = q1;
  this[2] = q2;
  this[3] = q3;
  this[4] = q4;
  this[5] = q5;
  this[6] = q6;
  this[7] = q7;
  this[8] = q8;
  this[9] = q9;
  this[10] = q10;
}

function question(question,answer) {
  this.question = question;
  this.answer = answer;
}

parent.Register(self.name,"startTest");
function startTest(newLevel) {
  currentLevel=newLevel;
  currentQuestion=1;
  document.forms[0].answer.value="";
  document.forms[0].score.value=0;
  displayQuestion();
}

function displayQuestion() {
  ask = test[currentLevel][currentQuestion].question;
  answer = test[currentLevel][currentQuestion].answer;
  toOutput = "" + currentQuestion + ". What is " + ask + "?";
  document.forms[0].answer.value = "";
  window.open("display.htm","output");
}

parent.Register(self.name,"output");
function output() {
  return toOutput;
}

function checkAnswer(form) {
  answer = form.answer.value;
  correctAnswer = test[currentLevel][currentQuestion].answer;
  ask = test[currentLevel][currentQuestion].question;
  score = form.score.value;
```

continues

Listing 8.12. continued

```
    if (eval(answer) == correctAnswer) {
      toOutput = "Correct!";
      score ++;
      form.score.value = score;
    } else {
      toOutput = "Sorry! " + ask + " is " + correctAnswer + ".";
    }
    window.open("display.htm","output");
    if (currentQuestion < 10) {
      currentQuestion ++;
      setTimeout("displayQuestion()",3000);
    } else {
      toOutput = "You're Done!<BR>You're score is " + score + " out of 10.";
      setTimeout("window.open('display.htm','output')",3000);
      form.answer.value="";
      form.score.value="0";
    }
  }

  function welcome() {
    toOutput = "Welcome!";
    window.open("display.htm","output");
  }

  parent.Register(self.name,"help");
  function help(message) {
    self.status = message;
    return true;
  }

// STOP HIDING FROM OTHER BROWSERS -->
</SCRIPT>

</HEAD>

<BODY BGCOLOR="#FFFFFF" TEXT="#0000FF" onLoad="welcome();">

<FORM METHOD=POST>
<CENTER>
<STRONG>Type You're Answer Here:</STRONG><BR>
<INPUT TYPE=text NAME=answer SIZE=30
➥onFocus="help('Enter your answer here.');"><P>
<A HREF="#" onClick="checkAnswer(document.forms[0]);"
➥onMouseOver="return help('Click here to check your answer.');">
➥Check Answer</A><P>
<INPUT TYPE=text NAME=score VALUE="0" SIZE=10 onFocus="this.blur();">
</FORM>

</BODY>

</HTML>
```

Similarly, level.htm requires changes:

TYPE **Listing 8.13. Updating the `level.htm` file.**

```
<!-- SOURCE CODE OF level.htm -->
<HTML>

<HEAD>
<SCRIPT LANGUAGE="JavaScript">
<!-- HIDE FROM OTHER BROWSERS

function help(message) {
  self.status = message;
  return true;
}

// STOP HIDING FROM OTHER BROWSERS -->
</SCRIPT>

</HEAD>

<BODY BGCOLOR="#000000" TEXT="#FFFFFF" LINK="#FFFFFF"
➥ALINK="#FFFFFF" VLINK="#FFFFFF">
<CENTER>
<STRONG>
Select a level here:<BR>
<A HREF="#" onClick="parent.Exec('startTest',1);"
➥onMouseOver="return
➥parent.Exec('help','Start test at level one.');">LEVEL ONE</A>
<A HREF="#" onClick="parent.Exec('startTest',2);"
➥onMouseOver="return parent.Exec('help',
➥'Start test at level two.');">LEVEL TWO</A>
<A HREF="#" onClick="parent.Exec('startTest',3);"
➥onMouseOver="return parent.Exec('help',
➥'Start test at level three.');">LEVEL THREE</A>
</STRONG>
</CENTER>
</BODY>

</HTML>
```

OUTPUT These changes produce results like those in Figure 8.9.

ANALYSIS In order to implement the interactive help in the math test, you have to make only minor changes to both HTML files.

In `form.htm`, you have added the `help()` function to the header and made two changes in the body of the document. You have added an `onFocus` event handler to the answer field. The event handler calls `help()` to display a help message.

Figure 8.9.

Using
onMouseOver *and*
the status
property to display
help messages in
the Navigator
window's status
bar.

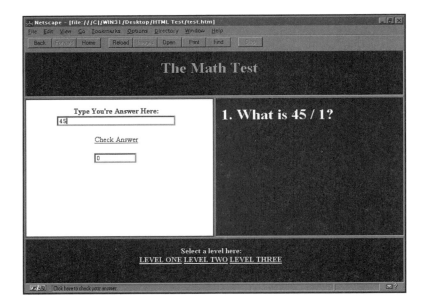

You have also changed the button to a hypertext link so that you can use the onMouseOver event handler to display another help message. There are several points to note in the following line:

```
<A HREF="#" onClick="checkAnswer(document.forms[0]);"
➥onMouseOver="return help('Click here to check your answer.');">
➥Check Answer</A>
```

First, in the call to checkAnswer(), you can't pass the argument this.form because the hypertext link is not a form element. For this reason, you use document.forms[0] to explicitly identify the form.

The second point to notice is that you have an empty anchor in the attribute HREF="#". When a user clicks on the link, only the onClick event handler executes, but because there is no URL specified, the page doesn't change.

NOTE

For changes to the status bar to take effect in an onMouseOver event, you need to return a value of true from the event handler. This isn't true in other event handlers, such as onFocus.

8

TIP

Instead of using the onClick event handler, you can use a special type of URL to call JavaScript functions and methods:

```
<A HREF="JavaScript:checkAnswer(document.forms[0])">.
```

8

In level.htm, you make similar changes. You simply have added the help function to the file's header and changed the three form buttons to three hypertext links with appropriate onMouseOver event handlers.

NOTE

Notice when you try these scripts that status messages stay displayed until another message is displayed in the status bar, even when the condition that caused the message to be displayed has ended.

Color in Navigator 2.0

The various HTML color attributes and tags (BGCOLOR, FGCOLOR, VLINKCOLOR, ALINKCOLOR, LINKCOLOR, FONT COLOR) and their related JavaScript methods (bgColor(), fgColor(), vlinkColor(), alinkColor(), linkColor(), fontColor()) can take both RGB triplets and selected color names as their values.

Table 8.7 is a list of selected Netscape color words and their corresponding RGB triplets. The complete list of color words can be found in the JavaScript document at the Netscape Web site (see Appendix A).

Table 8.7. Color words in Navigator 2.0.

Color Name	RGB Triplet	Color Name	RGB Triplet
antiquewhite	FA EB D7	ivory	FF FF F0
aqua	00 FF FF	lemonchiffon	FF FA CD
azure	F0 FF FF	lightblue	AD D8 E6
beige	F5 F5 DC	lightyellow	FF FF E0
black	00 00 00	magenta	FF 00 FF
blue	00 00 FF	maroon	80 00 00
brown	A5 2A 2A	mediumpurple	93 70 DB
chartreuse	7F FF 00	mediumturquoise	48 D1 CC
cornflowerblue	64 95 ED	moccasin	FF E4 B5

continues

Table 8.7. continued

Color Name	RGB Triplet	Color Name	RGB Triplet
crimson	DC 14 3C	navy	00 00 80
darkcyan	00 8B 8B	orange	FF A5 00
darkgray	A9 A9 A9	papayawhip	FF EF D5
darkgreen	00 64 00	pink	FF C0 CB
darkpink	FF 14 93	rosybrown	BC 8F 8F
firebrick	B2 22 22	salmon	FA 80 72
floralwhite	FF FA F0	silver	C0 C0 C0
fuchsia	FF 00 FF	slateblue	6A 5A CD
gold	FF D7 00	tan	D2 B4 8C
greenyellow	AD FF 2F	tomato	FF 63 47
hotpink	FF 69 B4	yellow	FF FF 00
indigo	4B 00 82		

Summary

In this chapter you have covered several significant topics.

You now know how to divide the Navigator window into multiple independent sections and how to work with functions and values in different windows using the hIdaho Frameset.

In addition, you have taken a detailed look at the document object and learned about its properties, which give you information about colors used in a document, as well as information about the last modification date of a document, and the location of a document.

The window object, which is the parent object of the document object, provides you the ability to work with various aspects of windows and frames, including altering the text displayed in the window's status bar, setting timeouts to pause before evaluating expressions or calling functions, and opening and closing named windows.

In the Chapter 9, "Remember Where You've Been with Cookies," you are going to take a look at Cookies—a feature of Navigator 2.0 that enables you to store information about a page and recall it later when the user returns to the page.

Commands and Extensions Review

Command/Extension	Type	Description
FRAMESET	HTML tag	Defines a window or frame containing frames
ROWS	HTML attribute	Defines the number of rows in a FRAMESET tag
COLS	HTML attribute	Defines the number of columns in a FRAMESET tag
FRAME	HTML tag	Defines the source document for a frame defined in a FRAMESET container
SRC	HTML attribute	Indicates the URL of a document to load into a frame
NORESIZE	HTML attribute	Specifies that a frame is fixed in size and cannot be resized by the user
SCROLLING	HTML attribute	Indicates whether scroll bars are to be displayed in a frame (takes the value YES, NO or AUTO)
MARGINHEIGHT	HTML attribute	Specifies the vertical offset in pixels from the border of the frame
MARGINWIDTH	HTML attribute	Specifies the horizontal offset in pixels from the border of the frame
TARGET	HTML attribute	Indicates the frame or window for a document to load into—used with the A, FORM, BASE, and AREA tags
NOFRAMES	HTML tag	Indicates HTML code to be displayed in browsers that don't support frames; used in documents containing the FRAMESET container tags
frames	JavaScript property	Array of objects for each frame in a Navigator window
parent	JavaScript property	Indicates the parent frameset document of the currently loaded document

continues

Command/Extension	Type	Description
BODY	HTML Tag	Defines the main body of an HTML document
BACKGROUND	HTML attribute	Specifies URL of a background image in the BODY tag
BGCOLOR	HTML attribute	Specifies the background color for a document as a hexadecimal triplet or color name
FGCOLOR	HTML attribute	Specifies the foreground color for a document as a hexadecimal triplet or color name
LINK	HTML attribute	Specifies the color of link text
ALINK	HTML attribute	Specifies the color of active link text
VLINK	HTML attribute	Specifies the color of followed link text
alinkColor	JavaScript property	The color value of active links
anchors	JavaScript property	Array of objects corresponding to each named anchor in a document
bgColor	JavaScript property	The background color value of a document
fgColor	JavaScript property	The foreground color value of a document
forms	JavaScript property	Array of objects corresponding to each form in a document
lastModified	JavaScript property	As a string, the last date the document was modified
linkColor	JavaScript property	The color value of link text
links	JavaScript property	Array of objects corresponding to each link in a document
location	JavaScript property	Object defining the full URL of the document
title	JavaScript property	Title of the document represented as a string
vlinkColor	JavaScript property	The color value of followed links
hash	JavaScript property	An anchor name (location object)

Command/Extension	Type	Description
host	JavaScript property	Hostname and port of a URL (location object)
href	JavaScript property	Hostname of a URL (location object)
pathname	JavaScript property	File path from the URL (location object)
port	JavaScript property	Port number from the URL (location object)
protocol	JavaScript property	Protocol part of the URL (location object)
search	JavaScript property	Form data or query from the URL (location object)
assign()	JavaScript method	Sets location.href (location object)
toString()	JavaScript method	Returns location.href as a string (location object)
open()	JavaScript method	Opens a document for a particular MIME type (document object)
close()	JavaScript method	Closes a document for writing (document object)
clear()	JavaScript method	Clears a document window (document object)
self	JavaScript property	Refers to the current window
top	JavaScript property	The top-most parent window
status	JavaScript property	Text displayed in the status bar represented as a string
defaultStatus	JavaScript property	Default text displayed in the status bar
close()	JavaScript method	Closes the window (window object)
open()	JavaScript method	Opens a document in a named window (window object)
setTimeout()	JavaScript method	Pauses for a specified number of milliseconds and then evaluates an expression

8

continues

Command/Extension	Type	Description
clearTimeout()	JavaScript method	Cancels a previously set timeout
onMouseOver	Event handler	Specifies script to execute when the mouse pointer is over a hypertext link
location	JavaScript property	The location of the document currently loaded in a window

Q&A

Q If I use frames in my documents, will users of any other Web browsers be able to view my documents?

A At the present time, only Netscape Navigator 2.0 supports the FRAMESET and FRAMES tags. If you make effective use of the NOFRAMES tag, it is possible to design perfectly reasonable non-frame alternatives for the users of other browsers' software. Of course, if you are using JavaScript, your users must be using Navigator.

Q Is it possible to force changes in the relative size of frames using JavaScript?

A No. There are no mechanisms to force resizing of frames in JavaScript without reloading the document and dynamically changing the value of the ROWS and COLS attributes of the FRAMESET tag using document.write() or document.writeln().

Q Is it possible to set the status bar when the user points at a form button?

A No. At the present time, the <INPUT TYPE=button> tag does not support the onMouseOver event, which you use in the <A> tag to set the status bar when the mouse points at the link.

Exercises

1. Expand the math test example so that it presents the questions in a random order each time the user runs through the test.

2. Design a program that does the following:

   Splits the screen into two frames.

   In the first, enables the user to indicate a URL.

   Loads the URL into the second frame, and once it's loaded, displays the following information about it in the first frame: all color attributes, the title of the document, and the last date of modification.

3. What happens on the status bar in this script?

```
<HTML>

<HEAD>
<TITLE>Exercise 8.3</TITLE>

<SCRIPT LANGUAGE="JavaSCript">
<!-- HIDE FROM OTHER BROWSERS

function help(message) {
  self.status = message;
  return true;
}

function checkField(field) {
  if (field.value == "")
    help("Remember to enter a value in this field");
  else
    help("");
  return true;
}
// STOP HIDING FROM OTHER BROWSERS -->
</SCRIPT>

</HEAD>

<BODY>

<FORM METHOD=POST>
Name: <INPUT TYPE=text NAME="name" onFocus="help('Enter your name');"
            onBlur="checkField(this);">
Email: <INPUT TYPE=text NAME="email"
➥onFocus="help('Enter your email address');"
            onBlur="checkField(this);">
</FORM>

</BODY>

</HTML>
```

4. Extend Listing 8.9 and Listing 8.10. so that the user can specify any URL to be displayed using the specified color scheme. You will want to consider using the alternative method for the display() function.

Answers

1. In order to add random order to the tests, you need to add two things to the program: a function to produce a suitable random number and a method to keep track of which questions have already been asked. All the changes are to form.htm and should look like this:

```
<!-- SOURCE CODE OF form.htm -->
<HTML>
```

continues

```
<HEAD>
<SCRIPT LANGUAGE="JavaScript">
<!-- HIDE FROM OTHER BROWSERS

var currentLevel=1;
var currentQuestion=1;
var askedQuestion=0;
var toOutput = "";

// DEFINE LEVEL ONE
q1 = new question("1 + 3",4);
q2 = new question("4 + 5",9);
q3 = new question("5 - 4",1);
q4 = new question("7 + 3",10);
q5 = new question("4 + 4",8);
q6 = new question("3 - 3",0);
q7 = new question("9 - 5",4);
q8 = new question("8 + 1",9);
q9 = new question("5 - 3",2);
q10 = new question("8 - 3",5);
levelOne = new level(q1,q2,q3,q4,q5,q6,q7,q8,q9,q10);

// DEFINE LEVEL TWO
q1 = new question("15 + 23",38);
q2 = new question("65 - 32",33);
q3 = new question("99 + 45",134);
q4 = new question("34 - 57",-23);
q5 = new question("-34 - 57",-91);
q6 = new question("23 + 77",100);
q7 = new question("64 + 32",96);
q8 = new question("64 - 32",32);
q9 = new question("12 + 34",46);
q10 = new question("77 + 77",154);
levelTwo = new level(q1,q2,q3,q4,q5,q6,q7,q8,q9,q10);

// DEFINE LEVEL THREE
q1 = new question("10 * 7",70);
q2 = new question("15 / 3",5);
q3 = new question("34 * 3",102);
q4 = new question("33 / 2",16.5);
q5 = new question("100 / 4",25);
q6 = new question("99 / 6",16.5);
q7 = new question("32 * 3",96);
q8 = new question("48 / 4",12);
q9 = new question("31 * 0",0);
q10 = new question("45 / 1",45);
levelThree = new level(q1,q2,q3,q4,q5,q6,q7,q8,q9,q10);

// DEFINE TEST
test = new newTest(levelOne,levelTwo,levelThree);

function newTest(levelOne,levelTwo,levelThree) {
  this[1] = levelOne;
  this[2] = levelTwo;
  this[3] = levelThree;
}
```

8

```
function level(q1,q2,q3,q4,q5,q6,q7,q8,q9,q10) {
  this[1] = q1;
  this[2] = q2;
  this[3] = q3;
  this[4] = q4;
  this[5] = q5;
  this[6] = q6;
  this[7] = q7;
  this[8] = q8;
  this[9] = q9;
  this[10] = q10;
}

function question(question,answer) {
  this.question = question;
  this.answer = answer;
}

parent.Register(self.name,"startTest");
function startTest(newLevel) {
  currentLevel=newLevel;
  currentQuestion=1;
  clearArray(asked);
  askedQuestion = chooseQuestion();
  document.forms[0].answer.value="";
  document.forms[0].score.value=0;
  displayQuestion();
}

function displayQuestion() {
  ask = test[currentLevel][askedQuestion].question;
  answer = test[currentLevel][askedQuestion].answer;
  toOutput = "" + currentQuestion + ". What is " + ask + "?";
  document.forms[0].answer.value = "";
  window.open("display.htm","output");
}

parent.Register(self.name,"output");
function output() {
  return toOutput;
}

function checkAnswer(form) {
  answer = form.answer.value;
  correctAnswer = test[currentLevel][askedQuestion].answer;
  ask = test[currentLevel][askedQuestion].question;
  score = form.score.value;
  if (eval(answer) == correctAnswer) {
    toOutput = "Correct!";
    score ++;
    form.score.value = score;
  } else {
    toOutput = "Sorry! " + ask + " is " + correctAnswer + ".";
  }
  window.open("display.htm","output");
  if (currentQuestion < 10) {
```

continues

```
      currentQuestion ++;
      askedQuestion = chooseQuestion();
      setTimeout("displayQuestion()",3000);
    } else {
      toOutput = "You're Done!<BR>You're score is " +
➥score + " out of 10.";
      setTimeout("window.open('display.htm','output')",3000);
      form.answer.value="";
      form.score.value="0";
    }
}

function welcome() {
  toOutput = "Welcome!";
  window.open("display.htm","output");
}

asked = new createArray(10);

function createArray(num) {
  for (var j=1; j<=num; j++)
    this[j] = false;
  this.length=num;
}

function clearArray(toClear) {
  for (var j=1; j<=toClear.length; j++)
    toClear[j] = false;
}

function chooseQuestion() {
  choice = (getNumber() % 10) + 1;
  while (asked[choice]) {
    choice = (getNumber() % 10) + 1;
  }
  asked[choice] = true;
  return choice;
}

function getNumber() {
  var time = new Date();
  return time.getSeconds();
}

// STOP HIDING FROM OTHER BROWSERS -->
</SCRIPT>

</HEAD>

<BODY BGCOLOR="#FFFFFF" TEXT="#0000FF" onLoad="welcome();">

<FORM METHOD=POST>
<CENTER>
<STRONG>Type You're Answer Here:</STRONG><BR>
<INPUT TYPE=text NAME=answer SIZE=30><P>
<INPUT TYPE=button NAME=done VALUE="Check Answer"
```

8

```
➥onClick="checkAnswer(this.form);"><P>
Correct Answers So Far:<BR>
<INPUT TYPE=text NAME=score VALUE="0" SIZE=10>
</FORM>

</BODY>

</HTML>
```

You've added four functions to the script, as well as made a few other subtle changes. First, you've added a simple createArray() function that enables you to create the asked array. You use this array to keep track of questions already asked. Each element is set to false until that question is asked.

The clearArray() function takes an array as an argument and simply sets each element to false.

The chooseQuestion() function adds the ability to randomly select a question. The function uses the getNumber() function (which returns the seconds from the current time) to create a pseudo-random number. The while loop keeps selecting numbers until it finds one that has a false entry in the asked array.

Once an available question has been found, the appropriate entry in asked is set to true, and the number of the question is returned.

In addition to these three functions, you have made some other small changes. You have added a global variable called askedQuestion. This variable indicates the index of the question you have asked. currentQuestion becomes the sequential number of the question to be displayed to the user.

In the startTest() function, you add the lines

```
clearArray(asked);
askedQuestion = chooseQuestion();
```

which clear the asked array to false and then select a question.

In displayQuestion(), you have switched to using askedQuestion in place of currentQuestion as an index to the test[currentLevel] object, and in the function checkAnswer(), you have made the same change.

In checkAnswer(), you have also changed the way the function selects the next question:

```
currentQuestion ++;
askedQuestion = chooseQuestion();
setTimeout("displayQuestion()",3000);
```

This simply chooses a random question and then calls displayQuestion().

2. The following frameset and HTML document produce the desired results, as shown in Figure 8.10.

```
<!-- MAIN FRAMESET FILE -->

<HTML>

<HEAD>
<TITLE>Exercise 8.2</TITLE>
</HEAD>

<FRAMESET COLS="25%,*">
  <FRAME SRC="info.htm">
  <FRAME SRC="blank.htm" NAME="display">
</FRAMESET>

</HTML>
```

The HTML document would look like this:

```
<!-- SOURCE CODE FOR info.htm -->

<HTML>

<HEAD>
<SCRIPT LANGUAGE="JavaScript">
<!-- HIDE FROM OTHER BROWSERS

function loadSite(form) {
  var url = form.url.value;
  doc = open(url,"display");
  form.title.value = doc.document.title;
  form.date.value = doc.document.lastModified;
  form.bg.value = doc.document.bgColor;
  form.fg.value = doc.document.fgColor;
  form.link.value = doc.document.linkColor;
  form.alink.value = doc.document.alinkColor;
  form.vlink.value = doc.document.vlinkColor;
}

// STOP HIDING FROM OTHER BROWSERS -->
</SCRIPT>
</HTML>

<BODY>

<FORM METHOD=POST>
URL: <INPUT TYPE=text NAME="url"><P>
<INPUT TYPE=button NAME=load VALUE="Load URL"
➥onClick="loadSite(this.form);"><P>
Title: <INPUT TYPE=text NAME="title"
➥onFocus="this.blur();"><P>
Last Modified: <INPUT TYPE=text NAME="date" onFocus="this.blur();"><P>
Background Color: <INPUT TYPE=text NAME="bg"
➥onFoucs="this.blur();"><P>
```

```
Text Color: <INPUT TYPE=text NAME="fg" onFocus="this.blur();"><P>
Link Color: <INPUT TYPE=text NAME="link" onFocus="this.blur();"><P>
Active Link Color: <INPUT TYPE=text NAME="alink"
➥onFocus="this.blur();"><P>
Followed Link Color: <INPUT TYPE=text NAME="vlink"
➥onFocus="this.blur();">
</FORM>

</BODY>

</HTML>
```

Figure 8.10.

Testing colors on a document selected by the user.

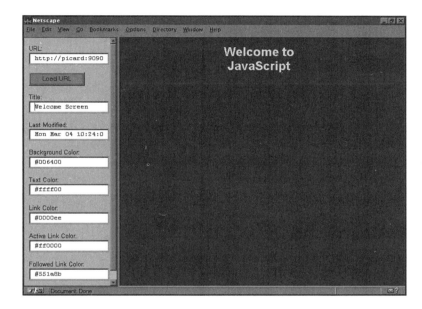

You use one simple function to achieve the desired result: loadSite(). The function loads the specified URL into the display frame using window.open().

Once this is done, you can use the properties of the document object to display the desired information into fields in the HTML form.

In the form in the body of the HTML document, you use the onClick event handler in the button to call the loadSite() function. The display fields for the information about the document all have the event handler onFocus="this.blur();" to make sure the user can't alter the information.

3. This script partially addresses the problem in Listings 8.12 and 8.13—that the help messages remain displayed even after you remove mouse focus from a link or remove focus from a field. This particular script displays a help message when the user gives focus to a field. When focus is removed, either a warning message is displayed or the status bar is cleared.

4. The following script makes the necessary changes to enable the user to specify a
   URL to be displayed in the lower frame:

```
<HTML>

<HEAD>

<SCRIPT LANGUAGE="JavaScript">
<!-- HIDE FORM OTHER BROWSERS

function display(form) {
  parent.output.document.bgColor = form.bg.value;
  parent.output.document.fgColor = form.fg.value;
  parent.output.document.linkClor = form.link.value;
  parent.output.document.alinkColor = form.alink.value;
  parent.output.document.vlinkColor = form.vlink.value;
}

function loadPage(url) {
  var toLoad = url.value;
  if (url.value == "")
    toLoad = "sample.htm";
  open (toLoad,"output");
}

// STOP HIDING SCRIPT -->
</SCRIPT>

</HEAD>

<BODY>

<CENTER>

<SCRIPT LANGUAGE="JavaScript">
<!-- HIDE FROM OTHER BROWSERS

document.write('<H1>The Color Picker</H1>');
document.write('<FORM METHOD=POST>');
document.write('Enter Colors:<BR>');

document.write('Background: <INPUT TYPE=text NAME="bg"
➥VALUE="' + document.bgColor + '"> ... ');
document.write('Text: <INPUT TYPE=text NAME="fg"
➥VALUE="' + document.fgColor + '"><BR>');
document.write('Link: <INPUT TYPE=text NAME="link"
➥VALUE ="' + document.linkColor + '"> ...');
document.write('Active Link: <INPUT TYPE=text NAME="alink"
➥VALUE="' + document.alinkColor + '"><BR>');
document.write('Followed Link: <INPUT TYPE="text" NAME="vlink"
➥VALUE ="' + document.vlinkColor + '"><BR>');
document.write('Test URL: <INPUT TYPE="text" SIZE=40 NAME="url"
➥VALUE="" onChange="loadPage(this);"><BR>');
document.write('<INPUT TYPE=button VALUE="TEST"
➥onClick="display(this.form);">');

document.write('</FORM>');
```

8

```
// STOP HIDING FROM OTHER BROWSERS -->
</SCRIPT>

</CENTER>

</BODY>

</HTML>
```

You have made two simple changes to the script. In addition to the display() function, you have added the loadPage() function, which loads a URL into the lower frame using window.open(). If the user provides no value for the URL, the standard sample file is loaded.

In the form, you have added a text field for the URL with an onChange event handler that calls loadPage(). You also need to change the frameset to load the appropriate sample page into the lower frame:

```
<HTML>

<HEAD>
<TITLE>Exercise 8.4</TITLE>
</HEAD>

<FRAMESET ROWS="45%,*">
  <FRAME SRC="pick.htm">
  <FRAME SRC="sample.htm" NAME="output">
</FRAMESET>

</HTML>
```

From the Web:

Michael Yu's Civic Car Viewer

Michael Yu's Civic Car viewing program provides you with a good example of how to combine frames with JavaScript. It's located at

`http://www-leland.stanford.edu/~guanyuan/public/car/car.html`

The premise behind the program is simple: In one frame, a view of a Honda Civic is displayed. In the other frame, the user has four directional controls to rotate the view in steps in any direction: up, down, left, or right.

In achieving this, Yu has made use of a simple file-naming scheme, the `windows.location` property, and the `frames` array.

The program in Listing W3.1 produces results similar to those in Figures W3.1 and W3.2.

Listing W3.1. Source code for Michael's Civic Car Viewer page.

Parent frameset:

```
<HTML>
<head>
<title> Car View 3D</title>
</head>

<FRAMESET ROWS="18%, 72%, 10%">
     <FRAME SRC="head.html" NAME="head" TARGET="head" SCROLLING="no">

     <FRAMESET COLS="68%, 32%">
        <FRAME NAME="left" SRC="left.html" NORESIZE>
        <FRAME NAME="right" SRC="right.html" NORESIZE>

     </FRAMESET>
     <FRAME SRC="tail.html" NAME="tail" SCROLLING="no">
</FRAMESET>

<noframes>

<h2 align="center">Sorry, Netscape 2.0b3 (Beta 3) required.</h2>

</noframes>

</BODY></HTML>
```

The file `right.html`:

```
<html>
<title>control pad</title>

<BODY BGCOLOR="ffffff" LINK="#0000FF" ALINK="#D9D919" VLINK="#871F78">

<form method="post">

<center>
<br>
<h3> Rotation<br>Control Panel</h3>
<br>
You can use the following control panel to rotate the civic car.
<br>
<div align="center">
<table border=0 cellspacing=0 cellpadding=0>
<tr>
  <td></td>
  <td><input type="button" name="upmiddle" value="U" onclick="up()"></td>
  <td></td>
</tr>
<tr>
  <td><input type="button" name="middleleft" value="L" onclick="left()"></td>
  <td></td>
  <td><input type="button" name="middleright" value="R" onclick="right()"></td>
</tr>
<tr>
```

```
    <td></td>
    <td><input type="button" name="downmiddle" value="D" onclick="down()">
    <td></td>
</tr>
</table>
</div>
<br>
<a href="http://www-leland.stanford.edu/~guanyuan/michael.html" target="_top">
<img src="cycleimages.gif">
</a>

</center>

</form>

<script language="LiveScript">
  var ud=0;
  var lr=0;
  var chars="012345678";

function up(){
  getcar(1,0);
  return 0;
}

function down(){
  getcar(-1,0);
  return 0;
}

function left(){
  getcar(0,1);
  return 0;
}

function right(){
 getcar(0,-1);
  return 0;
}

function getcar( myud, mylr){

   ud=ud+myud;
   lr=lr+mylr;
   if (lr == 8) { lr=0;};
   if (lr == -1) { lr=7;};
   if (ud == 3) { ud=1; lr=4+lr;};
   if (ud == -1) { ud=1; lr=lr+4;};
   if (lr > 7) { lr=lr-8;};


   parent.frames[1].location="http://www-leland.stanford.edu/~guanyuan/public/
➥car/car"+chars.substring(ud,ud+1)+ "_"+chars.substring(lr,lr+1)+".html";
    return 0;
}
```

continues

Listing W3.1. continued

```
  </script>

  </body>
  </html>
```

OUTPUT The Civic Car Viewer uses two main working frames across the center of the window: The car is displayed on the left, and the rotation controls are in the right hand frame.

Figure W3.1.

Michael's Civic Car Viewer provides interactivity between frames.

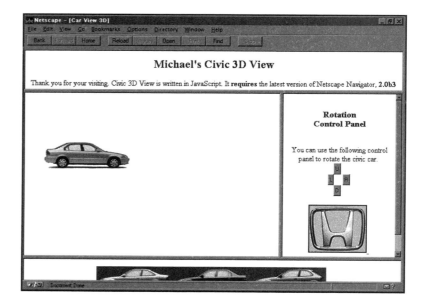

ANALYSIS Although the Civic Car Viewer may seem simple at first glance, it provides a good example of how to build easy-to-use programs using multiple frames. It is interesting to note that the program does not follow Netscape's recommendation of placing function definitions in the header of the HTML file. This means it is possible that a user could press one of the four buttons before a function has been evaluated.

All the image files are named carA_B.html where A and B are integers. A represents the up-down axis and can have values from 1 to 3, and B represents the left-right axis and can have values from 0 to 7.

The script uses three global variables:

```
var ud=0;
var lr=0;
var chars="012345678";
```

ud and lr are used to keep track of the current viewing angle of the car. The variable chars is used to build the URL for a new view, as you will see later.

Figure W3.2.

The user selects a rotation control on the right, and the image on the left updates.

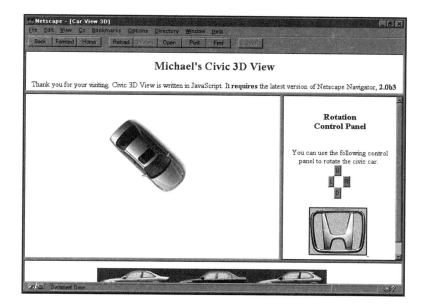

The primary function is getcar(). This function accepts two arguments myud and mylr, which represent changes to the values of ud and lr:

```
ud=ud+myud;
lr=lr+mylr;
```

Once the changes to the values are made, a series of if statements check whether the new value is outside the acceptable range for each variable; if it is, the command block of the if statement wraps the value around to the other end of the range. For instance, if lr is 8, it becomes 0:

```
if (lr == 8) { lr=0;};
if (lr == -1) { lr=7;};
if (ud == 3) { ud=1; lr=4+lr;};
if (ud == -1) { ud=1; lr=lr+4;};
if (lr > 7) { lr=lr-8;};
```

Once this has been done, the function is ready to open the new view in the left frame using

```
parent.frames[1].location=
➥"http://www-leland.stanford.edu/~guanyuan/public/car/car"
➥+chars.substring(ud,ud+1)+"_"+chars.substring(lr,lr+1)+".html";
```

The command uses parent to look at the parent frameset and the frames array to explicitly choose the desired frame. It then sets the location property to the new URL.

TIP

> An easy way to load a new page in a window or frame is to set the `location` property. This automatically causes the new URL to load into the window or frame.

NOTE

> Because the left frame is named, the script could just as easily have used the form `parent.left.location`.

The actual filename is built with the portion of the URL expression which reads:

```
car"+chars.substring(ud,ud+1)+"_"+chars.substring(lr,lr+1)+".html"
```

The `substring()` method is used to select single digits from the `chars` variable based on the values of `ud` and `lr`, respectively.

Each of the four buttons in the form calls one of four functions: `up()`, `down()`, `left()`, or `right()`. These functions all work in the same way. They call `getcar()` with appropriate arguments based on the direction, and then they return a value `0`. The value returned by the function is incidental because the value is never used anywhere in the script.

Michael Yu's Civic Car Viewer is a concrete example of how combining frames and JavaScript makes it possible to create interactive applications. By taking advantage of frames to build sophisticated interfaces and combining that with JavaScript's ability to generate dynamic URLs, it is possible to extend the simple Web metaphor into something more diverse and powerful.

DAY 5

Chapter 9

Remember Where You've Been with Cookies

One of the challenges of writing applications for the World Wide Web has been the inability of the Web to maintain *state*. That is, after a user sends a request to the server and a Web page is returned, the server forgets all about the user and the page she has just downloaded.

If the user clicks on a link, the server doesn't have background information about what page the user is coming from and, more importantly, if the user returns to the page at a later date, there is no information available to the server about the user's previous actions on the page.

Maintaining state can be important to developing complex interactive applications. Several sites work around this problem using complex server-end CGI scripts. However, Navigator 2.0 addresses the problem with *cookies*: a method of storing information locally in the browser and sending it to the server whenever the appropriate pages are requested by the user.

JavaScript provides the capability to work with client-side state information stored as cookies.

In addition to cookies, JavaScript offers the navigator object, which provides information about the version of the browser a user has and, in the future, will likely include methods to customize the browser.

The information available in the navigator object can be useful for a number of purposes, including ensuring that users are using a version of the browser that supports all the features of a script.

In this chapter, we take a detailed look at using cookies in the JavaScript applications as well as how to use the navigator object, including

- [ ] What cookies are
- [ ] Examples of using cookies
- [ ] Cookies and CGI
- [ ] Using cookies in JavaScript
- [ ] Information provided by the navigator object

What Are Cookies?

Cookies provide a method to store information at the client side and have the browser provide that information to the server along with a page request.

NOTE The term *cookies* has no special significance. It is just a name in the same way Java is just a name for Sun's object-oriented programming language.

In order to understand how the mechanism works, it is important to have a basic understanding of how servers and clients communicate on the World Wide Web using the *hypertext transfer protocol* (HTTP).

HTTP and How It Works

The hypertext transfer protocol is fairly simple. When a user requests a page, an HTTP request is sent to the server. The request includes a header that defines several pieces of information, including the page being requested.

The server returns an HTTP response that also includes a header. The header contains information about the document being returned, including its MIME type (such as text/html for a standard HTML page or image/gif for a GIF file).

These headers all contain one or more fields of information in a basic format:

```
Field-name: Information
```

Cookies and HTTP Headers

Cookie information is shared between the client browser and a server using fields in the HTTP headers. The way it works is fairly simple—in theory.

When the user requests a page for the first time, a cookie (or more than one cookie) can be stored in the browser by a Set-Cookie entry in the header of the response from the server. The Set-Cookie field includes the information to be stored in the cookie along with several optional pieces of information, including an expiry date, path, and server information, and if the cookie requires security.

Then, when the user requests a page in the future, if a matching cookie is found among all the stored cookies, the browser sends a Cookie field to the server in a request header. The header will contain the information stored in that cookie.

Cookie **and** Set-Cookie

The Set-Cookie and Cookie fields use a fairly simple syntax to transfer significant information between the client and server.

Set-Cookie takes the form:

```
Set-Cookie: name=VALUE; expires=DATE; path=PATH; domain=DOMAIN; secure
```

The name=VALUE entry is the only required piece of information that must be included in the Set-Cookie field. This is simply a string of characters defining information to be stored in the cookie for later transmission back to the server. The string cannot contain semicolons, commas, or spaces.

All the other entries in the Set-Cookie field are optional and are outlined in Table 9.1.

Table 9.1. Optional attributes for Set-Cookie.

Name	Description
expires=DATE	Specifies the expiry date of a cookie. After this date the cookie will no longer be stored by the client or sent to the server (DATE takes the form Wdy, DD-Mon-YY HH:MM:SS GMT—dates are only stored in Greenwich Mean Time). By default, the value of expires is set to the end of the current Navigator session.

continues

Table 9.1. continued

Name	Description
path=*PATH*	Specifies the path portion of URLs for which the cookie is valid. If the URL matches both the path and domain, then the cookie is sent to the server in the request header. (If left unset, the value of path is the same as the document that set the cookie).
domain=*DOMAIN*	Specifies the domain portion of URLs for which the cookie is valid. The default value for this attribute is the domain of the current document setting the cookie.
secure	Specifies that the cookie should only be transmitted over a secure link (i.e. to HTTP servers using the SSL protocol—known as HTTPS servers).

By comparison, the Cookie field in a request header contains only a set of name-value pairs for the requested URL:

```
Cookie: name1=VALUE1; name=VALUE2 ...
```

It is important to realize that multiple Set-Cookie fields can be sent in a single response header from the server.

NOTE

A cookie that has the same path and name as an existing cookie will overwrite the old one—this can be used as a way of erasing cookies—by writing a new one with an expiry date that has already passed.

There are some limitations on the use of cookies. Navigator 2.0 will store only 300 cookies in total. Within that 300, each cookie is limited to four kilobytes in length, including all the optional attributes, and only 20 cookies will be stored for each domain. When the number of cookies is exceeded, the browser will delete the least recently used and when the length of a cookie is too long, the cookie is trimmed to fit.

Examples of How Cookies Are Used

There are several ways that cookies can be used to enhance interactive applications.

For instance, there are sites using cookies to implement shopping carts. That is, a user traverses multiple pages at a site and selects items he wants to buy. The selections are stored in cookies until a JavaScript script or CGI script is executed to total up the purchases.

Other applications that could use cookies include

- Reminder calendars that use cookies to store appointments and other messages.
- Country tours that users can take during several visits to a Web site—cookies are used to remember where the user left off.
- Adventure games that use cookies to keep track of pertinent character data and the current state of the game.

Cookies and CGI Scripts

In order for cookies to be useful, it is necessary for the server to be able to take advantage of the cookie information it receives and for the server to be able to generate cookie headers if they are needed.

This is primarily done by using CGI scripts.

For instance, if you want to provide a custom search tool that would search World Wide Web indexes selected by the user, you would need to develop a system that follows this basic pattern:

1. User calls the site by using an URL that requests a CGI script.
2. The script checks whether it is the user's first time at the site by checking whether there is a `Cookie` field in the HTTP request header.
3. If there is no cookie, the script sends back a new search page with all choices unselected and an empty search field.
4. If there is a `Cookie` field, the script interprets the cookie and returns a page with all the user's previous choices selected.
5. When the user conducts a search, the script returns the search results along with a `Set-Cookie` field in the header to reset the cookie to the newly selected values that the user used for the search.

This type of application could produce results similar to Figures 9.1 and 9.2.

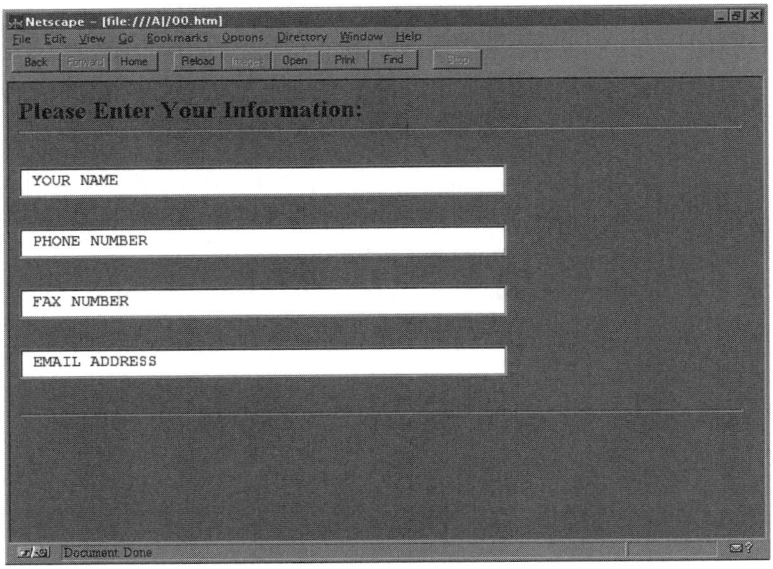

Figure 9.1.

If the user has never visited the URL, a page with a new form is sent to the user.

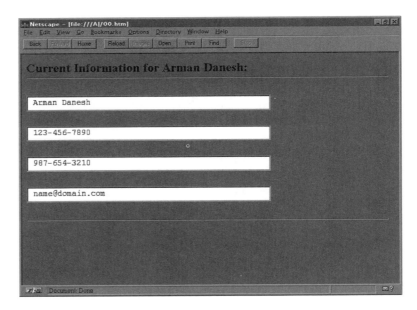

Figure 9.2.

On subsequent visits, the user receives a page in the same state as he or she last left it.

To implement this type of server-side processing for cookies may require significant increases in the load on a Web server. With this model, most pages are being built dynamically based on receiving cookie information in the header.

9

This is in contrast to typical Web pages, which are static and all the server needs to do is send the correct file to the client without any additional processing.

Using Cookies in JavaScript

In JavaScript, however, cookies become available for processing by the *client*.

JavaScript makes the `cookie` property of the `document` object available for processing. The `cookie` property exposes all the attributes of cookies for the page to the script and enables the script to set new cookies. In this way much, if not all, of the server-end processing that would be done to take advantage of cookies can now be done by the client in a JavaScript script.

The `cookie` property simply contains a string with the value that would be sent out in a `Cookie` field for that page.

As a string, it can be manipulated like any other string literal or variable using the methods and properties of the `string` object.

NOTE

> In Chapter 10, "Strings, Math, and the History List," we will take a detailed look at the `string` object and all of its methods and properties.

By assigning values to `document.cookie`, it is possible to create new cookies. The value of the string assigned to the `cookie` property should be the same as what would be sent by the server in the `Set-Cookie` header field.

For instance, if you create two cookies named `cookie1` and `cookie2` as follows:

```
document.cookie = "cookie1=First_cookie";
document.cookie = "cookie2=Second_cookie";
```

then `document.write(document.cookie)` would produce output that looks like this:

```
cookie1=First_cookie; cookie2=Second_cookie
```

If you want to set optional properties such as the expiry date or path, you can use a command like:

```
document.cookie = 'cookie1=First_cookie;
➥expires=Mon, 01-Jul-95 12:00:00 GMT; path="/"';
```

This would create a cookie named `cookie1` that expires at noon on 1 July 1995 and is valid for all documents in the default domain because the path is set to the top-level directory for the domain.

Of course, times are likely to be set using offsets from the current time. For instance, you may want an expiry date one day or one year from the current date. You can use the methods of the Date object to achieve this:

```
expires = new Date();
expires.setTime (expires.getTime() + 24 * 60 * 60 * 365 * 1000);
document.cookie = "cookie2=Second_cookie; expires=" + expires.toGMTString();
```

These commands use the Date object to set a time one year after today by adding 24×60×60×365×1000 (the number of milliseconds in one year) to the current date and time. You can then use expires.toGMTString() to return the date string in GMT time as required by the cookie.

NOTE

setTime(), getTime(), and toGMTString() are methods of the Date() object, which is discussed in more detail later in this chapter.

Storing User Choices in Cookies

In this example, you are going to use cookies to expand the functionality of the script you created in Exercise 8.4 in the previous chapter.

In Exercise 8.4, you extended the simple color testing application to include the capability for the user to select a URL to test the colors.

In this example you further extend the script so that if a user has entered a URL, it is stored in a cookie, as are the colors. The next time the user returns to the page, the URL is recalled, loaded, and displayed with the stored colors. The expiry date for a cookie should be 30 days from the current date.

In order to achieve this, you need to do several things. You need to save the colors and URLs as cookies whenever they are changed. You also need a function that can decode the cookie when the page is loaded for the first time.

Listing 9.1 includes these additions.

 TYPE   **Listing 9.1. Keeping track of the user's color choices.**

```
<HTML>

<HEAD>

<SCRIPT LANGUAGE="JavaScript">
<!-- HIDE FORM OTHER BROWSERS
```

```
    var expires = new Date();
    expires.setTime (expires.getTime() + 24 * 60 * 60 * 30 * 1000);
    var expiryDate = expires.toGMTString();

    function display(form) {
      parent.output.document.bgColor = form.bg.value;
      parent.output.document.fgColor = form.fg.value;
      parent.output.document.linkClor = form.link.value;
      parent.output.document.alinkColor = form.alink.value;
      parent.output.document.vlinkColor = form.vlink.value;
    }

    function loadPage(url) {
      var toLoad = url.value;
      if (url.value == "")
        toLoad = "sample.htm";
      open (toLoad,"output");
    }

    function newCookie(name,value) {
      document.cookie = name + "=" + value + "; expires=" + expiryDate;
    }

    function getCookie(name) {
      var cookieFound = false;
      var start = 0;
      var end = 0;
      var cookieString = document.cookie;

      var i = 0;

      // SCAN THE COOKIE FOR name
      while (i <= cookieString.length) {
        start = i;
        end = start + name.length;
        if (cookieString.substring(start,end) == name) {
          cookieFound = true;
          break;
        }
        i++;
      }

      // IS name FOUND?
      if (cookieFound) {
        start = end + 1;
        end = document.cookie.indexOf(";",start);
        if (end < start)
          end = document.cookie.length;
        return document.cookie.substring(start,end);
      }
      return "";
    }

    // STOP HIDING SCRIPT -->
    </SCRIPT>
```

continues

Listing 9.1. continued

```
</HEAD>

<BODY onLoad="loadPage(document.forms[0].url); display(document.forms[0]);">

<CENTER>

<SCRIPT LANGUAGE="JavaScript">
<!-- HIDE FROM OTHER BROWSERS

document.write('<H1>The Color Picker</H1>');
document.write('<FORM METHOD=POST>');
document.write('Enter Colors:<BR>');

var thisCookie = ((document.cookie != "") && (document.cookie != null));

var bg = (thisCookie) ? getCookie("bg") : document.bgColor;
var fg = (thisCookie) ? getCookie("fg") : document.fgColor;
var link = (thisCookie) ? getCookie("link") : document.linkColor;
var alink = (thisCookie) ? getCookie("alink") : document.alinkColor;
var vlink = (thisCookie) ? getCookie("vlink") : document.vlinkColor;
var url = (thisCookie) ? getCookie("url") : "sample.htm";

document.write('Background: <INPUT TYPE=text NAME="bg" VALUE="' + bg + '"
➥onChange="newCookie(this.name,this.value);"> ... ');
document.write('Text: <INPUT TYPE=text NAME="fg" VALUE="' + fg + '"
➥onChange="newCookie(this.name,this.value);"><BR>');
document.write('Link: <INPUT TYPE=text NAME="link" VALUE ="' + link + '"
➥onChange="newCookie(this.name,this.value);"> ...');
document.write('Active Link: <INPUT TYPE=text NAME="alink" VALUE="' + alink + '"
➥onChange="newCookie(this.name,this.value);"><BR>');
document.write('Followed Link: <INPUT TYPE="text" NAME="vlink" VALUE ="' + vlink
➥+ '" onChange="newCookie(this.name,this.value);"><BR>');
document.write('Test URL: <INPUT TYPE="text" SIZE=40 NAME="url" VALUE="' + url +
➥'" onChange="newCookie(this.name,this.value); loadPage(this);"><BR>');
document.write('<INPUT TYPE=button VALUE="TEST"
➥onClick="display(this.form);">');

document.write('</FORM>');

// STOP HIDING FROM OTHER BROWSERS -->
</SCRIPT>

</CENTER>

</BODY>

</HTML>
```

ANALYSIS   In order to use cookies to store the current state for the color tester application, you have to add two new functions (newCookie() and getCookie()) to the header, as well as alter the script that dynamically generates the HTML form in the upper frame. The other two functions remain unchanged.

The `newCookie()` Function

The `newCookie()` function is the simpler of the two new functions. It stores a cookie given a name and value as arguments. The `expiryDate` variable is a global variable created by taking the current date, adding 30 days, and then converting it to a string in Greenwich Mean Time using `toGMTString()`:

```
var expires = new Date();
expires.setTime (expires.getTime() + 24 * 60 * 60 * 30 * 1000);
var expiryDate = expires.toGMTString();
```

The `getCookie()` Function

The `getCookie()` function is designed to return a particular cookie value. What makes this somewhat complicated is that `document.cookie` contains a string of name-value pairs separated by a semicolon followed by a space.

In order to find the particular value you want and return it, you need to do some relatively sophisticated processing on the `document.cookie` string.

```
function getCookie(name) {
  var cookieFound = false;
  var start = 0;
  var end = 0;
  var cookieString = document.cookie;
```

You start by declaring the variables. `cookieFound` is a Boolean variable, which you use to keep track of whether a name-value pair matching the argument has been found. `start` and `end` are used to hold indexes for the `substring()` function and `cookieString` holds the value of `document.cookie` simply because it is a little easier to read—it's my personal preference.

```
  var i = 0;

  // SCAN THE COOKIE FOR name
  while (i <= cookieString.length) {
    start = i;
    end = start + name.length;
    if (cookieString.substring(start,end) == name) {
      cookieFound = true;
      break;
    }
    i++;
  }
```

This loop is fairly simple. You use `i` as the counter and simply loop through `cookieString` character by character and check the `substring` starting at `i` that is the length of the name you're looking for. If there is a match, you set `cookieFound` to `true` and break out of the loop.

```
// IS name FOUND?
  if (cookieFound) {
    start = end + 1;
```

```
    end = document.cookie.indexOf(";",start);
    if (end < start)
      end = document.cookie.length;
    return document.cookie.substring(start,end);
  }
```

If you've found a cookie that matches the name you are looking for, then you set `start` to the value of `end + 1`—this means you are starting after the equal sign that follows the name. Next you use `indexOf()` to look for the semicolon that may be ending the cookie (unless it is the last cookie in the string). You store the value in `end`.

We will see more of the `string.indexOf()` method in Chapter 10 when we discuss the `string` object in more detail. The method takes two arguments: `indexOf(string,startIndex)` and starts searching for *string* from the index *startIndex*. The value returned is the index where *string* first occurs. If `indexOf()` doesn't find the character it is looking for, it returns a value of zero.

Once you have a value for `end`, you check if a semicolon was found. If not, you know the name-value pair is the last in the list and you can set `end` to the last character in `cookieString`, which is the value of `cookieString.length`.

Finally, you return the substring indicated by `start` and `end`.

```
  return "";
}
```

If you haven't found a cookie, you simply return an empty string.

The Body of the Document

All of the HTML output is done from a JavaScript script in the body of the document.

```
<BODY onLoad="loadPage(document.forms[0].url); display(document.forms[0]);">

<CENTER>

<SCRIPT LANGUAGE="JavaScript">
<!-- HIDE FROM OTHER BROWSERS

document.write('<H1>The Color Picker</H1>');
document.write('<FORM METHOD=POST>');
document.write('Enter Colors:<BR>');
```

Here you output the title and set up the form.

```
var thisCookie = ((document.cookie != "") && (document.cookie != null));

var bg = (thisCookie) ? getCookie("bg") : document.bgColor;
var fg = (thisCookie) ? getCookie("fg") : document.fgColor;
var link = (thisCookie) ? getCookie("link") : document.linkColor;
var alink = (thisCookie) ? getCookie("alink") : document.alinkColor;
var vlink = (thisCookie) ? getCookie("vlink") : document.vlinkColor;
var url = (thisCookie) ? getCookie("url") : "sample.htm";
```

The form elements are built dynamically so that the contents of each field match any existing cookies. If there is no cookie, then the contents of the color fields will match the defaults for the browser.

You do this by checking whether the cookie exists and then using conditional expressions to assign values to several variables, that will be used later to build the actual form elements. If cookies exist, you get the values by calling getCookie(). If not, you use the appropriate color properties of the document object, except in the case of url which you assign to a default URL.

```
document.write('Background: <INPUT TYPE=text NAME="bg" VALUE="' + bg + '"
➥onChange="newCookie(this.name,this.value);"> ... ')
document.write('Text: <INPUT TYPE=text NAME="fg" VALUE="' + fg + '"
➥onChange="newCookie(this.name,this.value);"><BR>');
document.write('Link: <INPUT TYPE=text NAME="link" VALUE ="' + link + '"
➥onChange="newCookie(this.name,this.value);"> ...');
document.write('Active Link: <INPUT TYPE=text NAME="alink" VALUE="' + alink + '"
➥onChange="newCookie(this.name,this.value);"><BR>');
document.write('Followed Link: <INPUT TYPE="text" NAME="vlink" VALUE ="' + vlink
➥+ '" onChange="newCookie(this.name,this.value);"><BR>');
document.write('Test URL: <INPUT TYPE="text" SIZE=40 NAME="url" VALUE="' + url +
➥'" onChange="newCookie(this.name,this.value); loadPage(this);"><BR>');
document.write('<INPUT TYPE=button VALUE="TEST"
➥onClick="display(this.form);">');
```

Once you have calculated the initial values for the form fields, you use document.write() to output the HTML for each field. In each text entry field you use onChange to store a new cookie when the user changes the value of the field. The button calls display() on a click event.

Encoding Cookies

As I mentioned earlier, the information stored in the name-value pair of a cookie cannot contain any spaces. This poses something of a limitation because many applications will need to store complete phrases or strings containing spaces in cookies.

The solution to this lies in encoding the illegal characters in a cookie. Netscape suggests using an encoding scheme such as that used in URL strings.

However, any coding scheme will work. For instance, alternative characters such as % or + could be used for spaces and a similar approach could be taken for other illegal characters, such as semicolons.

Any script that is going to build cookies using white spaces and other illegal characters, or that is going to read similar cookies, will need to include methods for dealing with these characters.

JavaScript provides the escape() and unescape() methods, which take a string as an argument. escape() returns the string encoded like an URL and unescape() translates it back from this encoding.

An easier recipe for cookies.

It should be clear now that some type of standardized method for creating new
cookies, reading existing cookies, and encoding cookies would make writing scripts
much easier.

Just as he wrote the hIdaho Frameset, Bill Dortch has developed a set of freely
available functions to perform all these tasks. The functions are available at `http://`
`www.hidaho.com/cookies/cookie.txt`.

The source code is reproduced on the CD-ROM:

```
<script language="javascript">
<!-- begin script
//
//  Cookie Functions - Second Helping  (21-Jan-96)
//  Written by:  Bill Dortch, hIdaho Design <bdortch@netw.com>
//  The following functions are released to the public domain.
//
//  The Second Helping version of the cookie functions dispenses with
//  my encode and decode functions, in
➥favor of JavaScript's new built-in
//  escape and unescape functions,
➥which do more complete encoding, and
//  which are probably much faster.
//
//  The new version also extends the SetCookie function, though in
//  a backward-compatible manner, so if you used the First Helping of
//  cookie functions as they were written,
➥you will not need to change any
//  code, unless you want to take advantage of the new capabilities.
//
//  The following changes were made to SetCookie:
//
//  1.  The expires parameter is now optional - that is, you can omit
//      it instead of passing it null to expire the cookie at the end
//      of the current session.
//
//  2.  An optional path parameter has been added.
//
//  3.  An optional domain parameter has been added.
//
//  4.  An optional secure parameter has been added.
//
//  For information on the significance of these parameters, and
//  and on cookies in general, please refer to the official cookie
//  spec, at:
//
//      http://www.netscape.com/newsref/std/cookie_spec.html
//
//
// "Internal" function to return the decoded value of a cookie
//
```

9

```
function getCookieVal (offset) {
  var endstr = document.cookie.indexOf (";", offset);
  if (endstr == -1)
    endstr = document.cookie.length;
  return unescape(document.cookie.substring(offset, endstr));
}


//
//  Function to return the value of the cookie specified by "name".
//    name - String object containing the cookie name.
//    returns - String object containing the cookie value, or null if
//      the cookie does not exist.
//
function GetCookie (name) {
  var arg = name + "=";
  var alen = arg.length;
  var clen = document.cookie.length;
  var i = 0;
  while (i < clen) {
    var j = i + alen;
    if (document.cookie.substring(i, j) == arg)
      return getCookieVal (j);
    i = document.cookie.indexOf(" ", i) + 1;
    if (i == 0) break;
  }
  return null;
}


//
//  Function to create or update a cookie.
//    name - String object object containing the cookie name.
//    value - String object containing the cookie value.  May contain
//      any valid string characters.
//    [expires] - Date object containing the
➥expiration data of the cookie.  If
//      omitted or null, expires the cookie
➥at the end of the current session.
//    [path] - String object indicating the path
➥for which the cookie is valid.
//      If omitted or null, uses the path of the calling document.
//    [domain] - String object indicating
➥the domain for which the cookie is
//      valid.  If omitted or null,
➥uses the domain of the calling document.
//    [secure] - Boolean (true/false) value
➥Indicating whether cookie transmission
//      requires a secure channel (HTTPS).
//
//  The first two parameters are required.
➥The others, if supplied, must
//  be passed in the order listed above.
➥To omit an unused optional field,
//  use null as a place holder.
➥For example, to call SetCookie using name,
```

9

```
//   value and path, you would code:
//
//       SetCookie ("myCookieName", "myCookieValue", null, "/");
//
//   Note that trailing omitted parameters
➥do not require a placeholder.
//
//   To set a secure cookie for path "/myPath", that expires after the
//   current session, you might code:
//
//       SetCookie (myCookieVar, cookieValueVar, null,
➥"/myPath", null, true);
//
function SetCookie (name, value) {
  var argv = SetCookie.arguments;
  var argc = SetCookie.arguments.length;
  var expires = (argc > 2) ? argv[2] : null;
  var path = (argc > 3) ? argv[3] : null;
  var domain = (argc > 4) ? argv[4] : null;
  var secure = (argc > 5) ? argv[5] : false;
  document.cookie = name + "=" + escape (value) +
    ((expires == null) ? "" :
➥("; expires=" + expires.toGMTString())) +
((path == null) ? "" : ("; path=" + path)) +
    ((domain == null) ? "" : ("; domain=" + domain)) +
    ((secure == true) ? "; secure" : "");
}

//   Function to delete a cookie.
➥(Sets expiration date to current date/time)
//     name - String object containing the cookie name
//
function DeleteCookie (name) {
  var exp = new Date();
  exp.setTime (exp.getTime() - 1);  // This cookie is history
  var cval = GetCookie (name);
  document.cookie = name + "=" + cval + ";
➥expires=" + exp.toGMTString();
}

// end script -->
</script>
```

The source code should be included in the header of any document that includes
scripts that work with cookies.

Although Dortch has done a good job of documenting each of the functions in the
comments of the source code, we will run through them all in the next few sections.

The getCookieVal() function.

This function is an internal function called by GetCookie(). Given the index of the
first character of the value of a name-value pair in a cookie, it returns the value as
an unencoded string.

9

The function uses the unescape method to decode the value.

The GetCookie() function.

The getCookie() function is used to retrieve the value of a particular cookie. It takes the name of the cookie as an argument and returns the value. If the cookie doesn't exist, the function returns a null value.

The SetCookie() function.

This function can be used to create a new cookie or to update an existing cookie. The function requires two arguments and can take several optional arguments:

```
setCookie(name,value,expires,path,domain,secure)
```

where expires, path, domain, and secure are optional parameters, and name and value are required. name, value, path, and domain should be strings. expires should be passed as a Date object and secure should be a Boolean value.

The order of the arguments is important, so if you want to leave out a particular value in the middle of the order, you should pass the null value as a placeholder.

The DeleteCookie() function.

This function does just what the name suggests: deletes the cookies specified by a name argument. The cookie is deleted by updating it with an expiry date equal to the current date and time.

Building a News Search Page

You are now going to use cookies to develop a more sophisticated application.

Most users of the World Wide Web are well aware that the Web can be a great source of the latest news. However, finding just the right news can be a little daunting. The process can take loading a variety of news providers' Web pages to get all the information you want.

Using a combination of cookies and frames, you are going to build an application that provides news from multiple sources in one browser window.

The concept is simple: The screen is divided into two main sections—the left side contains a form for manipulating the application, and the right side contains three frames displaying the news sources selected by the user.

In the control frame, users should be provided with three drop-down selection lists to enable them to select the news sources for each of the three frames on the right. In addition, users should be able to add news sources to the list, as well as delete sources from the list.

Cookies are used to store the list of news sources, as well as the currently selected sources for each frame.

The application is created using scripts in two files: the top-level frameset called news.htm (see Listing 9.2) and the main control file that you will call control.htm (see Listing 9.3). The file wait.htm is a placeholder that is displayed when the three news source frames on the right side are first created (see Listing 9.4).

TYPE   **Listing 9.2. The parent frameset (news.htm).**

```
<!-- SOURCE CODE FOR TOP-LEVEL FRAMESET -->
<HTML>

<HEAD>
<TITLE>Example 9.2</TITLE>

<SCRIPT LANGUAGE="JavaScript">
<!-- HIDE FROM OTHER BROWSERS
//
//   WE NEED TO INCLUDE THE COOKIE FUNCTIONS
//
//
//   Cookie Functions - Second Helping  (21-Jan-96)
//   Written by:  Bill Dortch, hIdaho Design <bdortch@netw.com>
//   The following functions are released to the public domain.
//

// "Internal" function to return the decoded value of a cookie
//
function getCookieVal (offset) {
  var endstr = document.cookie.indexOf (";", offset);
  if (endstr == -1)
    endstr = document.cookie.length;
  return unescape(document.cookie.substring(offset, endstr));
}

//
//   Function to return the value of the cookie specified by "name".
//
function GetCookie (name) {
  var arg = name + "=";
  var alen = arg.length;
  var clen = document.cookie.length;
  var i = 0;
  while (i < clen) {
    var j = i + alen;
    if (document.cookie.substring(i, j) == arg)
      return getCookieVal (j);
    i = document.cookie.indexOf(" ", i) + 1;
    if (i == 0) break;
  }
  return null;
}
```

9

```
//
//   Function to create or update a cookie.
//
function SetCookie (name, value) {
  var argv = SetCookie.arguments;
  var argc = SetCookie.arguments.length;
  var expires = (argc > 2) ? argv[2] : null;
  var path = (argc > 3) ? argv[3] : null;
  var domain = (argc > 4) ? argv[4] : null;
  var secure = (argc > 5) ? argv[5] : false;
  document.cookie = name + "=" + escape (value) +
    ((expires == null) ? "" : ("; expires=" + expires.toGMTString())) +
    ((path == null) ? "" : ("; path=" + path)) +
    ((domain == null) ? "" : ("; domain=" + domain)) +
    ((secure == true) ? "; secure" : "");
}

//   Function to delete a cookie. (Sets expiration date to current date/time)
//
function DeleteCookie (name) {
  var exp = new Date();
  exp.setTime (exp.getTime() - 1);  // This cookie is history
  var cval = GetCookie (name);
  document.cookie = name + "=" + cval + "; expires=" + exp.toGMTString();
}

//
//   END OF THE COOKIE FUNCTIONS. OUR SCRIPT STARTS HERE.
//

function getURL(frame) {
  var name = GetCookie(frame);
  return GetCookie(name);
}

function initialize() {
  if (GetCookie("sites") == null) {
    var expiryDate = new Date();
    expiryDate.setTime(expiryDate.getTime() + (365 * 24 * 60 * 60 * 1000));
    SetCookie("sites","CNN,USA-Today,Yahoo",expiryDate,"/");
    SetCookie("CNN","http://www.cnn.com/",expiryDate,"/");
    SetCookie("USA-Today","http://www.usatoday.com/",expiryDate,"/");

    SetCookie("Yahoo","http://www.yahoo.com/headlines/news/",expiryDate,"/");
    SetCookie("frameOne","CNN",expiryDate,"/");
    SetCookie("frameTwo","USA-Today",expiryDate,"/");
    SetCookie("frameThree","Yahoo",expiryDate,"/");
    SetCookie("number","3",expiryDate,"/");
  }
}


initialize();
```

continues

Listing 9.2. continued

```
var frameOne = getURL("frameOne");
var frameTwo = getURL("frameTwo");
var frameThree = getURL("frameThree");

// STOP HIDING HERE -->
</script>

</HEAD>

<FRAMESET COLS="35%,*" onLoad="parent.frames['frameOne'].location=frameOne;
➥parent.frames['frameTwo'].location=frameTwo;
➥parent.frames['frameThree'].location=frameThree;">
  <FRAME SRC="control.htm" NAME="control">
  <FRAMESET ROWS="33%,33%,*">
    <FRAME SRC="wait.htm" NAME="frameOne">
    <FRAME SRC="wait.htm" NAME="frameTwo">
    <FRAME SRC="wait.htm" NAME="frameThree">
  </FRAMESET>
</FRAMESET>


</HTML>
```

TYPE **Listing 9.3. The source code for** `control.htm.`

```
<!-- SOURCE CODE FOR control.htm -->
<HTML>

<HEAD>
<TITLE>Example 9.3</TITLE>

<SCRIPT LANGUAGE="JavaScript">
<!-- HIDE FROM OTHER BROWSERS
//
//   WE NEED TO INCLUDE THE COOKIE FUNCTIONS
//
//
//   Cookie Functions - Second Helping  (21-Jan-96)
//   Written by:  Bill Dortch, hIdaho Design <bdortch@netw.com>
//   The following functions are released to the public domain.
//

// "Internal" function to return the decoded value of a cookie
//
function getCookieVal (offset) {
  var endstr = document.cookie.indexOf (";", offset);
  if (endstr == -1)
    endstr = document.cookie.length;
  return unescape(document.cookie.substring(offset, endstr));
}
```

9

```
//
//   Function to return the value of the cookie specified by "name".
//
function GetCookie (name) {
  var arg = name + "=";
  var alen = arg.length;
  var clen = document.cookie.length;
  var i = 0;
  while (i < clen) {
    var j = i + alen;
    if (document.cookie.substring(i, j) == arg)
      return getCookieVal (j);
    i = document.cookie.indexOf(" ", i) + 1;
    if (i == 0) break;
  }
  return null;
}

//
//   Function to create or update a cookie.
//
function SetCookie (name, value) {
  var argv = SetCookie.arguments;
  var argc = SetCookie.arguments.length;
  var expires = (argc > 2) ? argv[2] : null;
  var path = (argc > 3) ? argv[3] : null;
  var domain = (argc > 4) ? argv[4] : null;
  var secure = (argc > 5) ? argv[5] : false;
  document.cookie = name + "=" + escape (value) +
    ((expires == null) ? "" : ("; expires=" + expires.toGMTString())) +
    ((path == null) ? "" : ("; path=" + path)) +
    ((domain == null) ? "" : ("; domain=" + domain)) +
    ((secure == true) ? "; secure" : "");
}

//   Function to delete a cookie. (Sets expiration date to current date/time)
//
function DeleteCookie (name) {
  var exp = new Date();
  exp.setTime (exp.getTime() - 1);  // This cookie is history
  var cval = GetCookie (name);
  document.cookie = name + "=" + cval + "; expires=" + exp.toGMTString();
}

//
//   END OF THE COOKIE FUNCTIONS. OUR SCRIPT STARTS HERE.
//

function getURL(frame) {
  var name = GetCookie(frame);
  return GetCookie(name);
}

var expiryDate = new Date();
```

continues

Listing 9.3. continued

```javascript
expiryDate.setTime(expiryDate.getTime() + (365 * 24 * 60 * 60 * 1000));

var number = parseInt(GetCookie("number"));
var siteList = GetCookie("sites");
var sites = new createArray(number);
sites = extractSites(siteList,number);

function createArray(num) {
  for (var i=1; i <= num; i++)
    this[i] = "";
  this.length = num;
}

function extractSites(list,num) {
  var results = new createArray(num);
  var first = 0;
  var last = 0;
  for (var i = 1; i <= num; i ++) {
    first = (i == 1) ? 0 : last+1;
    last = (i == num) ? list.length : list.indexOf(",",first+1);
    results[i] = list.substring(first,last);
  }
  return results;
}

function makeList() {
  var result = "";
  for (var i = 1; i <= number; i++) {
    result += sites[i];
    result += (i == number) ? "" : ",";
  }
  return result;
}

function getList(frame) {
  var result = '<SELECT NAME="' + frame + '" onChange="loadURL(this);">';
  for (var i = 1; i<=number; i++) {
    result += '<OPTION';
    result += (GetCookie(frame) == sites[i]) ? " SELECTED" : "";
    result += ">" + sites[i] + "\n";
  }
  result += "</SELECT>";
  return result;
}

function addURL(form) {
  if ((form.name.value == "") || (form.name.value == null)) {
    return1
  }
  var name = form.name.value;
  var url = form.url.value;
  SetCookie(name,url,expiryDate,"/");
  sites[++number] = name;
  SetCookie("sites",makeList(),expiryDate,"/");
```

9

```
      SetCookie("number",number,expiryDate,"/");
      window.open("control.htm","control");
    }

    function deleteURL(form) {
      var name = form.name.value;
      var gone = false;
      for (var i=1; i<=number; i++) {
        if (sites[i] == name) {
          gone = true;
          number--;
          for (var j=i; j<=number; j++) {
            sites[j] = sites[j+1];
          }
          sites[number+1] = null;
          break;
        }
      }
      if (gone) {
        SetCookie("number",number,expiryDate,"/");
        SetCookie("sites",makeList(),expiryDate,"/");
        var today = new Date();
        SetCookie(name,GetCookie(name),today,"/");
      }
      window.open("control.htm","control");
    }

    function loadURL(field) {
      var frame = field.name;
      var index = field.selectedIndex;
      var name = field.options[index].text;
      var url = GetCookie(name);
      window.open(url,frame);
      SetCookie(frame,name,expiryDate,"/");
    }

    // Set things up before building forms
    var oneList = "";
    var twoList = "";
    var threeList = "";

    oneList = getList("frameOne");
    twoList = getList("frameTwo");
    threeList = getList("frameThree");

    // STOP HIDING HERE -->
    </script>

    </HEAD>

    <BODY>

    <H1>The<BR>News<BR>Source</H1>

    <SCRIPT LANGUAGE="JavaScript">
```

continues

Listing 9.3. continued

```
<!-- HIDE FROM OTHER BROWSERS

document.write("<FORM METHOD=POST>");
document.write("Source One:");
document.write(oneList);
document.write("</FORM>");
document.write("<FORM METHOD=POST>");
document.write("<BR>");
document.write("Source Two:")
document.write(twoList);
document.write("</FORM>");
document.write("<FORM METHOD=POST>");
document.write("<BR>");
document.write("Source Three:");
document.write(threeList);
document.write("</FORM>");

// STOP HIDING -->
</SCRIPT>

<BR>
<FORM METHOD=POST>

Name:
<INPUT TYPE="text" NAME="name">
<BR>
URL:
<INPUT TYPE="text" NAME="url">
<BR>
<INPUT TYPE="button" VALUE="Add URL" onClick="addURL(this.form);">
<BR>
<INPUT TYPE="button" VALUE="Delete URL" onClick="deleteURL(this.form);">

</FORM>

</BODY>

</HTML>
```

TYPE **Listing 9.4. Creating a Wait message.**

```
<!-- SOURCE CODE FOR wait.htm -->
<HTML>

<BODY>
<H1>Please Wait ...</H1>
</BODY>

</HTML>
```

9

OUTPUT   The results should look like Figures 9.3 and 9.4.

Figure 9.3.

Using cookies to create a user-oriented custom news sources Web page.

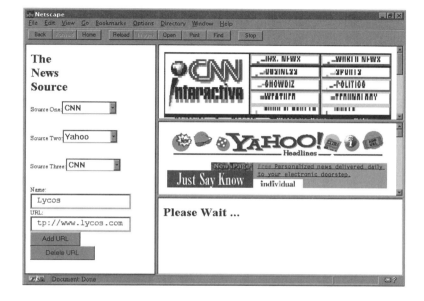

Figure 9.4.

Users can add a new URL and automatically update selection lists.

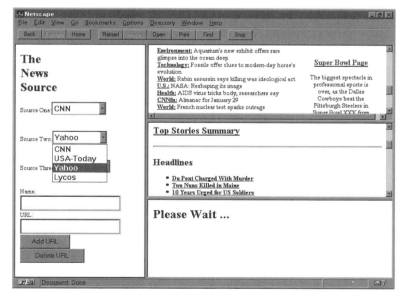

ANALYSIS   This program is somewhat complex in that it uses dynamically generated HTML, both in the parent frameset and the main HTML file in the control frame. Both files include Bill Dortch's cookie functions because the scripts in both files need to access the cookies.

In order to understand how the application works, you need to understand how you are using cookies to store all the information.

You need to keep track of the following information:

- [ ] A name and URL for each option in the selection lists
- [ ] The last loaded (selected) option for each of the three frames
- [ ] A list of all the names of the options
- [ ] The number of options currently available

All this information is stored in cookies. You keep an *optionName=url* cookie for each option. In addition, you have three cookies of the form *frameName=optionName* for each of the frames. The list of all names is stored in the form sites=*optionName1,optionName2,optionName3*, and so on, where the list is comma-separated and encoded using Bill Dortch's functions. The number of options is stored in the cookie number=*numberOfOptions*.

In the parent frameset, you have written two functions of your own, as well as building the HTML for the entire frameset using the document.write() method.

```
function getURL(frame) {
  var name = GetCookie(frame);
  return GetCookie(name);
}
```

The getURL() function accepts a frame name as a parameter. It first gets the name of the option for the frame from the appropriate cookie and then gets the URL for that option name with another call to GetCookie(). The URL is returned.

```
function initialize() {
  if (GetCookie("sites") == null) {
    var expiryDate = new Date();
    expiryDate.setTime(expiryDate.getTime() + (365 * 24 * 60 * 60 * 1000));
    SetCookie("sites","CNN,USA-Today,Yahoo",expiryDate,"/");
    SetCookie("CNN","http://www.cnn.com/",expiryDate,"/");
    SetCookie("USA-Today","http://www.usatoday.com/",expiryDate,"/");

    SetCookie("Yahoo","http://www.yahoo.com/headlines/news/",expiryDate,"/");
    SetCookie("frameOne","CNN",expiryDate,"/");
    SetCookie("frameTwo","USA-Today",expiryDate,"/");

    SetCookie("frameThree","Yahoo",expiryDate,"/");
    SetCookie("number","3",expiryDate,"/");
  }
}
```

The `initialize()` function is the first function called in the script. It simply checks whether any sites are currently stored as cookies using `if (GetCookies("sites") == null)`. If there are no sites stored, the function defines an initial list of three options and stores all the relevant information in the appropriate cookies.

After calling `initialize()` to ensure you have sites stored in cookies, you use `getURL()` to extract the URLs for the three news frames from the cookies.

Finally, the three URLs are loaded into their respective frames by using an `onLoad` event handler in the `FRAMESET` tag. This ensures that all the frames are loaded and ready when you attempt to open the URLs in them. The parent frameset itself divides the right-hand column into three frames where you load `wait.htm` as a placeholder until the various news sources begin to load. In the left-column frame you load `control.htm`, which is the main application:

```
<FRAMESET COLS="35%,*" onLoad="parent.frames['frameOne'].location=frameOne;
➥parent.frames['frameTwo'].location=frameTwo;
➥parent.frames['frameThree'].location=frameThree;">
  <FRAME SRC="control.htm" NAME="control">
  <FRAMESET ROWS="33%,33%,*">
    <FRAME SRC="wait.htm" NAME="frameOne">
    <FRAME SRC="wait.htm" NAME="frameTwo">
    <FRAME SRC="wait.htm" NAME="frameThree">
  </FRAMESET>
</FRAMESET>
```

Once the frameset is built, you use `getURL()` to extract the URLs for the three news frames from the cookies. Then you use `window.open()` to open the appropriate URL in each frame.

The file `control.htm` (refer back to Listing 9.3) is where all the interactive work of the application takes place. The file includes several HTML forms that provide the three drop-down selection lists—one for each of the three news frames—and a simple form to add and remove URLs from the list.

In order to implement all of the functionality you need, `control.htm` includes several additional functions in the header of the file.

```
var expiryDate = new Date();
expiryDate.setTime(expiryDate.getTime() + (365 * 24 * 60 * 60 * 1000));

var number = parseInt(GetCookie("number"));
var siteList = GetCookie("sites");
var sites = new createArray(number);
sites = extractSites(siteList,number);

function createArray(num) {
  for (var i=1; i <= num; i++)
    this[i] = "";
  this.length = num;
}
```

You start by setting up all the global variables you are going to need throughout the script. `expiryDate` is set to one year after the current date and is used whenever you create new cookies or update existing ones.

The variable `number` contains the number of options in the selection lists and is initially extracted from the appropriate cookie using `GetCookie()`. Also, `siteList` is the string of option names from the `sites` cookie. It is passed to `extractSites` to fill up the array `sites`, which is used throughout the script to reference option names.

You have used a standard `createArray()` type function to build the array `sites`.

```
function extractSites(list,num) {
  var results = new createArray(num);
  var first = 0;
  var last = 0;
  for (var i = 1; i <= num; i ++) {
    first = (i == 1) ? 0 : last+1;
    last = (i == num) ? list.length : list.indexOf(",",first+1);
    results[i] = list.substring(first,last);
  }
  return results;
}
```

The `extractSites()` function accepts two arguments: the string of comma-separated option names and the number of options in the list. It returns an array of option names.

The real work of the function all takes place in the `for` loop. The loop is repeated once for each of the options in the list. The first step is to figure out the index of the first character of the next option name in the list. The command `first = (i == 1) ? 0 : last+1;` does this by checking whether the loop counter is still at the start (equal to 1). If it is, the value of `first` is zero; otherwise, it is one character past the last character of the previous name, which was stored in `last`.

The index of the last character is calculated in a similar way using the command:

```
last = (i == num) ? list.length : list.indexOf(",",first+1);
```

This command checks whether the counter is at its final value. If it is, then `last` should be set to the last character in the string using `list.length`. Otherwise, the `indexOf()` method is used to find the next comma in the string.

These two lines are a good example of using conditional expressions to write what would otherwise be a set of bulkier `if-else` statements.

Once `first` and `last` are calculated, then the next entry in the array is set using `list.substring()` to extract the option name from the string.

Finally, the array `results` is returned as the result of the function.

```
function makeList() {
  var result = "";
  for (var i = 1; i <= number; i++) {
    result += sites[i];
    result += (i == number) ? "" : ",";
  }
  return result;
}
```

`makeList()` is used to perform exactly the opposite function of `extractSites()`. Given the array of option names stored in the global array `sites`, it returns a single string containing a comma-separated list of options.

This is done, again, in a single `for` loop that loops through each entry in the array and adds it to the `result` variable using the `+=` concatenation operator. The command

```
result += (i == number) ? "" : ",";
```

uses a conditional expression to make sure that a comma is added only after an entry from the array, if it is not the last entry in the array.

```
function getList(frame) {
  var result = '<SELECT NAME="' + frame + '" onChange="loadURL(this);">';
  for (var i = 1; i<=number; i++) {
    result += '<OPTION';
    result += (GetCookie(frame) == sites[i]) ? " SELECTED" : "";
    result += ">" + sites[i] + "\n";
  }
  result += "</SELECT>";
  return result;
}
```

The `getList()` function is used to build the drop-down selection menus for each of the three frames based on the current cookie settings. The function accepts a frame name as an argument and returns, as a single string, the SELECT HTML container, complete with all options set and the appropriate one preselected.

The function uses the `frame` argument to correctly set the NAME attribute of the SELECT tag. The `onChange` event handler contains the function call to load a new URL when the user chooses a new option.

The `for` loop in the function builds the list of options. It does this by looping through each option and adding an OPTION tag to the string. It then uses `sites[i]` to add the name to be displayed for each option. The command

```
result += (GetCookie(frame) == sites[i]) ? " SELECTED" : "";
```

checks if the current option is stored in the cookie for the frame. If it is, then the SELECTED attribute is added to the OPTION tag so that that option will appear selected initially.

```
function addURL(form) {
  if ((form.name.value == "") || (form.name.value == null)) {
    return1
  }
  var name = form.name.value;
  var url = form.url.value;
  SetCookie(name,url,expiryDate,"/");
  sites[++number] = name;
  SetCookie("sites",makeList(),expiryDate,"/");
  SetCookie("number",number,expiryDate,"/");
  window.open("control.htm","control");
}
```

addURL() is invoked when the user clicks on the Add URL button near the bottom of the frame. It adds a new entry to the selection lists for each frame.

Given the form object as an argument, the addURL() function extracts the name and URL from the fields in the form and then sets the cookie for that name, as well as updates the sites array and stores new sites and number cookies.

Notice the use of the unary increment operator in sites[++number] = name; to increment the value of the number variable before using it as an index to sites. This effectively adds a new entry to sites before the next line:

```
SetCookie("sites",makeList(),expiryDate,"/");
```

This line updates the sites cookie by calling makeList() to build a comma-separated string out of the updated array.

Finally, the function reloads control.htm into control to rebuild the selection menus.

```
function deleteURL(form) {
  var name = form.name.value;
  var gone = false;
  for (var i=1; i<=number; i++) {
    if (sites[i] == name) {
      gone = true;
      number--;
      for (var j=i; j<=number; j++) {
        sites[j] = sites[j+1];
      }
      sites[number+1] = null;
      break;
    }
  }
  if (gone) {
    SetCookie("number",number,expiryDate,"/");
    SetCookie("sites",makeList(),expiryDate,"/");
    var today = new Date();
    SetCookie(name,GetCookie(name),today,"/");
  }
  window.open("control.htm","control");
}
```

In this excerpt, the deleteURL() function removes an entry from the list of options.

This process is actually a bit more complicated than adding a new URL to the list because a little bit of work needs to be done to remove an entry from the middle of the array and then close up the hole that this creates in the array.

The function uses a for loop to move through the array. The if statement checks whether the current entry matches the one you want to delete.

If there is a match, then the work begins. gone is set to true so that later in the function you know a match was found—after all, the user could incorrectly type the name of the entry to delete. Next, number is decreased to reflect the fact that the number of entries in the list will decrease by one. Another for loop is used to count from the current index of the entry you are deleting to the new value of number (that is, one before the current last entry in the array).

The command sites[j] = sites[j+1]; copies the array entry immediately following the current entry into the current entry. In this way, you fill in the hole created by removing an entry.

Finally, after the for loop finishes, you set the previous last entry to the null value with sites[number+1] = null;.

Once you finish the for loop, if you have found an entry to delete, you update the sites and number cookies just as you did in addURL() and then you remove the cookie for the deleted entry by updating it with an expiry date equal to the current date and time.

```
function loadURL(field) {
  var frame = field.name;
  var url = GetURL(frame);
  open(url,frame);
  SetCookie(frame,name,expiryDate,"/");
}
```

The loadURL() function is invoked when the user changes the value of one of the selection lists. It receives the field object for the selection list as an argument.

Based on this information, it can extract the frame name, which is actually the NAME value of the selection element. Using this information, you can call getURL() to get the URL for that frame.

Once you have this information, you can open the URL in the frame and then update the cookie for that frame to reflect the new selection by the user.

```
// Set things up before building forms
var oneList = "";
var twoList = "";
var threeList = "";

oneList = getList("frameOne");
twoList = getList("frameTwo");
threeList = getList("frameThree");
```

The last thing you do in the header of the document is set up three variables containing the selection lists for the three different news source frames by calling getList().

```
document.write("<FORM METHOD=POST>");
document.write("Source One:");
document.write(oneList);
document.write("</FORM>");
document.write("<FORM METHOD=POST>");
document.write("<BR>");
document.write("Source Two:")
document.write(twoList);
document.write("</FORM>");
document.write("<FORM METHOD=POST>");
document.write("<BR>");
```

```
document.write("Source Three:");
document.write(threeList);
document.write("</FORM>");
```

In the body of the document, you use scripts to build each of the three drop-down selection lists. Each list is a separate form, but could just as easily have been a single form.

```
<FORM METHOD=POST>

Name:
<INPUT TYPE="text" NAME="name">
<BR>
URL:
<INPUT TYPE="text" NAME="url">
<BR>
<INPUT TYPE="button" VALUE="Add URL" onClick="addURL(this.form);">
<BR>
<INPUT TYPE="button" VALUE="Delete URL" onClick="deleteURL(this.form);">

</FORM>
```

The last element in the document is the form used to add and delete entries from the list of options. The form contains two text entry fields and two buttons that invoke either addURL() or deleteURL() in their onClick event handlers.

The navigator Object

As mentioned at the beginning of this chapter, the navigator object makes information about the current version of Navigator available to scripts.

The navigator object is currently one of the most poorly documented objects in JavaScript. Although there are indications that the available properties, and perhaps methods, will expand with future versions of JavaScript, today it offers four properties that are outlined in Table 9.2.

Table 9.2. Properties of the navigator object.

Name	Description
appName	The name of the application in which the page is loaded represented as a string (i.e. "Netscape").
appVersion	The version information of the current browser as a string in the form "2.0 (Win16; I)" where 2.0 is the version number, Win16 is the platform, and I indicates the international version (as opposed to U for the domestic version).
appCodeName	The code name of the current browser (i.e. "Mozilla").
userAgent	The user agent for the current browser as a string in the form "Mozilla/ 2.0 (Win16; I)".

9

In order to understand the significance of this information, it is important to understand the concept of the user agent. In the initial communication between the client and the server during an HTTP request, the browser sends the user agent string to the server. That information becomes available on the server for a number of uses, including processing by CGI scripts or for delivering specific versions of the pages based on the nature of the client browser.

The user agent information has two parts separated by a slash: a code name for the browser and the version information for the browser. This is the information stored in the `appCodeName` and `appVersion` properties. For instance, `"TOME"` would represent the current version of Navigator 2.0 for Windows 3.1.

Using the `navigator` **Properties**

At first, it may seem as though this information serves little practical use—but it can be very useful.

For instance, during the beta development of the Navigator 2.0 browser, releases of new versions of the beta were quite frequent. Each version supported new features of JavaScript and fixed problems with earlier implementations, which sometimes created incompatibilities.

Many page authors are now using the properties of the `navigator` object to check whether the browsers being used will support the features used in the script. If not, users are alerted so that they don't try to run the script and get errors—or even find Netscape, or their PCs, crashing.

For example, if a page should only be run with Navigator 2.0.0 beta 6a on any platform and beta 6a is the latest version, the HTML file should look like this:

```
<HTML>

<HEAD>
<TITLE>navigator Example</TITLE>

<SCRIPT LANGUAGE="JavaScript">
<!-- HIDE FROM OTHER BROWSERS

function checkBrowser() {
  if ((navigator.appVersion.substring(0,6) != "2.0b6a") &&
➡(navigator.appName != "Netscape"))
alert("Please use version 2.0b6a of the Netscape Navigator
➡web browser with this page.");
}


Rest of script

// STOP HIDING FROM OTHER BROWSERS -->
</SCRIPT>
```

```
</HEAD>

<BODY onLoad="checkBrowser();">

HTML code

</BODY>

</HTML>
```

Similarly, in the future, if different browsers support JavaScript, they may offer different features or additional objects, and the use of the navigator object can help script authors ensure that their scripts run on the largest number of browsers while also taking advantage of the unique features of each.

Summary

In this chapter, you learned about an extremely useful feature of JavaScript: the cookie property.

Using the cookie property, scripts can set and read cookies that store state information in the client browser. Using cookies, you can retain information between sessions to produce applications that outlive the currently loaded document and even the current browser session.

Once again, Bill Dortch has provided the JavaScript community with a set of freely available functions that make setting and retrieving cookies easier.

In addition to cookies, you took a look at the navigator object and how it can be used to ensure that users are using the appropriate browser for your scripts.

In the next chapter, we take a look at a variety of objects and features of JavaScript that we haven't covered in detail yet, including the string object, the Math object, and the history object.

Commands and Extensions Review

Command/Extension	Type	Description
Set-Cookie	HTTP header	Sets cookies in the client browser—part of an HTTP response header
Cookie	HTTP header	Returns cookies to the server—part of an HTTP request header

expires	Set-Cookie attribute	Indicates the expiry date for a cookie (in GMT)
path	Set-Cookie attribute	Used to set the path for files applicable to a cookie
domain	Set-Cookie attribute	Used to set the domain for files applicable to a cookie
secure	Set-Cookie attribute	Specifies that a cookie should be transmitted only on secure links
cookie	JavaScript property	String containing the value of cookies for the current document
indexOf()	JavaScript method	A method of the string object that returns the index of the next occurrence of a substring in a string
escape()	JavaScript method	Encodes a string using URL encoding
unescape()	JavaScript method	Decodes a string encoded using URL encoding
appName	JavaScript property	The name of the browser application as a string
appVersion	JavaScript property	The version number and platform of the browser as a string
appCodeName	JavaScript property	The code name of the browser as a string
userAgent	JavaScript property	The user agent string for the browser
link()	JavaScript method	Method of the string object that encloses the string in an \<A> HTML tag
fontcolor()	JavaScript method	Method of the string object that sets the HTML font color for the string

9

Q&A

Q How can I be sure that other people's applications and scripts won't overwrite the cookies that I have created?

A If you are setting cookies with the specific path of your document, then it is possible for other documents to create cookies with the same name, domain, and path. However, these cookies do not overwrite your cookies. Instead, `document.cookies` will contain two entries with the same name, but different values. Only a script in the file in the same original location can overwrite cookies created by that file.

Q Can I rely on cookies to store information vital to my application between sessions?

A Not really. While most users will not delete their browsers or change browsers between sessions—which would mean the loss of cookie information—there are too many variables to be sure that your cookies still will be present when the user next returns to your page. For instance, cookies could have been added exceeding the limits, and your cookies could be the ones that get deleted. It is generally good to write your scripts in such a way that if the cookies you are looking for no longer exist, you can perform alternate actions and recreate the cookies.

Q Why does the `navigator` object have both the `appName` and `appCodeName` properties? They seem to be pretty much the same thing in different forms.

A While it's true that generally you can glean the same information from both properties (such as Mozilla for Netscape, and so on), it is not always the case that you will know that the code name for Lynx or the application name for a less well-known browser. Having both properties, you have the maximum information available to determine the client browser.

Exercises

1. A user loads the page `http://sample.page/sample/file.html` on 1 January 1996 at noon (GMT), and a script in it contains the following lines:

```
document.cookie = "user=joe; expires=Wed,
➥31-Jan-96 00:00:00 GMT; path=/";
document.cookie = "message=hello";
document.cookie = "food=lasagna; expires=Wed, 31-Jan-96 00:00:00 GMT;
➥domain=another.site; path=/anotherpath/";
document.cookie = "color=blue; expires=Tue, 02-Jan-96 12:00:00 GMT;
➥domain=sample.page; path=/sample/";
```

If the user accesses the following pages at the following times, what will be displayed by the command `document.write(document.cookie)`:

9

a. `http://sample.page/otherfile.html` on 3 January

b. `http://sample.page/sample/file.html` on 31 January at noon (GMT)

c. `http://another.site/anotherfile.html` on 31 January at 11:59 a.m.

2. Extend your script in Listings 9.2 through 9.4 (the news sources example) so that some sort of error checking takes place. If the user tries to add an entry with no URL, the user should get an error. In addition, if the user tries to add more than 10 entries to the list, prompt the user for the name of an entry to replace and check the name to make sure it is valid before proceeding.

3. Design a page that asks questions of first-time visitors (or those who haven't visited for more than 30 days). Ask for their favorite color and their favorite food (from a list of options) and then customize the Web page to include the specified background color and a picture of the food indicated.

Every time users come to the page within 30 days of their last visit, build the specified page without asking for the information.

Answers

1. The following strings would be displayed:

   a. `user=joe.`

   b. There are no cookies—user expired at midnight, 12 hours earlier.

   c. There are no cookies—The only cookie set for this site is at a lower level path than the user is accessing.

2. All the changes are needed in the `addURL()` function:

```
function addURL(form) {
  var name = form.name.value;
  var url = form.url.value;
  if ((name == "") || (name == null) || (url == "") ||
➥(url == null)) {
alert ("Please Enter both a name and URL.");
    form.name.focus();
    return;
  }
  if (number == 10) {
    var delete = prompt("Cannot enter more than 10 items.\n
➥Enter the name of an entry to replace or enter nothing
➥to stop adding" + name + ".","");
if ((delete == "") || (delete == null)) {
      form.name.focus();
      return;
    }
    var i=1;
    while (i <= number) {
```

```
    if (sites[i] == delete) {
      form.name.value = delete;
      deleteURL(form);
      form.name.value = name;
      break;
    }
    if (i == number) {
        delete = prompt("No such entry to delete. Cannot enter more
➡than 10 items.\nEnter the name of an entry to replace or
➡enter nothing to stop adding" + name + ".","");

i = 0;
    }
      i++;
    }
  }
  SetCookie(name,url,expiryDate,"/");
  sites[++number] = name;
  SetCookie("sites",makeList(),expiryDate,"/");
  SetCookie("number",number,expiryDate,"/");
  window.open("control.htm","control");
}
```

You can add the following elements to the function to perform the necessary error checking and to make sure the user doesn't enter too many elements.

```
if ((name == "") || (name == null) || (url == "") || (url == null)) {
    alert ("Please Enter both a name and URL.");
    form.name.focus();
    return;
  }
```

This if statement checks whether either field is the empty string or the null value. If the result is true, then an alert message is displayed, focus is returned to the form, and the function ends with the return statement.

The next if statement handles the 10-item limitation on the list. The work that takes place if there are already 10 entries in the list is a bit more complex than the previous if statement.

```
    var delete = prompt("Cannot enter more than 10 items.\n
➡Enter the name of an entry to replace or enter nothing
➡to stop adding" + name + ".","");
```

The first step is to ask users what to do because there are too many entries already. They can either provide an item to replace or they can cancel the addition. The user's selection is stored in the delete variable.

```
if ((delete == "") || (delete == null)) {
    form.name.focus();
    return;
  }
```

Once the user responds, the script immediately checks whether the user has decided to cancel the addition of the new entry by entering nothing in the prompt dialog box. If the user is canceling, then focus is returned to the form, and the function exits with the return statement.

```
var i=1;
    while (i <= number) {
      if (sites[i] == delete) {
        form.name.value = delete;
        deleteURL(form);
        form.name.value = name;
        break;
      }
```

The `while` loop is used to check whether the entry the user wants to replace actually exists. This is done by looping through each entry in the array. The first step, then, is to check whether the current entry matches the user's selection. If it does, then the value of `delete` is temporarily stored in the name field of the form, `deleteURL()` is called, and then the name field is returned to its previous value. The `break` statement ends the `while` loop.

```
    if (i == number) {
      delete = prompt("No such entry to delete. Cannot enter more
➤than 10 items.\nEnter the name of an entry to replace or
➤enter nothing to stop adding" + name + ".","");
    i = 0;
      }
```

The next step in the loop is to see if you have exhausted all the entries in the list. You check this with the condition `if (i == number)`. If the last entry has been reached without a match in the previous `if` statement, then the user is again prompted to enter an item to replace or to enter an empty string. Then the counter is reset to start checking again.

3. The following script achieves the desired effect. The output looks like Figures 9.5 and 9.6.

```
<HTML>

<HEAD>
<TITLE>Exercise 9.3</TITLE>

<SCRIPT LANGUAGE="JavaScript">
<!-- HIDE FROM OTHER BROWSERS
//
//  WE NEED TO INCLUDE THE COOKIE FUNCTIONS
//
//
//  Cookie Functions - Second Helping  (21-Jan-96)
//  Written by:  Bill Dortch, hIdaho Design <bdortch@netw.com>
//  The following functions are released to the public domain.
//
// "Internal" function to return the decoded value of a cookie
//
function getCookieVal (offset) {
  var endstr = document.cookie.indexOf (";", offset);
  if (endstr == -1)
    endstr = document.cookie.length;
  return unescape(document.cookie.substring(offset, endstr));
}
```

```
//
//   Function to return the value of the cookie specified by "name".
//
function GetCookie (name) {
  var arg = name + "=";
  var alen = arg.length;
  var clen = document.cookie.length;
  var i = 0;
  while (i < clen) {
    var j = i + alen;
    if (document.cookie.substring(i, j) == arg)
      return getCookieVal (j);
    i = document.cookie.indexOf(" ", i) + 1;
    if (i == 0) break;
  }
  return null;
}

//
//   Function to create or update a cookie.
//
function SetCookie (name, value) {
  var argv = SetCookie.arguments;
  var argc = SetCookie.arguments.length;
  var expires = (argc > 2) ? argv[2] : null;
  var path = (argc > 3) ? argv[3] : null;
  var domain = (argc > 4) ? argv[4] : null;
  var secure = (argc > 5) ? argv[5] : false;
  document.cookie = name + "=" + escape (value) +
    ((expires == null) ? "" : ("; expires=" +
➥expires.toGMTString())) +
((path == null) ? "" : ("; path=" + path)) +
    ((domain == null) ? "" : ("; domain=" + domain)) +
    ((secure == true) ? "; secure" : "");
}

//   Function to delete a cookie.
➥(Sets expiration date to current date/time)
//
function DeleteCookie (name) {
  var exp = new Date();
  exp.setTime (exp.getTime() - 1);  // This cookie is history
  var cval = GetCookie (name);
  document.cookie = name + "=" + cval + ";
➥expires=" + exp.toGMTString();
}

//
//   END OF THE COOKIE FUNCTIONS. OUR SCRIPT STARTS HERE.
//

var expiryDate = new Date();
expiryDate.setTime(expiryDate.getTime() + (30 * 24 * 60 * 60 * 1000));

var food = new createArray(3);
food[1] = "Beets";
food[2] = "Jello-Pudding";
food[3] = "Cockroaches";
```

```
function createArray(num) {
  this.length = num;
  for (var i = 1; i <= num; i++)
    this[i] = "";
}

function listArray(stuff) {
  var result = "";
  for (var i = 1; i <= stuff.length; i++)
    result += i + ". " + stuff[i] + "/";
  return result;
}

var color = "";
var favFood = "";

function initialize() {
  if (GetCookie("color") == null) {
    color = prompt("Enter your favorite Netscape color.","A Color");
    SetCookie("color",color,expiryDate);
    var foodNum = prompt("Food: - " + listArray(food),"0");
    favFood = food[foodNum];
    SetCookie("food",favFood,expiryDate);
  } else {
    color = GetCookie("color");
    SetCookie("color",color,expiryDate);
    favFood = GetCookie("food");
    SetCookie("food",favFood,expiryDate);
  }
}

// STOP HIDING HERE -->
</SCRIPT>

</HEAD>

<SCRIPT LANGUAGE="JavaScript">
<!-- HIDE FROM OTHER BROWSERS

initialize();

document.write('<BODY BGCOLOR="' + color + '">');

document.write("<CENTER>")

document.write('<IMG SRC="' + favFood + '.gif">');

// STOP HIDING -->
</SCRIPT>

<H1>Welcome to the favorite food and color page</H1>

</CENTER>

</BODY>

</HTML>
```

Figure 9.5.

The script prompts the first-time visitor for the color and food information.

Figure 9.6.

On subsequent visits, information stored in the cookies automatically formats the page.

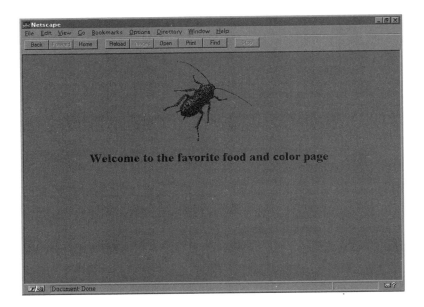

The logic behind this script is rather simple, but it provides an example of how to rebuild cookies after they expire and how to keep cookies current when it is relevant to do so.

The createArray() and listArray() functions should be obvious. listArray() returns a string containing all the items in an array numerically listed by their index numbers in the array. This is used to prompt users for their food choices.

The initialize() function is where all the work takes place. The function checks for the existence of the color cookie. If the cookie doesn't exist, the program prompts users for the food and color information and stores it in the appropriate cookies, as well as setting the color and favFood global variables for use in the body of the document.

If the cookies exist, the values are loaded into color and favFood and then the cookies are updated so that their expiry dates get reset to 30 days into the future.

In the body of the document, a script is used to set the BGCOLOR attribute of the BODY tag and the SRC attribute of the IMG tag based on the color and favFood variables.

9

From the Web:

James Thiele's Reminder Calendar

James Thiele has designed a simple reminder calendar as an example of using cookies in JavaScript. The calendar is available at

```
http://www.eskimo.com/~jet/javascript/calendar_js.html
```

Rather than being a full-fledged application, this page provides simple functionality, yet is a compelling example of how cookies can extend the value of a script beyond time and session constraints.

The program (see Listing W4.1) displays a calendar of the current month, much the same as in Dave Eisenberg's calendar example. When users click on any of the days in the calendar, they either can enter a reminder for that day, or are alerted of their previously entered reminder.

When the user reloads the page or returns to it later in the month, the days with reminders are displayed in a different color.

Listing W4.1. Source code for James Thiele's Reminder Calendar.

```
<HTML>
<HEAD>
<SCRIPT LANGUAGE="JavaScript">


<!-- to hide script contents from old browsers

//
//  Cookie Functions
//  Written by:  Bill Dortch, hIdaho Design
//  The following functions are released to the public domain.
//

//
// "Internal" function to encode cookie value.  This permits cookies to
// contain whitespace, comma and semicolon characters.
//
function encode (str) {
  var dest = "";
  var len = str.length;
  var index = 0;
  var code = null;
  for (var i = 0; i < len; i++) {
    var ch = str.charAt(i);
    if (ch == " ") code = "%20";
    else if (ch == "%") code = "%25";
    else if (ch == ",") code = "%2C";
    else if (ch == ";") code = "%3B";
    else if (ch == "\b") code = "%08";
    else if (ch == "\t") code = "%09";
    else if (ch == "\n") code = "%0A";
    else if (ch == "\f") code = "%0C";
    else if (ch == "\r") code = "%0D";
    if (code != null) {
      dest += str.substring(index,i) + code;
      index = i + 1;
      code = null;
    }
  }
  if (index < len)
    dest += str.substring(index, len);
  return dest;
}

//
// "Internal" function to decode cookie values.
//
function decode (str) {
  var dest = "";
  var len = str.length;
  var index = 0;
  var code = null;
  var i = 0;
```

```
  while (i < len) {
    i = str.indexOf ("%", i);
    if (i == -1)
      break;
    if (index < i)
      dest += str.substring(index, i);
    code = str.substring (i+1,i+3);
    i += 3;
    index = i;
    if (code == "20") dest += " ";
    else if (code == "25") dest += "%";
    else if (code == "2C") dest += ",";
    else if (code == "3B") dest += ";";
    else if (code == "08") dest += "\b";
    else if (code == "09") dest += "\t";
    else if (code == "0A") dest += "\n";
    else if (code == "0C") dest += "\f";
    else if (code == "0D") dest += "\r";
    else {
      i -= 2;
      index -= 3;
    }
  }
  if (index < len)
    dest += str.substring(index, len);
  return dest;
}


//
// "Internal" function to return the decoded value of a cookie
//
function getCookieVal (offset) {
  var endstr = document.cookie.indexOf (";", offset);
  if (endstr == -1)
    endstr = document.cookie.length;
  return decode(document.cookie.substring(offset, endstr));
}


//
//  Function to return the value of the cookie specified by "name".
//    name - String object containing the cookie name.
//
function GetCookie (name) {
  var arg = name + "=";
  var alen = arg.length;
  var clen = document.cookie.length;
  var i = 0;
  while (i < clen) {
    var j = i + alen;
    if (document.cookie.substring(i, j) == arg)
      return getCookieVal (j);
    i = document.cookie.indexOf(" ", i) + 1;
    if (i == 0) break;
  }
  return null;
}
```

continues

Listing W4.1. continued

```
//
//   Function to create or update a cookie.
//     name - String object object containing the cookie name
//     value - String object containing the cookie value.  May contain
//        any valid sting characters, including whitespace, commas and quotes.
//     expires - Date object containing the expiration data of the cookie,
//        or null to expire the cookie at the end of the current session.
//
function SetCookie (name, value, expires) {
  document.cookie = name + "=" + encode(value) + ((expires == null) ? "" :
➥("; expires=" + expires.toGMTString()));
}

//   Function to delete a cookie. (Sets expiration date to current date/time)
//     name - String object containing the cookie name
//
function DeleteCookie (name) {
  var exp = new Date();
  var cval = GetCookie (name);
  document.cookie = name + "=" + cval + "; expires=" + exp.toGMTString();
}


function intro()
{
   document.write  ("<CENTER>");

   document.writeln("<BR>");
   document.write  ("<H1>");
   document.write  ("Reminder Calendar");
   document.writeln("</H1>");
   document.writeln("</CENTER>");
   document.writeln("<h2>How to use the Reminder Calendar:</h2>");
   document.writeln("<ul><li>Click on a  date to add a reminder");
   document.writeln("    <li>Click on that date again to see the reminder");
   document.writeln("    <li>Reload the page to see dates with
➥reminders in different colors");
   document.writeln("</ul>");

   document.writeln("<h2>Notes:</h2>");
   document.writeln("<ul><li>Lame user interface");
   document.writeln("    <li>Can't delete a reminder");
   document.writeln("    <li>Reminders disappear in about 24 hours");
   document.writeln("</ul>");

   document.writeln("<h2>This is mostly a programming example of:</h2>");
   document.writeln("<ul><li>Using cookies in JavaScript");
   document.writeln("    <li>Using text links to call a
➥function, not open a URL");
   document.writeln("</ul>");

   document.writeln("<h2>Credits:</h2>");
   document.writeln("<ul><li>Cookie Functions written by:
➥<A href='mailto:bdortch@netw.com'>Bill Dortch</A>, hIdaho Design");
   document.writeln("<ul>The functions are at:");
```

```
    document.writeln("     <li>Code: <A href='http://www.hidaho.com/cookies/
cookie.txt'>
➥http://www.hidaho.com/cookies/cookie.txt</A>");
    document.writeln("     <li>Demo: <A href='http://www.hidaho.com/cookies/
cookie.html'>
➥http://www.hidaho.com/cookies/cookie.html</A>");
    document.writeln("</ul>");
    document.writeln("     <li>Reminder Calendar by
➥James Thiele who can be reached:");
    document.writeln("     <UL><LI>at his home page ");
    document.writeln("          <A href='http://www.eskimo.com/~jet'>
➥http://www.eskimo.com/~jet</A>");
    document.writeln("          <LI> via email at ");
    document.writeln("          <address><A href='mailto:jet@eskimo.com'>
➥jet@eskimo.com</a></address></p>");
    document.writeln("</ul>");
}


function arrayOfDaysInMonths(isLeapYear)
{
    this[0] = 31;
    this[1] = 28;
    if (isLeapYear)
                this[1] = 29;
    this[2] = 31;
    this[3] = 30;
    this[4] = 31;
    this[5] = 30;
    this[6] = 31;
    this[7] = 31;
    this[8] = 30;
    this[9] = 31;
    this[10] = 30;
    this[11] = 31;
}

function daysInMonth(month, year)
{
                                        // do the classic leap year calculation
    var isLeapYear = (((year % 4 == 0) &&
➥(year % 100 != 0)) || (year % 400 == 0));
    var monthDays  = new arrayOfDaysInMonths(isLeapYear);

    return monthDays[month];
}


function calendar()
{
    var monthNames = "JanFebMarAprMayJunJulAugSepOctNovDec";
    var today      = new Date();
    var day        = today.getDate();
    var month      = today.getMonth();
    var year       = today.getYear() + 1900;
```

continues

Listing W4.1. continued

```
     figure out how many days this month will have...
var numDays    = daysInMonth(month, year);

// and go back to the first day of the month...
var firstDay   = today;
    firstDay.setDate(1);
// and figure out which day of the week it hits...
var startDay = firstDay.getDay();

var column = 0;

// Start the calendar table
document.write("<CENTER>");
document.write("<TABLE BORDER>");
document.write("<TR><TH COLSPAN=7>");
document.write(monthNames.substring(3*month, 3*(month + 1)) + " " + year);
document.write("<TR><TH>Sun<TH>Mon<TH>Tue<TH>Wed<TH>Thu<TH>Fri<TH>Sat");

// put blank table entries for days of week before beginning of the month
document.write("<TR>");
for (i=1; i < startDay; i++)
{
   document.write("<TD>");
   column++;
}

for (i=1; i <= numDays; i++)
{
   // Write the day
   var s = "" + i;
   if ((GetCookie("d"+i) != null))
     // s = s.fontcolor(document.vlinkColor);
     s = s.fontcolor("#FF0000");
   s = s.link("javascript:dayClick(" + i + ")")
     document.write("<TD>" + s);

   // Check for end of week/row
   if (++column == 7)
   {
      document.write("<TR>"); // start a new row
      column = 0;
   }
}
document.write("</TABLE>");
document.writeln("</CENTER>");
}


////////////////////////////
//////// dayClick //////////
////////////////////////////
function dayClick(day)
{
      var expdate = new Date ();
```

```
                expdate.setTime (expdate.getTime() + (24 * 60 * 60 * 1000));
➥// 24 hrs from now
        var prefix                = "d";
        var theCookieName         = prefix + day;
        var theDayclickedReminder = GetCookie(theCookieName);

    if (theDayclickedReminder != null) {
        alert("The reminder for day " + day + " is:"  + theDayclickedReminder);
    } // end if

        if (confirm("Do you wish to enter a reminder for day " +
➥day + " of this month?"))
        {
                x = prompt("Enter a reminder for day "+ day +
➥" of this month", theDayclickedReminder);
        SetCookie (theCookieName, x, expdate);
    } // end if
}


// --> <!-- end hiding contents from old browsers   -->

</SCRIPT>

<TITLE>James Thiele's Calendar reminders
</TITLE>
</HEAD>

<BODY>

<SCRIPT LANGUAGE="JavaScript">


<!--  to hide script contents from old browsers

// Write the intro
// Write the calendar
calendar();
document.write("<HR>");
intro();
// --> <!-- end hiding contents from old browsers   -->

</SCRIPT>

<IMG SRC="../RainbowLine.gif">
<A href="index.html"><IMG SRC="javascriptlogo.gif">To JavaScript stuff</A>
<br><em>Page last modified 24 Jan 96</em>

</BODY>
</HTML>
```

OUTPUT The results look like Figures W4.1 and W4.2.

Figure W4.1.
A reminder prompt dialog appears when users click a date for the first time.

Figure W4.2.
In future visits, the days with reminders are displayed in a different color.

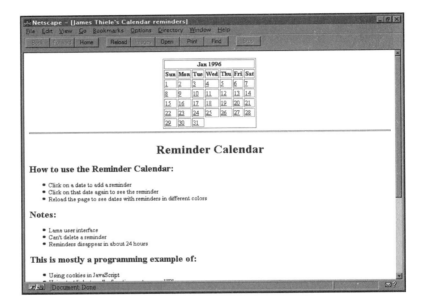

ANALYSIS The first thing you notice is that Thiele is using an early version of Bill Dortch's cookie function set. This version was written before JavaScript included the `escape()` and `unescape()` functions, which forced Dortch to write his own functions, `encode()` and `decode()`, to perform the encoding of values.

In any case, the newer version of Dortch's functions is backward compatible and could replace the old version in this script without affecting its operation in newer browsers.

Thiele has written five functions to implement his calendar program: `intro()`, `arrayOfDaysInMonth()`, `daysInMonth()`, `calendar()`, and `dayClick()`.

In addition, he builds most of the body of his HTML document using a JavaScript script:

```
<SCRIPT LANGUAGE="JavaScript">

<!-- to hide script contents from old browsers

// Write the intro
// Write the calendar
```

```
calendar();
document.write("<HR>");
intro();
// --> <!-- end hiding contents from old browsers  -->

</SCRIPT>
```

This script is quite simple: it calls `calendar()` to display the calendar, it draws a horizontal line, and then it calls `intro()`, which displays most of the rest of the text of the script.

The `intro()` Function

This function needs little discussion. It is just a static collection of `document.write()` statements that output the introductory information about the application.

The `arrayOfDaysInMonth()` Function

The `arrayOfDaysInMonth()` function simply creates a twelve-element array containing the number of days in each calendar month. It accepts one boolean variable as an argument. This enables it to correctly set the number of days in February based on whether or not it is a leap year.

The `daysInMonth()` Function

This function takes two arguments—the month and year—and uses these to determine if it is a leap year. It then creates an array of days in each month of the particular year and returns the number of days in the specified month.

The `calendar()` Function

The `calendar()` function is where some of the more complex processing occurs.

```
var monthNames = "JanFebMarAprMayJunJulAugSepOctNovDec";
var today      = new Date();
var day        = today.getDate();
var month      = today.getMonth();
var year       = today.getYear() + 1900;

// figure out how many days this month will have...
var numDays    = daysInMonth(month, year);

// and go back to the first day of the month...
var firstDay   = today;
    firstDay.setDate(1);
// and figure out which day of the week it hits...
var startDay = firstDay.getDay();

var column = 0;
```

As you might expect, the function starts by setting up key variables for use throughout the function. These include a string of month names—the same technique you saw in Dave Eisenberg's calendar script.

The firstDay Date object is used to get the day of the week of the first day of the month and store it in startDay.

```
// Start the calendar table
document.write("<CENTER>");
document.write("<TABLE BORDER>");
document.write("<TR><TH COLSPAN=7>");
document.write(monthNames.substring(3*month, 3*(month + 1)) + " " + year);
document.write("<TR><TH>Sun<TH>Mon<TH>Tue<TH>Wed<TH>Thu<TH>Fri<TH>Sat");

// put blank table entries for days of week before beginning of the month
document.write("<TR>");
for (i=1; i < startDay; i++)
{
    document.write("<TD>");
    column++;
}
```

After building the header of the table, which holds the calendar for the month, the for loop inserts blank cells for each of the unused days of the week before the first day of the month.

```
for (i=1; i <= numDays; i++)
{
    // Write the day
    var s = "" + i;
    if ((GetCookie("d"+i) != null))
      // s = s.fontcolor(document.vlinkColor);
      s = s.fontcolor("#FF0000");
      s = s.link("javascript:dayClick(" + i + ")")
        document.write("<TD>" + s);

    // Check for end of week/row
    if (++column == 7)
    {
        document.write("<TR>"); // start a new row
        column = 0;
    }
}
```

Next, another for loop repeats for each day in the month. For each day, a cell is created and the number is displayed with a hypertext link to the URL javascript:dayClick(number). This is done by using the string's link method to add the URL. As you will see in Chapter 10, "Strings, Math, and the History List," if the link method is used, then the value of the string is surrounded by an appropriate <A> HTML container tag.

NOTE

> Notice the use of the `javascript:` URL. This type of URL can be used to call a function in the current document. When used in the HREF attribute of the `<A>` tag, this is often an alternative to using the `onClick` event handler. It can also be used in the open location dialog box of the Navigator browser to test what a line of JavaScript code will evaluate to. In this case, the result of evaluating an expression is displayed in the browser window.

Similarly, the `fontcolor()` method adds the appropriate HTML tags to the value of the string. In this case, the `fontcolor()` method is called only if the cookie for that day has been previously set with a reminder.

The final `if` statement checks whether you have reached the last column, and if so, closes the row, opens a new row in the table, and resets the `column` counter.

The `dayClick()` Function

This function handles both prompting for a reminder and displaying existing reminders. It is invoked when the user clicks on a date. It accepts the date as an argument.

```
        var expdate = new Date ();
            expdate.setTime (expdate.getTime() + (24 * 60 * 60 * 1000));
➡// 24 hrs from now
        var prefix               = "d";
        var theCookieName        = prefix + day;
        var theDayclickedReminder = GetCookie(theCookieName);
```

The function starts by setting up its variables, including an expiry date for cookies and a value of the cookie for the selected date.

```
    if (theDayclickedReminder != null) {
        alert("The reminder for day " + day + " is:"  + theDayclickedReminder);
    } // end if
```

If the value of the cookie is not `null`, then the reminder is displayed in an alert dialog box.

```
        if (confirm("Do you wish to enter a reminder for day " +
➡day + " of this month?"))
        {
                x = prompt("Enter a reminder for day "+ day +
➡" of this month", theDayclickedReminder);
        SetCookie (theCookieName, x, expdate);
    } // end if
```

If the value of the cookie is null, then users are asked if they wish to enter a reminder for the current day and, if they do, they are further prompted for the text of the reminder. The reminder is then stored in a cookie. Notice the use of the confirm() call as the condition of the if statement—confirm() returns a value of true or false based on the user's response.

Chapter 10

Strings, Math, and the History List

Up to this point in the book, you have learned about the major objects and tools of JavaScript. Even so, this leaves several useful objects undiscovered.

In this chapter you are going to take a detailed look at some of the objects that you have been introduced to only briefly earlier in the book. These include the string object, the Math object, and the history object.

Every string in JavaScript is an object. The string object offers properties and methods to perform a variety of manipulations on a given string. These include methods for searching a string, extracting substrings, and applying HTML tags to the content of the string.

The Math object provides those functions and methods necessary to perform mathematical calculations. These range from the PI value to methods for all the trigonometric functions.

The history object is a bit different in that it doesn't involve the manipulation of information the way the string and Math objects do. The history object reflects the information in the browser's history list.

In this chapter you will learn the details of each of these object's properties and methods plus:

☐ How to manipulate the content of strings
☐ How to perform advanced mathematical calculations with the Math object
☐ How to build dynamic forward and back buttons—in any frame

The string Object

You already have considerable experience working with strings. You have used them throughout the book, you understand how to represent string literals, and you even know some of the basic techniques for examining the content of strings.

Even with the substring() and indexOf() methods which you saw earlier, though, you haven't reached the true possibilities of working with the string object.

The length Property

The string object has only one property: length. The length property is an integer value reflecting the number of characters in the string. Because the index of the first character in a string is zero, this means the length property is one greater than the index of the last character in the string.

For example, the string "Hello" has a length of five. The index of the first character ("H") is 0, and the index of the last character ("o") is 4.

Methods of the string Object

The flexibility and power of the string object rest in the wide variety of methods available to manipulate the content of the string. Table 10.1 outlines the methods available in the string object.

Table 10.1. Methods of the string object.

Name	Description
anchor()	Surrounds the string with an anchor A tag.
big()	Surrounds the string with the HTML BIG tag.
blink()	Surrounds the string with the HTML BLINK tag.
bold()	Surrounds the string with the HTML B tag.
charAt()	Given an index as an argument, returns the character at the specified index.

10

Name	Description
fixed()	Surrounds the string with the HTML TT tag to make it display as a fixed-width font.
fontcolor()	Surrounds the string with the HTML <FONT COLOR=*color*> and </FONT> tags to make it display in the specified color.
fontsize()	Surrounds the string with the HTML <FONT SIZE=size> and </FONT> tags to make it display in the desired font size.
indexOf()	Given a string and an initial index, returns the index of the next occurrence of the string after the initial index.
italics()	Surrounds the string with the HTML I tag.
lastIndexOf()	Given a string and a starting index, returns the index of the last occurrence of the string starting the search backwards at the starting index.
link()	Given a URL, surrounds the string with an A tag to create a hypertext link.
small()	Surrounds the string with the HTML SMALL tag.
strike()	Surrounds the string with the HTML STRIKE tag.
sub()	Surrounds the string with the HTML SUB tag.
substring()	Given two indexes, returns the substring starting at the first index and ending with the character before the last index. If the second index is greater, the substring starts with the second index and ends with the character before the first index; if the two indexes are equal, returns the empty string.
sup()	Surrounds the string with the HTML SUP tag.
toLowerCase()	Makes the entire string lowercase.
toUpperCase()	Makes the entire string uppercase.

10

The HTML Methods

As you can see in Table 10.1, many of the methods of the string object are designed to add HTML tags to the content of the string so that when you display the string, it is suitably formatted. This can make the JavaScript code easier to read than if all the string assignments contained HTML tags, with the actual text to be displayed using document.write() or document.writeln().

The way these functions work is to return a new string containing the additional HTML tags. So, if you have a string variable named sample with the value "test", sample.big() returns "<BIG>test</BIG>" but sample still has a value of "test".

For instance, the following JavaScript commands output the text "Hello!" in large, blinking, bold letters:

```
var sample = "Hello!";
var sampleBig = sample.big();
var sampleBlink = sampleBig.blink();
var sampleBold = sampleBlink.bold();
document.write(sampleBold);
```

The following text displays the same word but as a hypertext link to the file: http://some.domain/some/file.html

```
var sample = "Hello!";
sample = sample.link("http://some.domain/some/file.html");
document.write(sample);
```

Because these methods return strings, you can also string together a series of methods and rewrite the first example as

```
var sample = "Hello!";
document.write(sample.big().blink().bold());
```

To give you a better idea of what these methods actually do to the content of your strings, the script in Listing 10.1 displays the actual content of the strings using the XMP tag to force the browser not to interpret any HTML in the output.

TYPE

Listing 10.1. Applying HTML tags with JavaScript's string object.

```
<HTML>

<HEAD>
<TITLE>HTML method example</TITLE>
</HEAD>

<BODY>

<SCRIPT LANGUAGE="JavaScript">
<!-- HIDE FROM OTHER BROWSERS

var sample = "hello";

document.write("<XMP>" + sample.italics() + "</XMP>");
document.write(sample.italics());

document.write("<XMP>" + sample.blink() + "</XMP>");
document.write(sample.italics());

document.write("<XMP>" + sample.anchor("test") + "</XMP>");
document.write(sample.anchor("test"));

document.write("<XMP>" + sample.fontsize(7) + "</XMP>");
document.write(sample.fontsize(7));
```

10

```
document.write("<XMP>" + sample.bold().strike() + "</XMP>");
document.write(sample.bold().strike());

document.write("<XMP>" + sample.fontcolor("iceblue").big().sup() + "</XMP>");
document.write(sample.fontcolor("iceblue").big().sup());

// STOP HIDING FROM OTHER BROWSERS -->
</SCRIPT>

</BODY>

</HTML>
```

OUTPUT   The script produces results like those in Figure 10.1.

Figure 10.1.

The HTML methods of the string *object return new strings containing the appropriate HTML tags.*

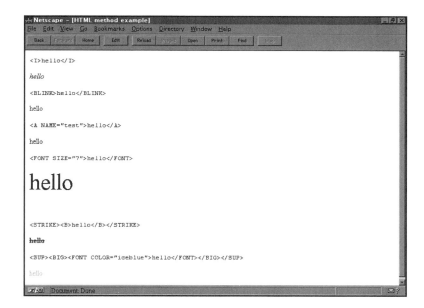

ANALYSIS   In this script, you are using various methods of the string object and the value returned by these methods. The script contains the examples in pairs of document.write() statements. The first output is the result of a method call surrounded by the XMP HTML container tags. The XMP tag ensures that any content inside the container is displayed without any processing. In this way, any HTML inside the container is simply displayed as regular text rather than treated as HTML.

The second line of each pair calls the same method but this time without the surrounding XMP tags so that the user can see what the result looks like when treated as HTML.

The `substring()` Method

You have seen the `substring()` method several times in previous chapters. You first saw the `substring()` method in Exercise 6.3 when you used it to verify input in a form.

To review, the method takes two integer arguments and returns the string starting at the first argument and ending at the character before the second argument. Where the first argument is larger, the process is reversed, and the substring starts at the second argument and continues until one before the first argument. When both arguments are equal, an empty string is returned.

For instance, if you have a string named `sample` with a value `"Hello!"`, then `sample.substring(0,3)` is `"Hel"`, `sample.substring(3,0)` is `"Hel"`, and `sample.substring(2,4)` has the value `"ll"`.

The Case Methods

The `string` object has two methods for changing the case of characters in a string. `toLowerCase()` returns a new string with all characters in lowercase. Similarly, `toUpperCase()` returns a copy of the string with all characters uppercase.

For instance, if the variable `sample` is `"tEsT"`, then `sample.toLowerCase()` is `"test"`, and `sample.toUpperCase()` is `"TEST"`.

Using a combination of these methods and the `substring()` method, you can achieve more interesting results. If you want to take a string and make the first character uppercase and the rest lowercase, you could use the following technique:

```
var sample = "tEsT";
var newSample = sample.substring(0,1).toUpperCase() +
➥sample.substring(1,sample.length).toLowerCase();
```

Other Methods

The `string` object has three other methods: `indexOf()`, `lastIndexOf()`, and `charAt()`.

You saw the `indexOf()` method in Chapter 9, "Remember Where You've Been with Cookies." Simply, given two arguments (a string and an index) the method starts searching the `string` object from the index and looks for the first occurrence of the string that has been passed to it as an argument. It returns the index of this occurrence.

This is best understood by example: If you have a string named `sample` with the value `"Greetings! Welcome to Navigator 2.0! Enjoy!"`, then `sample.indexOf("Wel",2)` would return a value of 13 and `sample.lastIndexOf("!",sample.length - 3)` would return a value of 35.

What happens in the first example is that the method starts searching the string sample from index 2 (the first "e" in "Greetings"). It checks if the phrase "Wel" starts at that index and if not, it moves to the next character (index 3) and tries again. This is repeated until the character at index 13, where a match is found.

The send example is similar, but it moves backwards through the string looking for a match. In this case it starts at the 3 character from the end ("o" in "Enjoy") and moves back until it finds a "!".

The other method, charAt(), is almost the reverse of this process. Given an index as an argument, it returns the character at that location. This is easier to use to extract a single character from a string than the substring() method.

For instance, with the above string, both sample.charAt(3) and sample.substring(3,4) have the value of "e".

With these methods, you can now develop tools to enable users to play with HTML to see how it looks. Using two frames, you will build an application that enables users to enter text in the left frame and select from a list of HTML attributes. They will see the text displayed with the combined attributes in the right frame, along with the actual HTML code needed to produce the results. Listings 10.2 through 10.4 contain the script files for the program.

In order to do this, you need a top-level frameset which looks like Listing 10.2.

TYPE **Listing 10.2. Top-level frameset.**

```
<HTML>

<HEAD>
<TITLE>Listing 10.2</TITLE>
</HEAD>

<FRAMESET COLS="50%,*">
  <FRAME SRC="htmlform.html" NAME="choose">
  <FRAME SRC="sample.html" NAME="output">
</FRAMESET>

</HTML>
```

The htmlform.html file is where all the work is done.

TYPE **Listing 10.3. The htmlform.html file.**

```
<HTML>

<HEAD>
```

continues

Listing 10.3. continued

```
<SCRIPT LANGUAGE="JavaScript">
<!-- HIDE FROM OTHER BROWSERS

function display(form) {
  var format = form.toDisplay.value;
  var doc = parent.output;

  format = (form.big.checked) ? format.big() : format;
  format = (form.blink.checked) ? format.blink() : format;
  format = (form.bold.checked) ? format.bold() : format;
  format = (form.fixed.checked) ? format.fixed() : format;
  format = (form.italics.checked) ? format.italics() : format;
  format = (form.small.checked) ? format.small() : format;
  format = (form.strike.checked) ? format.strike() : format;
  format = (form.sup.checked) ? format.sup() : format;
  format = (form.sub.checked) ? format.sub() : format;
  format = (form.color.value == "") ? format.fontcolor("black") :
➥format.fontcolor(form.color.value);
  format = (form.size.value == "") ? format.fontsize(3) :
➥format.fontsize(form.size.value);

  var result = "<CENTER>The HTML code: <XMP>";
  result += format;
  result += "</XMP> looks like:<P>"
  result += format;
  result += "</CENTER>";

  doc.document.open("text/html");
  doc.document.write(result);
  doc.document.close();

}

// STOP HIDING -->
</SCRIPT>

<BODY BGCOLOR="aquamarine">

<CENTER>
<H1>The HTML tester page</H1>
Please enter some text, select some attributes and
➥enter a color and size (from 1 to 7).
The display will update dynamically.
<BR>
</CENTER>
<FORM METHOD=POST>

<TEXTAREA NAME="toDisplay" ROWS=10 COLS=35 WRAP=SOFT
➥onChange="display(this.form);">
Enter Text Here
</TEXTAREA><BR>
<INPUT TYPE="checkbox" NAME="big" onClick="display(this.form);">Big<BR>
<INPUT TYPE="checkbox" NAME="blink" onClick="display(this.form);">Blinking<BR>
<INPUT TYPE="checkbox" NAME="bold" onClick="display(this.form);">Bold<BR>
<INPUT TYPE="checkbox" NAME="fixed"
➥onClick="display(this.form);">Fixed Width<BR>
```

10

```
<INPUT TYPE="checkbox" NAME="italics" onClick="display(this.form);">Italics<BR>
<INPUT TYPE="checkbox" NAME="small" onClick="display(this.form);">Small<BR>
<INPUT TYPE="checkbox" NAME="strike"
➥onClick="display(this.form);">Striked Out<BR>
<INPUT TYPE="checkbox" NAME="sub" onClick="display(this.form);">Subscript<BR>
<INPUT TYPE="checkbox" NAME="sup" onClick="display(this.form);">SuperScript<BR>
Font Color: <INPUT TYPE="text" NAME="color" VALUE="black"
➥onChange="display(this.form);"><BR>
Font Size (1 to 7): <INPUT TYPE="text" NAME="size" VALUE="3"
➥onChange="display(this.form);">

</FORM>

<SCRIPT LANGUAGE="JavaScript">
<!-- HIDE FROM OTHER BROWSERS

display(document.forms[0]);

// STOP HIDING -->
</SCRIPT>

</BODY>

</HTML>
```

10

The file `sample.html` is just a blank HTML file to fill the window when the frame is initially loaded.

TYPE **Listing 10.4. The source code for `sample.html`.**

```
<HTML>

<BODY BGCOLOR="#FFFFFF">
</BODY>

</HTML>
```

OUTPUT This script produces results like those in Figure 10.2.

ANALYSIS This program not only highlights the effect of the previous example but also some of the methods and techniques you learned in previous chapters.

All the work is done in the file `htmlform.html` (Listing 10.3). The program only really does one task—displays information based on the content of a form—so only one function, `display()`, is necessary.

```
function display(form) {
  var format = form.toDisplay.value;
  var doc = parent.output;
```

Figure 10.2.

Using methods from the `string` *object to dynamically test different combinations of HTML attributes.*

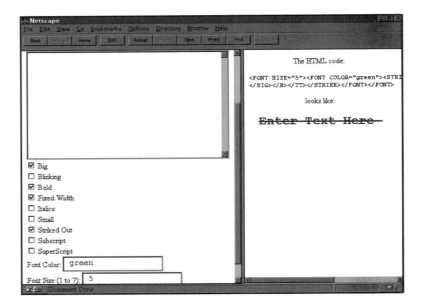

You start by setting up the global variable `format`. You use this variable to hold the entire text and HTML tags to be tested. You start by assigning the content of the `textarea` input field, which contains the text you are going to test.

You also define `doc` to be equal to the object `parent.output`. `parent.output` refers to the second frame in the frameset and is effectively the `window` object for that frame. In this way, you can use `doc` instead of `parent.output`. For instance, `doc.document.write()` is the same as `parent.output.document.write()`.

```
format = (form.big.checked) ? format.big() : format;
format = (form.blink.checked) ? format.blink() : format;
format = (form.bold.checked) ? format.bold() : format;
format = (form.fixed.checked) ? format.fixed() : format;
format = (form.italics.checked) ? format.italics() : format;
format = (form.small.checked) ? format.small() : format;
format = (form.strike.checked) ? format.strike() : format;
format = (form.sup.checked) ? format.sup() : format;
format = (form.sub.checked) ? format.sub() : format;
format = (form.color.value == "") ? format.fontcolor("black") :
➡format.fontcolor(form.color.value);
format = (form.size.value == "") ? format.fontsize(3) :

➡format.fontsize(form.size.value);
```

This section of code looks complex at first glance, but in reality, it is simple. You start by checking whether any of the checkboxes are checked. Because the `checkbox` object's `checked` property is a boolean value, you can use it as the condition for a conditional expression, which performs the appropriate method and then assigns the result back to `format`.

10

Next, you apply the appropriate `fontcolor()` and `fontsize()` methods based on the form content. If either field is empty, you use a default value.

```
var result = "<CENTER>The HTML code: <XMP>";
result += format;
result += "</XMP> looks like:<P>"
result += format;
result += "</CENTER>";

doc.document.open("text/html");
doc.document.write(result);
doc.document.close();
```

The final task is to output the results. The string `result` holds the complete output for the second frame. Then you use `document.open()` to open a new output stream in the second frame for the HTML MIME type. You write the results to the frame and close the stream with `document.close()`.

```
<FORM METHOD=POST>

<TEXTAREA NAME="toDisplay" ROWS=10 COLS=35 WRAP=SOFT
➥onChange="display(this.form);">
Enter Text Here
</TEXTAREA><BR>
<INPUT TYPE="checkbox" NAME="big" onClick="display(this.form);">Big<BR>
<INPUT TYPE="checkbox" NAME="blink" onClick="display(this.form);">Blinking<BR>
<INPUT TYPE="checkbox" NAME="bold" onClick="display(this.form);">Bold<BR>
<INPUT TYPE="checkbox" NAME="fixed"
➥onClick="display(this.form);">Fixed Width<BR>
<INPUT TYPE="checkbox" NAME="italics" onClick="display(this.form);">Italics<BR>
<INPUT TYPE="checkbox" NAME="small" onClick="display(this.form);">Small<BR>
<INPUT TYPE="checkbox" NAME="strike"
➥onClick="display(this.form);">Striked Out<BR>
<INPUT TYPE="checkbox" NAME="sub" onClick="display(this.form);">Subscript<BR>
<INPUT TYPE="checkbox" NAME="sup" onClick="display(this.form);">SuperScript<BR>
Font Color: <INPUT TYPE="text" NAME="color" VALUE="black"
➥onChange="display(this.form);"><BR>
Font Size (1 to 7): <INPUT TYPE="text" NAME="size" VALUE="3"

➥onChange="display(this.form);">
```

The form is simple. When any text field changes, you call `display()` and when any checkbox is clicked, you also call `display()`. No buttons are needed.

NOTE

> When using a form with no buttons like this, realize that in the version of Navigator 2.0 currently available, it is necessary to remove focus from a text field for a change event to be triggered.

```
<SCRIPT LANGUAGE="JavaScript">
<!-- HIDE FROM OTHER BROWSERS

display(document.forms[0]);

// STOP HIDING -->
</SCRIPT>
```

You end the body of the HTML file with a one-line script that calls `display()` for the first time to update the second frame with the contents of the form. This also could have been done in the `onLoad` event handler.

Creating Search and Replace Tools

Anyone familiar with UNIX will miss many of the powerful text searching and matching tools found in the operating system and in scripting languages such as Perl, Awk, and sed. Although JavaScript provides the `indexOf()`, `lastIndexOf()`, `charAt()`, and `substring()` methods to help manipulate string contents, it doesn't provide powerful search and replace capabilities.

In this example, you extend the functionality of JavaScript's text manipulation capabilities with simple `search` and `replace` functions.

The `search` function should be able to search for words both in a case sensitive and case insensitive manner and should be able to search for whole words or substrings in words. Likewise, the `replace` function should be able to replace a word or substring, paying attention to case in the original text or ignoring it.

The `search` function should return `true` or `false`, and the `replace` function should return a new string with the result of the replace.

Listing 10.5 is the source code for these search and replace functions.

TYPE   **Listing 10.5. Searching and replacing in JavaScript.**

```
<SCRIPT LANGUAGE="JavaScript">
<!-- HIDE FROM OTHER BROWSERS

// SET UP ARGUMENTS FOR FUNCTION CALLS
//
var caseSensitive = true;
var notCaseSensitive = false;
var wholeWords = true;
var anySubstring = false;


// SEARCH FOR A TERM IN A TARGET STRING
//
```

```
// search(targetString,searchTerm,caseSensitive,wordOrSubstring)
//
// where caseSenstive is a boolean value and wordOrSubstring is a boolean
// value and true means whole words, false means substrings
//
function search(target,term,caseSens,wordOnly) {

  var ind = 0;
  var next = 0;

  if (!caseSens) {
    term = term.toLowerCase();
    target = target.toLowerCase();
  }

  while ((ind = target.indexOf(term,next)) >= 0) {
    if (wordOnly) {
      var before = ind - 1;
      var after = ind + term.length;
      if (!(space(target.charAt(before)) && space(target.charAt(after)))) {
        next = ind + term.length;
        continue;
      }
    }
    return true;
  }

  return false;

}

// SEARCH FOR A TERM IN A TARGET STRING AND REPLACE IT
//
// replace(targetString,oldTerm,newTerm,caseSensitive,wordOrSubstring)
//
// where caseSenstive is a boolean value and wordOrSubstring is a boolean
// value and true means whole words, false means substrings
//
function replace(target,oldTerm,newTerm,caseSens,wordOnly) {

  var work = target;
  var ind = 0;
  var next = 0;

  if (!caseSens) {
    oldTerm = oldTerm.toLowerCase();
    work = target.toLowerCase();
  }

  while ((ind = work.indexOf(oldTerm,next)) >= 0) {
    if (wordOnly) {
      var before = ind - 1;
      var after = ind + oldTerm.length;
      if (!(space(work.charAt(before)) && space(work.charAt(after)))) {
        next = ind + oldTerm.length;
        continue;
      }
```

10

continues

Listing 10.5. continued

```
    }
    target = target.substring(0,ind) + newTerm +
    ➥target.substring(ind+oldTerm.length,target.length);
    work = work.substring(0,ind) + newTerm +
    ➥work.substring(ind+oldTerm.length,work.length);
    next = ind + newTerm.length;
    if (next >= work.length) { break; }
  }

  return target;

}

// CHECK IF A CHARACTER IS A WORD BREAK AND RETURN A BOOLEAN VALUE
//
function space(check) {

  var space = " .,/<>?!`';:@#$%^&*()=-¦[]{}" + '"' + "\\\n\t";

  for (var i = 0; i < space.length; i++)
    if (check == space.charAt(i)) { return true; }

  if (check == "") { return true; }
  if (check == null) { return true; }

  return false;

}

// STOP HIDING -->
</SCRIPT>
```

To demonstrate how these functions work, you can set up a simple search and replace application using the functions in Listing 10.6.

TYPE Listing 10.6. Using the search and replace functions.

```
<HTML>

<HEAD>
<TITLE>Listing 10.6</TITLE>

<SCRIPT LANGUAGE="JavaScript">
<!-- HIDE FROM OTHER BROWSERS

// SET UP ARGUMENTS FOR FUNCTION CALLS
//
var caseSensitive = true;
var notCaseSensitive = false;
var wholeWords = true;
var anySubstring = false;
```

10

```
// SEARCH FOR A TERM IN A TARGET STRING
//
// search(targetString,searchTerm,caseSensitive,wordOrSubstring)
//
// where caseSenstive is a boolean value and wordOrSubstring is a boolean
// value and true means whole words, false means substrings
//
function search(target,term,caseSens,wordOnly) {

  var ind = 0;
  var next = 0;

  if (!caseSens) {
    term = term.toLowerCase();
    target = target.toLowerCase();
  }

  while ((ind = target.indexOf(term,next)) >= 0) {
    if (wordOnly) {
      var before = ind - 1;
      var after = ind + term.length;
      if (!(space(target.charAt(before)) && space(target.charAt(after)))) {
        next = ind + term.length;
        continue;
      }
    }
    return true;
  }

  return false;

}

// SEARCH FOR A TERM IN A TARGET STRING AND REPLACE IT
//
// replace(targetString,oldTerm,newTerm,caseSensitive,wordOrSubstring)
//
// where caseSenstive is a boolean value and wordOrSubstring is a boolean
// value and true means whole words, false means substrings
//
function replace(target,oldTerm,newTerm,caseSens,wordOnly) {

  var work = target;
  var ind = 0;
  var next = 0;

  if (!caseSens) {
    oldTerm = oldTerm.toLowerCase();
    work = target.toLowerCase();
  }

  while ((ind = work.indexOf(oldTerm,next)) >= 0) {
    if (wordOnly) {
      var before = ind - 1;
      var after = ind + oldTerm.length;
      if (!(space(work.charAt(before)) && space(work.charAt(after)))) {
```

10

continues

Listing 10.6. continued

```
          next = ind + oldTerm.length;
          continue;
        }
      }
      target = target.substring(0,ind) + newTerm +
      ➥target.substring(ind+oldTerm.length,target.length);
      work = work.substring(0,ind) + newTerm +
      ➥work.substring(ind+oldTerm.length,work.length);
      next = ind + newTerm.length;
      if (next >= work.length) { break; }
    }

  return target;

}

// CHECK IF A CHARACTER IS A WORD BREAK AND RETURN A BOOLEAN VALUE
//
function space(check) {

  var space = " .,/<>?!`';:@#$%^&*()=-¦[]{}" + '"' + "\\\n\t";

  for (var i = 0; i < space.length; i++)
    if (check == space.charAt(i)) { return true; }

  if (check == "") { return true; }
  if (check == null) { return true; }

  return false;

}

// STOP HIDING -->
</SCRIPT>

</HEAD>

<BODY>

<TABLE WIDTH=100%>

<TR>

<TD VALIGN=TOP>
<DIV ALIGN=CENTER>
<H1>Search</H1>

<FORM METHOD=POST>

<SCRIPT LANGUAGE="JavaScript">
<!-- HIDE FROM OTHER BROWSERS

function doSearch(form) {
  var result = search(form.initial.value,form.term.value,
➥form.casesens.checked,form.word.checked);
```

```
  alert ((result) ? "Found!" : "Not Found!");
}

// STOP HIDING -->
</SCRIPT>

<TEXTAREA NAME="initial" ROWS=2 COLS=30>Search Text</TEXTAREA><BR>
Search For: <INPUT TYPE="text" NAME="term"><BR>
<INPUT TYPE="checkbox" NAME="casesens"> Case Sensitive
<INPUT TYPE="checkbox" NAME="word"> Whole Word Search<BR>
<INPUT TYPE="button" VALUE="SEARCH" onClick="doSearch(this.form);">
</FORM>
</DIV>

</TD>

<TD VALIGN=TOP>
<DIV ALIGN=CENTER>
<H1>Replace</H1>

<FORM METHOD=POST>

<SCRIPT LANGUAGE="JavaScript">
<!-- HIDE FROM OTHER BROWSERS

function doReplace(form) {

  form.result.value =
  ➥replace(form.initial.value,form.oldterm.value,form.newterm.value,
  ➥form.casesens.checked,form.word.checked);

}

// STOP HIDING -->
</SCRIPT>

<TEXTAREA NAME="initial" ROWS=2 COLS=30>Search Text</TEXTAREA><BR>
<TEXTAREA NAME="result" ROWS=2 COLS=30>Result Text</TEXTAREA><BR>
Search For: <INPUT TYPE="text" NAME="oldterm"><BR>
Replace With: <INPUT TYPE="text" NAME="newterm"><BR>
<INPUT TYPE="checkbox" NAME="casesens"> Case Sensitive
<INPUT TYPE="checkbox" NAME="word"> Whole Word Search<BR>
<INPUT TYPE="button" VALUE="REPLACE" onClick="doReplace(this.form);">
</FORM>
</DIV>

</TD>

</TR>

</TABLE>

</BODY>

</HTML>
```

10

OUTPUT This script produces results like those in Figure 10.3.

Figure 10.3.
The search *and* replace *functions can be used in any JavaScript application.*

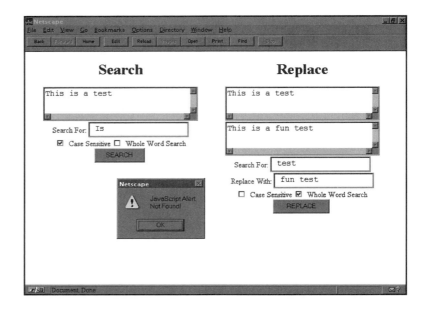

ANALYSIS You use three functions to implement the search and replace system: search(), replace(), and space().

search() and replace() use a similar approach to handling their tasks, but differ in the specific actions they take when they find the term they are looking for.

The replace() Function

The replace() function takes five arguments: the string to work on, the term to search for, the term to replace it with, and two boolean values. The two boolean values indicate whether to pay attention to the case of letters in searching and whether to search only for whole words (if not, substrings will be matched and replaced).

```
var work = target;
var ind = 0;
var next = 0;
```

As would be expected, you start by setting up the work variables.

```
if (!caseSens) {
  oldTerm = oldTerm.toLowerCase();
  work = target.toLowerCase();
}
```

10

Then you check whether you are paying attention to case. If not, you change the search term and the string to search to lowercase, using the toLowerCase() method. This means that case is ignored in the searches because any variation in case in either string has been removed.

```
while ((ind = work.indexOf(oldTerm,next)) >= 0) {
  if (wordOnly) {
    var before = ind - 1;
    var after = ind + oldTerm.length;
    if (!(space(work.charAt(before)) && space(work.charAt(after)))) {
      next = ind + oldTerm.length;
      continue;
    }
  }
```

All the work is done in the preceding while loop. In the condition of the while loop, you search the target string for the next occurrence of the search term, store the index in ind, and see if it is greater than zero.

If you have found an occurrence of the term, you next check if you are searching for whole words or substrings. If you are searching for whole words, you use the space() function to check if the characters before and after the word boundary are word breaks. If they aren't, you update next to the index of the character after the term you just found and start the loop again.

```
    target = target.substring(0,ind) + newTerm +
    ➥target.substring(ind+oldTerm.length,target.length);
    work = work.substring(0,ind) + newTerm +
    ➥work.substring(ind+oldTerm.length,work.length);
    next = ind + newTerm.length;
    if (next >= work.length) { break; }
  }
```

If you reach this point in the loop, then you have found a term you want to replace. You use the substring method to update both the string itself and change the variable next to the index of the character after the term you have just added.

Finally, you check if you have reached the end of the target string, and if not, you run the loop again to look for another occurrence.

The search() Function

This function is similar in structure to the replace() function. The differences lie in the while loop:

```
while ((ind = target.indexOf(term,next)) >= 0) {
  if (wordOnly) {
    var before = ind - 1;
    var after = ind + term.length;
    if (!(space(target.charAt(before)) && space(target.charAt(after)))) {
      next = ind + term.length;
      continue;
    }
```

```
    }
    return true;
  }

  return false;
```

As before, you perform the search for the search term using the `indexOf()` method in the condition of the `while` loop. Again, you check if you are searching for whole words, and if you are, you check for word boundaries. If you haven't found a complete word, you prepare to search again and return to the top of the loop with the `continue` statement.

If you get beyond the `if` statements, you have found an occurrence of the term and return a `true` value from the function. If you finish the `while` loop without returning `true`, then you haven't found a match and you return a `false` value.

The `space()` Function

The `space()` function plays a support role for `search()` and `replace()`.

Given a character as an argument, the function checks whether it is one of a series of characters considered word breaks or delimiters. If it is, the function returns `true`—otherwise, it returns a `false` value.

The way this is done is simple. All the possible word breaks are stored in the string `space`. A `for` loop goes through the string, character by character and compares each character to the argument. If there is a match, a `true` result is returned.

After the loop, a comparison is made between the argument and either the empty string or the `null` value. If these are `true`, the function returns a `true` value as well.

If you have failed all these conditions, then a `false` value is returned because the argument character is not a word break.

If the programmer wants to change the definition of a word break, he or she simply has to change the declaration of the variable `space`.

The `Math` Object

Where the `string` object enables you to work with text literals, the `Math` object provides methods and properties to move beyond the simple arithmetic manipulations offered by the arithmetic operators.

Among the features offered by the `Math` object are several special values such as `PI`, natural logarithms, and common square roots, trigonometric methods, rounding methods, an absolute value method, and more.

10

Table 10.2 outlines all the properties and methods of the Math object.

Table 10.2. Properties and methods of the Math object.

Name	Description
E	Euler's constant—the base of natural logarithms (roughly 2.718).
LN10	The natural logarithm of 10 (roughly 2.302).
LN2	The natural logarithm of 2 (roughly 0.693).
PI	The ratio of the circumference of a circle to the diameter of the same circle (roughly 3.1415).
SQRT1_2	The square root of 1/2 (roughly 0.707).
SQRT2	The square root of 2 (roughly 1.414).
abs()	Calculates the absolute value of a number.
acos()	Calculates the arc cosine of a number—returns result in radians.
asin()	Calculates the arc sine of a number—returns result in radians.
atan()	Calculates the arc tangent of a number—returns result in radians.
ceil()	Returns the next integer greater than or equal to a number.
cos()	Calculates the cosine of a number.
exp()	Calculates e to the power of a number.
floor()	Returns the next integer less than or equal to a number.
log()	Calculates the natural logarithm of a number.
max()	Returns the greater of two numbers—takes two arguments.
min()	Returns the least of two numbers—takes two arguments.
pow()	Calculates the value of one number to the power of a second number—takes two arguments.
random()	Returns a random number between zero and one. Presently, this is implemented only in UNIX versions of Navigator 2.0.
round()	Rounds a number to the nearest integer.
sin()	Calculates the sine of a number.
sqrt()	Calculates the square root of a number.
tan()	Calculates the tangent of a number.

10

Some of these functions require further discussion.

The Trigonometric Methods

You will notice that the trigonometric methods, such as `acos()` and `sin()` use radians to measure the size of angles instead of the more familiar degrees.

This isn't too difficult to handle. Where you have 360 degrees in a circle, there are 2×PI (or roughly 6.283) radians in a circle.

So, where the arc tangent of 1 is 45 degrees, in radians, the result is roughly 0.785398.

The `log()` and `exp()` Methods

The `log()` and `exp()` functions are related in that they use e, Euler's constant, as their base.

The relationship between logarithms and exponential expressions is that if `log(a) = b`, then `exp(b) = a`.

The `abs()` Method

The absolute value method returns the positive value of a number. That is, it removes a negative sign from a number so that `abs(4)` and `abs(-4)` both have a value of `4`.

Calculating Geometric Measurements

To highlight some of these math functions, you are going to build a simple calculator that calculates the angles and the lengths of the sides of a right angle triangle and calculates the area, diameter, and circumference of a circle.

In order to do this, you will use the trigonometric functions and `PI`.

As a reminder, with a right angle triangle, if you want to calculates the sine, cosine, or tangent of any of the other two angles, you can use the following formulas:

sine = opposite side / hypotenuse

cosine = adjacent side / hypotenuse

tangent = opposite side / adjacent side

The script should be able to fill in all the information about the shapes when there is sufficient information in the relevant form. The results of Listing 10.7 look like Figure 10.4.

TYPE Listing 10.7. Using the trigonometric functions.

```
<HTML>

<HEAD>
<TITLE>Example 10.7</TITLE>

<SCRIPT LANGUAGE="JavaScript">
<!-- HIDE FROM OTHER BROWSERS

function circle(form,changed) {

  with (Math) {
    var area = form.area.value;
    var diameter = form.diameter.value;
    var circumfrence = form.circumfrence.value;

    if (changed == "area") {
      var radius = sqrt(area / PI);
      diameter = 2 * radius;
      circumfrence = PI * diameter;
    }

    if (changed == "diameter") {
      area = PI * (diameter / 2) * (diameter / 2);
      circumfrence = PI * diameter;
    }

    if (changed == "circumfrence") {
      diameter = circumfrence / PI;
      area = PI * (diameter / 2) * (diameter / 2);
    }

    form.area.value = area;
    form.diameter.value = diameter;
    form.circumfrence.value = circumfrence;

  }

}

var toDegrees = 360 / (Math.PI * 2);
var toRadians = (Math.PI * 2) / 360;

function angle(form,changed) {

  with (Math) {

    var angle = (changed == "angleA") ? form.angleA.value *
    ➥toRadians : form.angleB.value;
    var otherAngle = (90 * toRadians) - angle;
    var hypotenuse = form.hypotenuse.value;
    var sine = sin(angle);
    var opposite = sine * hypotenuse;
    var cosine = cos(angle);
    var adjacent = cosine * hypotenuse;
```

continues

Listing 10.7. continued

```
            if (changed == "angleA") {
              form.angleB.value = otherAngle * toDegrees;
              form.sideA.value = adjacent;
              form.sideB.value = opposite;
            } else {
              form.angleA.value = otherAngle * toDegrees;
              form.sideB.value = adjacent;
              form.sideC.value = opposite;
            }

        }

    }

    function side(form,changed) {

      with (Math) {

        var side = (changed == "sideA") ? form.sideA.value : form.sideB.value;
        var hypotenuse = form.hypotenuse.value;
        var otherSide = sqrt(pow(hypotenuse,2) - pow(side,2));
        var angle = acos(side/hypotenuse);
        var otherAngle = acos(otherSide/hypotenuse);

        if (changed == "sideA") {
          form.sideB.value = otherSide;
          form.angleA.value = angle * toDegrees;
          form.angleB.value = otherAngle * toDegrees;
        } else {
          form.sideA.value = otherSide;
          form.angleB.value = angle * toDegrees;
          form.angleA.value = otherAngle * toDegrees;
        }

      }

    }

    function hyp(form) {

      angle(form,"angleA");

    }

    // STOP HIDING FROM OTHER BROWSERS -->
    </SCRIPT>

    </HEAD>
```

```
<BODY>

<TABLE WIDTH="100%">

<TR>

<TD>
<H1>Circle</H1>
<FORM METHOD=POST>
Area: <INPUT TYPE="text" NAME="area" VALUE=0
➥onChange="circle(this.form,this.name);"><BR>
Diameter: <INPUT TYPE="text" NAME="diameter" VALUE=0
➥onChange="circle(this.form,this.name);"><BR>
Circumfrence: <INPUT TYPE="text" NAME="circumfrence" VALUE=0
➥onChange="circle(this.form,this.name);">
</FORM>
</TD>

<TD>
<H1>Triangle</H1>
<FORM METHOD=POST>
Angle A: <INPUT TYPE="text" NAME="angleA" VALUE=45
➥onChange="angle(this.form,this.name);"><BR>
Angle B: <INPUT TYPE="text" NAME="angleB" VALUE=45
➥onChange="angle(this.form,this.name);"><BR>
Side A: <INPUT TYPE="text" NAME="sideA" VALUE=1
➥onChange="side(this.form,this.name);"><BR>
Side B: <INPUT TYPE="text" NAME="sideB" VALUE=1
➥onChange="side(this.form,this.name);"><BR>
Hypotenuse: <INPUT TYPE="text" NAME="hypotenuse" VALUE=1.414
➥onChange="hyp(this.form);">
</FORM>
</TD>

</TR>

</TABLE>

</BODY>

</HTML>
```

OUTPUT Figure 10.4 shows the result.

ANALYSIS This script is rather simple, but it shows how to use the methods and properties available in the Math object.

Of the two forms, the circle form is the simpler because it has less information to deal with. The following two sections analyze the two functions.

Figure 10.4.
Using the Math *object
to perform more
complex mathematical
calculations.*

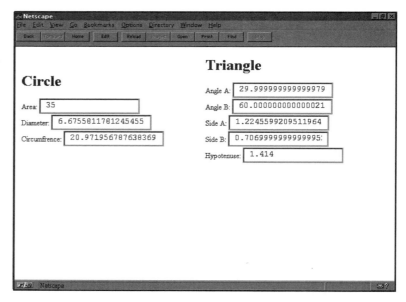

The `circle()` Function

The `circle()` function takes two arguments: the `form` object and the name of the field that
was just changed. The calculations are based on the name of this field.

```
with (Math) {
   var area = form.area.value;
   var diameter = form.diameter.value;
   var circumfrence = form.circumfrence.value;
```

You start by extracting whatever information is in the form and storing it in local variables.
Notice the use of the `with (Math)` command. This enables all of the `Math` properties and
methods in the function to be used without the `Math` prefix.

TIP

> The `with` command makes it easy to write command blocks that use
> properties and methods of a single object repeatedly. For instance, if
> you use `with (object) { command block }` then inside the command
> block, the methods and properties of *object* can be referred to as
> *methodName* and *propertyName* without the leading *object*.

10

```
if (changed == "area") {
  var radius = sqrt(area / PI);
  diameter = 2 * radius;
  circumfrence = PI * diameter;
}

if (changed == "diameter") {
  area = PI * (diameter / 2) * (diameter / 2);
  circumfrence = PI * diameter;
}

if (changed == "circumfrence") {
  diameter = circumfrence / PI;
  area = PI * (diameter / 2) * (diameter / 2);
}
```

The three if statement blocks simply calculate the other two fields based on the value of the changed field. All of these use two basic formulas:

> Area of Circle = PI×radius×radius
>
> Circumference of Circle = PI×diameter

Notice the use of the sqrt() method without the preceding Math prefix, which is made possible with the earlier with (Math) command.

```
form.area.value = area;
form.diameter.value = diameter;
form.circumfrence.value = circumfrence;
```

Once the calculation is done, you can reassign the results to the form.

Working with the Triangle

The triangle function assumes that you are working with a right angle triangle. This means the angle across from the hypotenuse is always 90 degrees.

The relationship between the remaining angles and sides is that sideA is adjacent to angleA and sideB is adjacent to angleB.

Before you can proceed to calculate the information in this form, you need to be able to convert between degrees and radians. All the trigonometric functions either take a radian value as a parameter or return a radian value. Users, on the other hand, are likely to prefer working in degrees.

You get around this by using the variables toDegrees and toRadians which represent the number of degrees per radian and the number of radians per degree:

```
var toDegrees = 360 / (Math.PI * 2);
var toRadians = (Math.PI * 2) / 360;
```

The `angle()` function is called whenever you change one of the two angle values. It uses the fact that all the angles of a triangle add up to 180 degrees to calculate the remaining angle. Then, using the `sin()` and `cos()` methods and the formulas for sine and cosine, the program calculates the length of the opposite and adjacent sides for the changed angle.

Finally, based on which angle was changed, the results are assigned to the correct form field.

The `side()` function plays a similar role when either `sideA` or `sideB` is changed. Using the value of the changed side and the value of the hypotenuse, you can calculate the value of the third side using the formula:

sideA×sideA + sideB×sideB = hypotenuse×hypotenuse

Once you have the value for the three sides, you can use the `acos()` method and the formula for cosine to calculate the value of the two angles.

The `hypotenuse` function simply calculates what the value of `sideA` and `sideB` should be based on the current angle settings by calling `angle(form, "angleA")`. You could just as easily have made the call `angle(form, "angleB")`.

The forms in the body of the HTML file are fairly simple. They call the appropriate function in the `onChange` event handler for each text field.

Working with the History List

When you use the Navigator browser, you will notice the history list, which is accessible under the Go menu.

The `history` object makes this list accessible in JavaScript. Early versions of JavaScript made the actual URLs in the list available to the script, but this was too large a security hole because it could be used by malicious scripts to steal information to access some secure Web sites. In addition, it could be used to breach privacy by supplying a page author with information about what sites a visitor had previously visited.

The current version of the `history` object provides methods for working with the list without actually reflecting the value of URLs and entries into a script.

Properties and Methods of the `history` Object

Table 10.3 outlines the properties and methods available in the `history` object.

Table 10.3. Properties and methods of the `history` object.

Name	Description
`length`	The length of the history list
`back()`	Loads the previous URL in the history list
`forward()`	Loads the next URL in the history list
`go()`	Loads the URL indicated by an offset from the current place in the history list

For instance, `history.back()` goes to the previous page while `history.go(-3)` goes back to the page visited three pages ago (like clicking the Back button three times on the Navigator toolbar) and `history.go(2)` goes two URLs forward in the list.

The `history.go()` method can also take a string instead of an integer as an argument. When a string is used, the method loads the nearest entry in the history that contains the string as part of its URL. The matching of the string against the URL is case insensitive.

One of the more popular uses of the `history` object is to provide back and forward buttons in individual frames or dynamic back buttons, which take users back to the last page they were on.

Summary

Manipulating data has been the focus of much of this chapter.

Using the `string` object, you now know how to add HTML tags using methods, how to change the case of a string, and how to search for the string and perform basic search and replace functions.

The `Math` object enables you to extend the type of mathematical calculations you can perform to include trigonometry, logarithms, and square roots and also provides several values as properties, including `PI`, `E`, and `LN2`.

The `history` object is a little different. By providing the ability to jump to URLs in the history list (without breaching security by providing the actual URL information), it is possible to build dynamic back and forward buttons into documents.

In the next chapter you will put everything you have learned together into producing a fun cartoon face drawing program.

Commands and Extensions Review

Command/Extension	Type	Description
anchor()	JavaScript method	Surrounds the string with an anchor A tag.
big()	JavaScript method	Surrounds the string with the HTML BIG tag.
blink()	JavaScript method	Surrounds the string with the HTML BLINK tag.
bold()	JavaScript method	Surrounds the string with the HTML B tag.
charAt()	JavaScript method	Given an index as an argument, returns the character at the specified index.
fixed()	JavaScript method	Surrounds the string with the HTML TT tag to make it display as a fixed-width font.
fontcolor()	JavaScript method	Surrounds the string with the HTML <FONT COLOR=color> and </FONT> tags to make it display in the specified color.
fontsize()	JavaScript method	Surrounds the string with the HTML <FONT SIZE=size> and </FONT> tags to make it display in the desired font size.
indexOf()	JavaScript method	Given a string and an initial index, returns the index of the next occurrence of the string after the initial index.
italics()	JavaScript method	Surrounds the string with the HTML I tag.
lastIndexOf()	JavaScript method	Given a string and a starting index, returns the index of the last occurrence of the string starting the search backward at the starting index.

10

Command/Extension	Type	Description
link()	JavaScript method	Given a URL, surrounds the string with an A tag to create a hypertext link
small()	JavaScript method	Surrounds the string with the HTML SMALL tag.
strike()	JavaScript method	Surrounds the string with the HTML STRIKE tag.
sub()	JavaScript method	Surrounds the string with the HTML SUB tag.
substring()	JavaScript method	Given two indexes, returns the substring starting at the first index and ending with the character before the last index. If the second index is greater, the substring starts with the second index and ends with the character before the first index; if the two indexes are equal, returns the empty string.
sup()	JavaScript method	Surrounds the string with the HTML SUP tag.
toLowerCase()	JavaScript method	Makes the entire string lowercase.
toUpperCase()	JavaScript method	Makes the entire string uppercase.
E	JavaScript property	Euler's constant—the base of natural logarithms (roughly 2.718).
LN10	JavaScript property	The natural logarithm of 10 (roughly 2.302).
LN2	JavaScript property	The natural logarithm of 2 (roughly 0.693).
PI	JavaScript property	The ratio of the circumference of a circle to the diameter of the same circle (roughly 3.1415).
SQRT1_2	JavaScript property	The square root of 1/2 (roughly 0.707).

continues

10

Command/Extension	Type	Description
SQRT2	JavaScript property	The square root of 2 (roughly 1.414).
abs()	JavaScript method	Calculates the absolute value of a number.
acos()	JavaScript method	Calculates the arc cosine of a number—returns result in radians.
asin()	JavaScript method	Calculates the arc sine of a number—returns result in radians.
atan()	JavaScript method	Calculates the arc tangent of a number—returns result in radians.
ceil()	JavaScript method	Returns the next integer greater than or equal to a number.
cos()	JavaScript method	Calculates the cosine of a number.
exp()	JavaScript method	Calculates e to the power of a number.
floor()	JavaScript method	Returns the next integer less than or equal to a number.
log()	JavaScript method	Calculates the natural logarithm of a number.
max()	JavaScript method	Returns the greater of two numbers—takes two arguments.
min()	JavaScript method	Returns the least of two numbers—takes two arguments.
pow()	JavaScript method	Calculates the value of one number to the power of a second number—takes two arguments.
random()	JavaScript method	Returns a random number between zero and one. Presently, this is implemented only in UNIX versions of Navigator 2.0.
round()	JavaScript method	Rounds a number to the nearest integer.
sin()	JavaScript method	Calculates the sine of a number.
sqrt()	JavaScript method	Calculates the square root of a number.

Command/Extension	Type	Description
`tan()`	JavaScript method	Calculates the tangent of a number.
`length`	JavaScript method	The length of the history list. Also used in the `string` object to provide the value of the string.
`back()`	JavaScript method	Loads the previous URL in the history list.
`forward()`	JavaScript method	Loads the next URL in the history list.
`go()`	JavaScript method	Loads the URL indicated by an offset from the current place in the history list.

10

Exercises

1. What would the output of the following code segment look like assuming there were no HTML tags elsewhere in the file affecting the output?

```
var sample = "test.";
sample.big();
sample.blink();
sample.bold();
sample.strike();
sample.fontsize(7);
document.write(sample.italics());
```

2. In the text searching and replacing functions (Listing 10.5 through 10.6), we have left out a critical feature: a wildcard. Extend the search and replace script to add a simple wildcard capability to the `search()` function. Use the following criteria:

   ☐ Use the asterisk character for your wildcard.

   ☐ The wildcard represents zero or more of any letter.

   ☐ Only one wildcard is enabled in a search term.

   ☐ Wildcards are valid only in the middle of a search term: `"text*"` and `"*text"` are not valid—catch this and inform the user.

   If you search the string `"Hello there"` for `"lo*e"` you should get a match as you would with `"H*lo"`, but `"the*h"` would not succeed.

3. What are the lines of code necessary to implement a dynamic forward and back button in an HTML page. The buttons should work just like the ones in the Navigator toolbar. (Hint: you need only one form with two buttons to do this.)

Answers

1. The phrase `"test."` would print in italics. All the other `method()` calls are useless. Remember that these methods return the new value. They do not directly alter the string. So, the results of all the other method calls went unassigned and unused. If we change the code to read

```
var sample = "test.";
sample = sample.big();
sample = sample.blink();
sample = sample.bold();
sample = sample.strike();
sample = sample.fontsize(7);
document.write(sample.italics());
```

then all the attributes will be applied to the displayed text.

2. The new search function would look like this:

```
function search(target,term,caseSens,wordOnly) {

  var ind = 0;
  var ind2 = 0;
  var next = 0;
  var wildcard = -1;
  var firstTerm = "";
  var secondTerm = "";

  if (!caseSens) {
    term = term.toLowerCase();
    target = target.toLowerCase();
  }

  if ((wildcard = term.indexOf("*",0)) >= 0) {

    if (!checkWildCards(term)) {
      alert("Improper use of the wildcard character.");
      return false;
    }

    firstTerm = term.substring(0,wildcard);
    secondTerm = term.substring(wildcard+1,term.length);

    while ((ind = target.indexOf(firstTerm,next)) >= 0) {
      var afterFirst = ind + firstTerm.length;

      ind2 = target.indexOf(secondTerm,afterFirst);
      if (ind2 < 0) { break; }

      if (wordOnly) {
        for (var i = ind+firstTerm.length; i <= ind2 - 1; i++)
          if (space(target.charAt(i))) {
            next = i + 1;
            continue;
          }
```

```
            var before = ind - 1;
            var after = ind2 + secondTerm.length;
            if (!(space(target.charAt(before)) && space(target.charAt(after))))
          ➡ {
              next = ind2 + secondTerm.length;
              if (next >= target.length) { break; }
              continue;
            }
          }
        return true;
      }

      return false;

    }

    while ((ind = target.indexOf(term,next)) >= 0) {
      if (wordOnly) {
        var before = ind - 1;
        var after = ind + term.length;
        if (!(space(target.charAt(before)) && space(target.charAt(after)))) {
          next = ind + term.length;
          continue;
        }
      }
      return true;
    }

    return false;
}
```

You would also need to add the `checkWildCards()` function:

```
function checkWildCards(term) {

  if (term.charAt(0) == "*") { return false; }
  if (term.charAt(term.length-1) == "*") { return false; }

  var first = term.indexOf("*",0);
  if (term.indexOf("*",first+1) >= 0) { return false; }

  return true;

}
```

You have not changed the basic functionality of the `search()` function. Rather, you have added a component in the middle which handles the wildcard searches. If there is no wildcard in the search term, the search functions operate in the same way as they did before, simply bypassing the wildcard section.

Assuming you have found a wildcard character, you perform an altered search, which is based on the simple search performed when there is no wildcard.

You start by checking that the use of the wildcard character is valid by calling `checkWildCards()`. If everything is correct, then you split the search term into two terms: the portion before the wildcard and the portion after it.

You then search for the first term in the condition of the `while` loop. If the first term occurs, you look for the second term. If the second term isn't there, you have no match and break out of the loop. Otherwise, you check if you are doing a whole word search. If you are, the function performs a check on the character before the occurrence of the first term and after the occurrence of the second term for word delimiter characters using the `space()` function. You also check that there are no word delimiters between the two terms. If the search fails either of these tests, you jump back to the top of the loop to continue searching the target string.

Otherwise, if you get past the `wordOnly` `if` statement, you know you have found a match and return a `true` value from the function.

3. The code

```
<FORM METHOD=POST>
<INPUT TYPE=button VALUE="BACK" onClick="history.back();">
<INPUT TYPE=button VALUE="FORWARD" onClick="history.forward();">
</FORM>
```

will implement dynamic forward and back buttons.

DAY

6

Chapter 11

Having Fun with JavaScript

In this chapter you are going to apply some of what you have learned to build a simple application that demonstrates how, with very basic JavaScript, it is possible to create the impression of a sophisticated interactive application.

You are going to design an application that enables users to build their own cartoon faces out of a library of existing eyes, noses, and mouths. No drawing skill is required for the user.

The Specifications

The application has several basic requirements:

- ☐ Display each piece of the face in a separate frame while the user is experimenting.
- ☐ Provide a button to build the complete face in a separate window which the user can then print out or save as a complete HTML file which displays the face.

☐ Provide a random face button which causes the script to build a random face from
among the possible faces.

Building the Application

In order to build this face program, you need to define the frameset, which contains all the
elements of the interface and application.

To do this, use the frameset in Listing 11.1.

TYPE   **Listing 11.1 The parent frameset.**

```
<FRAMESET ROWS="150,150,150,*">

  <FRAMESET COLS="400,*">
    <FRAME SRC="eye1.gif" NAME="eye" MARGINHEIGHT=0
➥MARGINWIDTH=0 SCROLLING="no">
    <FRAME SRC="eyes.htm" MARGINHEIGHT=0 MARGINWIDTH=0 SCROLLING="auto">
  </FRAMESET>

  <FRAMESET COLS="400,*">
    <FRAME SRC="nose1.gif" NAME="nose" MARGINHEIGHT=0
➥MARGINWIDTH=0 SCROLLING="no">
    <FRAME SRC="noses.htm" MARGINHEIGHT=0 MARGINWIDTH=0 SCROLLING="auto">
  </FRAMESET>

  <FRAMESET COLS="400,*">
    <FRAME SRC="mouth1.gif" NAME="mouth" MARGINHEIGHT=0
➥MARGINWIDTH=0 SCROLLING="no">
    <FRAME SRC="mouths.htm" MARGINHEIGHT=0 MARGINWIDTH=0 SCROLLING="auto">
  </FRAMESET>

  <FRAME SRC="build.htm">

</FRAMESET>
```

This sets up a four-row grid. The top three rows are each divided into two columns: The left
side displays the current selection for the eyes, nose, or mouth, and the right side presents all
the available choices.

The bottom row is where the control buttons to build the face and generate a random face
appear.

Based on this, you need to create four other HTML files (see Listings 11.2 through 11.5)
which are the basis of the program: eyes.htm, noses.htm, mouths.htm and build.htm.

TYPE **Listing 11.2. Source code for** `eyes.htm.`

```html
<!-- SOURCE CODE FOR eyes.htm -->

<BODY BGCOLOR="iceblue">

  <TABLE BORDER=0>

    <TR>

      <TD><A HREF="eye1.gif" TARGET="eye">
      <IMG SRC="eye1sample.gif" BORDER=0></A></TD>

      <TD><A HREF="eye2.gif" TARGET="eye">
      <IMG SRC="eye2sample.gif" BORDER=0></A></TD>

    </TR>

    <TR>

      <TD><A HREF="eye3.gif" TARGET="eye"">
      <IMG SRC="eye3sample.gif" BORDER=0></A></TD>

      <TD><A HREF="eye4.gif" TARGET="eye">
      <IMG SRC="eye4sample.gif" BORDER=0></A></TD>

    </TR>

  </TABLE>

</BODY>
```

TYPE **Listing 11.3. The source code for** `noses.htm.`

```html
<!-- SOURCE CODE FOR noses.htm -->

<BODY BGCOLOR="iceblue">

  <TABLE BORDER=0>

    <TR>

      <TD><A HREF="nose1.gif" TARGET="nose">
      <IMG SRC="nose1sample.gif" BORDER=0></A></TD>

      <TD><A HREF="nose2.gif" TARGET="nose">
      <IMG SRC="nose2sample.gif" BORDER=0></A></TD>

    </TR>

    <TR>
```

continues

Listing 11.3. continued

```
<TD><A HREF="nose3.gif" TARGET="nose">
<IMG SRC="nose3sample.gif" BORDER=0></A></TD>

<TD><A HREF="nose4.gif" TAGRET="nose">
<IMG SRC="nose4sample.gif" BORDER=0></A></TD>

</TR>

</TABLE>

</BODY>
```

TYPE   ## Listing 11.4. The source code for `mouths.htm`.

```
<!-- SOURCE CODE FOR mouths.htm -->

<BODY BGCOLOR="iceblue">

<TABLE BORDER=0>

<TR>

<TD><A HREF="mouth1.gif" TARGET="mouth">
<IMG SRC="mouth1sample.gif" BORDER=0></A></TD>

<TD><A HREF="mouth2.gif" TAGRET="mouth">
<IMG SRC="mouth2sample.gif" BORDER=0></A></TD>

</TR>

<TR>

<TD><A HREF="mouth3.gif" TARGET="mouth">
<IMG SRC="mouth3sample.gif" BORDER=0></A></TD>

<TD><A HREF="mouth4.gif" TARGET="mouth">
<IMG SRC="mouth4sample.gif" BORDER=0></A></TD>

</TR>

</TABLE>

</BODY>
```

11

The file `build.htm` (Listing 11.5) provides the controls in the bottom frame:

TYPE **Listing 11.5. The source code for `build.htm`.**

```
<!-- SOURCE CODE FOR build.htm -->

<HEAD>

<SCRIPT LANGUAGE="JavaScript">
<!-- HIDE FROM OTHER BROWSERS

function buildFace() {

  var eye = parent.eye.location;
  var nose = parent.nose.location;
  var mouth = parent.mouth.location;

  var face = window.open("","builtFace","width=400,height=450");
  face.document.open("text/html");
  face.document.write('<IMG SRC="' + eye + '">');
  face.document.write('<IMG SRC="' + nose + '">');
  face.document.write('<IMG SRC="' + mouth + '">');
  face.document.close();

}

function randomFace() {

  var eye = "eye" + getRandom() + ".gif";
  var nose = "nose" + getRandom() + ".gif";
  var mouth = "mouth" + getRandom() + ".gif";

parent.eye.location = eye;
parent.nose.location = nose;
parent.mouth.location = mouth;

}

function getRandom() {

  today = new Date();
  var bigNumber = today.getSeconds() * today.getTime() *
➥Math.sqrt(today.getMinutes());
  var randomNum = (bigNumber % 4) + 1;

  return Math.floor(randomNum);

}

// STOP HIDING -->
</SCRIPT>

</HEAD>
```

continues

Listing 11.5. continued

```
<BODY BGCOLOR="#000000" TEXT="iceblue">
<FORM METHOD=POST>
<CENTER>
<INPUT TYPE="button" VALUE="Build This Face" onClick="buildFace();">
<INPUT TYPE="button" VALUE="Make A Random Face" onClick="randomFace();">
</CENTER>
</FORM>
</BODY>
```

OUTPUT   The results of this application appear similar to Figures 11.1 and 11.2.

Figure 11.1.
Choosing a facial feature updates the relevant frame on the left.

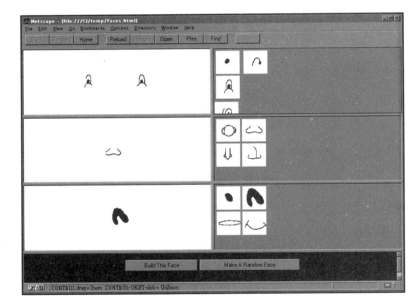

ANALYSIS   The first thing to notice about the four HTML documents is that three of them—eyes.htm, noses.htm, and mouths.htm—are very similar.

This is because all three files play the same role: They present options for the user to select each of three parts of the face.

Each file displays four options in a 2×2 table. Each of the small images displayed is, in fact, a link targeted to the appropriate frame on the left. When the user clicks on one of the sample images, the full-size version of that feature is displayed in the corresponding frame on the left.

11

You use JavaScript in the build.htm document. Here you have three functions related to the two buttons displayed in the bottom frame of the frameset: buildFace(), randomFace(), and getRandom().

buildFace() and randomFace() are called by the event handlers of the two buttons:

```
<INPUT TYPE="button" VALUE="Build This Face" onClick="buildFace();">
<INPUT TYPE="button" VALUE="Make A Random Face" onClick="randomFace();">
```

Figure 11.2.
Clicking on the build button causes a new window to open.

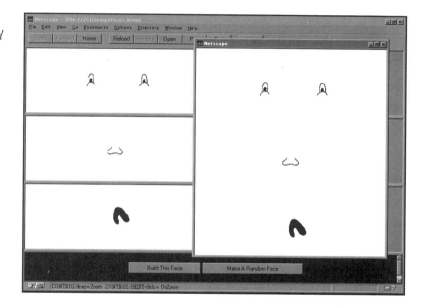

The buildFace() Function

The buildFace() function takes the three pieces of the face in the three frames and displays them in a single new window. This function needs to find out which files are displayed in each of the three left frames and then builds a single HTML file that displays the three files in a single window.

```
function buildFace() {

  var eye = parent.eye.location;
  var nose = parent.nose.location;
  var mouth = parent.mouth.location;

  var face = window.open("","builtFace","width=400,height=450");
  face.document.open("text/html");
  face.document.write('<IMG SRC="' + eye + '">');
  face.document.write('<IMG SRC="' + nose + '">');
```

```
face.document.write('<IMG SRC="' + mouth + '">');
face.document.close();

}
```

The function starts by getting the URLs of the three selected facial features with the `location` property of the `frame` object, as in the example `var eye = parent.eye.location;`. You use the fact that you can address object properties by name in the structure `parent.eye` to reference each frame.

Once this is done, a new window of the desired size is opened using

```
var face =window.open("","builtFace","width=400,height=450");
```

This command specifies the size of the window in pixels using the optional windows attributes argument. The new object for this window is called `face` so that you can later use commands such as `face.document.write()`.

Once the window is open, you open an HTML output stream using `face.document.open("text/html")` and then write out the three image tags based on the URLs you got earlier. Finally, you close the document output stream.

The `randomFace()` Function

The `randomFace()` function simply selects three random facial features and then opens them in the appropriate frames. This is done by calling the `getRandom()` function, which returns a number from 1 to 4, and then building three filenames, such as `var eye = "eye" + getRandom() + ".gif"`.

```
function randomFace() {

  var eye = "eye" + getRandom() + ".gif";
  var nose = "nose" + getRandom() + ".gif";
  var mouth = "mouth" + getRandom() + ".gif";

parent.eye.location = eye;
parent.nose.location = nose;
parent.mouth.location = mouth;

}
```

Once this is done, the three files are opened using `window.open()`.

The `getRandom()` Function

The `getRandom()` function is designed to return a random number from one to four. This is done by creating a new `Date` object for the current date and time, getting a large number by multiplying together different elements of the `Date` object, and then taking the modulus by four and adding one, as shown in the following lines.

```
function getRandom() {

  today = new Date();
  var bigNumber = today.getSeconds() * today.getTime() *
➡Math.sqrt(today.getMinutes());
  var randomNum = (bigNumber % 4) + 1;

  return Math.floor(randomNum);

}
```

The result is a pseudo-random number from one to four (because the modulus returns a number greater than or equal to zero and less than four). The use of `Math.floor()` ensures that the number returned is an integer.

Moving Beyond the Basic Script

There are a couple of limitations to the current script that you might like to improve:

☐ You have fixed the number of available eyes, noses, and mouths at four each. The program should be easily extendible to any number of eyes, noses, and mouths, and the number of each feature should be able to vary.

☐ Each time you build a face, it opens in the same window as the last face you built. The program should open each face in a different window.

☐ Users should be able to save the current face, and when they first come to the page, that face should be loaded as the default first face.

More Than Four Choices

In order to expand the script to support more than four choices for each feature, you need to make changes to each of the HTML files, including the parent frameset.

You start by adding a small script to the parent frameset (Listing 11.1).

```
<SCRIPT LANGUAGE="JavaScript">
<!-- HIDE FROM OTHER BROWSERS

var numEyes = 4;
var numNoses = 4;
var numMouths = 4;

// STOP HIDING -->
</SCRIPT>
```

This script is where you set the number of options for each of the three facial features. That way, if you want to add or remove choices, you only need to change these three numbers, and the whole program will work.

Next, you need to alter the three files eyes.htm, noses.htm, and mouths.htm (Listings 11.2 through 11.4) so that you use JavaScript to dynamically build two-row tables, regardless of the number of choices.

By way of example, this is what eyes.htm would look like:

```
<BODY BGCOLOR="iceblue">

  <TABLE BORDER=0>

    <TR>

    <SCRIPT LANGUAGE="JavaScript">
    <!-- HIDE FORM OTHER BROWSERS

    for (var i = 1; i <= Math.floor(parent.numEyes / 2); i ++) {
      document.write('<TD><A HREF="eye' + i + '.gif" TARGET="eye">');

      document.write('<IMG SRC="eye' + i + 'sample.gif" BORDER=0></A></TD>');
    }

    // STOP HIDING -->
    </SCRIPT>

    </TR>

    <TR>

    <SCRIPT LANGUAGE="JavaScript">
    <!-- HIDE FROM OTHER BROWSERS

    for (var i = Math.floor(parent.numEyes / 2) + 1;
 ➡️i <= parent.numEyes; i ++) {
      document.write('<TD><A HREF="eye' + i + '.gif" TARGET="eye">');

      document.write('<IMG SRC="eye' + i + 'sample.gif" BORDER=0></A></TD>');
    }

    // STOP HIDING -->
    </SCRIPT>

    </TR>

  </TABLE>

</BODY>
```

What you have added are two short scripts that build the table cells for each row of the table. The first script builds cells for each image from the first to the halfway point in the available list, and the second builds from there to the end. You use Math.floor() to ensure that you are building filenames out of integer values.

Finally, you need to alter the `randomFace()` and `getRandom()` functions in `build.htm` (Listing 11.5). `getRandom()` now takes an argument which is the range it is supposed to return (that is, from 1 to num). `randomFace()` passes the appropriate variable from the parent frameset for each function call to `getRandom()`.

```
function randomFace() {

  var eye = "eye" + getRandom(parent.numEyes) + ".gif";
  var nose = "nose" + getRandom(parent.numNoses) + ".gif";
  var mouth = "mouth" + getRandom(parent.numMouths) + ".gif";

parent.eye.location = eye;
parent.nose.location = nose;
parent.mouth.location = mouth;

}

function getRandom(num) {

  today = new Date();
  var bigNumber = today.getSeconds() * today.getTime() *
➥Math.sqrt(today.getMinutes());
  var randomNum = bigNumber % num + 1;

  return Math.floor(randomNum);

}
```

Building Faces in Multiple Windows

In order to build each face in a new window, you need to make far fewer changes than you made to support the variable number of choices for each facial attribute.

All the changes are made to the file `build.htm`. You add a global variable called `windowNumber`, which you increment for each window you open. Then you make one change to the function `buildFace()` on the line where you open the window:

```
var face = window.open("","builtFace" + windowNumber ++,"width=400,height=450");
```

This builds a new window name based on the value of `windowNumber` and then increments `windowNumber` by one. Remember that the unary increment operator (++) after an expression first evaluates the expression (in this case, that is simply `windowNumber`) and then increments the expression.

NOTE

Navigator includes a special target `_blank` which, when used in conjunction with `window.open()`, opens a new window. For instance, `window.open("","_blank")` opens a new empty window.

Summary

To help you see all the changes you have made, here is the source code including all the changes. I am only including eyes.htm (and not noses.htm or mouths.htm) because the changes are the same in these three files.

TYPE **Listing 11.6. Final version of eyes.htm.**

```html
<!-- SOURCE CODE FOR PARENT FRAMESET -->


<HEAD>

<SCRIPT LANGUAGE="JavaScript">
<!-- HIDE FROM OTHER BROWSERS

var numEyes = 4;
var numNoses = 4;
var numMouths = 4;

// STOP HIDING -->
</SCRIPT>

</HEAD>

<FRAMESET ROWS="150,150,150,*">

  <FRAMESET COLS="400,*">
    <FRAME SRC="eye1.gif" NAME="eye" MARGINHEIGHT=0
➥MARGINWIDTH=0 SCROLLING="no">
    <FRAME SRC="eyes.htm" MARGINHEIGHT=0 MARGINWIDTH=0 SCROLLING="auto">
  </FRAMESET>

  <FRAMESET COLS="400,*">
    <FRAME SRC="nose1.gif" NAME="nose" MARGINHEIGHT=0
➥MARGINWIDTH=0 SCROLLING="no">
    <FRAME SRC="noses.htm" MARGINHEIGHT=0 MARGINWIDTH=0 SCROLLING="auto">
  </FRAMESET>

  <FRAMESET COLS="400,*">
    <FRAME SRC="mouth1.gif" NAME="mouth" MARGINHEIGHT=0
➥MARGINWIDTH=0 SCROLLING="no">
    <FRAME SRC="mouths.htm" MARGINHEIGHT=0 MARGINWIDTH=0 SCROLLING="auto">
  </FRAMESET>

  <FRAME SRC="build.htm">

</FRAMESET>

<!-- SOURCE CODE FOR build.html -->

<HEAD>
```

11

```
<SCRIPT LANGUAGE="JavaScript">
<!-- HIDE FROM OTHER BROWSERS

var windowNumber = 1;

function buildFace() {

  var eye = parent.eye.location;
  var nose = parent.nose.location;
  var mouth = parent.mouth.location;

  var face = window.open("","builtFace" +
➥windowNumber ++,"width=400,height=450");
  face.document.open("text/html");
  face.document.write('<IMG SRC="' + eye + '">');
  face.document.write('<IMG SRC="' + nose + '">');
  face.document.write('<IMG SRC="' + mouth + '">');
  face.document.close();

}

function randomFace() {

  var eye = "eye" + getRandom(parent.numEyes) + ".gif";
  var nose = "nose" + getRandom(parent.numNoses) + ".gif";
  var mouth = "mouth" + getRandom(parent.numMouths) + ".gif";

parent.eye.location = eye;
parent.nose.location = nose;
parent.mouth.location = mouth;

}

function getRandom(num) {

  today = new Date();
  var bigNumber = today.getSeconds() * today.getTime() *
➥Math.sqrt(today.getMinutes());
  var randomNum = Math.floor(bigNumber % num);

  return randomNum + 1;

}

// STOP HIDING -->
</SCRIPT>

</HEAD>

<BODY BGCOLOR="#000000" TEXT="iceblue">
<FORM METHOD=POST>
<CENTER>
<INPUT TYPE="button" VALUE="Build This Face" onClick="buildFace();">
<INPUT TYPE="button" VALUE="Make A Random Face" onClick="randomFace();">
</CENTER>
```

continues

Listing 11.6. continued

```
</FORM>
</BODY>

<!-- SOURCE CODE FOR eyes.html -->

<BODY BGCOLOR="iceblue">

  <TABLE BORDER=0>

    <TR>

    <SCRIPT LANGUAGE="JavaScript">
    <!-- HIDE FORM OTHER BROWSERS

    for (var i = 1; i <= Math.floor(parent.numEyes / 2); i ++) {
      document.write('<TD><A HREF="eye' + i + '.gif" TARGET="eye">');

      document.write('<IMG SRC="eye' + i + 'sample.gif" BORDER=0></A></TD>');
    }

    // STOP HIDING -->
    </SCRIPT>

    </TR>

    <TR>

    <SCRIPT LANGUAGE="JavaScript">
    <!-- HIDE FROM OTHER BROWSERS

    for (var i = Math.floor(parent.numEyes / 2) + 1;
➡i <= parent.numEyes; i ++) {
document.write('<TD><A HREF="eye' + i + '.gif" TARGET="eye">');

      document.write('<IMG SRC="eye' + i + 'sample.gif" BORDER=0></A></TD>');
    }

    // STOP HIDING -->
    </SCRIPT>

    </TR>

  </TABLE>

</BODY>
```

Exercises

1. We still have one more addition to make: the ability to save a face and have it displayed as the first face when the user returns to the site. Extend the application so that there is a third button at the bottom to save the current face and change the loading procedure so that the saved face is loaded each time the user arrives at the site.

Answer

1. As you might have expected, the solution lies in cookies. In the file build.htm, you need to add a function called saveFace(), which saves the three filenames in three separate cookies. Define the path for the cookies to be "/" so all the files in your application have access to the cookies. Use Bill Dortch's cookie functions to handle the dirty work of saving and retrieving the cookies.

   Next, extend the parent frameset file so that it loads a blank file into each of three frames on the left and then uses an onLoad event handler to call a function called loadFace() to retrieve the relevant cookies and load the files into the empty frames.

   The resulting HTML documents look like Listing 11.7.

Listing 11.7. The final version of the parent frameset.

```
<!-- SOURCE CODE OF PARENT FRAMESET -->

<HEAD>

<SCRIPT LANGUAGE="JavaScript">
<!-- HIDE FROM OTHER BROWSERS

//
//  Cookie Functions - Second Helping  (21-Jan-96)
//  Written by:  Bill Dortch, hIdaho Design <bdortch@netw.com>
//  The following functions are released to the public domain.
//
// "Internal" function to return the decoded value of a cookie
//
function getCookieVal (offset) {
  var endstr = document.cookie.indexOf (";", offset);
  if (endstr == -1)
    endstr = document.cookie.length;
  return unescape(document.cookie.substring(offset, endstr));
}
```

continues

Listing 11.7. continued

```
//
//   Function to return the value of the cookie specified by "name".
//     name - String object containing the cookie name.
//     returns - String object containing the cookie value, or null if
//        the cookie does not exist.
//
function GetCookie (name) {
  var arg = name + "=";
  var alen = arg.length;
  var clen = document.cookie.length;
  var i = 0;
  while (i < clen) {
    var j = i + alen;
    if (document.cookie.substring(i, j) == arg)
      return getCookieVal (j);
    i = document.cookie.indexOf(" ", i) + 1;
    if (i == 0) break;
  }
  return null;
}

//
//   Function to create or update a cookie.
//     name - String object object containing the cookie name.

//     value - String object containing the cookie value.  May contain
//        any valid string characters.
//     [expires] - Date object containing the expiration data of the cookie.
//        If omitted or null, expires the cookie at the end of the current
➥session.
//     [path] - String object indicating the path for which the cookie is
➥valid.
//        If omitted or null, uses the path of the calling document.
//     [domain] - String object indicating the domain for which the cookie
//        is valid.  If omitted or null, uses the domain of the calling
➥document.
//     [secure] - Boolean (true/false) value
➥indicating whether cookie transmission
//        requires a secure channel (HTTPS).
//
//   The first two parameters are required.  The others, if supplied, must
//   be passed in the order listed above.  To omit an unused optional field,
//   use null as a place holder.  For example, to call SetCookie using name,
//   value and path, you would code:
//
//       SetCookie ("myCookieName", "myCookieValue", null, "/");
//
//   Note that trailing omitted parameters do not require a placeholder.
//
//   To set a secure cookie for path "/myPath", that expires after the
//   current session, you might code:
//
//       SetCookie (myCookieVar, cookieValueVar, null, "/myPath", null,
➥true);
//
```

11

```
function SetCookie (name, value) {
  var argv = SetCookie.arguments;
  var argc = SetCookie.arguments.length;
  var expires = (argc > 2) ? argv[2] : null;
  var path = (argc > 3) ? argv[3] : null;
  var domain = (argc > 4) ? argv[4] : null;
  var secure = (argc > 5) ? argv[5] : false;
  document.cookie = name + "=" + escape (value) +
    ((expires == null) ? "" : ("; expires=" + expires.toGMTString())) +
    ((path == null) ? "" : ("; path=" + path)) +
    ((domain == null) ? "" : ("; domain=" + domain)) +
    ((secure == true) ? "; secure" : "");
}

//  Function to delete a cookie. (Sets expiration date to current date/
➥time)
//     name - String object containing the cookie name
//
function DeleteCookie (name) {
  var exp = new Date();
  exp.setTime (exp.getTime() - 1);  // This cookie is history
  var cval = GetCookie (name);
  document.cookie = name + "=" + cval + "; expires=" + exp.toGMTString();
}

var numEyes = 4;
var numNoses = 4;
var numMouths = 4;

function loadFace() {

      var eye = GetCookie("eye");
      if ((eye == null) || (eye == "")) { eye = "eye1.gif"; }
      parent.eye.location = eye;

      var nose = GetCookie("nose");
      if ((nose == null) || (nose == "")) { nose = "nose1.gif"; }
      parent.nose.location = nose;

      var mouth = GetCookie("mouth");
      if ((mouth == null) || (mouth == "")) { mouth = "mouth1.gif"; }
      parent.mouth.location = mouth;

}

// STOP HIDING -->
</SCRIPT>

</HEAD>

<FRAMESET ROWS="150,150,150,*" onLoad="loadFace();">

  <FRAMESET COLS="400,*">
    <FRAME SRC="blank.htm" NAME="eye" MARGINHEIGHT=0
➥MARGINWIDTH=0 SCROLLING="no">
```

continues

Listing 11.7. continued

```
   <FRAME SRC="eyes.htm" MARGINHEIGHT=0 MARGINWIDTH=0 SCROLLING="auto">
 </FRAMESET>

 <FRAMESET COLS="400,*">
   <FRAME SRC="blank.htm" NAME="nose" MARGINHEIGHT=0
➥MARGINWIDTH=0 SCROLLING="no">
   <FRAME SRC="noses.htm" MARGINHEIGHT=0 MARGINWIDTH=0 SCROLLING="auto">
 </FRAMESET>

 <FRAMESET COLS="400,*">
   <FRAME SRC="blank.htm" NAME="mouth" MARGINHEIGHT=0
➥MARGINWIDTH=0 SCROLLING="no">
   <FRAME SRC="mouths.htm" MARGINHEIGHT=0 MARGINWIDTH=0 SCROLLING="no">
 </FRAMESET>

 <FRAME SRC="build.htm">

 <SCRIPT LANGUAGE="JavaScript">
 <!-- HIDE FROM OTHER BROWSERS


 // STOP HIDING -->
 </SCRIPT>

</FRAMESET>
```

TYPE **Listing 11.8. Revised version of** `build.htm`.

```
<!-- SOURCE CODE FOR build.html -->

<HEAD>

<SCRIPT LANGUAGE="JavaScript">
<!-- HIDE FROM OTHER BROWSERS

//
//  Cookie Functions - Second Helping   (21-Jan-96)
//  Written by:  Bill Dortch, hIdaho Design <bdortch@netw.com>
//  The following functions are released to the public domain.
//
//
// "Internal" function to return the decoded value of a cookie
//
function getCookieVal (offset) {
  var endstr = document.cookie.indexOf (";", offset);
  if (endstr == -1)
    endstr = document.cookie.length;
  return unescape(document.cookie.substring(offset, endstr));
}
```

```
//
//  Function to return the value of the cookie specified by "name".
//    name - String object containing the cookie name.
//    returns - String object containing the cookie value, or null if
//       the cookie does not exist.
//
function GetCookie (name) {
  var arg = name + "=";
  var alen = arg.length;
  var clen = document.cookie.length;
  var i = 0;
  while (i < clen) {
    var j = i + alen;
    if (document.cookie.substring(i, j) == arg)
      return getCookieVal (j);
    i = document.cookie.indexOf(" ", i) + 1;
    if (i == 0) break;
  }
  return null;
}


//
//  Function to create or update a cookie.
//    name - String object object containing the cookie name.

//    value - String object containing the cookie value.  May contain
//       any valid string characters.
//    [expires] - Date object containing the expiration data of the cookie.
//       If omitted or null, expires the cookie at the end of the
➥current session.
//    [path] - String object indicating the path for which the cookie is
➥valid.
//       If omitted or null, uses the path of the calling document.
//    [domain] - String object indicating the domain for which the cookie
➥//       is valid.  If omitted or null, uses the domain of the calling
➥document.
//    [secure] - Boolean (true/false) value
➥indicating whether cookie transmission
//       requires a secure channel (HTTPS).
//
//  The first two parameters are required.  The others, if supplied, must
//  be passed in the order listed above.  To omit an unused optional field,
//  use null as a place holder.  For example, to call SetCookie using name,
//  value and path, you would code:
//
//      SetCookie ("myCookieName", "myCookieValue", null, "/");
//
//  Note that trailing omitted parameters do not require a placeholder.
//
//  To set a secure cookie for path "/myPath", that expires after the
//  current session, you might code:
//
```

continues

Listing 11.8. continued

```
//      SetCookie (myCookieVar, cookieValueVar, null, "/myPath", null,
➡true);
//
function SetCookie (name, value) {
  var argv = SetCookie.arguments;
  var argc = SetCookie.arguments.length;
  var expires = (argc > 2) ? argv[2] : null;
  var path = (argc > 3) ? argv[3] : null;
  var domain = (argc > 4) ? argv[4] : null;
  var secure = (argc > 5) ? argv[5] : false;
  document.cookie = name + "=" + escape (value) +
    ((expires == null) ? "" : ("; expires=" + expires.toGMTString())) +
    ((path == null) ? "" : ("; path=" + path)) +
    ((domain == null) ? "" : ("; domain=" + domain)) +
    ((secure == true) ? "; secure" : "");
}

//  Function to delete a cookie. (Sets expiration date to current date/
➡time)
//     name - String object containing the cookie name
//
function DeleteCookie (name) {
  var exp = new Date();
  exp.setTime (exp.getTime() - 1);   // This cookie is history
  var cval = GetCookie (name);
  document.cookie = name + "=" + cval + "; expires=" + exp.toGMTString();
}

var windowNumber = 1;

function buildFace() {

  var eye = parent.eye.location;
  var nose = parent.nose.location;
  var mouth = parent.mouth.location;

  var face = window.open("","builtFace" +
➡windowNumber ++,"width=400,height=450");
  face.document.open("text/html");
  face.document.write('<IMG SRC="' + eye + '">');
  face.document.write('<IMG SRC="' + nose + '">');
  face.document.write('<IMG SRC="' + mouth + '">');
  face.document.close();

}

function randomFace() {

  var eye = "eye" + getRandom(parent.numEyes) + ".gif";
  var nose = "nose" + getRandom(parent.numNoses) + ".gif";
  var mouth = "mouth" + getRandom(parent.numMouths) + ".gif";
```

11

```
parent.eye.location = eye;
parent.nose.location = nose;
parent.mouth.location = mouth;

}

function getRandom(num) {

  today = new Date();
  var bigNumber = today.getSeconds() * today.getTime() *
➥Math.sqrt(today.getMinutes());
  var randomNum = Math.floor(bigNumber % num);

  return randomNum + 1;

}

function saveFace() {

  var eye = parent["eye"].location;
  var nose = parent["nose"].location;
  var mouth = parent["mouth"].location;

  var expiry = new Date;
  expiry.setTime(expiry.getTime() + 365*24*60*60*1000);

  SetCookie("eye",eye,expiry,"/");
  SetCookie("nose",nose,expiry,"/");
  SetCookie("mouth",mouth,expiry,"/");

}

// STOP HIDING -->
</SCRIPT>

</HEAD>

<BODY BGCOLOR="#000000" TEXT="iceblue">
<FORM METHOD=POST>
<CENTER>
<INPUT TYPE="button" VALUE="Build This Face" onClick="buildFace();">
<INPUT TYPE="button" VALUE="Make A Random Face" onClick="randomFace();">
<INPUT TYPE="button" VALUE="Save This Face" onClick="saveFace();">
</CENTER>
</FORM>
</BODY>
```

You may also want to extend the form in build.htm to add a button to load a saved face:

```
<INPUT TYPE="button" VALUE="Load Saved Face" onClick="parent.loadFace();">
```

From the Web:

Michal Sramka's Matches Game

Michal Sramka has used JavaScript to produce one of the traditional games used in many programming courses: the matches game. His game is on-line at

```
http://www.sanet.sk/~ms/js/matches.html
```

The rules of the game are simple: There is a supply of matches—in this case the number is selected by the user. The user and the computer take turns taking one, two, or three matches in an attempt to force the other player to take the last match. If you take the last match, you lose. If the computer is forced to take it, then you win.

In Sramka's example, he has developed a fairly sophisticated table-based interface that makes extensive use of JavaScript.

Listing W5.1. Source code for Michal Sramka's Matches Game.

```html
<html>
<head>
<title>JavaScript</title>
</head>

<body onload="welcome()" onunload="bye()">

<script language="JavaScript">
<!-- Begin
function welcome() {
  document.game.help.value=" Please enter
➥number of matches and click Start game.";
document.game.number.focus();
  window.defaultStatus="JavaScript Safety Matches Game"; }

function bye() {
  window.defaultStatus=""; }

function come_on() {
  if(document.game.number.value<5) alert("Must be more than 4");
  else {
    document.game.help.value="                Wow, it's your turn. Click 1, 2 or 3.";
    document.game.count.value=document.game.number.value; } }

function letsgo(yourchoice) {
  var date=new Date(),mychoice;
  if(document.game.count.value-yourchoice<=1) {
    document.game.help.value="                        You win !";
    document.game.count.value=1; }
  else {
    if(document.game.count.value%4==0) {
      if(yourchoice==1) mychoice=2;
      else {
        if(date.getSeconds()%2==0) mychoice=3;
        else mychoice=1; } }
    else if(document.game.count.value%4==1) mychoice=4-yourchoice;
    else if(document.game.count.value%4==2) {
      if(yourchoice==2) mychoice=3;
      else {
        if(date.getSeconds()%2==0) mychoice=1;
        else mychoice=2; } }
    else {
      if(yourchoice==1) mychoice=1;
      else {
        if(date.getSeconds()%2==0) mychoice=2;
        else mychoice=3; } }
    if(document.game.count.value-yourchoice<4)
➥ mychoice=document.game.count.value-yourchoice-1;
document.game.count.value-=yourchoice+mychoice;
    document.game.me.value=" "+mychoice;
  if(document.game.count.value==1) document.game.help.value=
➥"          I took "+mychoice+" matches and win this game !";
else document.game.help.value=
➥"          I took "+mychoice+" matches. It's your turn again."; } }
```

```
// End -->
</script>

<center>

<h1>Safety Matches Game</h1>
This is a very easy game. It's avaliable as JavaScript Applet as well as
<a href="/~milan/JAVA/matches.html">Java Applet</a><br>
At first choose the number of matches. Then you have to take 1, 2 or 3
matches by clicking on the appropriate button. The Master will do the
same. Who takes the last match - LOSE !<p>

<form name="game">
<table border="3" cellpadding="0" cellspacing="2">
<tr>
<td align="left">How many matches ?</td>
<td align="right"><input type="text" name="number" size="10">
➥<input type="button" name="start" value=" Start game "
➥onclick="if(confirm('Really start new game ?')) come_on()"></td>
</tr>
<tr>
<td align="center" colspan="2"><input type="text" name="help" size="55"></td>
</tr>
<tr>
<td align="left">Counter:</td>
<td align="right"><input type="text" name="count" size="10"></td>
</tr>
<tr>
<td align="left">Your Choice:</td>
<td align="right"><input type="button" name="one"
➥value=" 1 " onclick="letsgo(1)"><input type="button"
➥name="two" value=" 2 " onclick="letsgo(2)">
➥<input type="button" name="three" value=" 3 " onclick="letsgo(3)"></td>
</tr>
<tr>
<td align="left">My Choice:</td>
<td align="right"><input type="text" name="me" size="3"></td>
</tr>
</table>
</form>

<hr><b><i><a href="/~ms/ms.html">Michal Sramka</a>'s
➥<a href="/~ms/js/">JavaScript Archive</a></i></b>
</center>
</body>
</html>
```

OUTPUT The script produces results similar to those in W5.1.

Figure W5.1.

Michal Sramka's Matches Game.

ANALYSIS To understand Sramka's program, you need to start by looking at the table, which is the primary interface for the game.

```
<form name="game">
<table border="3" cellpadding="0" cellspacing="2">
<tr>
<td align="left">How many matches ?</td>
<td align="right"><input type="text" name="number" size="10">
➡<input type="button" name="start" value=" Start game "
➡onclick="if(confirm('Really start new game ?')) come_on()"></td>
</tr>
<tr>
<td align="center" colspan="2"><input type="text" name="help" size="55"></td>
</tr>
<tr>
<td align="left">Counter:</td>
<td align="right"><input type="text" name="count" size="10"></td>
</tr>
<tr>
<td align="left">Your Choice:</td>
<td align="right"><input type="button" name="one" value=" 1 "
➡onclick="letsgo(1)"><input type="button" name="two"
➡value=" 2 " onclick="letsgo(2)"><input type="button"
➡name="three" value=" 3 " onclick="letsgo(3)"></td>
</tr>
<tr>
<td align="left">My Choice:</td>
<td align="right"><input type="text" name="me" size="3"></td>
</tr>
</table>
</form>
```

There is a Start button that confirms the user wants to start and then calls come_on(). If a new game starts, it uses the number in the number field to determine the number of matches in the game. The help text field is the primary display point for messages about the status of the game. The count field is used to display the number of matches left in the current game. There are three buttons that the user uses to select the number of matches he wants to take each turn. The me field is used to display the computer's choice each round.

There are four functions in the main script: welcome(), bye(), come_on(), and letsgo(). The welcome() and bye() functions display welcome and farewell messages and are invoked from the BODY tag's onLoad and onUnload event handler.

The come_on() function is called when the user decides to start a new game.

```
function come_on() {
  if(document.game.number.value<5) alert("Must be more than 4");
  else {
    document.game.help.value="          Wow, it's your turn. Click 1, 2 or 3.";
    document.game.count.value=document.game.number.value; } }
```

The function checks that the value in number is valid (greater than or equal to 5). If not, the user is alerted to choose another number. Otherwise, the help field informs the user that it is his turn, and the count field is updated with the starting number of matches.

The real work of the game takes place in letsgo(). The function is invoked when the user clicks on one of the three buttons to select a number of matches to take. The function takes one argument: the number of matches selected by the user.

The first step is to declare the global variables and objects: date and mychoice. The next step is to check if the user has won, by subtracting the selected number from the value in the count field and comparing it to 1.

```
function letsgo(yourchoice) {
  var date=new Date(),mychoice;
  if(document.game.count.value-yourchoice<=1) {
    document.game.help.value="                You win !";
    document.game.count.value=1; }
```

If the user has won, the help field is updated with an appropriate message, and the single match left is displayed in count.

Assuming the user hasn't won, the next step is to decide the computer's next play.

```
  else {
    if(document.game.count.value%4==0) {
      if(yourchoice==1) mychoice=2;
      else {
        if(date.getSeconds()%2==0) mychoice=3;
        else mychoice=1; } }
```

To do this, see if the number of matches left was a multiple of four before the user selected. If it was, and the user chose one match, then the computer chooses two. Otherwise, the computer makes a random choice between one and three matches.

```
   else if(document.game.count.value%4==1) mychoice=4-yourchoice;
```

If the remainder of dividing the number (before the user's choice) by four is one, then the computer selects the result of subtracting the user's choice from four.

```
   else if(document.game.count.value%4==2) {
     if(yourchoice==2) mychoice=3;
     else {
       if(date.getSeconds()%2==0) mychoice=1;
       else mychoice=2; } }
```

If the remainder is two, and if the user chose two, the computer chooses three matches. Otherwise, it makes a random choice between one and two.

```
   else {
     if(yourchoice==1) mychoice=1;
     else {
       if(date.getSeconds()%2==0) mychoice=2;
       else mychoice=3; } }
```

If the remainder is three, and the user chose one match, the computer follows suit and chooses one. Otherwise, a random choice is made between two and three.

```
   if(document.game.count.value-yourchoice<4)
➥mychoice=document.game.count.value-yourchoice-1;
document.game.count.value-=yourchoice+mychoice;
   document.game.me.value=" "+mychoice;
   if(document.game.count.value==1) document.game.help.value=
➥"         I took "+mychoice+" matches and win this game !";
else document.game.help.value=

➥"         I took "+mychoice+" matches. It's your turn again."; } }
```

Finally, if the user's play results in the number of remaining matches being less than four, then the computer chooses the number of remaining matches less one.

The function then updates the value of the count field and displays the computer's choice in me. Then a check is made to see if the computer has won. If the number of remaining matches is one, then the computer has won, and a message is displayed in help to that effect. Otherwise, a message informing the user of how many matches the computer took is displayed in help.

Chapter **12**

Creating a Spreadsheet in JavaScript

In this chapter, you are going to apply what you have learned to developing another application—a general-purpose spreadsheet.

Although you have experienced creating, and have seen examples of specific-function calculators, JavaScript's capability to work with forms and its math functions are not limited to these types of applications.

Using forms and cookies, you can create a general-purpose spreadsheet that retains its formulas between sessions.

The Specifications

The spreadsheet has several basic requirements:

☐ It should have a reasonable number of fields—not so many that users with small displays will have trouble, but not so few as to be less than useful. A good number appears to be roughly 100.

- [ ] The columns and rows should be numbered—one with numerals and one with letters.
- [ ] Users should be able to create formulas, or expressions, for any of the fields that use values from other fields to calculate their own values.
- [ ] Formulas should be able to include mathematical operators, as well as any of the methods of the Math object. Basically, any legal JavaScript mathematical expression should be acceptable.
- [ ] Users should be able to change or delete any expression.
- [ ] Expressions should be saved between sessions so that users can come back and continue using their spreadsheets.

What You Need to Do

In order to implement a spreadsheet with these requirements, you need to do several things before you start writing the script.

You need to decide the structure of expressions, how to store expressions, and how to handle changes to information in the spreadsheet.

The obvious choice for saving expressions is using cookies, and you will use Bill Dortch's functions again to achieve this. Each function should be stored in a cookie named by the field it is attached to in the spreadsheet.

For instance, if an expression is created for field A6, then a cookie named A6 should be created with the expression stored as a string for the value of the cookie. You will use an expiry date one year in the future to ensure that cookies are available between sessions.

Of course, you are limited by the number of cookies you can store for a given page and need to keep track of them so you don't accidentally delete important expressions by enabling the user to add too many expressions. You can do this by using one cookie as a counter to keep track of how many expressions have been created so far on the page.

The syntax for expressions is simple: the value of another field can be referenced simply by using the field's name followed by a semicolon. So, the expression A1; * B7; would multiply the value in field A1 by the value in field B7.

Every time the value of a form field is changed, you need to be able to reevaluate all expressions. Likewise, if the definition of an expression is changed, a new expression is created, or an expression is deleted, all expressions need to be reevaluated because the change could potentially affect any of the formulas. Listing 12.1 contains the script for the program.

12

TYPE Listing 12.1. A general-purpose spreadsheet.

```
<HTML>

<HEAD>
<TITLE>Chapter 12</TITLE>

<SCRIPT LANGUAGE="JavaScript">
<!-- HIDE FROM OTHER BROWSERS
//
//   Cookie Functions - Second Helping   (21-Jan-96)
//   Written by:  Bill Dortch, hIdaho Design <bdortch@netw.com>
//   The following functions are released to the public domain.

//
//   "Internal" function to return the decoded value of a cookie
//
function getCookieVal (offset) {
  var endstr = document.cookie.indexOf (";", offset);
  if (endstr == -1)
    endstr = document.cookie.length;
  return unescape(document.cookie.substring(offset, endstr));
}

//
//   Function to return the value of the cookie specified by "name".
//
function GetCookie (name) {
  var arg = name + "=";
  var alen = arg.length;
  var clen = document.cookie.length;
  var i = 0;
  while (i < clen) {
    var j = i + alen;
    if (document.cookie.substring(i, j) == arg)
      return getCookieVal (j);
    i = document.cookie.indexOf(" ", i) + 1;
    if (i == 0) break;
  }
  return null;
}

//
//   Function to create or update a cookie.
//
function SetCookie (name, value) {
  var argv = SetCookie.arguments;
  var argc = SetCookie.arguments.length;
  var expires = (argc > 2) ? argv[2] : null;
  var path = (argc > 3) ? argv[3] : null;
  var domain = (argc > 4) ? argv[4] : null;
  var secure = (argc > 5) ? argv[5] : false;
  document.cookie = name + "=" + escape (value) +
    ((expires == null) ? "" : ("; expires=" + expires.toGMTString())) +
    ((path == null) ? "" : ("; path=" + path)) +
    ((domain == null) ? "" : ("; domain=" + domain)) +
```

continues

Listing 12.1. continued

```
          ((secure == true) ? "; secure" : "");
    }

    //  Function to delete a cookie. (Sets expiration date to current date/time)
    //     name - String object containing the cookie name
    //
    function DeleteCookie (name) {
      var exp = new Date();
      exp.setTime (exp.getTime() - 1);  // This cookie is history
      var cval = GetCookie (name);
      document.cookie = name + "=" + cval + "; expires=" + exp.toGMTString();
    }

    // END OF COOKIE FUNCTIONS

    // SEARCH AND REPLACE FUNCTIONS
    //
    // SET UP ARGUMENTS FOR FUNCTION CALLS
    //
    var caseSensitive = true;
    var notCaseSensitive = false;
    var wholeWords = true;
    var anySubstring = false;


    // SEARCH FOR A TERM IN A TARGET STRING
    //
    // search(targetString,searchTerm,caseSensitive,wordOrSubstring)
    //
    // where caseSenstive is a boolean value and wordOrSubstring is a boolean
    // value and true means whole words, false means substrings
    //
    function search(target,term,caseSens,wordOnly) {

      var ind = 0;
      var next = 0;

      if (!caseSens) {
        term = term.toLowerCase();
        target = target.toLowerCase();
      }

      while ((ind = target.indexOf(term,next)) >= 0) {
        if (wordOnly) {
          var before = ind - 1;
          var after = ind + term.length;
          if (!(space(target.charAt(before)) && space(target.charAt(after)))) {
            next = ind + term.length;
            continue;
          }
        }
        return true;
      }
```

12

```
    return false;

}

// SEARCH FOR A TERM IN A TARGET STRING AND REPLACE IT
//
// replace(targetString,oldTerm,newTerm,caseSensitive,wordOrSubstring)
//
// where caseSenstive is a boolean value and wordOrSubstring is a boolean
// value and true means whole words, false means substrings
//
function replace(target,oldTerm,newTerm,caseSens,wordOnly) {

  var work = target;
  var ind = 0;
  var next = 0;

  if (!caseSens) {
    oldTerm = oldTerm.toLowerCase();
    work = target.toLowerCase();
  }

  while ((ind = work.indexOf(oldTerm,next)) >= 0) {
    if (wordOnly) {
      var before = ind - 1;
      var after = ind + oldTerm.length;
      if (!(space(work.charAt(before)) && space(work.charAt(after)))) {
        next = ind + oldTerm.length;
        continue;
      }
    }
    target = target.substring(0,ind) + newTerm +
    ➥target.substring(ind+oldTerm.length,target.length);
    work = work.substring(0,ind) + newTerm +
    ➥work.substring(ind+oldTerm.length,work.length);
next = ind + newTerm.length;
    if (next >= work.length) { break; }
  }

  return target;

}

// CHECK IF A CHARACTER IS A WORD BREAK AND RETURN A BOOLEAN VALUE
//
function space(check) {

  var space = " .,/<>?!`';:@#$%^&*()=-¦[]{}" + '"' + "\\\n\t";

  for (var i = 0; i < space.length; i++)
    if (check == space.charAt(i)) { return true; }

  if (check == "") { return true; }
  if (check == null) { return true; }

  return false;
```

continues

Listing 12.1. continued

```
  }

  // END OF SEARCH AND REPLACE FUNCTIONS

  // MAIN BODY OF SCRIPT
  //
  // Set up global variables
  //
  var width = 8;
  var height = 12;
  var letters = "ABCDEFGHIJKLMNOPQRSTUVWXYZ";

  // Set up Expiry Date for cookies
  //
  var expiryDate = new Date();
  expiryDate.setTime(expiryDate.getTime() + 365*24*60*60*1000);
  var deleteExpiry = new Date();
  deleteExpiry.setTime(deleteExpiry.getTime() - 1);

  // Function to calculate the spreadsheet
  //
  function calculate(form) {

    var expField = "";
    var expression = "";

    // Check each field for an expression and if there is one, evaluate it
    for (var x = 0; x < width; x ++) {
      for (var y = 1; y <= height; y ++) {
        expField = letters.charAt(x) + y;
        if ((expression = GetCookie(expField)) != null)
          form[expField].value = evaluateExp(form,expression);
      }
    }

  }

  // Function to evaluate an expression
  //
  function evaluateExp(form,expression) {

    var column = "";
    var index = 0;
    var nextExpField;
    var nextExpression = "";
    var nextResult = "";

    // Scan the expression for field names
    for (var x = 0; x < width; x ++) {
      column = letters.charAt(x);
      index = 0;
      index = expression.indexOf(column,index);

      // If we find a field name, evaluate it
      while(index >= 0) {
```

12

```
      // Check if the field has an expression associated with it
      nextExpField = expression.substring(index,expression.indexOf(";",index));

      // If there is an expression, evaluate--
➥otherwise grab the value of the field
  if ((nextExpression = GetCookie(nextExpField)) != null) {
          nextResult = evaluateExp(form,nextExpression);
      } else {
        nextResult = form[nextExpField].value;
        if ((nextResult == "") || (nextResult == null))
          nextResult = "0";
      }

      // Replace the field name with the result
      nextExpField = nextExpField + ";";
      nextResult = "(" + nextResult + ")";
      expression = replace(expression,nextExpField,nextResult,
➥notCaseSensitive,anySubstring);

      // Check if we have reached the end of the expression
      index = index + nextResult.length;
      if (index >= expression.length - 1) { break; }

      // If not, search for another field name
      index = expression.indexOf(column,index);
    }
  }

  // Evaluate the expression
  with (Math) {
    var result = eval(expression);
  }

  // Return the result
  return result;

}

// Function to save an expression
//
function saveExp(form) {

  var numExp = GetCookie("numExpressions");

  // Check the number of saved expressions
  if (numExp == "19") {
    alert("Too many expressions. Delete One first");
  } else {

    // If there is room, save the expression and update
➥the number of expressions
SetCookie(form.expField.value,form.expression.value,expiryDate);
    numExp = parseInt(numExp) + 1;
    SetCookie("numExpressions",numExp,expiryDate);

    // Recalculate the spreadsheet
    calculate(document.spreadsheet);
```

continues

12

Listing 12.1. continued

```
        alert("Expession for field " + form.expField.value + " is saved.");

    }

}

// Function to delete an expression
//
function deleteExp(form) {

  var numExp = GetCookie("numExpressions");
  var expression = GetCookie(form.expField.value);

  // Check if there is an expression to delete for the field
  if (expression != null) {

    // There is, so set the expiry date
    SetCookie(form.expField.value,"",deleteExpiry);
    numExp = parseInt(numExp) - 1;
    SetCookie("numExpressions",numExp,expiryDate);

    // Update the field and recalculate the spreadsheet
    document.spreadsheet[form.expField.value].value = "";
    calculate(document.spreadsheet);

    alert("Expession for field " + form.expField.value + " is removed.");

  }

}

// Function to build form
//
function buildForm() {

  var numExp = 0;

  // Check if this is a new spreadsheet. If it is,
➥set the number of expressions to zero
  if ((numExp = GetCookie("numExpressions")) == null) {
    SetCookie("numExpressions",0,expiryDate);
  }

  // Build row header
  document.write("<TR><TD></TD>");
  for (var x = 0; x < width; x++) {
    document.write("<TD><DIV ALIGN=CENTER>" +
➥letters.charAt(x) + "</DIV></TD>");
}
  document.write("</TR>");

  // Build each field -- each is the same, with a different name
  for (var y = 1; y <= height; y++) {
    document.write("<TR><TD>" + y + "</TD>");
    for (var x = 0; x < width; x++) {
      document.write('<TD><INPUT TYPE=text SIZE=10 NAME="' +
```

12

```
➥letters.charAt(x) + y + '" onChange="calculate(this.form);"></TD>');
//SetCookie(letters.charAt(x) + y,"",deleteExpiry);
      }
      document.write("</TR>");
   }

}

// STOP HIDING -->
</SCRIPT>

</HEAD>

<BODY BGCOLOR="iceblue">

<CENTER>

<FORM METHOD=POST NAME="spreadsheet">
<TABLE BORDER=0>

<SCRIPT LANGUAGE="JavaScript">
<!-- HIDE FROM OTHER BROWSERS

buildForm();

// STOP HIDING -->
</SCRIPT>

</TABLE>
</FORM>
<HR>

<FORM METHOD=POST>
<TABLE BORDER=1>

<TR>
<TD><DIV ALIGN=CENTER>Field Name</DIV></TD>
<TD><DIV ALIGN=CENTER>Expression</DIV></TD>
</TR>

<TR>
<TD><DIV ALIGN=CENTER><INPUT TYPE=text SIZE=10 NAME="expField"
   onChange="var exp = GetCookie(this.value); this.form.expression.value =
➥(exp == null) ? '' : exp;"></DIV></TD>
<TD><DIV ALIGN=CENTER><INPUT TYPE=text SIZE=50 NAME="expression"></DIV></TD>
<TD><DIV ALIGN=CENTER><INPUT TYPE=button VALUE="Apply"
➥onClick="saveExp(this.form);"></DIV></TD>
<TD><DIV ALIGN=CENTER><INPUT TYPE=button VALUE="Delete"
➥onClick="deleteExp(this.form);"></DIV></TD>
</TR>

</TABLE>
</FORM>
</CENTER>

</BODY>

</HTML>
```

12

OUTPUT The results of this script appear like those in Figures 12.1 and 12.2.

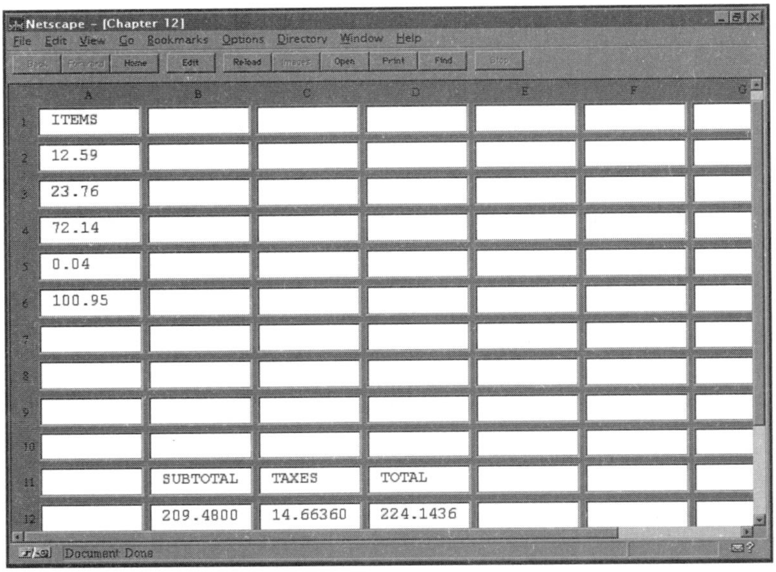

Figure 12.1.
*Building complex
spreadsheets using
mathematical
expressions.*

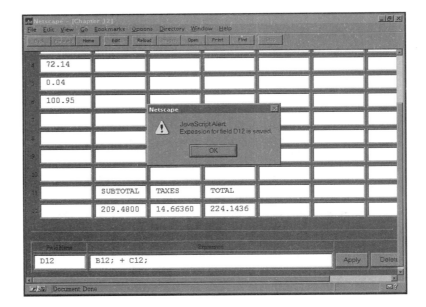

Figure 12.2.
*The small form at
the bottom can be
used to create,
update, and
delete expressions.*

12

You have used five functions to create the spreadsheet application. In addition, you have included Bill Dortch's cookie functions and the search and replace functions you built in Chapter 10, "Strings, Math, and the History List."

Using these, the `calculate()`, `evaluateExp()`, `saveExp()`, `deleteExp()`, and `buildForm()` functions do everything you need.

Before you look at the functions, you need to look at the body of the HTML document to understand the different interface components accessible to the user.

The document consists of two forms: the spreadsheet and the expression update form. The spreadsheet form is built dynamically by a small script which calls `buildForm()`. You use an HTML table to create a nicely formatted spreadsheet layout, as shown in the following segment.

```
<BODY BGCOLOR="iceblue">

<CENTER>

<FORM METHOD=POST NAME="spreadsheet">
<TABLE BORDER=0>

<SCRIPT LANGUAGE="JavaScript">
<!-- HIDE FROM OTHER BROWSERS

buildForm();

// STOP HIDING -->
</SCRIPT>

</TABLE>
</FORM>
<HR>
```

The second form is also in a table and is used to create, update, or delete expressions. It contains two text entry fields—one for the field name and one for the expression—and two buttons, Apply and Delete, which invoke the `saveExp()` and `deleteExp()` functions respectively (shown in Figure 12.2).

In addition, when the value of the `expField` field changes, you check if there is a stored cookie for that field, and if there is, display the expression in the `expression` field. Otherwise, you store an empty string in the `expression` field.

```
<FORM METHOD=POST>
<TABLE BORDER=1>

<TR>
<TD><DIV ALIGN=CENTER>Field Name</DIV></TD>
<TD><DIV ALIGN=CENTER>Expression</DIV></TD>
</TR>

<TR>
```

```
<TD><DIV ALIGN=CENTER><INPUT TYPE=text SIZE=10 NAME="expField"
  onChange="var exp = GetCookie(this.value); this.form.expression.value =
➥(exp == null) ? '' : exp;"></DIV></TD>
<TD><DIV ALIGN=CENTER><INPUT TYPE=text SIZE=50 NAME="expression"></DIV></TD>
<TD><DIV ALIGN=CENTER><INPUT TYPE=button VALUE="Apply"
➥onClick="saveExp(this.form);"></DIV></TD>
<TD><DIV ALIGN=CENTER><INPUT TYPE=button VALUE="Delete"
➥onClick="deleteExp(this.form);"></DIV></TD>
</TR>

</TABLE>
</CENTER>
</FORM>

</BODY>
```

Setting Up the Global Variables

In addition to the functions, you have several global variables you use to keep track of
information throughout the script:

```
var width = 8;
var height = 12;
var letters = " ABCDEFGHIJKLMNOPQRSTUVWXYZ ";

// Set up Expiry Date for cookies
//
var expiryDate = new Date();
expiryDate.setTime(expiryDate.getTime() + 365*24*60*60*1000);
var deleteExpiry = new Date();
deleteExpiry.setTime(deleteExpiry.getTime() - 1);
```

The width and height variables define the size of the spreadsheet. Eight columns and 12 rows
fit well on an 800×600 pixel display. Only notebook users with 640×480 displays may need
a smaller spreadsheet.

The letters string contains the letters of the alphabet which are used to name the columns
of the form. Each letter is extracted by its index (the column number minus one) when it is
needed. You include the whole alphabet because this gives you the flexibility to increase the
number of columns in the form simply by increasing the value of width.

expiryDate and deleteExpiry are the Date objects used for setting and deleting the cookies.
expiryDate is set to one year from the current date, and deleteExpiry is set to one millisecond
before the current time.

The calculate() Function

The calculate() function is probably the main function of the script. This function is called
every time you want to reevaluate the form when a value changes or an expression is added,

updated, or deleted. The function takes one argument: the `form` object for the spreadsheet form.

The structure of the function is quite simple. You have two nested `for` loops: one for each column using variable `x` and one for each row using variable `y`. For each combination of row and column you build the field name with `letters.charAt(x) + y`. Notice that the first `for` statement loops from zero to one less than the number of columns, which means `x` is the index of the appropriate letter in the `letters` string.

```
// Function to calculate the spreadsheet
//
function calculate(form) {

  var expField = "";
  var expression = "";

  // Check each field for an expression and if there is one, evaluate it
  for (var x = 0; x < width; x ++) {
    for (var y = 1; y <= height; y ++) {
      expField = letters.charAt(x) + y;
```

You then check if there is an expression stored in the cookie with the name of the field. You store the result of the `GetCookie()` call in the variable `expression` and compare this to `null`. If it is not `null`, you have an expression, and you evaluate the expression by calling `evaluateExp()`. `evaluateExp()` returns the evaluated expression, and you directly store that value in the appropriate field in the form.

Notice the use of the `form[expField]` structure to refer to the appropriate field in the form. As you learned earlier in the book, object properties can be referred to in three ways:

`objectName.propertyName`

`objectName["propertyName"]`

`objectName[propertyIndexNumber]`

The second form uses a string literal between the brackets, and in Listing 12.1, the value of `expField` is a string literal.

```
if ((expression = GetCookie(expField)) != null)
        form[expField].value = evaluateExp(form,expression);
    }
  }

}
```

The `evaluateExp()` Function

This is, perhaps, the most heavily used function in the script (with the exception of the cookie functions).

Given two arguments—the form object for the spreadsheet and the expression to be evaluated—the evaluateExp() function returns the value of the expression based on the current content of the spreadsheet.

```
// Function to evaluate an expression
//
function evaluateExp(form,expression) {

  var column = "";
  var index = 0;
  var nextExpField;
  var nextExpression = "";
  var nextResult = "";
```

You start with a for loop which iterates through each of the letters that name the columns. Inside that loop, you check whether there is an occurrence of the letter in the expression. If there is, it means that there is a reference to a field in that column that you need to handle.

You check for an occurrence of the letter by using indexOf() and storing the results in index.

```
  // Scan the expression for field names
  for (var x = 0; x < width; x ++) {
    column = letters.charAt(x);
    index = 0;
    index = expression.indexOf(column,index);
```

The while loop executes only when a field for the current column has been found—that is, index must be greater than zero.

Inside the loop, you get the field name by using substring() from index to the first occurrence of a semicolon (;), which marks the end of the field name. Given this value, you check whether there is an expression for that field and store the expression in nextExpression. If there is an expression, you call evaluateExp() recursively to get the value for that expression and store the result in nextResult.

If there is no expression for the field, you get the value of nextResult directly from the form. If this value is a null value or an empty string, you change nextResult to zero.

```
// If we find a field name, evaluate it
    while(index >= 0) {

      // Check if the field has an expression associated with it
      nextExpField = expression.substring(index,expression.indexOf(";",index));

      // If there is an expression, evaluate--
➦otherwise grab the value of the field
if ((nextExpression = GetCookie(nextExpField)) != null) {
        nextResult = evaluateExp(form,nextExpression);
      } else {
        nextResult = form[nextExpField].value;
        if ((nextResult == "") ¦¦ (nextResult == null))
          nextResult = "0";
      }
```

Once you have a value for nextResult, you can replace the occurrence of the field in the expression with the value of nextResult using the replace() function. Make sure that you also replace the semicolon after the field name and add parentheses to nextResult so that when the expression is evaluated, the value of nextResult is correctly evaluated and not affected by the rules of operator precedence.

For instance, if you have an expression A1; * B1; and B1 has the value of C1; + D1;, then, without adding the brackets, A1 would be multiplied by C1 and the result added to D1, when what you really want is to add C1 to D1 first and have the result multiplied by A1.

```
// Replace the field name with the result
    nextExpField = nextExpField + ";";
    nextResult = "(" + nextResult + ")";
    expression = replace(expression,nextExpField,nextResult,
➥notCaseSensitive,anySubstring);
```

Once you have updated the expression, you check whether you have reached the end of the expression by updating index to the character after the newly replaced value and compare this to the index of the last character in the expression.

If you haven't reached the end of the string, you check for another occurrence of the current letter with indexOf() and return to the condition at the top of the while loop.

```
    // Check if we have reached the end of the expression
    index = index + nextResult.length;
    if (index >= expression.length - 1) { break; }

    // If not, search for another field name
    index = expression.indexOf(column,index);
  }
}
```

Once you finish the for loop, you are ready to evaluate the expression. You use with(Math) so that any methods from the Math object that occurred in the expression don't require the presence of the Math prefix.

You evaluate the expression using the eval() statement.

```
// Evaluate the expression
with (Math) {
  var result = eval(expression);
}

// Return the result
return result;

}
```

12

The `saveExp()` Function

The `saveExp()` function saves an expression in a cookie when the user clicks the Apply button in the lower form, which is used to create and manipulate expressions. The function takes the `form` object for the expression as an argument.

The function starts by checking the number of expressions that have already been saved. If the number is already 19, the limit, then you inform the user that she needs to delete another expression if she wants to save this one.

```
// Function to save an expression
//
function saveExp(form) {

  var numExp = GetCookie("numExpressions");

  // Check the number of saved expressions
  if (numExp == "19") {
    alert("Too many expressions. Delete One first");
  } else {
```

If you have room to save the expression, then save it by getting the name of the cookie directly from the appropriate field in the form and getting the expression in the same way. You also update the number of expressions by one and update the cookie containing this value (notice the use of `parseInt()` to change the string returned by `GetCookie()` into an integer).

```
// If there is room, save the expression and
➥update the number of expressions
SetCookie(form.expField.value,form.expression.value,expiryDate);
    numExp = parseInt(numExp) + 1;
    SetCookie("numExpressions",numExp,expiryDate);
```

Finally, you recalculate the spreadsheet by calling `calculate()` and then inform the user that the expression has been saved.

```
    // Recalculate the spreadsheet
    calculate(document.spreadsheet);

    alert("Expession for field " + form.expField.value + " is saved.");

  }

}
```

The `deleteExp()` Function

Just as `saveExp()` saved an expression, `deleteExp()` deletes the expression indicated by a field name in the form. Again, it takes the `form` object as an expression and is invoked when the user clicks on the Delete button.

12

You start by checking whether there is an expression stored in that field. If there is, you save a new cookie with the same name but use deleteExpiry as the expiry date. You also decrease the number of expressions by one and update the cookie containing the number.

```
// Function to delete an expression
//
function deleteExp(form) {

  var numExp = GetCookie("numExpressions");
  var expression = GetCookie(form.expField.value);

  // Check if there is an expression to delete for the field
  if (expression != null) {

    // There is, so set the expiry date
    SetCookie(form.expField.value,"",deleteExpiry);
    numExp = parseInt(numExp) - 1;
    SetCookie("numExpressions",numExp,expiryDate);
```

Once the cookie has been deleted, you recalculate the spreadsheet and inform the user the task is done in the same way as the saveExp() function.

```
    // Update the field and recalculate the spreadsheet
    document.spreadsheet[form.expField.value].value = "";
    calculate(document.spreadsheet);

    alert("Expession for field " + form.expField.value + " is removed.");

  }

}
```

The buildForm() Function

The buildForm() function is the last function in Listing 12.1. It is called from inside the body of the HTML file and builds the HTML of the spreadsheet form, which is displayed in a table.

Using JavaScript to dynamically build the table is the best approach because each field is repetitive and because you want to be able to build the spreadsheet table to match the width and height variables if they get changed.

You start by determining whether this is a new spreadsheet by checking if there is any value stored in the cookie holding the number of expressions. If there isn't a value, you save a zero value there to initialize the spreadsheet.

```
// Function to build form
//
function buildForm() {

  var numExp = 0;

  // Check if this is a new spreadsheet.
```

```
➤If it is, set the number of expressions to zero
if ((numExp = GetCookie("numExpressions")) == null) {
    SetCookie("numExpressions",0,expiryDate);
  }
```

Next, you build the header row for the table which contains a blank field at the start, and then a field for each column with the appropriate letter centered in the field. You do this with a `for` loop that extracts each letter from the `letters` string.

```
// Build row header
document.write("<TR><TD></TD>");
for (var x = 0; x < width; x++) {
    document.write("<TD><DIV ALIGN=CENTER>" +
➤letters.charAt(x) + "</DIV></TD>");
}
    document.write("</TR>");
```

Once the table header is output, you use two nested `for` loops to build each row of the table with the number in the first field and then blank text input fields in the rest of the table cells in the row.

The names of the text entry fields are created using `letters.charAt(x) + y`.

```
// Build each field -- each is the same, with a different name
for (var y = 1; y <= height; y++) {
    document.write("<TR><TD>" + y + "</TD>");
    for (var x = 0; x < width; x++) {
      document.write('<TD><INPUT TYPE=text SIZE=10 NAME="' +
➤letters.charAt(x) + y + '"onChange="calculate(this.form);"></TD>');
}
    document.write("</TR>");
  }

}
```

Beyond the Basic Script

The basic script works but it has several limitations, including the following:

- ☐ Efficiency—Most users, especially those on Windows platforms, will notice that your script is a little slow and that actions create a noticeable lag to update the spreadsheet.

- ☐ Error checking—This script doesn't check that the syntax of the expressions is valid. It doesn't check that fields contain numeric values when it evaluates expressions and doesn't check for circular expressions (expressions that depend on each other to evaluate and will cause infinite recursion).

- ☐ Title—If you tried to create a spreadsheet including titles, you will notice that when you come back to the spreadsheet, the values of these title fields are lost.

12

In addition to these limitations, there are several features you could add to the spreadsheet to make it more useful:

☐ Ranges—Most spreadsheets enable formulas to include ranges in their expressions. (For instance, A1; ... A5; might be the total of the values in all fields from A1 to A5.)

☐ Clear—This application provides no easy way for the user to clear all the field values and all the expressions and start from scratch.

Improving Efficiency

The main efficiency bottleneck is in the calculate() function. In this function, you use two nested for loops to iterate through all 96 fields in the form. For each, you call GetCookie() to check whether the field has an expression, and if it does, you call evaluateExp().

This is inefficient, however. You end up calling GetCookie() for each empty field in the form, which in the example, means at least 77 unneeded calls to GetCookie() each time you change a value in the form.

If you have a way to know which fields have expressions without checking each field in the spreadsheet, you could avoid all these unnecessary calls to GetCookie().

To do this, you can take one more of the cookies and use it to store a list of fields that contain expressions. For instance, a semicolon delimited list such as A1;B11;C10; could be used.

In order to do this, you need to make changes to calculate(), saveExp(), and deleteExp().

In the calculate() function, you make a fundamental change to the logic of the function:

```
function calculate(form) {

  var index = 0;
  var next = 0;
  var expField = "";
  var expression = "";
  var fieldList = GetCookie("fieldList");

  if (fieldList != null) {
    while (index != fieldList.length) {
      next = fieldList.indexOf(";",index);
      expField = fieldList.substring(index,next);
      expression = GetCookie(expField);
      form[expField].value = evaluateExp(form,expression);
      index = next + 1;
    }
  }

}
```

12

You get the field list from the `fieldList` cookie. If it is `null`, there are no expressions and no evaluation is needed. Otherwise, you enter a `while` loop that continues until the index reaches the end of the `fieldList` string.

Inside the `while` loop, you scan for the next semicolon using `indexOf()` and extract the substring from `index` to the character before the semicolon. This value is the field name of an expression which you then get from the cookie, evaluate, and store in `form[expField].value`.

You then increment `index` to the character after the semicolon.

The `saveExp()` and `deleteExp()` functions both have similar changes. In the `saveExp()` function, you need to add a few lines to handle the extra cookie containing the field list, as well as change the maximum number of cookies to 18 to make room for the `fieldList` cookie.

You handle updating the `fieldList` cookie by first checking if there is a list already. If not, you simply create the list with the current field name. If there is a list, you remove the field name from the list by replacing it with an empty string and then add it back in. In this way, you don't get double occurrences of any field name in the list.

```
function saveExp(form) {

  var expField = form.expField.value;
  var fieldList = GetCookie("fieldList");
  var numExp = GetCookie("numExpressions");

  // Check the number of saved expressions
  if (numExp == "18") {
    alert("Too many expressions. Delete One first");
  } else {

    // If there is room, save the expression and
➥update the number of expressions
SetCookie(form.expField.value,form.expression.value,expiryDate);
    numExp = parseInt(numExp) + 1;
    SetCookie("numExpressions",numExp,expiryDate);
    expField += ";"
    if (fieldList == null) {
      fieldList = expField;
    } else {
      fieldList = replace(fieldList,expField,"",notCaseSensitive,anySubstring);
      fieldList += expField;
    }
    SetCookie("fieldList",fieldList,expiryDate);

    // Recalculate the spreadsheet
    calculate(document.spreadsheet);

    alert("Expession for field " + form.expField.value + " is saved.");

  }

}
```

The deleteExp() function works in a similar manner:

```
function deleteExp(form) {

  var fieldList = GetCookie("fieldList");
  var expField = form.expField.value;
  var numExp = GetCookie("numExpressions");
  var expression = GetCookie(form.expField.value);

  // Check if there is an expression to delete for the field
  if (expression != null) {

    // There is, so set the expiry date
    SetCookie(form.expField.value,"",deleteExpiry);
    numExp = parseInt(numExp) - 1;
    SetCookie("numExpressions",numExp,expiryDate);
    expField += ";";
    fieldList = replace(fieldList,expField,"",notCaseSensitive,anySubstring);
    SetCookie("fieldList",fieldList,expiryDate);

    // Update the field and recalculate the spreadsheet
    document.spreadsheet[form.expField.value].value = "";
    calculate(document.spreadsheet);

    alert("Expession for field " + form.expField.value + " is removed.");

  }

}
```

To delete the entry from the field list and update the cookie, you simply use the replace() function to delete the name and replace it with an empty string before updating the fieldList cookie.

Adding Title Fields

In order to save title fields, treat them as expressions so they get saved as cookies. The structure you will use is to have the first character of the title expression be a double-quote character.

Then, you can simply update the evaluateExp() function to return the rest of the string when it encounters this syntax:

```
function evaluateExp(form,expression) {

  var column = "";
  var index = 0;
  var nextExpField;
  var nextExpression = "";
  var nextResult = "";

  if (expression.charAt(0) == '"') {
    return(expression.substring(1,expression.length));
  }
```

```
  // Scan the expression for field names
  for (var x = 0; x < width; x ++) {
    column = letters.charAt(x);
    index = 0;
    index = expression.indexOf(column,index);

    // If we find a field name, evaluate it
    while(index >= 0) {

      // Check if the field has an expression associated with it
      nextExpField = expression.substring(index,expression.indexOf(";",index));

      // If there is an expression, evaluate.
➥Otherwise grab the value of the field
if ((nextExpression = GetCookie(nextExpField)) != null) {
        nextResult = evaluateExp(form,nextExpression);
      } else {
        nextResult = form[nextExpField].value;
        if ((nextResult == "") || (nextResult == null))
          nextResult = "0";
      }

      // Replace the field name with the result
      nextExpField = nextExpField + ";";
      nextResult = "(" + nextResult + ")";
      expression = replace(expression,nextExpField,
➥nextResult,notCaseSensitive,anySubstring);

      // Check if we have reached the end of the expression
      index = index + nextResult.length;
      if (index >= expression.length - 1) { break; }

      // If not, search for another field name
      index = expression.indexOf(column,index);
    }
  }

  // Evaluate the expression
  with (Math) {
    var result = eval(expression);
  }

  // Return the result
  return result;

}
```

You have added only one step to the evaluateExp() function. Before you attempt to evaluate the expression as a mathematical expression, you check the first character for a double quotation mark. If you find one, you simply return the rest of the expression string.

Checking for Errors

By way of example, you are going to perform some very basic error checking.

There are two places you need to check for errors. First, you need to make sure that the user has entered a legitimate expression in the expression field.

Here, if the user has entered a mathematical expression, you will check basic syntax—that is, that the field names use capital letters and end with a semicolon and also that you don't have a circular expression.

To make the script easier to read, do this in a separate function and call the function from the main `if` statement in `saveExp()`:

```
if (numExp == "18") {
  alert("Too many expressions. Delete One first");
} else {

  if (!checkExp(form.expression.value,expField + ";")) { return }

  // If there is room, save the expression and
➥update the number of expressions
SetCookie(form.expField.value,form.expression.value,expiryDate);
  numExp = parseInt(numExp) + 1;
  SetCookie("numExpressions",numExp,expiryDate);
  expField += ";"
  if (fieldList == null) {
    fieldList = expField;
  } else {
    fieldList = replace(fieldList,expField,"",notCaseSensitive,anySubstring);
    fieldList += expField;
  }
  SetCookie("fieldList",fieldList,expiryDate);

  // Recalculate the spreadsheet
  calculate(document.spreadsheet);

  alert("Expession for field " + form.expField.value + " is saved.");

}
```

The line

```
if (!checkExp(form.expression.value,expField + ";")) { return }
```

calls `checkExp()` which checks the expression in question and, if it finds an error, alerts the user and returns `false`. Otherwise, it returns `true`. By checking whether you get a `false` value from `checkExp()`, you are able to exit out of the function before saving the new expression.

The main work of error checking takes place in the function `checkExp()`:

```
function checkExp(expression,expField) {

  var index =0;
```

```
var next = 0;
var checkNum = 0;
var otherExpField = ""
var otherExp = "";
var lowerColumn = ""

if (expression.charAt(0) == '"') { return true; }

for (var x = 0; x < width; x++) {
  index =0;
  column = letters.charAt(x);
  lowerColumn = column.toLowerCase();

  // Check for field in this column
  index = expression.indexOf(column,0);
  if (index < 0) {
    index = expression.indexOf(lowerColumn,0);
  }

  // If we have a reference to this column, check the syntax
  while (index >= 0) {

    next = index + 1;

    // Check if letter is followed by a number,
➥if not assume it is a Math method
checkNum = parseInt(expression.charAt(next));
    if ((checkNum == 0) && (expression.charAt(next) != "0") &&
➥(expression.charAt(index) == lowerColumn)) {
if (next + 1 == expression.length) { break; }
      index = expression.indexOf(column,next+1);
      if (index < 0) {
        index = expression.indexOf(lowerColumn,next+1);
      }
      continue;
    }

    // It is not a Math method so check that the letter was uppercase
    if (expression.charAt(index) == lowerColumn) {
      alert("Field names must use uppercase letters.");
      return false;
    }

    // The letter was uppercase, so check that we have
➥only numbers followed by a semicolon
while(expression.charAt(++next) != ";") {
      checkNum = parseInt(expression.charAt(next));
      if ((checkNum == 0) && (expression.charAt(next) != "0")) {
        alert("Field name format is incorrect (should be like A12; or B9;).");
        return false;
      }
      if (next == expression.length - 1) {
        alert("Field name format is incorrect (should be like A12; or B9;).");
        return false;
      }
    }
```

12

```
      otherExpField = expression.substring(index,next);

      // Check for a circular expression
      otherExp = GetCookie(otherExpField);
      if (otherExp != null) {
        if (search(otherExp,expField,caseSensitive,anySubstring)) {
          alert("You have created a circular expression
➥with field " + otherExpField + ".");
return false;
        }
      }

      if (next + 1 == expression.length) { break; }

      index = expression.indexOf(column,next+1);
      if (index < 0) {
        index = expression.indexOf(lowerColumn,next+1);
      }

    }

  }

  return true;

}
```

This function is divided into several steps. It starts by checking whether you have a string expression (which starts with a double quotation mark). If you do, it returns true.

If you don't have a string expression, then you need to check the mathematical expression according to the criteria previously outlined. To do this, you use a for loop which loops through each of the letters that are column names and performs a series of checks based on that column.

```
index =0;
column = letters.charAt(x);
lowerColumn = column.toLowerCase();

// Check for field in this column
index = expression.indexOf(column,0);
if (index < 0) {
  index = expression.indexOf(lowerColumn,0);
}
```

You first assign the column name to the variable column. You also assign the lowercase version of the same letter to lowerColumn because you will also need to deal with lowercase versions of the same letter.

You then check for an occurrence of either the uppercase or lowercase letter using indexOf() and assign the index to the variable index. You then enter a while loop that performs the main checking. The condition of the while loop means it will repeat as long as you continue to find instances of the letter.

12

```
     // If we have a reference to this column, check the syntax
     while (index >= 0) {

       next = index + 1;

       // Check if letter is followed by a number,
➥if not assume it is a Math method
checkNum = parseInt(expression.charAt(next));
       if ((checkNum == 0) && (expression.charAt(next) != "0") &&
➥(expression.charAt(index) == lowerColumn)) {
if (next + 1 == expression.length) { break; }
         index = expression.indexOf(column,next+1);
         if (index < 0) {
           index = expression.indexOf(lowerColumn,next+1);
         }
         continue;
       }
```

The first check in the while loop is to see if the character immediately following the letter is a number. If it is not a number—which would make it the start of a field reference—you assume it refers to a method or property from the Math object.

NOTE

> This is not a perfect assumption. To correctly check, you would need to assure that whatever character string you find is actually part of the Math object.

You perform this check by passing the character through parseInt() and then check if the result is zero. If it is, you also check if the actual character is zero and make sure that the letter you found is a lowercase letter (since all the Math methods start with lowercase letters).

Having passed all these conditions, you make the assumption that this is a Math method and you scan forward for another occurrence of the letter and then return to the top of the loop with the continue statement.

```
     // It is not a Math method so check that the letter was uppercase
     if (expression.charAt(index) == lowerColumn) {
       alert("Field names must use uppercase letters.");
       return false;
     }
```

If you get by the first if statement, you know you have a letter followed by a number, which means the user is trying to reference a field name. The first thing you do is check if the user is using an uppercase letter; if not, you alert the user and return a false value.

```
     // The letter was upper case, so check that we
➥have only numbers followed by a semicolon
while(expression.charAt(++next) != ";") {
       checkNum = parseInt(expression.charAt(next));
       if ((checkNum == 0) && (expression.charAt(next) != "0")) {
```

12

```
        alert("Field name format is incorrect (should be like A12; or B9;).");
        return false;
      }
      if (next == expression.length - 1) {
        alert("Field name format is incorrect (should be like A12; or B9;).");
        return false;
      }
    }
```

Next, you move forward through the expression, checking each character. If you find a non-numeric character before you reach a semicolon, then you know that you have an invalid reference, so you alert the user and return a `false` value. Likewise, if you reach the end of the expression without hitting a semicolon, you also know you have an incorrect form, and you do the same thing.

```
    otherExpField = expression.substring(index,next);

    // Check for a circular expression
    otherExp = GetCookie(otherExpField);
    if (otherExp != null) {
      if (search(otherExp,expField,caseSensitive,anySubstring)) {
        alert("You have created a circular expression
with field " + otherExpField + ".");
return false;
      }
    }
```

The last check you perform is to look for a circular expression. You extract the field name that you are currently looking at and use it to get any existing expression for that field. If the field has an expression, you search it using `search()` to see if the expression refers back to the field you are trying to add an expression to. If it does, you have a circular expression, and you inform the user and return a `false` value again.

For instance, if the user is trying to define the expression A1-B1 in field A1, this would create a circular expression; so the user needs to be informed, and the expression should not be saved.

```
if (next + 1 == expression.length) { break; }

    index = expression.indexOf(column,next+1);
    if (index < 0) {
      index = expression.indexOf(lowerColumn,next+1);
    }

  }
```

Finally, you check whether you have reached the end of the expression and if not, search for another occurrence of the letter, store the index in `index`, and return to the top of the `while` loop.

The other place you need to perform error checking is in the `evaluateExp()` function. Here, you need to make sure that the values of fields being used in expressions are numeric. You do this in the main `if` statement in the `while` loop:

12

```
        if ((nextExpression = GetCookie(nextExpField)) != null) {
          nextResult = evaluateExp(form,nextExpression);
          if ("" + nextResult == "error") {
            return "error";
          }
        } else {
          nextResult = form[nextExpField].value;
          if ((nextResult == "") || (nextResult == null)) {
            nextResult = "0";
          } else {
            // Check if this is a numeric expression
            var checkNum = parseInt(nextResult);
            if ((checkNum == 0) && (nextResult.charAt(0) != "0")) {
              return "error";
            }
          }
        }

      }
```

When you get back a value of calling evaluateExp(), you check that the result is not "error". If it is "error", you simply return "error" back up the chain of function calls.

If you are getting a value directly from a form field and the field is not empty, you check whether the value is a number by applying parseInt() to the value and checking the result. If you don't have a numeric expression, you return "error".

Summary

In this chapter we have put together a complete, workable spreadsheet application using only the commands and JavaScript objects learned in this book. This demonstrates the power of JavaScript as an easy-to-use and flexible scripting language.

To help you put together the program you have just built, I am including the complete source code of the program, including all the changes you just made. In the exercises later in this chapter you will extend the features of this application even further.

```
<HTML>

<HEAD>
<TITLE>Chapter 12</TITLE>

<SCRIPT LANGUAGE="JavaScript">
<!-- HIDE FROM OTHER BROWSERS
//
//   Cookie Functions - Second Helping  (21-Jan-96)
//   Written by:  Bill Dortch, hIdaho Design <bdortch@netw.com>
//   The following functions are released to the public domain.

//
// "Internal" function to return the decoded value of a cookie
//
```

```
function getCookieVal (offset) {
  var endstr = document.cookie.indexOf (";", offset);
  if (endstr == -1)
    endstr = document.cookie.length;
  return unescape(document.cookie.substring(offset, endstr));
}

//
//  Function to return the value of the cookie specified by "name".
//
function GetCookie (name) {
  var arg = name + "=";
  var alen = arg.length;
  var clen = document.cookie.length;
  var i = 0;
  while (i < clen) {
    var j = i + alen;
    if (document.cookie.substring(i, j) == arg)
      return getCookieVal (j);
    i = document.cookie.indexOf(" ", i) + 1;
    if (i == 0) break;
  }
  return null;
}

//
//  Function to create or update a cookie.
//
function SetCookie (name, value) {
  var argv = SetCookie.arguments;
  var argc = SetCookie.arguments.length;
  var expires = (argc > 2) ? argv[2] : null;
  var path = (argc > 3) ? argv[3] : null;
  var domain = (argc > 4) ? argv[4] : null;
  var secure = (argc > 5) ? argv[5] : false;
  document.cookie = name + "=" + escape (value) +
    ((expires == null) ? "" : ("; expires=" + expires.toGMTString())) +
    ((path == null) ? "" : ("; path=" + path)) +
    ((domain == null) ? "" : ("; domain=" + domain)) +
    ((secure == true) ? "; secure" : "");
}

//  Function to delete a cookie. (Sets expiration date to current date/time)
//    name - String object containing the cookie name
//
function DeleteCookie (name) {
  var exp = new Date();
  exp.setTime (exp.getTime() - 1);  // This cookie is history
  var cval = GetCookie (name);
  document.cookie = name + "=" + cval + "; expires=" + exp.toGMTString();
}

// END OF COOKIE FUNCTIONS

// SEARCH AND REPLACE FUNCTIONS
//
```

12

continues

```
// SET UP ARGUMENTS FOR FUNCTION CALLS
//
var caseSensitive = true;
var notCaseSensitive = false;
var wholeWords = true;
var anySubstring = false;


// SEARCH FOR A TERM IN A TARGET STRING
//
// search(targetString,searchTerm,caseSensitive,wordOrSubstring)
//
// where caseSenstive is a boolean value and wordOrSubstring is a boolean
// value and true means whole words, false means substrings
//
function search(target,term,caseSens,wordOnly) {

  var ind = 0;
  var next = 0;

  if (!caseSens) {
    term = term.toLowerCase();
    target = target.toLowerCase();
  }

  while ((ind = target.indexOf(term,next)) >= 0) {
    if (wordOnly) {
      var before = ind - 1;
      var after = ind + term.length;
      if (!(space(target.charAt(before)) && space(target.charAt(after)))) {
        next = ind + term.length;
        continue;
      }
    }
    return true;
  }

  return false;

}

// SEARCH FOR A TERM IN A TARGET STRING AND REPLACE IT
//
// replace(targetString,oldTerm,newTerm,caseSensitive,wordOrSubstring)
//
// where caseSenstive is a boolean value and wordOrSubstring is a boolean
// value and true means whole words, false means substrings
//
function replace(target,oldTerm,newTerm,caseSens,wordOnly) {

  var work = target;
  var ind = 0;
  var next = 0;

  if (!caseSens) {
    oldTerm = oldTerm.toLowerCase();
    work = target.toLowerCase();
```

12

```javascript
  }

  while ((ind = work.indexOf(oldTerm,next)) >= 0) {
    if (wordOnly) {
      var before = ind - 1;
      var after = ind + oldTerm.length;
      if (!(space(work.charAt(before)) && space(work.charAt(after)))) {
        next = ind + oldTerm.length;
        continue;
      }
    }
    target = target.substring(0,ind) + newTerm +
➥target.substring(ind+oldTerm.length,target.length);
work = work.substring(0,ind) + newTerm +
➥work.substring(ind+oldTerm.length,work.length);
next = ind + newTerm.length;
    if (next >= work.length) { break; }
  }

  return target;

}

// CHECK IF A CHARACTER IS A WORD BREAK AND RETURN A BOOLEAN VALUE
//
function space(check) {

  var space = " .,/<>?!`';:@#$%^&*()=-¦[]{}" + '"' + "\\\n\t";

  for (var i = 0; i < space.length; i++)
    if (check == space.charAt(i)) { return true; }

  if (check == "") { return true; }
  if (check == null) { return true; }

  return false;

}

// END OF SEARCH AND REPLACE FUNCTIONS

// MAIN BODY OF SCRIPT
//
// Set up global variables
//
var width = 8;
var height = 12;
var letters = "ABCDEFGHIJKLMNOPQRSTUVWXYZ";

// Set up Expiry Date for cookies
//
var expiryDate = new Date();
expiryDate.setTime(expiryDate.getTime() + 365*24*60*60*1000);
var deleteExpiry = new Date();
deleteExpiry.setTime(deleteExpiry.getTime() - 1);

// Function to calculate the spreadsheet
```

continues

```
                 //
                 function calculate(form) {

                   var index = 0;
                   var next = 0;
                   var expField = "";
                   var expression = "";
                   var fieldList = GetCookie("fieldList");

                   if (fieldList != null) {
                     while (index != fieldList.length) {
                       next = fieldList.indexOf(";",index);
                       expField = fieldList.substring(index,next);
                       expression = GetCookie(expField);
                       form[expField].value = evaluateExp(form,expression);
                       index = next + 1;
                     }
                   }

                 }

                 // Function to evaluate an expression
                 //

                 function evaluateExp(form,expression) {

                   var column = "";
                   var index = 0;
                   var nextExpField;
                   var nextExpression = "";
                   var nextResult = "";

                   if (expression.charAt(0) == '"') {
                     return(expression.substring(1,expression.length));
                   }

                   // Scan the expression for field names
                   for (var x = 0; x < width; x ++) {
                     column = letters.charAt(x);
                     index = 0;
                     index = expression.indexOf(column,index);

                     // If we find a field name, evaluate it
                     while(index >= 0) {

                       // Check if the field has an expression associated with it
                       nextExpField = expression.substring(index,expression.indexOf(";",index));

                       // If there is an expression, evaluate--otherwise grab the value of the
                 field
                       if ((nextExpression = GetCookie(nextExpField)) != null) {
                         nextResult = evaluateExp(form,nextExpression);
                       } else {
                         nextResult = form[nextExpField].value;
                         if ((nextResult == "") || (nextResult == null))
                           nextResult = "0";
```

```
      }

      // Replace the field name with the result
      nextExpField = nextExpField + ";";
      nextResult = "(" + nextResult + ")";
      expression =
replace(expression,nextExpField,nextResult,notCaseSensitive,anySubstring);
      // Check if we have reached the end of the expression
      index = index + nextResult.length;
      if (index >= expression.length - 1) { break; }

      // If not, search for another field name
      index = expression.indexOf(column,index);
    }
  }

  // Evaluate the expression
  with (Math) {
    var result = eval(expression);
  }

  // Return the result
  return result;

}

// Function to save an expression
//
function saveExp(form) {

  var expField = form.expField.value;
  var fieldList = GetCookie("fieldList");
  var numExp = GetCookie("numExpressions");

  // Check the number of saved expressions
  if (numExp == "18") {
    alert("Too many expressions. Delete One first");
  } else {

    if (!checkExp(form.expression.value,expField + ";")) { return }

    // If there is room, save the expression and
➥update the number of expressions
SetCookie(form.expField.value,form.expression.value,expiryDate);
    numExp = parseInt(numExp) + 1;
    SetCookie("numExpressions",numExp,expiryDate);
    expField += ";"
    if (fieldList == null) {
      fieldList = expField;
    } else {
      fieldList = replace(fieldList,expField,"",notCaseSensitive,anySubstring);
      fieldList += expField;
    }
    SetCookie("fieldList",fieldList,expiryDate);

    // Recalculate the spreadsheet
```

continues

12

```
        calculate(document.spreadsheet);

        alert("Expession for field " + form.expField.value + " is saved.");

    }

}

// Function to delete an expression
//
function deleteExp(form) {

    var fieldList = GetCookie("fieldList");
    var expField = form.expField.value;
    var numExp = GetCookie("numExpressions");
    var expression = GetCookie(form.expField.value);

    // Check if there is an expression to delete for the field
    if (expression != null) {

        // There is, so set the expiry date
        SetCookie(form.expField.value,"",deleteExpiry);
        numExp = parseInt(numExp) - 1;
        SetCookie("numExpressions",numExp,expiryDate);
        expField += ";";
        fieldList = replace(fieldList,expField,"",notCaseSensitive,anySubstring);
        SetCookie("fieldList",fieldList,expiryDate);

        // Update the field and recalculate the spreadsheet
        document.spreadsheet[form.expField.value].value = "";
        calculate(document.spreadsheet);

        alert("Expession for field " + form.expField.value + " is removed.");

    }

}

// Function to build form
//
function buildForm() {

    var numExp = 0;

    // Check if this is a new spreadsheet. If it is,
➥set the number of expressions to zero
if ((numExp = GetCookie("numExpressions")) == null) {
        SetCookie("numExpressions",0,expiryDate);
    }

    // Build row header
    document.write("<TR><TD></TD>");
    for (var x = 0; x < width; x++) {
        document.write("<TD><DIV ALIGN=CENTER>" +
➥letters.charAt(x) + "</DIV></TD>");
}
```

```
    document.write("</TR>");

  // Build each field -- each is the same, with a different name
  for (var y = 1; y <= height; y++) {
    document.write("<TR><TD>" + y + "</TD>");
    for (var x = 0; x < width; x++) {
      document.write('<TD><INPUT TYPE=text SIZE=10 NAME="' +
➡letters.charAt(x) + y + '" onChange="calculate(this.form);"></TD>');
}
    document.write("</TR>");
  }

}


// Function check expressions
//

function checkExp(expression,expField) {

  var index =0;
  var next = 0;
  var checkNum = 0;
  var otherExpField = ""
  var otherExp = "";
  var lowerColumn = ""

  if (expression.charAt(0) == '"') { return true; }

  for (var x = 0; x < width; x++) {
    index =0;
    column = letters.charAt(x);
    lowerColumn = column.toLowerCase();

    // Check for field in this column
    index = expression.indexOf(column,0);
    if (index < 0) {
      index = expression.indexOf(lowerColumn,0);
    }

    // If we have a reference to this column, check the syntax
    while (index >= 0) {

      next = index + 1;

      // Check if letter is followed by a number, if not assume it is a Math
method
      checkNum = parseInt(expression.charAt(next));
      if ((checkNum == 0) && (expression.charAt(next) != "0") &&
(expression.charAt(index) == lowerColumn)) {
        if (next + 1 == expression.length) { break; }
        index = expression.indexOf(column,next+1);
        if (index < 0) {
          index = expression.indexOf(lowerColumn,next+1);
        }
        continue;
```

continues

12

```
        }

        // It is not a Math method so check that the letter was uppercase
        if (expression.charAt(index) == lowerColumn) {
          alert("Field names must use uppercase letters.");
          return false;
        }

        // The letter was uppercase, so check that we have only numbers followed
by a semicolon
        while(expression.charAt(++next) != ";") {
          checkNum = parseInt(expression.charAt(next));
          if ((checkNum == 0) && (expression.charAt(next) != "0")) {
            alert("Field name format is incorrect (should be like A12; or B9;).");
            return false;
          }
          if (next == expression.length - 1) {
            alert("Field name format is incorrect (should be like A12; or B9;).");
            return false;
          }
        }

        otherExpField = expression.substring(index,next);

        // Check for a circular expression
        otherExp = GetCookie(otherExpField);
        if (otherExp != null) {
          if (search(otherExp,expField,caseSensitive,anySubstring)) {
            alert("You have created a circular expression with field " +
otherExpField + ".");
            return false;
          }
        }

        if (next + 1 == expression.length) { break; }

        index = expression.indexOf(column,next+1);
        if (index < 0) {
          index = expression.indexOf(lowerColumn,next+1);
        }

      }

    }

    return true;

  }

  // STOP HIDING -->
  </SCRIPT>

  </HEAD>

  <BODY BGCOLOR="iceblue">

  <CENTER>
```

12

```
<FORM METHOD=POST NAME="spreadsheet">
<TABLE BORDER=0>

<SCRIPT LANGUAGE="JavaScript">
<!-- HIDE FROM OTHER BROWSERS

buildForm();

// STOP HIDING -->
</SCRIPT>

</TABLE>
</FORM>
<HR>

<FORM METHOD=POST>
<TABLE BORDER=1>

<TR>
<TD><DIV ALIGN=CENTER>Field Name</DIV></TD>
<TD><DIV ALIGN=CENTER>Expression</DIV></TD>
</TR>

<TR>
<TD><DIV ALIGN=CENTER><INPUT TYPE=text SIZE=10 NAME="expField"
   onChange="var exp = GetCookie(this.value); this.form.expression.value =
➥(exp == null) ? '' : exp;"></DIV></TD>
<TD><DIV ALIGN=CENTER><INPUT TYPE=text SIZE=50 NAME="expression"></DIV></TD>
<TD><DIV ALIGN=CENTER><INPUT TYPE=button VALUE="Apply"
➥onClick="saveExp(this.form);"></DIV></TD>
<TD><DIV ALIGN=CENTER><INPUT TYPE=button VALUE="Delete"
➥onClick="deleteExp(this.form);"></DIV></TD>
</TR>

</TABLE>
</FORM>
</CENTER>

</BODY>

</HTML>
```

12

Exercises

1. Earlier in the chapter we discussed adding two additional features: the Clear button and the range capability. Extend the script to add the Clear button.

2. Extend the script you just wrote in Exercise 1 to include the following range capability: When the user specifies the range, simply add up the values in all the fields in that range. You will need to define a syntax for ranges and then adjust the script to accommodate those changes. Try to define the syntax in such a way that it does not cause problems in the existing checkExp() function.

Answers

1. To add the clear function, add a single button to the second HTML form:

```
<FORM METHOD=POST>
<TABLE BORDER=1>

<TR>
<TD><DIV ALIGN=CENTER>Field Name</DIV></TD>
<TD><DIV ALIGN=CENTER>Expression</DIV></TD>
</TR>

<TR>
<TD><DIV ALIGN=CENTER><INPUT TYPE=text SIZE=10 NAME="expField"
   onChange="var exp = GetCookie(this.value); this.form.expression.value =
➥(exp == null) ? ''
: exp;"></DIV></TD>
<TD><DIV ALIGN=CENTER><INPUT TYPE=text SIZE=50 NAME="expression"></DIV></
TD>
<TD><DIV ALIGN=CENTER><INPUT TYPE=button VALUE="Apply"
onClick="saveExp(this.form);"></DIV></TD>
<TD><DIV ALIGN=CENTER><INPUT TYPE=button VALUE="Delete"
onClick="deleteExp(this.form);"></DIV></TD>
<TD><DIV ALIGN=CENTER><INPUT TYPE=button VALUE="Clear"
onClick="clearSpreadSheet();"></DIV></TD>
</TR>

</TABLE>
</FORM>
```

You then need to add a clearSpreadSheet() function:

```
function clearSpreadSheet() {

  var form = document.spreadsheet;

  var index = 0;
  var next = 0;
  var expField = "";
  var field = "";
  var fieldList = GetCookie("fieldList");

  // Clear Expression Cookies
  if (fieldList != null) {
    while (index != fieldList.length) {
      next = fieldList.indexOf(";",index);
      expField = fieldList.substring(index,next);
      SetCookie(expField,"",deleteExpiry);
      index = next + 1;
    }
  }

  SetCookie("fieldList","",deleteExpiry);
  SetCookie("numExpressions",0,expiryDate);

  // Clear form fields
```

12

```
    for (var x = 0; x < width; x++) {
      for (var y = 1; y <= height; y++) {
        field = letters.charAt(x) + y;
        form[field].value = "";
      }
    }

  }
```

There are two main steps in this function. First, you extract the field list from its cookie and loop through each of the expressions in the list the same way you did in the revised calculate() function. For each expression, you delete its cookie. Then you delete the field list cookie and set the number of expressions to zero.

Next, you use a set of nested for loops to place an empty string in each form text entry field in the spreadsheet.

2. In this solution, use a simple syntax for defining ranges:
   <fieldNameOne;fieldNametwo;>. If you want to define the sum of all fields from A1 to A6, you could use <A1;A6;>. Similarly, all fields from A1 to C1 would be <A1;C1;>. All ranges must be on the same row or column and must be indicated from lowest field to highest (that is, <C1;A1;> is invalid).

You add support for this range feature by adding a section to the evaluateExp() function:

```
function evaluateExp(form,expression) {

  var column = "";
  var index = 0;
  var nextExpField;
  var nextExpression = "";
  var nextResult = "";
  var next = 0;
  var firstField = "";
  var lastField = "";
  var rangeExp = ""

  if (expression.charAt(0) == '"') {
    return(expression.substring(1,expression.length));
  }

  // Check for ranges
  index = expression.indexOf("<",index);
  while (index >= 0) {
    next = expression.indexOf(">",index+1);
    nextExpField = expression.substring(index,next+1);
    firstField =
expression.substring(index+1,expression.indexOf(";",index+1));
    lastField = expression.substring
➥(expression.indexOf(";",index+1) + 1,next - 1);

    if (firstField.charAt(0) == lastField.charAt(0)) {
      var start = parseInt(firstField.substring(1,firstField.length));
      var end = parseInt(lastField.substring(1,lastField.length));
```

```
        nextResult = firstField.charAt(0) + start + ";";
        for (var i = start + 1; i <= end; i++)
          nextResult += " + " + firstField.charAt(0) + i + ";";
      } else {
        var tempChar = firstField.charAt(0);
        var start = letters.indexOf(tempChar,0);
        tempChar = lastField.charAt(0);
        var end = letters.indexOf(tempChar,0);
        nextResult = letters.charAt(start) +
➥firstField.substring(1,firstField.length) + ";";
for (var i = start + 1; i <= end; i++)
        nextResult += " + " + letters.charAt(i) +
➥firstField.substring(1,firstField.length) + ";";
}

    rangeExp = "<" + firstField + ";" + lastField + ";>";
    nextResult = "(" + nextResult + ")";
    expression = replace(expression,rangeExp,nextResult,
➥notCaseSensitive,anySubstring);
index += nextResult.length;
    if (index >= expression.length - 1) { break; }
    index = expression.indexOf("<",index);

  }

  // Scan the expression for field names
  for (var x = 0; x < width; x ++) {
    column = letters.charAt(x);
    index = 0;
    index = expression.indexOf(column,index);

    // If we find a field name, evaluate it
    while(index >= 0) {

      // Check if the field has an expression associated with it
      nextExpField =
expression.substring(index,expression.indexOf(";",index));

      // If there is an expression, evaluate--
➥otherwise grab the value of the field
if ((nextExpression = GetCookie(nextExpField)) != null) {
        nextResult = evaluateExp(form,nextExpression);
        if ("" + nextResult == "error") {
          return "error";
        }
      } else {
        nextResult = form[nextExpField].value;

        if ((nextResult == "") || (nextResult == null)) {
          nextResult = "0";
        } else {
          // Check if this is a numeric expression
          var checkNum = parseInt(nextResult);
          if ((checkNum == 0) && (nextResult.charAt(0) != "0")) {
            return "error";
          }
        }
```

12

```
    }

    // Replace the field name with the result
    nextExpField = nextExpField + ";";
    nextResult = "(" + nextResult + ")";
    expression = replace(expression,nextExpField,nextResult,
➥notCaseSensitive,anySubstring);

    // Check if we have reached the end of the expression
    index = index + nextResult.length;
    if (index >= expression.length - 1) { break; }

    // If not, search for another field name
    index = expression.indexOf(column,index);
    }
  }

  // Evaluate the expression
  with (Math) {
    var result = eval(expression);
  }

  // Return the result
  return result;

}
```

What you have done is add a section that replaces ranges with a mathematical expression. For instance, <A1;A4;> is replaced by (A1; + A2; + A3;). Once this is done, you can evaluate the expression in the same way you did before.

You check for ranges by scanning the string for the < character using indexOf(). All the processing takes place inside a while loop:

```
index = expression.indexOf("<",index);
while (index >= 0) {
  next = expression.indexOf(">",index+1);
  firstField =
expression.substring(index+1,expression.indexOf(";",index+1));
  lastField = expression.substring(expression.indexOf(";",index+1) +
➥1,next - 1);
```

You start by finding the end of the range by looking for >. Then you are able to extract the first field name and the last field name.

```
if (firstField.charAt(0) == lastField.charAt(0)) {
  var start = parseInt(firstField.substring(1,firstField.length));
  var end = parseInt(lastField.substring(1,lastField.length));
  nextResult = firstField.charAt(0) + start + ";";
  for (var i = start + 1; i <= end; i++)
    nextResult += " + " + firstField.charAt(0) + i + ";";
} else {
```

If you have a range on the same row (the first character of both lastField and firstField are the same), then you loop through each field in the range and build a mathematical expression that adds the fields.

```
        var tempChar = firstField.charAt(0);
        var start = letters.indexOf(tempChar,0);
        tempChar = lastField.charAt(0);
        var end = letters.indexOf(tempChar,0);
        nextResult = letters.charAt(start) +
►firstField.substring(1,firstField.length) + ";";
for (var i = start + 1; i <= end; i++)
        nextResult += " + " + letters.charAt(i) +
►firstField.substring(1,firstField.length) + ";";
}
```

If you don't have a range on the same row, then it must run down a single column. If it does, you build an expression appropriately.

```
        rangeExp = "<" + firstField + ";" + lastField + ";>";
        nextResult = "(" + nextResult + ")";
        expression = replace(expression,rangeExp,nextResult,
►notCaseSensitive,anySubstring);
index += nextResult.length;
    if (index >= expression.length - 1) { break; }
    index = expression.indexOf("<",index);

}
```

Finally, you use replace() to replace the range syntax with its mathematical equivalent. Then you see if you are at the end of the expression; if not, you scan for another range.

The range syntax you are using still enables checkExp() to accurately perform the checks it is making. However, you are not checking that the format of the range syntax is correct. For instance, you don't know that each open symbol < is matched with its partner >, and you don't know if extra characters have been introduced into the middle of the range structure.

You can add support for this in the checkExp() function. After you complete all of the checks, before you would return true, you can add a while loop that checks the range syntax:

```
  index = expression.indexOf("<",0);
  while (index >= 0) {
    next = index + 1;

    for (i = 1; i <= 2; i++) {
      thisLetter = expression.charAt(next);
      if (letters.indexOf(thisLetter,0) < 0) {
        alert("Incorrect Range format.");
        return false;
      }

      while(expression.charAt(++next) != ";") {
        checkNum = parseInt(expression.charAt(next));
        if ((checkNum == 0) && (expression.charAt(next) != "0")) {
          alert("Incorrect Range format.");
          return false;
        }
```

12

```
      }

      next ++;

    }

    if (expression.charAt(next) != ">") {
      alert("Incorrect Range format.");
      return false;
    }

    if (next + 1 == expression.length) { break; }
    index = expression.indexOf("<",next);

  }
```

The process of checking for errors is fairly simple. When you find occurrences of <, you first check the next letter to make sure it is a legitimate column name. If it is, you check that you have only numbers until a semicolon. Then you check if you have a valid letter again, and then check numbers again until another semicolon. Finally, you check for the closing >.

12

From the Web:

CCAS Indirect Cost Worksheet

CCAS Inc., which produces accounting software for Government Contractors, uses JavaScript to demonstrate one of the formulas included in its CCAS for Government Contractors financial and job cost accounting package.

The Indirect Cost Rate sheet is available at this site:

`http://www.ccas.com/ccasrate.html`

It provides a good example of building a complex worksheet using JavaScript.

The application uses one large form, spanning four separate tables, to guide the user through entering the required information for the form. The worksheet is designed to calculate the Fringe Benefit Rate, Overhead Rate, and G&A Rate based on information in the form. At the bottom of the page, the formulas being used are described. The source code for the CCAS Worksheet appears in Listing W6.1.

Listing W6.1. Source code for the CCAS Worksheet.

```
<HTML>
<HEAD>
<TITLE>CCAS Indirect Cost Rate Worksheet (JavaScript)</TITLE>

<SCRIPT LANGUAGE="LiveScript">


<!-- hide this script tag's contents from old browsers

function checkNumber(input, min, max, msg)
{
    msg = msg + " field has invalid data: " + input.value;

    var str = input.value;
    for (var i = 0; i < str.length; i++) {
        var ch = str.substring(i, i + 1)
        if ((ch < "0" || "9" < ch) && ch != '.') {
            alert(msg);
            return false;
        }
    }
    var num = 0 + str
    if (num < min || max < num) {
        alert(msg + " not in range [" + min + ".." + max + "]");
        return false;
    }
    input.value = str;
    return true;
}

function computeField(input)
{
    if (input.value != null && input.value.length != 0)
        input.value = "" + eval(input.value);
      computeForm(input.form);
}

function computeForm(form)
{
    if ((form.DL.value == null || form.DL.value.length == 0) ||
        (form.ODC.value == null || form.ODC.value.length == 0) ||
        (form.TFB.value == null || form.TFB.value.length == 0) ||
        (form.TOH.value == null || form.TOH.value.length == 0) ||
        (form.TGA.value == null || form.TGA.value.length == 0) ||
        (form.TBP.value == null || form.TBP.value.length == 0) ||
        (form.FBR.value == null || form.TBP.value.length == 0) ||
        (form.OHL.value == null || form.OHL.value.length == 0) ||
        (form.GAL.value == null || form.GAL.value.length == 0) ||
        (form.BPL.value == null || form.BPL.value.length == 0)) {
        form.FBR.value = "Incomplete data";
        form.OHR.value = "Incomplete data";
        form.GAR.value = "Incomplete data";
        return;
    }
```

```
if (!checkNumber(form.DL, 1,99999999, "Direct Labor") ||
    !checkNumber(form.ODC,0,99999999, "Other Direct Costs") ||
    !checkNumber(form.TFB,1,99999999, "Total Fringe Benefits") ||
    !checkNumber(form.TOH,1,99999999, "Total Overhead") ||
    !checkNumber(form.TGA,0,99999999, "Total G&A") ||
    !checkNumber(form.TBP,0,99999999, "Total B&P") ||
    !checkNumber(form.TBP,0,99999999, "Total B&P") ||
    !checkNumber(form.DLL,0,99999999, "Total B&P") ||
    !checkNumber(form.OHL,1,99999999, "Total Overhead Labor") ||
    !checkNumber(form.GAL,0,99999999, "Total G&A Labor") ||
    !checkNumber(form.BPL,0,99999999, "Total B&P Labor")) {
    form.FBR.value = "Invalid";
    form.OHR.value = "Invalid";
    form.GAR.value = "Invalid";
    return;
}

var i=form.DL.value *1
var j=form.ODC.value*1
form.TOTDIR.value=i + j
form.DLL.value=i

var k=form.TFB.value *1
var l=form.TOH.value *1
var m=form.TGA.value *1
var n=form.TBP.value *1
form.TOTIND.value=k + l + m + n
var z=i + j + k + l + m + n
form.TC.value=z

var o=form.OHL.value *1
var p=form.GAL.value *1
var q=form.BPL.value *1
var r=i + o + p + q
form.TOTLAB.value= r

var s=(k /  r)
form.FBR.value=s * 100

var t=(((i + o + q) * s) + l) / (i + q)
form.OHR.value= t * 100

var u=(m + n+ (p * s) + (t * q))
var z=z - u
var z= u / z
form.GAR.value=z * 100

form.DLB.value=i
var v=i * t
form.OHRB.value=v
form.OHRR.value=t * 100
form.ODCB.value=j
form.GARR.value=z * 100
var w=(i + v + j) * z
form.GARB.value=w
form.TCB.value=w + i + v + j
```

continues

Listing W6.1. continued

```
}

function clearForm(form)
{
    form.DL.value = "";
    form.ODC.value = "";
    form.TFB.value = "";
}

<!-- done hiding from old browsers -->


</SCRIPT>

<BODY BGCOLOR="#ffffff" TEXT="#020225"></HEAD>
<CENTER>
<FORM method=POST>
<TABLE BORDER=5 CELLSPACING=2 CELLPADDING=5 ALIGN=MIDDLE> <TR><TD><IMG SRC=
"ccaslogoTR.gif" WIDTH="343" HEIGHT="36" NATURALSIZEFLAG="3" ALIGN=bottom
➦alt="CCAS accounting solutions for Government Contractors"></TABLE><BR>

<H1>Indirect Cost Rate Worksheet</H1>
<IMG SRC="javatr.gif" alt="JavaScript(tm)"><BR><BR>
</Center>

<FONT SIZE=3>
In this JavaScript(tm) application, you can determine your indirect cost rates
➦based upon a commonly used (and DCAA accepted) rate structure.
➦This rate structure is one of several options that are included in
➦<A HREF="ccassw.html">CCAS for Government
Contractors</A><B>, "Internet Edition"</B>. Simply complete Steps 1 and 2, and
➦then in Step 3 calculate your indirect cost rates.  Be sure to review
➦the proof of the calculation and details of the calculation formulas
➦employed.<BR><BR>
Note that if this page (which requires Netscape 2.0b5 or later) is saved using
➦the "Save As...Format...Source" command from your browser's "File" menu,
➦it can be run locally when loaded into your browser using "Open File"--<B>
➦even without an active Internet connection.</B>
<P>

<CENTER>

<H2>Step 1-Enter Your Total Costs</H2>
<TABLE BORDER=6 CELLSPACING=2 CELLPADDING=3 ALIGN=MIDDLE>
<TR>
<TD><DIV ALIGN=CENTER><B>COST CATEGORY<BR>DESCRIPTION</B></DIV></TD>
<TD><DIV ALIGN=CENTER><B><br>AMOUNT</B></DIV></TD>
<TD><DIV ALIGN=CENTER><B>SUBTOTAL<br>(Computed)</B></DIV></TD>
</TR>
<TD><DIV ALIGN=CENTER><B>Total Costs From General Ledger</B></DIV> </TD>
</TR>
<TD><B>Direct Costs:</B></DIV> </TD>
</TR>
<TR>
<TD>A. <B>Total</B> Direct Labor</TD>
```

```
<TD><DIV ALIGN=CENTER><INPUT TYPE=TEXT NAME=DL  SIZE=15
➥onChange=computeField(this)></DIV></TD>
<TD><DIV ALIGN=CENTER> </TD></TR>
<TD>B. <B>Total</B> Other Direct Costs</TD>
<TD><DIV ALIGN=CENTER><INPUT TYPE=TEXT NAME=ODC SIZE=15
➥onChange=computeField(this)></DIV> </TD>
<TD><DIV ALIGN=CENTER></DIV> </TD></TR>
<TD><DIV ALIGN=RIGHT>Total Direct Costs</DIV></TD>
<TD><DIV ALIGN=CENTER> </DIV></TD>
<TD><DIV ALIGN=CENTER><INPUT TYPE=TEXT NAME=TOTDIR  SIZE=15></DIV> </TD></TR>
<TR>
<TD><B>Indirect Costs:</B> </TD>
</TR>
<TR>
<TD>C. <B>Total</B> Fringe Benefits</TD>
<TD><DIV ALIGN=CENTER><INPUT TYPE=TEXT NAME=TFB  SIZE=15
➥onChange=computeField(this)> </DIV></TD>
<TD><DIV ALIGN=CENTER></DIV> </TD></TR>
<TD>D. <B>Total</B>  Overhead</TD>
<TD><DIV ALIGN=CENTER><INPUT TYPE=TEXT NAME=TOH  SIZE=15></DIV> </TD>
<TD><DIV ALIGN=CENTER> </DIV></TD></TR>
<TD>E. <B>Total</B> G&A</TD>
<TD><DIV ALIGN=CENTER><INPUT TYPE=TEXT NAME=TGA SIZE=15></DIV> </TD>
<TD><DIV ALIGN=CENTER></DIV> </TD></TR>
<TD>F. <B>Total</B> B&P and IR&D</TD>
<TD><DIV ALIGN=CENTER><INPUT TYPE=TEXT NAME=TBP  SIZE=15> </DIV></TD>
<TD><DIV ALIGN=CENTER></DIV> </TD></TR>
<TD><DIV ALIGN=RIGHT>Total Indirect Costs</DIV></TD>
<TD><DIV ALIGN=CENTER> </DIV></TD>
<TD><DIV ALIGN=CENTER><INPUT TYPE=TEXT NAME=TOTIND  SIZE=15></DIV> </TD></TR>
<TD><DIV ALIGN=RIGHT>G.  Total Costs</DIV></TD>
<TD><DIV ALIGN=CENTER> </DIV></TD>
<TD><DIV ALIGN=CENTER><INPUT TYPE=TEXT NAME=TC  SIZE=15></DIV> </TD></TR>
</Table><br><br>

<H2>Step 2-Enter Your Total Labor Costs<BR> (subset of Total Costs)</H2>
<TABLE BORDER=6 CELLSPACING=2 CELLPADDING=3 ALIGN=MIDDLE>
<TR>
<TD><DIV ALIGN=CENTER><B>COST ELEMENT<BR>DESCRIPTION</B></DIV></TD>
<TD><DIV ALIGN=CENTER><B><br>AMOUNT</B></DIV></TD>
<TD><DIV ALIGN=CENTER><B>SUBTOTAL<br>(Computed)</B></DIV></TD></TR>
<TR>
<TD><DIV ALIGN=CENTER><B>Labor Costs from General Ledger</B></DIV> </TD>
</TR>
<TR><TD>A. <B>Total</B> Direct Labor (from Step 1)</TD>
<TD><DIV ALIGN=CENTER><INPUT TYPE=TEXT NAME=DLL  SIZE=15> </DIV></TD>
<TD><DIV ALIGN=CENTER> </TD></TR>
<TD>H. <B>Total</B> Overhead Labor</TD>
<TD><DIV ALIGN=CENTER><INPUT TYPE=TEXT NAME=OHL  SIZE=15> </DIV></TD>
<TD><DIV ALIGN=CENTER> </DIV></TD></TR>
<TD>I. <B>Total</B> G&A Labor</TD>
<TD><DIV ALIGN=CENTER><INPUT TYPE=TEXT NAME=GAL SIZE=15> </DIV></TD>
<TD><DIV ALIGN=CENTER> </DIV></TD></TR>
<TD>J. <B>Total</B> B&P and IR&D Labor</TD>
<TD><DIV ALIGN=CENTER><INPUT TYPE=TEXT NAME=BPL  SIZE=15> </DIV></TD>
```

continues

Listing W6.1. continued

```
<TD><DIV ALIGN=CENTER> </DIV></TD></TR>
<TD><DIV ALIGN=RIGHT>K.  Total Labor</DIV></TD>
<TD><DIV ALIGN=CENTER></DIV> </TD>
<TD><DIV ALIGN=CENTER><INPUT TYPE=TEXT NAME=TOTLAB  SIZE=15></DIV> </TD></TR>
</Table><br><br>
<A NAME="help">
(If you have difficulty running this worksheet on your Netscape 2.0b6a browser,
➥<A HREF="ccasratehelp.html">click here</A>.)
<BR><BR>

<H2>Step 3-Click on Compute for Rate Calculation Results</H2>
<INPUT TYPE="button" VALUE="Compute"   onClick=computeForm(this.form)>
<INPUT TYPE="reset"  VALUE="Reset"     onClick=clearForm(this.form)>
<BR><BR>
<TABLE BORDER=6 CELLSPACING=2 CELLPADDING=3 ALIGN=MIDDLE>
<TR>
<TD><DIV ALIGN=CENTER>Fringe Benefit Rate</DIV></TD>
<TD><DIV ALIGN=CENTER><INPUT TYPE=TEXT NAME=FBR  SIZE=15> </DIV></TD>
<TD><DIV ALIGN=CENTER>The Fringe Benefit Rate rate is generated to build the
➥Overhead and G&A rates and is not separately stated for pricing or
➥billing. See formulas, below.</DIV></TD></TR>
<TR>
<TD>Overhead Rate</TD>
<TD></TD>
<TD><DIV ALIGN=CENTER><INPUT TYPE=TEXT NAME=OHR  SIZE=15></DIV> </TD></TR>
<TR>
<TD>G&A Rate</TD>
<TD></TD>
<TD><DIV ALIGN=CENTER><INPUT TYPE=TEXT NAME=GAR  SIZE=15> </DIV></TD></TR>
</TABLE>

<BR><BR>


<H2>The Proof of the Calculated Rates</H2>
<TABLE BORDER=6 CELLSPACING=2 CELLPADDING=3 ALIGN=MIDDLE>
<TR>
<TD><DIV ALIGN=CENTER><B>COST ITEM</B></DIV></TD>
<TD><DIV ALIGN=CENTER><B>RATE%</B></DIV></TD>
<TD><DIV ALIGN=CENTER><B>AMOUNT</B></DIV></TD></TR>
<TR><TD> Direct Labor</TD>
<TD><DIV ALIGN=CENTER> </TD>
<TD><DIV ALIGN=CENTER><INPUT TYPE=TEXT NAME=DLB  SIZE=15> </DIV></TD>
</TR>
<TR>
<TD> Overhead on Direct Labor</TD>
<TD><DIV ALIGN=CENTER><INPUT TYPE=TEXT NAME=OHRR  SIZE=15> </DIV></TD>
<TD><DIV ALIGN=CENTER><INPUT TYPE=TEXT NAME=OHRB  SIZE=15> </DIV></TD>
</TR>
```

```
<TR><TD> Other Direct Costs</TD>
<TD><DIV ALIGN=CENTER> </TD>
<TD><DIV ALIGN=CENTER><INPUT TYPE=TEXT NAME=ODCB  SIZE=15> </DIV></TD>
</TR>
<TR>
<TD> G&A on Subtotal of Costs</TD>
<TD><DIV ALIGN=CENTER><INPUT TYPE=TEXT NAME=GARR  SIZE=15> </DIV></TD>
<TD><DIV ALIGN=CENTER><INPUT TYPE=TEXT NAME=GARB  SIZE=15> </DIV></TD>
</TR>
<TR><TD> Total Costs (see Step 1, above)</TD>
<TD><DIV ALIGN=CENTER> </TD>
<TD><DIV ALIGN=CENTER><INPUT TYPE=TEXT NAME=TCB  SIZE=15> </DIV></TD>
</TR>
</Table><br><br>

<H2>The Indirect Cost Rate Calculation Formulas <BR>
➥(Keyed to Cost Elements Above)</H2>
</CENTER>
<BR>
<B>Fringe Benefit Rate (FBR)</B>= C / K<BR><BR>
<B>Overhead Rate (OHR)</B>= (((A + H + J)  * FBR) + D) / (A + J)<BR><BR>
<B>G&A Rate</B>= ((I * FBR) + E + F + (J *OHR)) /
➥(G - ((I * FBR) + E + F + (J *OHR)))

<BR><BR>
</FORM>
<H5>

<img src="back.gif"><A HREF="ccassw.html">Back to CCAS Software</A><BR>
<P>
<CENTER>
<HR SIZE="6">
<A HREF="Default.html">CCAS's home page</A><P>
<A HREF="mailto:info@ccas.com"><IMG SRC="mbox.gif"
➥ALIGN=bottom WIDTH="32" HEIGHT=
"32" NATURALSIZEFLAG="3" Border="0"></A><BR>
Forward inquiries to <BR>
<A HREF="mailto:info@ccas.com">info@ccas.com</A> <BR>
<BR>
(c) 1996 CCAS, Inc. All rights reserved.
</H5>
</CENTER>
</BODY>
</HTML>
```

OUTPUT   The worksheet looks like Figures W6.1 through W6.4.

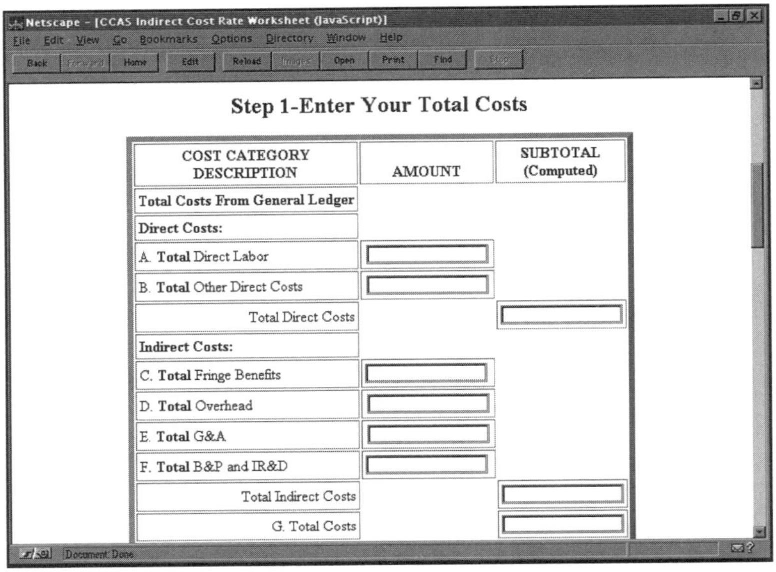

Figure W6.1.

The first form allows users to enter their total costs.

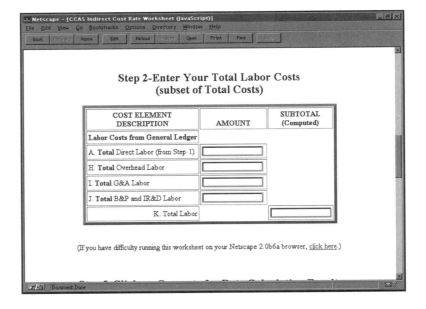

Figure W6.2.

Next, users enter their total labor costs.

Figure W6.3.
The third form allows users to compute the results.

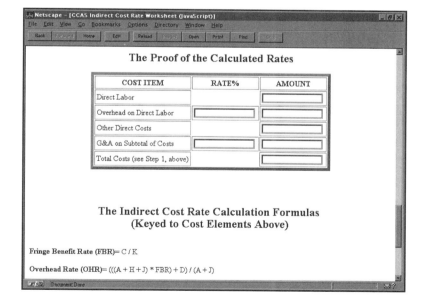

Figure W6.4.
The fourth form provides break-down proofs of the calculations.

ANALYSIS   The Indirect Cost Rate Sheet is built out of four functions. The HTML form itself is rather simple, consisting of a number of text input fields spanning four tables with a Compute button and a Reset button. Only three of the text fields have event handlers, which all call the same function: `computeField()`. This function makes calls to two of the other functions: `checkNumber()` and `computeForm()`. `clearForm()` is invoked when the user clicks on the Reset button.

The `checkNumber()` Function

This function takes four arguments and checks that a given number falls within a specified range. If not, it warns the user that a particular field contains invalid data.

```
function checkNumber(input, min, max, msg)
{
    msg = msg + " field has invalid data: " + input.value;
```

The function starts by building the message that will be displayed if there is an error.

```
    var str = input.value;
    for (var i = 0; i < str.length; i++) {
        var ch = str.substring(i, i + 1);
        if ((ch < "0" || "9" < ch) && ch != '.') {
            alert(msg);
            return false;
        }
    }
```

Next, the function scans each character of the `input` string to make sure it is a numeric value. This program was written before the `parseInt()` function became available in JavaScript, which could also be used with certain limitations, to check if a value was numeric.

If the value is not numeric, the user is alerted and a `false` value is returned by the function.

```
    var num = 0 + str;
    if (num < min || max < num) {
        alert(msg + " not in range [" + min + ".." + max + "]");
        return false;
    }
    input.value = str;
    return true;
}
```

The final step is to check whether the value falls within the specified range, and if not, to alert the user and return a `false` value.

The `computeField()` Function

This function is called by the event handler in three of the form fields. It ensures that the value stored in a field is a string by adding an empty string to the start of the field and then calling `computeForm()` to evaluate the whole form based on the new value of the field.

The `computeForm()` Function

The `computeForm()` function performs all the work of calculating the results of the three formulas.

```
function computeForm(form)
{
    if ((form.DL.value == null || form.DL.value.length == 0) ||
        (form.ODC.value == null || form.ODC.value.length == 0) ||
        (form.TFB.value == null || form.TFB.value.length == 0) ||
        (form.TOH.value == null || form.TOH.value.length == 0) ||
        (form.TGA.value == null || form.TGA.value.length == 0) ||
        (form.TBP.value == null || form.TBP.value.length == 0) ||
        (form.FBR.value == null || form.TBP.value.length == 0) ||
        (form.OHL.value == null || form.OHL.value.length == 0) ||
        (form.GAL.value == null || form.GAL.value.length == 0) ||
        (form.BPL.value == null || form.BPL.value.length == 0)) {
        form.FBR.value = "Incomplete data";
        form.OHR.value = "Incomplete data";
        form.GAR.value = "Incomplete data";
        return;
    }
```

The function starts by checking that certain critical fields contain valid data. If not, error messages are displayed in selected fields and the function returns.

```
    if (!checkNumber(form.DL, 1,99999999, "Direct Labor") ||
        !checkNumber(form.ODC,0,99999999, "Other Direct Costs") ||
        !checkNumber(form.TFB,1,99999999, "Total Fringe Benefits") ||
        !checkNumber(form.TOH,1,99999999, "Total Overhead") ||
        !checkNumber(form.TGA,0,99999999, "Total G&A") ||
        !checkNumber(form.TBP,0,99999999, "Total B&P") ||
        !checkNumber(form.TBP,0,99999999, "Total B&P") ||
        !checkNumber(form.DLL,0,99999999, "Total B&P") ||
        !checkNumber(form.OHL,1,99999999, "Total Overhead Labor") ||
        !checkNumber(form.GAL,0,99999999, "Total G&A Labor") ||
        !checkNumber(form.BPL,0,99999999, "Total B&P Labor")) {
        form.FBR.value = "Invalid";
        form.OHR.value = "Invalid";
        form.GAR.value = "Invalid";
        return;
    }
```

Next, the function checks that the values in selected fields fall within the desired range using `checkNumber()`. Again, if there is a problem, a message to that effect is displayed in selected text fields and the function exits.

```
    var i=form.DL.value *1
    var j=form.ODC.value*1
    form.TOTDIR.value=i + j
    form.DLL.value=i

    var k=form.TFB.value *1
    var l=form.TOH.value *1
    var m=form.TGA.value *1
    var n=form.TBP.value *1
    form.TOTIND.value=k + l + m + n
```

```
var z=i + j + k + l + m + n
form.TC.value=z

var o=form.OHL.value *1
var p=form.GAL.value *1
var q=form.BPL.value *1
var r=i + o + p + q
form.TOTLAB.value= r

var s=(k /  r)
form.FBR.value=s * 100

var t=(((i + o + q) * s) + l) / (i + q)
form.OHR.value= t * 100

var u=(m + n+ (p * s) + (t * q))
var z=z - u
var z= u / z
form.GAR.value=z * 100

form.DLB.value=i
var v=i * t
form.OHRB.value=v
form.OHRR.value=t * 100
form.ODCB.value=j
form.GARR.value=z * 100
var w=(i + v + j) * z
form.GARB.value=w
form.TCB.value=w + i + v + j
```

```
}
```

Finally, the function makes all the mathematical calculations and stores the results in the relevant fields.

The `clearForm()` Function

The `clearForm()` function simply clears three critical fields in the form by assigning empty strings to them.

DAY

7

Chapter 13

Navigator Gold—
A JavaScript
Development Tool

Now that you know how to develop large applications on the World Wide Web
using JavaScript, it would be useful to have sophisticated development tools for
JavaScript applications similar to the large number of powerful HTML editors,
validators, and assistants.

Although there are currently no editors or development tools specifically
designed for JavaScript, Netscape has begun development of Navigator Gold 2.0
(which became public beta in the spring of 1996). This product promises to
bring together the Navigator 2.0 browser with a comprehensive editing environment for developing Netscape-specific Web pages that support all the major
features of Navigator 2.0, including JavaScript.

In this chapter we take a look at Navigator Gold 2.0 as a development tool, both for HTML and for JavaScript. We discuss the following:

☐ The features of Navigator Gold 2.0

☐ Using Navigator Gold to develop HTML documents

☐ Developing JavaScript in Navigator Gold 2.0

☐ Other advanced features of Navigator Gold 2.0

☐ Limitations of Navigator Gold 2.0

An Introduction to Navigator Gold 2.0

Navigator Gold 2.0 could be seen as the advanced version of the Navigator 2.0 Web browser. Where Netscape is trying to position Navigator 2.0 as the complete Web browser and Internet tool for the Internet user, Navigator Gold 2.0 is being positioned as a key application for users to develop Web applications that take advantage of the special features of Navigator 2.0. Netscape expects to complete Navigator Gold 2.0 in the first half of 1996 and has indicated it intends to sell the product for a retail price of US$79.

These are the main features of Navigator Gold 2.0:

☐ An editing environment

☐ Drag-and-drop capability

☐ Distributed publishing

☐ JavaScript support

☐ Tutorials and guides for the novice developer

An Editing Environment

Navigator Gold adds a new editing window accessible from the File menu and from a new button on the Web browser's toolbar. Using the editor, it is possible to develop Web pages in a WYSIWYG (what you see is what you get) environment. The editor makes it easy to apply HTML tags in such a way as to completely avoid the intricacies of HTML tags. Figures 13.1 and 13.2 show what the same document looks like in the Web browser window and the editor window.

Drag-and-Drop Capability

Netscape has implemented drag-and-drop support throughout Navigator Gold 2.0. It is possible to drag images or links from the Web browser window to the editor window to develop pages quickly.

Figure 13.1.

Navigator Gold 2.0 supports standard browsing features found in Netscape Navigator.

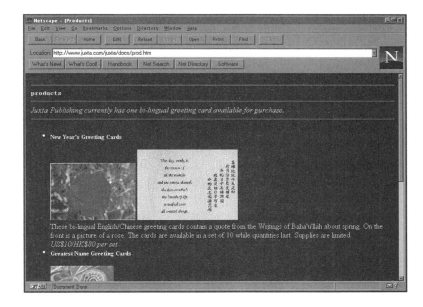

Figure 13.2.

In addition to browsing capabilities, documents can be opened in a built-in editor.

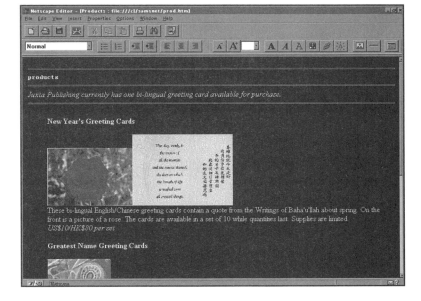

Distributed Publishing

Netscape has indicated that Navigator Gold will include a feature called One Button Publish, which will enable the simple uploading of Web pages developed with Navigator Gold to Internet Service Providers that support this feature.

JavaScript Support

Netscape claims that Navigator Gold 2.0 provides the industry's first JavaScript program editor. The built-in editor window will provide specific features and options particularly designed for JavaScript programming.

Tutorials and Guides for the Novice Developer

Netscape's promotions for Navigator Gold 2.0 include several on-line services. These include the Netscape Page Starter Site, which offers resources on the Web for page authors and the Netscape Page Wizard, which guides a novice developer through Web creation using simple questions, style guides, and pre-designed artwork. For more information about these, check out the Navigator Gold 2.0 handbook at

```
http://home.netscape.com/eng/mozilla/Gold/handbook.
```

The Relationship Between the Browser and Editor Windows

In order to take advantage of the features of Navigator Gold 2.0, it is necessary to understand the relationship between the browser and editor windows.

As with Navigator 2.0, the default window is the browser window. From the browser window, there are several ways to get to the editor window:

☐ Choose New Document from the File menu—This causes a new editor window to be opened with a blank document. The original browser window remains open.

☐ Click the Edit button—Changes the current browser window into an editor window and opens the document you were viewing. The Edit button is an addition to the toolbar in Navigator Gold's browser window.

☐ Choose Edit Document from the File menu—Changes the current browser window into an editor window and opens the document you were viewing.

☐ Choose Open File in Editor from the File menu—Opens an editor window containing the specified file. The original browser window and file remain open.

13

The Editor Window

The editor window is similar to the browser window. The document is displayed in a WYSIWYG mode similar to the browser window, and the user can specify the color of text, links, and other page elements.

Unlike the browser window, the editor window does not offer the same toolbar, location field, and directory buttons. Instead, the editor window offers the File/Edit toolbar, the Paragraph Format toolbar, and the Character Format toolbar, each of which can be individually displayed or hidden by the user.

The File/Edit Toolbar

The File/Edit toolbar provides buttons to perform the main file and editing functions, including opening and saving documents, switching to the browser window, cutting, copying and pasting, and printing documents. The File/Edit toolbar looks like Figure 13.3. Table 13.1 describes each button.

Figure 13.3.
The File/Edit toolbar.

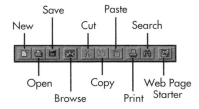

Table 13.1. The buttons on the File/Edit toolbar.

Button	Function
New	Opens a new document for editing
Open	Opens an existing document in a new editor window
Save	Saves the current document
Browse	Opens the current document in a new browser window
Cut	Cuts the selected items/section and saves it in the Clipboard
Copy	Copies the selected items/section to the Clipboard
Paste	Pastes the Clipboard contents into the current document
Print	Prints the current document
Search	Searches for text in the current document
Web Page Starter	Displays information about Web content creation

13

The Paragraph Format Toolbar

The Paragraph Format toolbar provides the basic buttons for applying HTML formatting tags to text. A drop-down list offers the main paragraph formats, including various header formats. Buttons offer a range of features, including unnumbered and numbered lists and paragraph alignment. The Paragraph Format toolbar looks like Figure 13.4. Table 13.2 describes each button.

Figure 13.4.

The Paragraph Format toolbar.

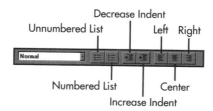

Table 13.2. The buttons on the Paragraph Format toolbar.

Button	Function
Unnumbered List	Create or change to an unnumbered list
Numbered List	Create or change to a numbered list
Increase Indent	Increase paragraph indent by one level
Decrease Indent	Decrease paragraph indent by one level
Left	Align text to the left
Center	Align text to the center
Right	Align text to the right

The Character Format Toolbar

The Character Format toolbar offers buttons to set the font size tag, the style of type including bold, italic, and fixed-width, as well as setting font color, creating links, and inserting images and horizontal rules. The Character Format toolbar looks like Figure 13.5. Table 13.3 describes each button.

Figure 13.5.

The Character Format toolbar.

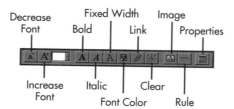

13

Table 13.3. The buttons on the Character Format toolbar.

Button	Function
Decrease Font	Decrease the font size
Increase Font	Increase the font size
Bold	Apply a bold style
Italic	Apply an italic style
Fixed Width	Make the type monospaced (fixed width)
Font Color	Select a font color
Link	Create a new link or modify an existing one
Clear	Clear all styles
Image	Insert an image
Rule	Insert a horizontal line
Properties	Open the object properties dialog box for the selected object

Pop-Up Menus

The other key feature of the editor window is context-sensitive pop-up menus. Pop-up menus on different objects provide quick access to a list of relevant commands and frequently used functions. Most objects in a document generate different pop-up menus, including links, images, and horizontal rules. Pop-up menus are accessed by right clicking on an object in the editor window.

Creating an HTML Document Using Navigator Gold 2.0

In order to understand better how the editor window works, you are going to create a new document using Navigator Gold 2.0.

The document you create will include an image, a horizontal rule, a link to another page, as well as header and body text and highlighted text using different character styles and different color text. The final page should look like the one in Figure 13.6.

13

Figure 13.6.

You are going to create this page using Navigator Gold 2.0.

Setting Up the Editor

The editor preferences dialog box can be opened from the Options menu. It offers the user the opportunity to set general options, as well as default display colors and backgrounds for the editor.

The two pages of the editor preferences dialog box look like Figures 13.7 and 13.8.

Figure 13.7.

General preferences.

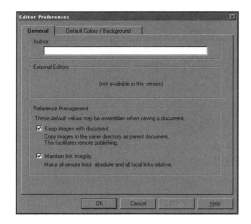

13

Figure 13.8.
Default Colors/Backgrounds.

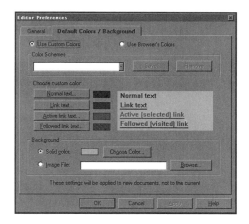

The general options include the default author of documents, as well as two options: Keep images with document (to copy all images to your local hard disk) and Maintain link integrity (to adjust links to work regardless of whether the file is saved locally or published to a Web site on the Internet).

For this document, select both Keep images with document and Maintain link integrity.

The Default Colors/Backgrounds screen also enables the user to set the colors used by the editor to display everything from normal text to link text, as well as the background.

Creating the File

As mentioned earlier, you can create a new document by selecting New Document from the File menu in the browser window. This opens a new editor window with a blank document but will not close the existing browser window.

Once the file is created, you can give it a filename by saving it—this can be done in the File menu or by choosing the save button on the File/Edit toolbar. It is important to save the file for many of Gold's link-related features to function correctly.

The document properties dialog box (in the Properties menu) enables you to set up several features of your HTML document, including header information, such as the title and the color and background information for the BODY tag.

The information in the dialog box is divided into two pages which can be selected by tabs: header (document) information and color/background information.

The document properties dialog box looks like Figures 13.9 and 13.10.

13

Figure 13.9.
Header information.

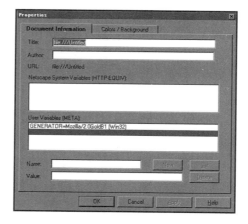

Figures 13.10.
Colors/Background.

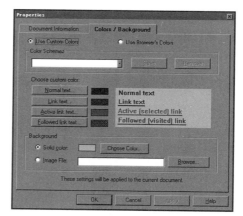

The Document Information screen allows the user to set information to include in the header of the HTML document. This includes the title of the document and the author.

For your document, you want to set the Title to Example 13.1 and the background color to whatever color you prefer.

Inserting the Image

There are two ways you can insert the desired image—drag an existing image from the browser window or insert a new image by choosing Image from the Insert menu (which is the same as clicking on the insert image button on the Character Format toolbar). You will use the latter.

13

When you choose to insert an image, you are presented with an image properties dialog box like the one in Figure 13.11.

Figure 13.11.

The image properties dialog box.

The image properties dialog box allows you to specify the image file, an alternate image file, and alternate text. In addition, the alignment of the image relative to the neighboring text, the size of the border, and the blank space around the image can be controlled.

The dialog box contains two browse buttons—one for the image file and one for the alternate image file.

If you want to, you could specify alternate text for text-based browsers, as well as the space around the image and the width of the border. If you want to make the image a link, you could select a link as well.

Inserting a Horizontal Line

You can insert a horizontal line by selecting the horizontal line button on the Character Format toolbar or by selecting Horizontal Line from the Insert menu. Once the line is inserted, you can right click on it to get a pop-up menu and then select Horizontal Line Properties to get the horizontal line properties dialog box, which looks like Figure 13.12.

The horizontal line properties dialog enables you to specify the alignment, width, height, and other properties of a horizontal line.

You aren't selecting anything special for this example except to choose a center alignment.

Figure 13.12.
*The horizontal
line properties
dialog box.*

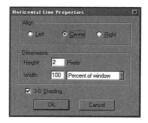

Inserting a Heading

By clicking next to the horizontal line you just inserted and pressing return, you can type in
the text of the header.

Next you need to apply the appropriate paragraph format. Paragraph formats apply to all
paragraphs in a selection. If no text is selected, then the format applies to the paragraph where
the cursor is.

By leaving the cursor in the paragraph you have just written, you can simply select the header
style you like from the drop-down list on the Paragraph Format toolbar.

You also want to change the words `"Netscape Navigator Gold"` in the paragraph to italics and
change the color to red. You can do this using character formatting features.

In order to apply character formats to selected text, you need to select the text you want to
work with. Next, you can select the italic style from the Character Format toolbar. Then you
can add the color red by clicking the color button on the toolbar or selecting Font Color from
the Properties menu.

When you do, you get the font color dialog box, which looks like Figure 13.13.

Figure 13.13.
*The font color
dialog box.*

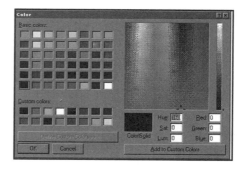

13

Inserting Body Text

Next you can click after the header you have just created, hit return, and enter the body text. You need to select the normal paragraph format from the drop-down list in the Paragraph Format toolbar to switch from the header style to normal text. You also need to turn off italics by clicking on the italics button in the Character Format toolbar and set the color back to black before you start typing.

Creating a Link

You want to turn the text here into a link to Netscape's home page. You can do this by selecting the text and clicking on the link button in the Character Format toolbar. When you do this, you get the modify/insert links dialog box like the one in Figure 13.14.

Figure 13.14.
The modify/insert links dialog box.

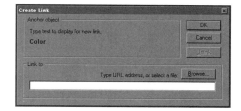

In this dialog box, you can specify a link. You can select a link by clicking on the Browser button or by typing a URL. In this case, you can enter the URL http://home.netscape.com/.

Save the File and View It

Now you can save the document by selecting the save button on the File/Edit toolbar or by selecting Save from the File menu.

If you want to view the source code of the document you have just created, select Document Source from the View menu. This opens a view source window, which looks like Figure 13.15.

Then you can view the document by selecting the browser button in the File/Edit dialog box. The document will be opened in the browser window.

Figure 13.15.

You can view the source code of any project.

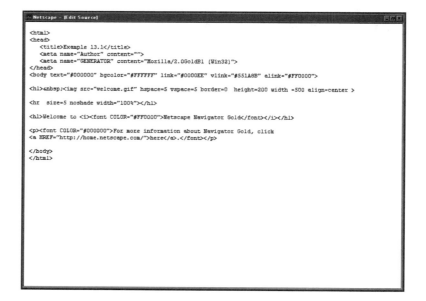

Developing JavaScript Applications in Navigator Gold 2.0

In the version of Navigator Gold 2.0 that is currently available, the JavaScript features of Gold are limited. Still, Navigator Gold 2.0 does offer the first integrated tools for working with both HTML and JavaScript and offers a few basic editing features especially well-suited to JavaScript editing.

For instance, when you indent a line using the Tab key, the editor remembers the level of indent and the next line will also be indented to the same point. The Shift+Tab combination enables you to back out to a higher level (that is, indent less). This feature can be useful in maintaining well-structured, easy-to-read JavaScript programs.

In addition, JavaScript code is treated as a character style, so you can type a script without the SCRIPT tags. Then, you can highlight the text and select JavaScript (client) from the character submenu of the Properties menu, and the SCRIPT tag will be inserted (but not displayed), and the color of the script text will change.

One drawback of the editor is that you need to hit Shift+Return (a soft return) at the end of each line. Otherwise, each line of your script will be contained in separate SCRIPT container tags.

13

Even so, in the current beta version of Navigator Gold, it is not practical to create new JavaScript pages using the editor window. Not only is there no direct way to put scripts into the header of the document, but it is not possible to add event handlers to various HTML tags.

Nonetheless, you can to use the editor to edit an existing JavaScript application by loading the page in the browser and then switching to the editor window by clicking on the Edit button. Then all of your SCRIPT containers will appear, and if you edit the existing files, they will remain properly contained in SCRIPT container tags.

Even so, event handlers in JavaScript tags will not appear, and it will be difficult to work with forms because Gold's form handling, especially related to JavaScript, is less than perfect in the current beta. Nonetheless, these aspects of editing and creating integrated JavaScript and HTML documents should be worked out by a later release of Navigator Gold.

Other Advanced Features of Navigator Gold 2.0

In addition to promising to offer JavaScript editing capabilities, Navigator Gold includes, or will include in a later version, several other advanced functions that can ease the Web page development process. These features include a one-button publish feature that will publish your page or pages to your service provider's Web server along with all related images and linked files.

Navigator Gold also promises to include the ability to create client-side image maps (one of the new features in Navigator 2.0), include audio files, and provide basic document management capabilities.

Limitations of Navigator Gold

At the current time, Navigator Gold is still in an early public beta release and is not complete. In this state, it has several limitations which restrict its usefulness as a complete HTML and JavaScript development tool:

- ☐ Editor window does not support frame display.
- ☐ Editor window does not display tables.
- ☐ Forms support in editor window is not stable.
- ☐ JavaScript capabilities are limited.
- ☐ Image alignment and text wrapping display support are not complete.

13

In addition to these shortcomings, many of which should be fixed by the release of the final version of Navigator Gold 2.0, there are several other limitations of the product, including:

☐ Not designed for site management: Navigator Gold 2 is designed for producing individual Web pages—it cannot be used to develop and maintain large sites with numerous internal links.

Summary

In this chapter, you learned the basics of using Navigator Gold 2.0 to create HTML pages, and we discussed how future versions of Gold will allow for integrated development of JavaScript scripts. Navigator Gold provides a separate WYSIWYG editing window which enables drag-and-drop editing, and provides tools for easy adjustment of object properties in a page through properties dialog boxes and toolbars.

In Chapter 14, "From JavaScript to Java—Looking into the Future," you are going to take a look at the relationship of JavaScript and Java, how to move from JavaScript to Java, how to bring Java and JavaScript together in an HTML document, and future developments of JavaScript.

Q&A

Q I have seen products that manage complete Web sites—not just pages. They track links between files and manage the directory structure. Can Navigator Gold 2.0 do this for me?

A No. Navigator Gold is not a site management tool. It is a browser with an integrated editor. Still, Navigator Gold does have features for managing the relationship between HTML files and inline images and can handle the conversion of relative and absolute links in files.

Q What I see in the editor window doesn't match the browser window. Why?

A The beta version of Navigator Gold currently available doesn't have a complete editor. Specifically, the editor window can't display some of the HTML tags supported by the browser window, including image alignment attributes and frames.

Q If I have Navigator Gold 2.0, is there any reason for me to have Navigator 2.0 as well?

A Not really. Navigator Gold includes the complete Navigator Web browser with the addition of an editor. You shouldn't find any need for Navigator as well.

13

Chapter 14

From JavaScript to Java—Looking into the Future

Now that you've mastered the essentials of JavaScript, it should be clear that JavaScript is a powerful tool for extending the functionality of basic HTML documents and creating sophisticated interactive applications.

Nonetheless, the questions remain: How do I do more? Can I move beyond JavaScript and extend its power?

In this chapter, we take a look at the future relationship between JavaScript and Java and how you can quickly and easily add Java applets to your pages today.

You'll learn about the following:

☐ The future `applet` object

☐ Basic Java concepts

☐ Using the `APPLET` tag to use pre-built Java applets

☐ Similarities between JavaScript and Java
☐ Where else JavaScript is headed

Integrating Java into JavaScript—The Future `applet` Object

When Sun and Netscape announced the creation of JavaScript in late 1995, they made a lot of noise about the role of JavaScript in gluing Java into Web pages.

Java applets, because they exist outside the context of the Web page itself, are unable to interact with the type of document, form, and window objects that JavaScript can work with. Java applets are simply assigned a space in the current page, like images are given a particular rectangle, and then they do their thing in that space.

Any interaction with the user requires the applet to provide its own alternatives to the HTML forms and links that JavaScript can so readily work with. Given this, JavaScript's role is supposed to become the link. By having access to all the document and browser objects, as well as having objects which provide hooks into each Java applet in a page, a JavaScript script can play the role of middleman and cause information generated by user or browser events outside the applet to be passed to any applet.

Pretty powerful stuff, overall.

In its current form, however, JavaScript provides no means by which to interact with Java applets. The version of JavaScript built into version 2.0 of Netscape Navigator doesn't provide the `applet` object. This is scheduled for inclusion in the next release of Navigator—due out later in 1996.

Still, this doesn't prevent JavaScript-enabled Web pages from taking advantage of Java applets and even from performing some basic manipulations that would seem to the user to interact with Java applets.

Basic Java Concepts

In order to be able to easily use in your Web pages applets that other people have written, you need to understand several fundamental things about Java.

First, Java is compiled. In order to build your own Java applets or to compile source code provided by friendly folk on the Web and in Usenet newsgroups, it is necessary to have a Java compiler.

14

Presently, the Java Development Kit is available for SPARC-based hardware running the Solaris operating system and 32-bit Windows platforms (namely, Windows 95 and Windows NT). The compiler and related files and documentation are available at

```
http://www.javasoft.com/
```

Other groups have ported the Java Development Kit to other platforms, such as Linux and the Mac OS.

Once the source code for an applet is compiled, it becomes a class file. Class files are not source code and contain objects that can be used in other programs or applets you build. The class file for a Java applet is what is downloaded to the browser and executed when a user loads a page containing the applet.

Presently, there are several large archives of freely available applets, which often include source code or even downloadable Java binary files. If you want to use these applets, you can download the source code and compile them yourself or download the actual class files. Information about using the Java compiler is included in the documentation at the Java Web page.

The leading archives can be found at this site:

```
http://www.gamelan.com/
```

and at the Java Web page itself.

NOTE

In looking though these archives, you will notice both Alpha and Beta applets (supported by Navigator 2.0). There have been two main stages in the development of Java. The Alpha applets are supported on the HotJava browser for Solaris and 32-bit Windows. The Beta applets and applets written to the final release API are supported by Netscape. Sun is encouraging Java developers to move from Alpha applets to the current specification. We will be discussing the current specification throughout this chapter.

In order to understand how to go about obtaining and preparing to use existing applets, you are going to prepare the Growing Text applet by Jamie Hall, which you will use for the rest of the chapter. This applet animates any string of text and causes it to grow from very small to very large. The page author can control several different options including color, font, and delay.

14

I am assuming that you have downloaded the Development Kit (which includes the compiler) from Sun's Java home page and have followed the installation instructions. The Development Kit is available for several platforms including Windows 95, the Mac OS, and Solaris. Navigator can run Java applets in its 32-bit Windows version, its UNIX versions, and the Mac version.

The Growing Text applet can be found on the Web at this site:

```
http://www1.mhv.net/~jamihall/java/GrowingText/GrowingText.html
```

You should download the source code, which looks like Listing 14.1 (remember—this is Java code and not a JavaScript script).

Listing 14.1. The Growing Text applet source code.

```
/*
 * GrowingText
 *
 * Feel free to re-use any part of this code.
 *
 * Jamie Hall, hallj@frb.gov  1/9/96
 *
 * Jamie Hall 2/2/96 - Added blur parameter
 */

/*
   Takes text, delay, fontName, fontBold, fontItalic, bgColor,
   and fgColor as parameters.  The following are the defaults:

   text       -  String displayed in applet     -  Growing Text
   delay      -  Milliseconds between updates    -  500
   fontName   -  Font style                      -  TimesRoman
   fontBold   -  Font boldness                   -  true
   fontItalic -  Font italics                    -  false
   bgColor    -  Background color (hex. number)  -  light Gray
   fgColor    -  Foreground color (hex. number)  -  black
   blur       -  Blurring effect                 -  false

   Note: 'random' can be used as the background or foreground color
   to generate a random color on each update.
 */

import java.awt.*;
import java.applet.*;

public class GrowingText extends Applet implements Runnable {
   String fontName = "TimesRoman", text = "Growing Text", bgColor, fgColor;
   Thread killme = null;
   boolean threadSuspended = false, blur = false;
   int fonts[] = { 8, 12, 14, 18, 24, 36 };
   int delay = 500, numFonts = 6, fontIndex = 0, fontStyle;
   Font appFont;
```

14

```
   public void init() {
     String param;
     boolean fontBold = true, fontItalic = false;

     param = getParameter("text");
     if (param != null) { text = param; }

     param = getParameter("delay");
     if (param != null) { delay = Integer.parseInt(param); }

     param = getParameter("fontName");
     if (param != null) { fontName = param; }

     param = getParameter("fontBold");
     if (param != null) { fontBold = param.equals("true"); }

     param = getParameter("fontItalic");
     if (param != null) { fontItalic = param.equals("true"); }

     fontStyle = (fontBold ? Font.BOLD : Font.PLAIN) +
       (fontItalic ? Font.ITALIC : Font.PLAIN);

     bgColor = getParameter("bgColor");
     if (bgColor == null) { bgColor = "Color.lightGray"; }
     setBackground(colorFromString(bgColor, Color.lightGray));

     fgColor = getParameter("fgColor");
     if (fgColor == null) { fgColor = "Color.black"; }
     setForeground(colorFromString(fgColor, Color.black));

     param = getParameter("blur");
     if (param != null) { blur = param.equals("true"); }

     /* Resize applet to fit string with largest font.
        Only works in JDK appletviewer, Netscape ignores it */
     /* FontMetrics fm =
➥getFontMetrics(new Font(fontName, fontStyle, fonts[numFonts-1]));
resize(fm.stringWidth(s) + 20, appFont.getSize() + 20); */
   }

   public void start() {
     if (killme == null) {
       killme = new Thread(this);
       killme.start();
     }
   }

   public void stop() {
     if (killme != null) {
       killme.stop();
       killme = null;
     }
   }
```

14

continues

Listing 14.1. continued

```java
public void run() {
  while (killme != null) {
    repaint();
    try { Thread.sleep(delay); } catch (InterruptedException e) {};
  }
  killme = null;
}

public void update(Graphics g) {
  if (blur) {
    if (fontIndex > numFonts - 1 ) {
      g.clearRect(0, 0, size().width, size().height);
    }
    paint(g);
  } else {
    g.clearRect(0, 0, size().width, size().height);
    paint(g);
  }
}

public void paint(Graphics g) {
  if (bgColor.equalsIgnoreCase("random")) {
    setBackground(colorFromString(bgColor, Color.lightGray));
  }

  if (fgColor.equalsIgnoreCase("random")) {
    setForeground(colorFromString(fgColor, Color.black));
  }

  if (fontIndex > numFonts - 1 ) {
    fontIndex = 0;
  }
  g.setFont(appFont = new Font(fontName, fontStyle, fonts[fontIndex++]));
  FontMetrics fm = getFontMetrics(appFont);

  g.drawString(text, (size().width - fm.stringWidth(text))/2,
    (size().height/2)+10);
}

public boolean mouseDown(Event evt, int x, int y) {
  if (threadSuspended) {
    killme.resume();
  } else {
    killme.suspend();
  }
  threadSuspended = !threadSuspended;
  return true;
}

public Color colorFromString(String str, Color defaultColor) {
  if (str.equalsIgnoreCase("random")) {
    return new Color((int)(Math.random() * 256),
➡ (int)(Math.random() * 256), (int)(Math.random() * 256));
  } else {
```

14

```
    try {
      Integer i = Integer.valueOf(str, 16);
      return new Color(i.intValue());
    } catch (NumberFormatException e) {
      return defaultColor;
    }
  }
}

  public String getAppletInfo() {
    return "GrowingText effect by Jamie M. Hall, 1996";
  }

}
```

OUTPUT The demonstration page for this applet looks like Figure 14.1.

Figure 14.1.
The Growing Text applet.

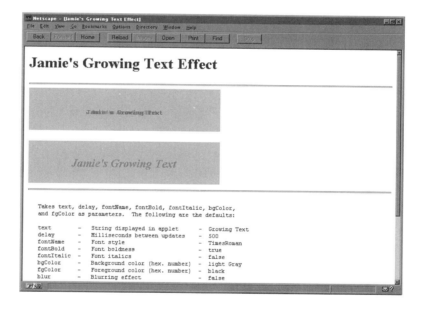

Once you have the source code, the next step is to compile it. On Windows 95 or NT systems, this involves running the program `javac` (which is the compiler). For instance, `javac GrowingText.java` will compile the Java source code file you downloaded. The result of this process should be a file called `GrowingText.class`. The `.class` files are Java binaries, and this is the actual executable applet used by the browser.

14

Incorporating Java Applets in HTML: The APPLET Tag

Including a JavaScript applet in an HTML file requires the use of the APPLET tag. The APPLET tag specifies the URL of the Java class file for the applet and tells the browser what size rectangular space to set aside for use by the applet. This is done using the attributes outlined in Table 14.1.

Table 14.1. Attributes of the APPLET tag.

Name	Description
CODE	Specifies the URL binary class file for the applet (this can be relative to the base URL specified with the CODEBASE attribute).
CODEBASE	Specifies the base URL for applets (this points to the directory containing applet code).
WIDTH	Specifies the width of the rectangle set aside for the applet.
HEIGHT	Specifies the height of the rectangle set aside for the applet.

The APPLET tag is a container tag. Any text between the opening and closing tags will be displayed by browsers that don't support the APPLET tag (that is, which don't support the beta version of Java).

In addition to defining the space in which the APPLET is able to operate, you can also pass parameters—which can be thought of as arguments—to the applet using the PARAM tag. You can include as many PARAM tags—which define name-value pairs for the parameters—as you want between the opening and closing APPLET tags. The PARAM tag takes the form:

```
<PARAM NAME="nameOfParameter" VALUE="valuePassedForParameter">
```

Using the GrowingText applet, which you compiled in Listing 14.1, you can now build a simple Web page that displays the applet in a 500×200 pixel rectangle with the words "Java Really Works" as the text used by the applet.

As you can see in the source code for the applet (Listing 14.1), several parameters are available for you to set:

```
Takes text, delay, fontName, fontBold, fontItalic, bgColor,
   and fgColor as parameters.  The following are the defaults:

   text       -   String displayed in applet      -   Growing Text
   delay      -   Milliseconds between updates     -   500
   fontName   -   Font style                       -   TimesRoman
   fontBold   -   Font boldness                    -   true
   fontItalic -   Font italics                     -   false
   bgColor    -   Background color (hex. number)   -   light Gray
   fgColor    -   Foreground color (hex. number)   -   black
   blur       -   Blurring effect                  -   false

   Note: 'random' can be used as the background or foreground color
   to generate a random color on each update.
```

For your Web page, you will use a delay of 250 milliseconds and bold type to test the blurring effect. Listing 14.2 shows how to combine the applet into a Web page.

TYPE

Listing 14.2. Combining the Growing Text applet into a Web page.

```
<HTML>

<HEAD>
<TITLE>Example 14.2</TITLE>
</HEAD>

<BODY>
<H1>Java Applet Example</H1>
<APPLET CODE="GrowingText.class" WIDTH=500 HEIGHT=200>
<PARAM NAME="text" VALUE="Java Really Works">
<PARAM NAME="delay" VALUE="250">
<PARAM NAME="bold" VALUE="true">
<PARAM NAME="blur" VALUE="true">
</APPLET>
</BODY>

</HTML>
```

OUTPUT   Figure 14.2 illustrates the effects of the script.

14

Figure 14.2.

The APPLET tag lets you define the space available to the applet.

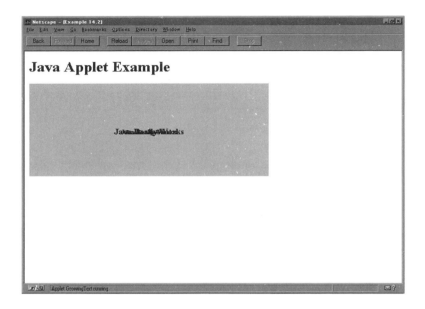

ANALYSIS There are several things to notice in this example. First, there are default values for many of the parameters, so you don't actually need any parameters to get the applet to work. The parameters are like optional arguments. In this case, you can use as few or as many as you like.

The Java applet continues to run until you leave the page or close Netscape.

Working with Java Today

Although the applet object is not available in the current version of JavaScript, it is still possible to create limited interaction between applets and the browser environment, using JavaScript.

For instance, with JavaScript's capability to dynamically generate HTML code, a form in one frame could easily reload a Java applet in another frame, with new parameters.

While this is not truly interacting with an applet while it is loaded and executing, it can produce the appearance that the applet is better integrated into a Web application.

To demonstrate how dynamically written HTML can be used to change the state of an applet in another frame, let's build a simple testing program for the Growing Text applet.

14

This program should enable the user to enter a string, select options from checkboxes, and fill in fields. When the user clicks on a Test button, the applet should be reloaded in a second frame with the new parameters. Listings 14.3 through 14.5 are the source code for this application.

TYPE   **Listing 14.3. The parent frameset.**

```
<!-- SOURCE CODE OF PARENT FRAMESET -->

<FRAMESET ROWS="50%,*">

  <FRAME SRC="javatest.html" NAME="form">
  <FRAME SRC="blank.html" NAME="applet">


</FRAMESET>
```

Listings 14.4 and 14.5 are the source code for `javatest.html` that provides a form to test different parameters of the applet and the code to display it.

TYPE   **Listing 14.4. Source code for the testing form.**

```
<!-- SOURCE CODE FOR JAVATEST.HTML -->

<HEAD>
<TITLE>Example 14.4</TITLE>
</HEAD>

<BODY BGCOLOR="#FFFFFF">
<H1>Growing Text Java Applet Tester</H1>
<FORM METHOD=POST>
Text to display: <INPUT TYPE=text NAME="text" SIZE=40><BR>
Delay between updates: <INPUT TYPE=text NAME="delay"><BR>
Font to use: <INPUT TYPE=text NAME="font" SIZE=40><BR>
<INPUT TYPE=checkbox NAME="bold"> Bold
<INPUT TYPE=checkbox NAME="blur"> Blur<BR>
<INPUT TYPE=button VALUE="Test Applet"
➥onClick="parent['applet'].location='applet.html';"> </FORM>
</BODY>

</HTML>
```

14

TYPE   **Listing 14.5. The code to display the applet.**

```
<!-- SOURCE CODE FOR applet.html -->

<BODY>
<SCRIPT LANGUAGE="JavaScript">
<!-- HIDE FROM OTHER BROWSERS
  document.write('<APPLET CODE="GrowingText.class" WIDTH=500 HEIGHT=200>');
  document.write('<PARAM NAME="text" VALUE="' +
➥parent["form"].document.forms[0].text.value + '">');
document.write('<PARAM NAME="delay" VALUE="' +
➥parent["form"].document.forms[0].delay.value + '">');
document.write('<PARAM NAME="fontName" VALUE="' +
➥parent["form"].document.forms[0].font.value + '">');
document.write('<PARAM NAME="boldBold" VALUE="' +
➥parent["form"].document.forms[0].bold.value + '">');
document.write('<PARAM NAME="blur" VALUE="' +
➥parent["form"].document.forms[0].blur.value + '">');
document.write('</APPLET>');
// STOP HIDING -->
</SCRIPT>
</BODY>
```

OUTPUT   The results appear in Figure 14.3.

Figure 14.3.
*Using JavaScript,
you can reload an
applet in another
frame with new
parameters.*

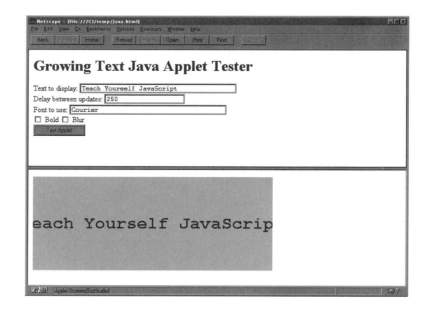

14

ANALYSIS   The process by which you update the applet parameters is fairly straight forward: In the upper frame, you load the form, which you use to change the parameters of the applet. In the lower frame, you load the file `applet.html` which builds the `APPLET` and `PARAM` tags in a script. The script in `applet.html` assigns the relevant `PARAM` values based on the values in the form in the other frame (using `parent["form"]` to reference the named frame).

The file `javatest.html` makes minimal use of JavaScript. The only place you use JavaScript is in the `onClick` event handler in the form button where you reload `applet.html` into the lower frame to get it to restart the applet with the new parameters.

From JavaScript to Java

For many of you, the next step after reading this book will be to look into learning Java. This isn't that outrageous an idea.

By learning JavaScript, you have learned the fundamental syntax used throughout Java. You are familiar with how Java commands are built, how to use loops, and how to build expressions.

Of course, Java is not the same as JavaScript. Besides being compiled and having access to the same set of objects JavaScript does, there are other significant differences:

☐ Static Typing: Where in JavaScript, variables acquire types, such as numbers or strings dynamically when you first use the variable, Java requires explicit definition of variables and their types before they get used in a program. This removes some of the flexibility of dynamic typing but ensures more rigid adherence to good programming style.

☐ Static Binding: In JavaScript, you are able to refer to objects in your scripts, that may not exist when the script is first loaded and checked for errors. In Java, a program will not compile unless all objects being referred to exist at the time of compilation.

☐ Object-orientation: JavaScript implements only a limited object model. Java takes this further to include classes and inheritance—two important aspects of true object-oriented programming.

The result of these and other more subtle differences between Java and JavaScript is that Java programming can be more complex and require more rigorous debugging and organization than JavaScript scripts.

At the same time, with Java it is possible to write complete standalone applications and to perform actions not possible with JavaScript.

14

NOTE

> The types of applications and applets being developed with Java are wide and varied. A quick glance through a Java archive, such as Gamelan, shows that the major categories of Java applet development include these areas:
>
> **Arts and Entertainment**: Applets range from portrait painting tools to interactive drag-and-drop poetry creators to simple drawing tools.
>
> **Business and Finance**: Numerous applets have been created for business applications including stock ticker tapes, real estate viewing tools, shopping carts, and spreadsheets.
>
> **Education**: The educational applications of Java today include rotatable, three-dimensional molecular models, an interactive abacus, an animated juggling tutorial, and multilingual word matching games.
>
> **Multimedia**: Multimedia is the most talked-about area of Java development and includes animation tools, fractal drawing applets, electronic publishing systems, audio players, and midi applications.
>
> **Network**: Applets in this area include terminal emulators and chat applications.
>
> **Utilities**: Utilities developed as Java applets range from font viewers to graphical calculators to clocks.

JavaScript into the Future

Currently, JavaScript is limited to products from Netscape. The most prominent use of JavaScript, which we have discussed throughout this book, is the use of the language for developing client-end applications that are integrated into HTML pages displayed in the Navigator 2.0 browser.

However, Netscape also has implemented JavaScript to use at the server end, much like CGI programming. Using the Netscape product called LiveWire—a server package for developing sophisticated interactive Web applications—it is possible to create CGI-like scripts using JavaScript. This simplifies Web development in many ways because programming at both ends can be done in the same language, rather than requiring the use of JavaScript for the client end of an application and using Perl, C, or another language for the server end.

At the client end, JavaScript should become increasingly powerful with the next release of Navigator later this year. Not only will the object hierarchy become richer, adding features

14

such as the `applet` object, but missing elements such as the `Math.random()` method will be migrated to all platforms.

At the same time, several plug-in developers have indicated they will provide access to their plug-ins in JavaScript in the form of objects that reflect attributes and functions of the plug-in. This can greatly enhance a JavaScript application by enabling it to work with a range of other file formats, such as Macromedia Director files, Acrobat files, and more.

NOTE

The following is a list of some of the plug-ins available for Navigator 2.0. Netscape makes a longer list available on the Web at

```
http://home.netscape.com/comprod/products/navigator/version
➥_2.0/plugins/index.html
```

Acrobat Amber Reader (Adobe): A viewer for Portable Document Format (PDF) files—Windows 95/NT

ASAP WebShow (Software Publishing Corporation): A viewer for viewing documents created with SPC's ASAP WordPower presentation software—Windows 95/3.1

Corel Vector Graphics (Corel): A viewer for Corel's CMX vector graphic format—Windows 95/NT

EarthTime (Starfish Software): A plug-in to display the local time in eight geographical locations along with an animated world map displaying daylight and darkness—Windows 95/NT

Envoy (Tumbleweed Software): A viewer for Envoy documents—Windows 95/3.1, Macintosh, Power Macintosh

FIGleaf Inline (Carberry Technology): A viewer for multiple graphics formats—including CGM, GIF, JPEG, TIFF, BMP, WMF, and EPS—that includes zooming, panning, and scrolling of graphics within Web pages—Windows 95/NT

Formula One/NET (Visual Components): An Internet-capable, Excel-compatible spreadsheet available within Navigator 2.0—Windows 95/NT/3.1

InterCAP Inline (InterCAP Graphics Systems): A plug-in version of InterCAP's MEtaLink RunTIme CGM viewer that supports zooming, panning, and animation—Windows 95/NT

PreVU (InterVU): An MPEG player that supports viewing of MPEG video files while downloading—Windows 95/NT

14

> **RealAudio** (Progressive Networks): A player for live, on-demand audio files—Windows 95/NT/3.1, Power Macintosh, UNIX (Irix 5.3, Solaris 2.4/2.5, SunOS 4.1.x, Linux 1.2.x or later)
>
> **Shockwave for Director** (Macromedia): A player for presentations created with Macromedia Director—Windows 95/3.1, Macintosh, Power Macintosh
>
> **VR Scout** (Chaco Communications): A plug-in to view VRML worlds in Navigator 2.0—Windows 95/NT
>
> **Word Viewer** (Inso): A viewer for Microsoft Word 6.0 and 7.0 documents—Windows 95/NT/3.1

In addition to these third-party plug-ins, Netscape has introduced Live3D, which promises to add three-dimensional, interactive capabilities to Navigator.

Live3D includes a VRML viewer and extends Java and JavaScript as well. In addition to supporting animation and multimedia (in the form of LiveMedia), Live3D extends the plug-in interface in Navigator to provide plug-ins with access to the 3D space as well as providing Java and JavaScript objects for developing interactive three-dimensional worlds. Live3D is based on the Moving Worlds VRML2.0 specification, which is being considered as a standard.

NOTE

> LiveMedia is Netscape's system for delivering real-time audio and video via Netscape software. Netscape will be making the framework available on the Internet and will try to have the technology adopted as an open Internet standard.

Summary

Having learned to use JavaScript, you looked in this chapter at the relationship between JavaScript and Java.

We discussed how the applet object, which will be available in a future version of Navigator, will enable JavaScript applications to interact with Java applets. You also learned how to incorporate existing Java applets into HTML pages and to use JavaScript to pass custom parameters to the applets you are using.

Finally, you took a look at how to make the move from JavaScript scripting to Java programming and considered the future development of JavaScript.

Q&A

Q **I'm running a PC with Windows 3.1 and lots of memory. When I try the Java examples in this chapter, they don't work. Why?**

A Java is supported only in the 32-bit Windows version of Navigator 2.0 (as well as the Mac and UNIX versions). If you are running Windows 3.1, you are out of luck. There is no known Java support for Windows 3.1 at this time.

Q **I want to develop an animated logo. Should I use Java or JavaScript?**

A Although there are examples of simple animations using JavaScript, JavaScript is not well-suited to the task. JavaScript animations suffer from speed problems as well as flickering and inconsistent timing. There are numerous well-developed, freely available Java applets for animating a series of GIF images, and these are much more suitable for generating animated logos. Check out the Gamelan archive at http://www.gamelan.com/ for examples of these applets.

Q **Why can't my Java applets see what is in my HTML forms?**

A This is where Java faces some limitations. It is not able to see elements of your Web pages, such as forms, links, colors, and so on. This is where JavaScript's role will grow in the future as it becomes able to pass this type of information to Java applets.

14

APPENDIX
A

JavaScript Reference Resources

The following is a list of selected JavaScript and Java reference resources on the Internet, organized by type of resource.

World Wide Web Sites

JavaScript Overview   Netscape's brief introduction to JavaScript, which includes pointers to several examples and a link to the JavaScript documentation.

```
http://home.netscape.com/comprod/products/navigator/version_2.0/
script/index.html
```

JavaScript Documentation　　Netscape's official JavaScript documentation and reference materials.

`http://home.netscape.com/eng/mozilla/Gold/handbook/javascript/index.html`

JavaScript Index　　A comprehensive index of JavaScript-related pages, including sites using JavaScript, teaching JavaScript, and offering JavaScript consulting and development services.

`http://www.c2.org/~andreww/javascript/`

JavaScript Library　　A growing library of JavaScript examples and applications available on the Web.

`http://www.c2.org/~andreww/javascript/lib/`

JavaScript PDF Documentation　　The JavaScript documentation from the Netscape Web site in Adobe Acrobat format for easy printing.

`http://www.ipst.com/docs.htm`

Morphic Molecules　　A collection of advanced information and mini-tutorials about different aspects of JavaScript.

`http://www.txdirect.net/users/everett/`

Learning JavaScript with Windows Help　　Offers a windows help with information for learning JavaScript.

`http://www.jchelp.com/javahelp/javahelp.htm`

JavaScript Tutorial　　A growing tutorial covering many aspects of JavaScript.

`http://ourworld.compuserve.com/homepages/vood/script.htm`

Gamelan　　A leading repository of Java applets, which also includes a JavaScript section.

`http://www.gamelan.com/`

Java Home Page　　Sun's source of official information about Java.

`http://java.sun.com/`

Mailing Lists

JavaHouse　　Focuses on Java with some coverage of JavaScript.

`http://www.center.nitech.ac.jp/ml/java-house/hypermail/0000`

JavaScript List Focuses on JavaScript (can be high volume).

`http://www.obscure.org/`

Subscribe by sending an e-mail to `majordomo@obscure.org` with "subscribe JavaScript" in the message body.

Newsgroups

`comp.lang.java` Discussion of Java with some JavaScript talk.

`news:comp.lang.java`

`comp.lang.javascript` Discussion of JavaScript.

`news:comp.lang.javascript`

Netscape's JavaScript Group Internal secure newsgroup discussing JavaScript.

`snews://secnews.netscape.com/netscape.devs-javascript`

APPENDIX B

JavaScript Language Reference

The first part of this reference is organized by object, with properties and methods listed by the object to which they apply. The second part covers independent functions in JavaScript not connected with a particular object, as well as operators in JavaScript and reserved words.

The anchor **Object**

See the anchors property of the document object.

The button **Object**

The button object reflects a push button from an HTML form in JavaScript.

Properties

☐ **name**   A string value containing the name of the button element.

☐ **value**   A string value containing the value of the button element.

Methods

☐ **click()**   Emulates the action of clicking on the button.

Event Handlers

☐ **onClick**   Specifies JavaScript code to execute when the button is clicked.

The checkbox Object

The checkbox object makes a checkbox from an HTML form available in JavaScript.

Properties

☐ **checked**   A boolean value indicating if the checkbox element is checked.

☐ **defaultChecked**   A boolean value indicating if the checkbox element is checked by default (i.e., it reflects the CHECKED attribute).

☐ **name**   A string value containing the name of the checkbox element.

☐ **value**   A string value containing the value of the checkbox element.

Methods

☐ **click()**   Emulates the action of clicking on the checkbox.

Event Handlers

☐ **onClick**   Specifies JavaScript code to execute when the checkbox is clicked.

The Date Object

The Date object provides mechanisms for working with dates and times in JavaScript. Instances of the object can be created with the syntax:

newObjectName = new Date(*dateInfo*)

where *dateInfo* is an optional specification of a particular date and can be one of the following:

"month day, year hours:minutes:seconds"

year, month, day

year, month, day, hours, minutes, seconds

The latter two options represent integer values.

If no *dateInfo* is specified, the new object will represent the current date and time.

Methods

- ☐ **getDate()** Returns the day of the month for the current Date object as an integer from 1 to 31.
- ☐ **getDay()** Returns the day of the week for the current Date object as an integer from 0 to 6 (where 0 is Sunday, 1 is Monday, etc.).
- ☐ **getHours()** Returns the hour from the time in the current Date object as an integer from 0 to 23.
- ☐ **getMinutes()** Returns the minutes from the time in the current Date object as an integer from 0 to 59.
- ☐ **getMonth()** Returns the month for the current Date object as an integer from 0 to 11 (where 0 is January, 1 is February, etc.).
- ☐ **getSeconds()** Returns the seconds from the time in the current Date object as an integer from 0 to 59.
- ☐ **getTime()** Returns the time of the current Date object as an integer representing the number of milliseconds since 1 January 1970 at 00:00:00.
- ☐ **getTimezoneOffset()** Returns the difference between the local time and GMT as an integer representing the number of minutes.
- ☐ **getYear()** Returns the year of the week for the current Date object as a two-digit integer representing the year less 1900.
- ☐ **parse(dateString)** Returns the number of milliseconds between January 1, 1970 at 00:00:00 and the date specified in *dateString*. *dateString* should take the format:

  `Day, DD Mon YYYY HH:MM:SS TZN`

  Mon DD, YYYY

- ☐ **setDate(*dateValue*)** Sets the day of the month for the current Date object. *dateValue* is an integer from 1 to 31.

☐ **setHours(*hoursValue*)**   Sets the hours for the time for the current Date object. *hoursValue* is an integer from 0 to 23.

☐ **setMinutes(*minutesValue*)**   Sets the minutes for the time for the current Date object. *minutesValue* is an integer from 0 to 59.

☐ **setMonth(*monthValue*)**   Sets the month for the current Date object. *monthValue* is an integer from 0 to 11 (where 0 is January, 1 is February, etc.).

☐ **setSeconds(*secondsValue*)**   Sets the seconds for the time for the current Date object. *secondsValue* is an integer from 0 to 59.

☐ **setTime(*timeValue*)**   Sets the value for the current Date object. *timeValue* is an integer representing the number of milliseconds since January 1, 1970 at 00:00:00.

☐ **setYear(*yearValue*)**   Sets the year for the current Date object. *yearValue* is an integer greater than 1900.

☐ **toGMTString()**   Returns the value of the current Date object in GMT as a string using Internet conventions in the form:

Day, DD Mon YYYY HH:MM:SS GMT

☐ **toLocaleString()**   Returns the value of the current Date object in the local time using local conventions.

☐ **UTC(*yearValue, monthValue, dateValue, hoursValue, minutesValue, secondsValue*)**   Returns the number of milliseconds since January 1, 1970 at 00:00:00 GMT. *yearValue* is an integer greater than 1900. *monthValue* is an integer from 0 to 11. *dateValue* is an integer from 1 to 31. *hoursValue* is an integer from 0 to 23. *minutesValue* and *secondsValue* are integers from 0 to 59. *hoursValue*, *minutesValue*, and *secondsValue* are optional.

The document Object

The document object reflects attributes of an HTML document in JavaScript.

Properties

☐ **alinkColor**   The color of active links as a string or a hexadecimal triplet.

☐ **anchors**   Array of anchor objects in the order they appear in the HTML document. Use anchors.length to get the number of anchors in a document.

☐ **bgColor**   The color of the document's background.

☐ **cookie**   A string value containing cookie values for the current document.

☐ **fgColor**   The color of the document's foreground.

- ☐ **forms**   Array of form objects in the order the forms appear in the HTML file. Use `forms.length` to get the number of forms in a document.
- ☐ **lastModified**   String value containing the last date of modification of the document.
- ☐ **linkColor**   The color of links as a string or a hexadecimal triplet.
- ☐ **links**   Array of link objects in the order the hypertext links appear in the HTML document. Use `links.length` to get the number of links in a document.
- ☐ **location**   A string containing the URL of the current document.
- ☐ **referrer**   A string value containing the URL of the calling document when the user follows a link.
- ☐ **title**   A string containing the title of the current document.
- ☐ **vlinkColor**   The color of followed links as a string or a hexadecimal triplet.

Methods

- ☐ **clear()**   Clears the document window.
- ☐ **close()**   Closes the current output stream.
- ☐ **open(mimeType)**   Opens a stream which allows `write()` and `writeln()` methods to write to the document window. *mimeType* is an optional string which specifies a document type supported by Navigator or a plug-in (i.e., `text/html`, `image/gif`, etc.).
- ☐ **write()**   Writes text and HTML to the specified document.
- ☐ **writeln()**   Writes text and HTML to the specified document followed by a newline character.

The form **Object**

The form object reflects an HTML form in JavaScript. Each HTML form in a document is reflected by a distinct instance of the form object.

Properties

- ☐ **action**   A string value specifying the URL to which the form data is submitted.
- ☐ **elements**   Array of objects for each form element in the order in which they appear in the form.
- ☐ **encoding**   String containing the MIME encoding of the form as specified in the `ENCTYPE` attribute.

☐ **method**   A string value containing the method of submission of form data to the server.

☐ **target**   A string value containing the name of the window that responses to form submissions are directed to.

Methods

☐ **submit()**   Submits the form.

Event Handlers

☐ **onSubmit**   Specifies JavaScript code to execute when the form is submitted. The code should return a true value to allow the form to be submitted. A false value prevents the form from being submitted.

The **frame** Object

The **frame** object reflects a frame window in JavaScript.

Properties

☐ **frames**   An array of objects for each frame in a window. Frames appear in the array in the order in which they appear in the HTML source code.

☐ **parent**   A string indicating the name of the window containing the frameset.

☐ **self**   A alternative for the name of the current window.

☐ **top**   An alternative for the name of the top-most window.

☐ **window**   An alternative for the name of the current window.

Methods

☐ **alert(*message*)**   Displays *message* in a dialog box.

☐ **close()**   Closes the window.

☐ **confirm(*message*)**   Displays *message* in a dialog box with OK and CANCEL buttons. Returns true or false based on the button clicked by the user.

☐ **open(url,name,features)**   Opens *url* in a window named *name*. If *name* doesn't exist, a new window is created with that name. **features** is an optional string argument containing a list of features for the new window. The feature list contains any of the following name-value pairs separated by commas and without additional spaces:

`toolbar=[yes,no,1,0]`	Indicates if the window should have a toolbar
`location=[yes,no,1,0]`	Indicates if the window should have a location field
`directories=[yes,no,1,0]`	Indicates if the window should have directory buttons
`status=[yes,no,1,0]`	Indicates if the window should have a status bar
`menubar=[yes,no,1,0]`	Indicates if the window should have menus
`scrollbars=[yes,no,1,0]`	Indicates if the window should have scroll bars
`resizable=[yes,no,1,0]`	Indicates if the window should be resizable
`width=pixels`	Indicates the width of the window in pixels
`height=pixels`	Indicates the height of the window in pixels

☐ **`prompt(message,response)`**   Displays *message* in a dialog box with a text entry field with the default value of *response*. The user's response in the text entry field is returned as a string.

☐ **`setTimeout(expression,time)`**   Evaluates *expression* after *time* where *time* is a value in milliseconds. The time out can be named with the structure:

`name = setTimeOut(expression,time)`

☐ **`clearTimeout(name)`**   Cancels the time out with the name *name*.

The `hidden` Object

The `hidden` object reflects a hidden field from an HTML form in JavaScript.

Properties

☐ **`name`**   A string value containing the name of the hidden element.

☐ **`value`**   A string value containing the value of hidden text element.

The `history` Object

The `history` object allows a script to work with the Navigator browser's history list in JavaScript. For security and privacy reasons, the actual content of the list is not reflected into JavaScript.

Properties

☐ **length** An integer representing the number of items on the history list.

Methods

☐ **back()** Goes back to the previous document in the history list.

☐ **forward()** Goes forward to the next document in the history list.

☐ **go(location)** Goes to the document in the history list specified by *location*. *location* can be a string or integer value. If it is a string, it represents all or part of a URL in the history list. If it is an integer, *location* represents the relative position of the document on the history list. As an integer, *location* can be positive or negative.

The link Object

The link object reflects a hypertext link in the body of a document.

Properties

☐ **target** A string value containing the name of the window or frame specified in the TARGET attribute.

Event Handlers

☐ **onClick** Specifies JavaScript code to execute when the link is clicked.

☐ **onMouseOver** Specifies JavaScript code to execute when the mouse is over the hypertext link

The location Object

The location object reflects information about the current URL.

Properties

☐ **hash** A string value containing the anchor name in the URL.

☐ **host** A string value containing the hostname and port number from the URL.

☐ **hostname** A string value containing the domain name (or numerical IP address) from the URL.

☐ **href** A string value containing the entire URL.

☐ **pathname** A string value specifying the path portion of the URL.

☐ **port** A string value containing the port number from the URL.

☐ **protocol** A string value containing the protocol from the URL (including the colon, but not the slashes).

☐ **search** A string value containing any information passed to a GET CGI-BIN call (i.e., information after the question mark).

The Math Object

The Math object provides properties and methods for advanced mathematical calculations.

Properties

☐ **E** The value of Euler's constant (roughly 2.718) used as the base for natural logarithms.

☐ **LN10** The value of the natural logarithm of 10 (roughly 2.302).

☐ **LN2** The value of the natural logarithm of 2 (roughly 0.693).

☐ **PI** The value of PI—used in calculating the circumference and area of circles (roughly 3.1415).

☐ **SQRT1_2** The value of the square root of one-half (roughly 0.707).

☐ **SQRT2** The value of the square root of two (roughly 1.414).

Methods

☐ **abs(number)** Returns the absolute value of *number*. The absolute value is the value of a number with its sign ignored so that abs(4) and abs(-4) both return 4.

☐ **acos(*number*)** Returns the arc cosine of *number* in radians.

☐ **asin(*number*)** Returns the arc sine of *number* in radians.

☐ **atan(*number*)** Returns the arc tangent of *number* in radians.

☐ **ceil(*number*)** Returns the next integer greater than *number*—in other words, rounds up to the next integer.

☐ **cos(number)** Returns the cosine of *number* where *number* represents an angle in radians.

☐ **exp(number)**   Returns the value of E to the power of *number*.

☐ **floor(*number*)**   Returns the next integer less than *number*—in other words, rounds down to the nearest integer.

☐ **log(number)**   Returns the natural logarithm of *number*.

☐ **max(number1,number2)**   Returns the greater of *number1* and *number2*.

☐ **min(number1,number2)**   Returns the smaller of *number1* and *number2*.

☐ **pow(number1,number2)**   Returns the value of *number1* to the power of *number2*.

☐ **random()**   Returns a random number between zero and one (at press time, this method only was available on UNIX versions of Navigator 2.0).

☐ **round(*number*)**   Returns the closest integer to *number*—in other words rounds to the closest integer.

☐ **sin(number)**   Returns the sine of *number* where *number* represents an angle in radians.

☐ **sqrt(*number*)**   Returns the square root of number.

☐ **tan(number)**   Returns the tangent of *number* where *number* represents an angle in radians.

The navigator **Object**

The navigator object reflects information about the version of Navigator being used.

Properties

☐ **appCodeName**   A string value containing the code name of the client (i.e., "Mozilla" for Netscape Navigator).

☐ **appName**   A string value containing the name of the client (i.e., "Netscape" for Netscape Navigator).

☐ **appVersion**   A string value containing the version information for the client in the form

versionNumber (platform; country)

For instance, Navigator 2.0, beta 6 for Windows 95 (international version), would have an appVersion property with the value "2.0b6 (Win32; I)".

☐ **userAgent**   A string containing the complete value of the user-agent header sent in the HTTP request. This contains all the information in appCodeName and appVersion:

Mozilla/2.0b6 (Win32; I)

The `password` **Object**

The `password` object reflects a password text field from an HTML form in JavaScript.

Properties

☐ **`defaultValue`**   A string value containing the default value of the password element (i.e., the value of the VALUE attribute).

☐ **`name`**   A string value containing the name of the password element.

☐ **`value`**   A string value containing the value of the password element.

Methods

☐ **`focus()`**   Emulates the action of focusing in the password field.

☐ **`blur()`**   Emulates the action of removing focus from the password field.

☐ **`select()`**   Emulates the action of selecting the text in the password field.

The `radio` **Object**

The `radio` object reflects a set of radio buttons from an HTML form in JavaScript. To access individual radio buttons, use numeric indexes starting at zero. For instance, individual buttons in a set of radio buttons named `testRadio` could be referenced by `testRadio[0]`, `testRadio[1]`, etc.

Properties

☐ **`checked`**   A boolean value indicating if a specific button is checked. Can be used to select or deselect a button.

☐ **`defaultChecked`**   A boolean value indicating if a specific button was checked by default (i.e., reflects the CHECKED attribute).

☐ **`length`**   An integer value indicating the number of radio buttons in the set.

☐ **`name`**   A string value containing the name of the set of radio buttons.

☐ **`value`**   A string value containing the value a specific radio button in a set (i.e., reflects the VALUE attribute).

Methods

☐ `click()`   Emulates the action of clicking on a radio button.

Event Handlers

☐ `onClick`   Specifies JavaScript code to execute when a radio button is clicked.

The reset Object

The reset object reflects a reset button from an HTML form in JavaScript.

Properties

☐ `name`   A string value containing the name of the reset element.

☐ `value`   A string value containing the value of the reset element.

Methods

☐ `click()`   Emulates the action of clicking on the reset button.

Event Handlers

☐ `onClick`   Specifies JavaScript code to execute when the reset button is clicked.

The select Object

The select object reflects a selection list from an HTML form in JavaScript.

Properties

☐ `length`   An integer value containing the number of options in the selection list.

☐ `name`   A string value containing the name of the selection list.

☐ `options`   An array reflecting each of the options in the selection list in the order they appear. The options property has its own properties:

`defaultSelected`   A boolean value indicating if an option was selected by default (i.e., reflects the SELECTED attribute).

index	An integer value reflecting the index of an option.
length	An integer value reflecting the number of options in the selection list.
name	A string value containing the name of the selection list.
options	A string value containing the full HTML code for the selection list.
selected	A boolean value indicating if the option is selected. Can be used to select or deselect an option.
selectedIndex	An integer value containing the index of the currently selected option.
text	A string value containing the text displayed in the selection list for a particular option.
value	A string value indicating the value for the specified option (i.e., reflects the VALUE attribute).

☐ **selectedIndex** Reflects the index of the currently selected option in the selection list.

Event Handlers

☐ **onBlur** Specifies JavaScript code to execute when the selection list loses focus.

☐ **onFocus** Specifies JavaScript code to execute when focus is given to the selection list.

☐ **onChange** Specifies JavaScript code to execute when the selected option in the list changes.

The string Object

The string object provides properties and methods for working with string literals and variables.

Properties

☐ **length** An integer value containing the length of the string expressed as the number of characters in the string.

Methods

☐ **anchor(*name*)** Returns a string containing the value of the string object surrounded by an A container tag with the NAME attribute set to *name*.

☐ **`big()`**   Returns a string containing the value of the string object surrounded by a BIG container tag.

☐ **`blink()`**   Returns a string containing the value of the string object surrounded by a BLINK container tag.

☐ **`bold()`**   Returns a string containing the value of the string object surrounded by a B container tag.

☐ **`charAt(index)`**   Returns the character at the location specified by *index*.

☐ **`fixed()`**   Returns a string containing the value of the string object surrounded by a FIXED container tag.

☐ **`fontColor(color)`**   Returns a string containing the value of the string object surrounded by a FONT container tag with the COLOR attribute set to *color* where *color* is a color name or an RGB triplet.

☐ **`fontSize(size)`**   Returns a string containing the value of the string object surrounded by a FONTSIZE container tag with the size set to *size*.

☐ **`indexOf(findString,startingIndex)`**   Returns the index of the first occurrence of *findString*, starting the search at *startingIndex* where *startingIndex* is optional— if it is not provided, the search starts at the start of the string.

☐ **`italics()`**   Returns a string containing the value of the string object surrounded by an I container tag.

☐ **`lastIndexOf(findString,startingIndex)`**   Returns the index of the last occurrence of *findString*. This is done by searching backwards from *startingIndex*. *startingIndex* is optional and assumed to be the last character in the string if no value is provided.

☐ **`link(href)`**   Returns a string containing the value of the string object surrounded by an A container tag with the HREF attribute set to *href*.

☐ **`small()`**   Returns a string containing the value of the string object surrounded by a SMALL container tag.

☐ **`strike()`**   Returns a string containing the value of the string object surrounded by a STRIKE container tag.

☐ **`sub()`**   Returns a string containing the value of the string object surrounded by a SUB container tag.

☐ **`substring(firstIndex,lastIndex)`**   Returns a string equivalent to the substring starting at *firstIndex* and ending at the character before *lastIndex*. If *firstIndex* is greater than *lastIndex*, the string starts at *lastIndex* and ends at the character before *firstIndex*.

☐ **`sup()`**   Returns a string containing the value of the string object surrounded by a SUP container tag.

☐ **toLowerCase()**   Returns a string containing the value of the string object with all character converted to lower case.

☐ **toUpperCase()**   Returns a string containing the value of the string object with all character converted to upper case.

The submit Object

The submit object reflects a submit button from an HTML form in JavaScript.

Properties

☐ **name**   A string value containing the name of the submit button element.

☐ **value**   A string value containing the value of the submit button element.

Methods

☐ **click()**   Emulates the action of clicking on the submit button.

Event Handlers

☐ **onClick**   Specifies JavaScript code to execute when the submit button is clicked.

The text Object

The text object reflects a text field from an HTML form in JavaScript.

Properties

☐ **defaultValue**   A string value containing the default value of the text element (i.e., the value of the VALUE attribute).

☐ **name**   A string value containing the name of the text element.

☐ **value**   A string value containing the value of the text element.

Methods

☐ **focus()**   Emulates the action of focusing in the text field.

☐ **blur()**   Emulates the action of removing focus from the text field.

☐ **select()**   Emulates the action of selecting the text in the text field.

Event Handlers

☐ **onBlur**   Specifies JavaScript code to execute when focus is removed from the field.

☐ **onChange**   Specifies JavaScript code to execute when the content of the field is changed.

☐ **onFocus**   Specifies JavaScript code to execute when focus is given to the field.

☐ **onSelect**   Specifies JavaScript code to execute when the user selects some or all of the text in the field.

The textarea Object

The textarea object reflects a multi-line text field from an HTML form in JavaScript.

Properties

☐ **defaultValue**   A string value containing the default value of the textarea element (i.e., the value of the VALUE attribute).

☐ **name**   A string value containing the name of the textarea element.

☐ **value**   A string value containing the value of the textarea element.

Methods

☐ **focus()**   Emulates the action of focusing in the textarea field.

☐ **blur()**   Emulates the action of removing focus from the textarea field.

☐ **select()**   Emulates the action of selecting the text in the textarea field.

Event Handlers

☐ **onBlur**   Specifies JavaScript code to execute when focus is removed from the field.

☐ **onChange**   Specifies JavaScript code to execute when the content of the field is changed.

☐ **onFocus**   Specifies JavaScript code to execute when focus is given to the field.

☐ **onSelect**   Specifies JavaScript code to execute when the user selects some or all of the text in the field.

The `window` Object

The `window` object is the top-level object for each window or frame and is the parent object for the document, location, and history objects.

Properties

- [ ] **`defaultStatus`** A string value containing the default value displayed in the status bar.
- [ ] **`frames`** An array of objects for each frame in a window. Frames appear in the array in the order in which they appear in the HTML source code.
- [ ] **`length`** An integer value indicating the number of frames in a parent window.
- [ ] **`name`** A string value containing the name of the window or frame.
- [ ] **`parent`** A string indicating the name of the window containing the frameset.
- [ ] **`self`** A alternative for the name of the current window.
- [ ] **`status`** Used to display a message in the status bar—this is done by assigning values to this property.
- [ ] **`top`** An alternative for the name of the top-most window.
- [ ] **`window`** An alternative for the name of the current window.

Methods

- [ ] **`alert(message)`** Displays *message* in a dialog box.
- [ ] **`close()`** Closes the window.
- [ ] **`confirm(message)`** Displays *message* in a dialog box with OK and CANCEL buttons. Returns true or false based on the button clicked by the user.
- [ ] **`open(url,name,features)`** Opens *url* in a window named *name*. If *name* doesn't exist, a new window is created with that name. *features* is an optional string argument containing a list of features for the new window. The feature list contains any of the following name-value pairs separated by commas and without additional spaces:

`toolbar=[yes,no,1,0]`	Indicates if the window should have a toolbar
`location=[yes,no,1,0]`	Indicates if the window should have a location field
`directories=[yes,no,1,0]`	Indicates if the window should have directory buttons

`status=[yes,no,1,0]`	Indicates if the window should have a status bar
`menubar=[yes,no,1,0]`	Indicates if the window should have menus
`scrollbars=[yes,no,1,0]`	Indicates if the window should have scroll bars
`resizable=[yes,no,1,0]`	Indicates if the window should be resizable
`width=pixels`	Indicates the width of the window in pixels
`height=pixels`	Indicates the height of the window in pixels

☐ **prompt(message,response)**   Displays *message* in a dialog box with a text entry field with the default value of *response*. The user's response in the text entry field is returned as a string.

☐ **setTimeout(expression,time)**   Evaluates *expression* after *time* where *time* is a value in milliseconds. The time out can be named with the structure

name = setTimeOut(*expression*,*time*)

☐ **clearTimeout(*name*)**   Cancels the time out with the name name.

Event Handlers

☐ **onLoad**   Specifies JavaScript code to execute when the window or frame finishes loading.

☐ **onUnload**   Specifies JavaScript code to execute when the document in the window or frame is exited.

Independent Functions, Operators, Variables, Literals, and Reserved Words

Independent Functions

☐ **escape(character)**   Returns a string containing the ASCII encoding of *character* in the form %xx where xx is the numeric encoding of the character.

☐ **eval(expression)**   Returns the result of evaluating *expression* where *expression* is an arithmetic expression.

☐ **isNaN(*value*)**   Evaluates value to see if it is NaN. Returns a boolean value. This function is only available on UNIX platforms where certain functions return NaN if their argument is not a number.

☐ **parseFloat(*string*)**   Converts *string* to a floating point number and returns the value. It continues to convert until it hits a non-numeric character and then returns the result. If the first character cannot be converted to a number, the function returns "NaN" (zero on Windows platforms).

☐ **parseInt(*string*,*base*)**   Converts *string* to an integer of base *base* and returns the value. It continues to convert until it hits a non-numeric character and then returns the result. If the first character cannot be converted to a number, the function returns "NaN" (zero on Windows platforms).

☐ **unescape(*string*)**   Returns a character based on the ASCII encoding contained in *string*. The ASCII encoding should take the form "%integer" or "hexadecimalValue".

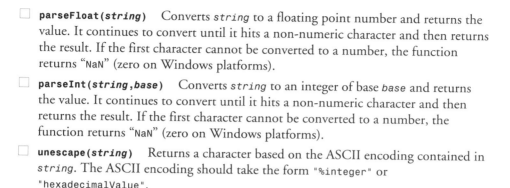

Operators

☐ **Assignment**   Table B.1 shows the assignment operators in JavaScript.

Table B.1. Assignment operators.

Operator	Description
=	Assigns value of the right operand to the left operand
+=	Adds the left and right operands and assigns the result to the left operand
-=	Subtracts the right operand from the left operand and assigns the result to the left operand
*=	Multiplies the two operands and assigns the result to the left operand
/=	Divides the left operand by the right operand and assigns the value to the left operand
%=	Divides the left operand by the right operand and assigns the remainder to the left operand

☐ **Arithmetic**   Table B.2 shows the arithmetic operators in JavaScript.

Table B.2. Arithmetic operators.

Operator	Description
+	Adds the left and right operands
-	Subtracts the right operand from the left operand
*	Multiplies the two operands

continues

Table B.2. continued

Operator	Description
/	Divides the left operand by the right operand
%	Divides the left operand by the right operand and evaluates to the remainder
++	Increments the operand by one (can be used before or after the operand)
--	Decreases the operand by one (can be used before or after the operand)
-	Changes the sign of the operand

☐ **Bitwise**   Bitwise operators deal with their operands as binary numbers but return JavaScript numerical value (see Table B.3).

Table B.3. Bitwise operators in JavaScript.

Operator	Description
AND (or &)	Converts operands to integers with 32 bits, pairs the corresponding bits and returns one for each pair of ones. Returns zero for any other combination
OR (or ¦)	Converts operands to integers with 32 bits, pairs the corresponding bits and returns one for each pair where one of the two bits is one. Returns zero if both bits are zero
XOR (or ^)	Converts operands to integer with 32 bits, pairs the corresponding bits and returns one for each pair where only one bit is one. Returns zero for any other combination.
<<	Converts the left operand to an integer with 32 bits and shifts bits to the left the number of bits indicated by the right operand—bits shifted off to the left are discarded and zeros are shifted in from the right
>>>	Converts the left operand to an integer with 32 bits and shifts bits to the right the number of bits indicated by the right operand—bits shifted off to the right are discarded and zeros are shifted in from the left

Operator	Description
>>	Converts the left operand to an integer with 32 bits and shifts bits to the right the number of bits indicated by the right operand—bits shifted off to the right are discarded and copies of the leftmost bit are shifted in from the left

Logical   Table B.4 shows the logical operators in JavaScript.

Table B.4. Logical operators.

Operator	Description
&&	Logical "and"—returns true when both operands are true, otherwise it returns false
||	Logical "or"—returns true if either operand is true. It only returns false when both operands are false
!	Logical "not"—returns true if the operand is false and false if the operand is true. This is a unary operator and precedes the operand.

Logical   Table B.5 shows the comparison operators in JavaScript.

Table B.5. Logical (comparison) operators.

Operator	Description
==	Returns true if the operands are equal
!=	Returns true if the operands are not equal
>	Returns true if the left operand is greater than the right operand
<	Returns true if the left operand is less than the right operand
>=	Returns true if the left operand is greater than or equal to the right operand
<=	Returns true if the left operand is less than or equal to the right operand

B

☐ **Conditional**   Conditional expressions take one form:

(condition) ? *val1* : *val2*

If `condition` is true, the expression evaluates to *val1*, otherwise it evaluates to *val2*.

☐ **String**   The concatenation operators (+) is one of two string operators. It evaluates to a string combining the left and right operands. The concatenation assignment operator (+=) is also available.

☐ **Operator Precedence**   JavaScript applies the rules of operator precedence as follows (from lowest to highest precedence):

comma (,)	bitwise and (&)
assignment operators (= += -= *=	equality (== !=)
/= %=)	relational (< <= > >=)
conditional (? :)	shift (<< >> >>>)
logical or (¦¦)	addition/subtraction (+ -)
logical and (&&)	multiply/divide/modulus (* / %)
bitwise or (¦)	negation/increment (! - ++ —)
bitwise xor (^)	call, member (() [])

Reserved Words

The following is list of reserved words in JavaScript. These terms either are used as keywords or are being kept for future use in JavaScript. You cannot define variables or functions with these names in your scripts.

abstract	float	public
boolean	for	return
break	function	short
byte	goto	static
case	if	super
catch	implements	switch
char	import	synchronized
class	in	this
const	instanceof	throw
continue	int	throws
default	interface	transient
do	long	true
double	native	try
else	new	var
extends	null	void
false	package	while
final	private	with
finally	protected	

Glossary

Applet: Small program, usually written in Java, that is downloaded as needed to extend the functionality of a Web page or a Web browser.

Array: An ordered, named set of values, indexed by number.

Associative Array: A named set of values in association pairs.

Boolean: A binary literal value which can be either true or false.

CGI (Common Gateway Interface): The standard mechanism for processing data entered in an HTML form on a Web server and returning the results.

Comments: Portions of a JavaScript script or an HTML file that are not interpreted or displayed.

Cookies: A method for saving client-side state information that is sent back to the server along with specific page requests.

Dialog Boxes: Small user interaction boxes which allow the user to react to information presented by an application or a script.

Events: Signals that are triggered when a particular user action occurs or when the browser has completed a specific task.

Event Handlers: Event handlers define the program code to execute when an event occurs.

Expression: A combination of variables, literals, and operators that evaluates to a single value.

Floating Point: A type of literal value that represents a number including a fractional portion (that is, the portion after a decimal place).

Forms: A standard HTML element which offers tools for the user to provide information through textboxes, checkboxes, radio buttons, selection lists, and buttons.

Frames: An extension to HTML developed by Netscape that allows the browser to be divided into discrete rectangular spaces, each of which contains separate files. Links in one frame can target the resulting file to another frame.

Functions: Stand-alone, reusable segments of program code that are not part of an object.

HTML (Hypertext Markup Language): A series of tags included in text files that define the structure of a Web document and its links to other documents. Web browsers interpret these tags to determine how to display a Web page.

Internet: A globe-spanning network of computer networks linking tens of millions of people worldwide.

Integer: A literal value expressing a number with no fraction component.

Instance: A particular occurrence of an object structure. Objects can have multiple instances that are independent of each other but share a similar structure of properties and methods.

Loops: A programming structure that allows a segment of code to be repeated a specified number of times or to be repeated until a specified condition exists.

Java: A compiled, object-oriented programming language developed by Sun Microsystems. Java is well-suited for developing distributed applications on the World Wide Web using applets.

JavaScript: An interpreted, object-based scripting language developed by Netscape Communications that adds interactivity to Web pages.

Literals: A literal expression of a value, including a number or a text string.

Methods: The segments of program code, or functions, tied to an object.

Null: A special literal value that represents the lack of any other value.

Object-oriented: A style of programming that links data to the processes that manipulate it.

Operators: Perform actions on one or more variables, literals, or expressions and evaluate to a single value.

Plug-ins: A technology that allows third-party vendors to develop extensions to Navigator 2.0. These extensions enable Navigator 2.0 to view additional formats or enable it to be used as the interface for complex applications, such as spreadsheets or image editors.

Properties: Refers to the data structures available in an object.

Recursion: A programming technique whereby a function or method calls itself one or more times.

Status Bar: The small bar at the bottom of the Navigator window where messages about the current action are displayed. JavaScript can write text to the status bar.

Strings: A literal value representing text.

Tables: A feature of HTML that allows the creation of structured tables of information with distinct columns and rows.

Variables: Named pieces of data of different types. The value of variables can be changed, and the value can be referred to by the name of the variable.

WWW (**World Wide Web**): A collection of millions of linked documents on the Internet exchanged using the Hypertext Transfer Protocol (HTTP). These documents include text, images, video, and sound.

INDEX

A V I A C O M S E R V I C E

The Information SuperLibrary™

| Bookstore | Search | What's New | Reference | Software | Newsletter | Company Overviews |

| Yellow Pages | Internet Starter Kit | HTML Workshop | Win a Free T-Shirt! | Macmillan Computer Publishing | Site Map | Talk to Us |

CHECK OUT THE BOOKS IN THIS LIBRARY.

You'll find thousands of shareware files and over 1600 computer books designed for both technowizards and technophobes. You can browse through 700 sample chapters, get the latest news on the Net, and find just about anything using our massive search directories.

All Macmillan Computer Publishing books are available at your local bookstore.

We're open 24-hours a day, 365 days a year.

You don't need a card.

We don't charge fines.

And you can be as **LOUD** as you want.

The Information SuperLibrary
http://www.mcp.com/mcp/   ftp.mcp.com

Teach Yourself the Internet in a Week, Second Edition

— *Neil Randall*

The combination of a structured, step-by-step approach and the excitement of exploring the world of the Internet make this tutorial and reference perfect for any user wanting to master the Net. Efficiently exploring the basics of the Internet, *Teach Yourself the Internet* takes users to the farthest reaches of the Internet with hands-on exercises and detailed instructions. Completely updated to cover Netscape, Internet-works, and Microsoft's Internet Assistant.

Price: $25.00 USA/$34.99 CDN   User Level: Beginner-Inter
ISBN: 0-672-30735-9   622 pages

Tricks of the Internet Gurus

— *Various Internet Gurus*

Best-selling title that focuses on tips and techniques that allow the reader to more effectively use the resources of the Internet. A must-have for the power Internet user, *Tricks of the Internet Gurus* offers tips, strategies, and techniques for optimizing use of the Internet. Features interviews with various Internet leaders.

Price: $35.00 USA/$47.95 CDN   User Level: Inter-Advanced
ISBN: 0-672-30599-2   809 pages

Teach Yourself More Web Publishing with HTML in a Week

— *Laura Lemay*

Ideal for those people who are ready for more advanced World Wide Web home page design! The sequel to *Teach Yourself Web Publishing with HTML*, *Teach Yourself More* explores the process of creating and maintaining Web presentations, including setting up tools and converters for verifying and testing pages. Teaches advanced HTML techniques and tricks in a clear, step-by-step manner with many practical examples. Highlights the Netscape extensions and HTML 3.0.

Price: $29.99 USA/$39.99 CDN   User Level: Inter-Advanced
ISBN: 1-57521-005-3   480 pages

The Internet Business Guide, Second Edition

— *Rosalind Resnick & Dave Taylor*

Updated and revised, this guide will inform and educate anyone on how they can use the Internet to increase profits, reach a broader market, track down business leads, and access critical information. Updated to cover digital cash, Web cybermalls, secure Web servers, and setting up your business on the Web, *The Internet Business Guide* includes profiles of entrepreneurs' successes (and failures) on the Internet. Improve your business by using the Internet to market products and services, make contacts with colleagues, cut costs, and improve customer service.

Price: $25.00 USA/$39.99 CDN   User Level: All Levels
ISBN: 1-57521-004-5   470 pages

Teach Yourself Netscape Web Publishing in a Week

— Wes Tatters

Teach Yourself Netscape Web Publishing in a Week is the easiest way to learn how to produce attention-getting, well-designed Web pages using the features provided by Netscape Navigator. Intended for both the novice and the expert, this book provides a solid grounding in HTML and Web publishing principles, while providing special focus on the possibilities presented by the Netscape environment. Learn to design and create attention-grabbing Web pages for the Netscape environment while exploring new Netscape development features such as frames, plug-ins, Java applets, and JavaScript!

Price: $39.99 USA/ $47.95 CDN   User Level: Beginner-Inter
ISBN: 1-57521-068-1   450 pages

Teach Yourself CGI Programming with Perl in a Week

— Eric Herrmann

This book is a step-by-step tutorial of how to create, use, and maintain Common Gateway Interfaces (CGI). It describes effective ways of using CGI as an integral part of Web development. Adds interactivity and flexibility to the information that can be provided through your Web site. Includes Perl 4.0 and 5.0, CGI libraries, and other applications to create databases, dynamic interactivity, and other enticing page effects.

Price: $39.99 USA/$53.99 CDN   User Level: Inter-Advanced
ISBN: 1-57521-009-6   500 pages

Teach Yourself Java in 21 Days

— Laura Lemay and Charles Perkins

The complete tutorial guide to the most exciting technology to hit the Internet in years—Java! A detailed guide to developing applications with the hot new Java language from Sun Microsystems, *Teach Yourself Java in 21 Days* shows readers how to program using Java and develop applications (applets) using the Java language. With coverage of Java implementation in Netscape Navigator and Hot Java, along with the Java Development Kit, including the compiler and debugger for Java, *Teach Yourself Java* is a must-have!

Price: $39.99 USA/$53.99 CDN   User Level: Inter-Advanced
ISBN: 1-57521-030-4   600 pages

Presenting Java

— John December

Presenting Java gives you a first look at how Java is transforming static Web pages into living, interactive applications. Java opens up a world of possibilities previously unavailable on the Web. You'll find out how Java is being used to create animations, computer simulations, interactive games, teaching tools, spreadsheets, and a variety of other applications. Whether you're a new user, a project planner, or developer, *Presenting Java* provides an efficient, quick introduction to the basic concepts and technical details that make Java the hottest new Web technology of the year!

Price: $25.00 USA/$34.95 CDN   User Level: All Levels
ISBN: 1-57521-039-8   207 pages

Netscape 2 Unleashed

— Dick Oliver, et. al.

This book provides a complete, detailed, and fully fleshed-out overview of the Netscape products. Through case studies and examples of how individuals, businesses, and institutions are using the Netscape products for Web development, *Netscape Unleashed* gives a full description of the evolution of Netscape from its inception to today, and its cutting-edge developments with Netscape Gold, LiveWire, Netscape Navigator 2.0, Java and JavaScript, Macromedia, VRML, Plug-ins, Adobe Acrobat, HTML 3.0 and beyond, security and Intranet systems.

Price: $49.99 USA/$61.95 CDN   User Level: All Levels
ISBN: 1-57521-007-X   Pages: 800 pages

The Internet Unleashed 1996

— Barron, Ellsworth, Savetz, et. al.

The Internet Unleashed 1996 is the complete reference to get new users up and running on the Internet while providing the consummate reference manual for the experienced user. *The Internet Unleashed 1996* provides the reader with an encyclopedia of information on how to take advantage of all the Net has to offer for business, education, research, and government. The companion CD-ROM contains over 100 tools and applications. The only book that includes the experience of over 40 of the world's top Internet experts, this new edition is updated with expanded coverage of Web publishing, Internet business, Internet multimedia and virtual reality, Internet security, Java, and more!

Price: $49.99 USA/$67.99 CDN   User Level: All Levels
ISBN: 1-57521-041-X   1,456 pages

The World Wide Web Unleashed 1996

— December and Randall

The World Wide Web Unleashed 1996 is designed to be the only book a reader will need to experience the wonders and resources of the Web. The companion CD-ROM contains over 100 tools and applications to make the most of your time on the Internet. Shows readers how to explore the Web's amazing world of electronic art museums, online magazines, virtual malls, and video music libraries, while giving readers complete coverage of Web page design, creation, and maintenance, plus coverage of new Web technologies such as Java, VRML, CGI, and multimedia!

Price: $49.99 USA/$67.99 CDN   User Level: All Levels
ISBN: 1-57521-040-1   1,440 pages

Teach Yourself Web Publishing with HTML in 14 Days, Premier Edition

— Laura Lemay

This book teaches everything about publishing on the Web. In addition to its exhaustive coverage of HTML, it also gives readers hands-on practice with more complicated subjects such as CGI, tables, forms, multimedia programming, testing, maintenance, and much more. CD-ROM is Mac- and PC-compatible and includes a variety of applications that help readers create Web pages using graphics and templates.

Price: $39.99 USA/$53.99 CDN   User Level: All Levels
ISBN: 1-57521-014-2   804 pages

Teach Yourself Web Publishing with HTML 3.0 in a Week, Second Edition

— Laura Lemay

Ideal for those people who are interested in the Internet and the World Wide Web—the Internet's hottest topic! This updated and revised edition teaches readers how to use HTML (Hypertext Markup Language) version 3.0 to create Web pages that can be viewed by nearly 30 million users. Explores the process of creating and maintaining Web presentations, including setting up tools and converters for verifying and testing pages. The new edition highlights the new features of HTML, such as tables and Netscape and Microsoft Explorer extensions. Provides the latest information on working with images, sound files, and video, and teaches advanced HTML techniques and tricks in a clear, step-by-step manner with many practical examples of HTML pages.

Price: $29.99 USA/$34.95 CDN   User Level: Beginner-Inter
ISBN: 1-57521-064-9   518 pages

Web Page Construction Kit (Software)

Create your own exciting World Wide Web pages with the software and expert guidance in this kit! Includes HTML Assistant Pro Lite, the acclaimed point-and-click Web page editor. Simply highlight text in HTML Assistant Pro Lite, and click the appropriate button to add headlines, graphics, special formatting, links, etc. No programming skills needed! Using your favorite Web browser, you can test your work quickly and easily without leaving the editor. A unique catalog feature allows you to keep track of interesting Web sites and easily add their HTML links to your pages. Assistant's user-defined toolkit also allows you to add new HTML formatting styles as they are defined. Includes the #1 best-selling Internet book, *Teach Yourself Web Publishing with HTML 3.0 in a Week, Second Edition,* and a library of professionally designed Web page templates, graphics, buttons, bullets, lines, and icons to rev up your new pages!

PC Computing magazine says, "If you're looking for the easiest route to Web publishing, HTML Assistant is your best choice."

Price: $39.95 US/$46.99 CAN   User Level: Beginner-Inter
ISBN: 1-57521-000-2   518 pages

HTML & CGI Unleashed

— John December & Marc Ginsburg

Targeted to professional developers who have a basic understanding of programming and need a detailed guide. Provides a complete, detailed reference to developing Web information systems. Covers the full range of languages—HTML, CGI, Perl C, editing and conversion programs, and more—and how to create commercial-grade Web Applications. Perfect for the developer who will be designing, creating, and maintaining a Web presence for a company or large institution.

Price: $49.99 USA/$53.99 CDN   User Level: Inter-Advanced
ISBN: 0-672-30745-6   830 pages

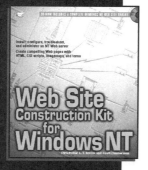

Web Site Construction Kit for Windows NT

— Christopher Brown and Scott Zimmerman

The Web Site Construction Kit for Windows NT has everything you need to set up, develop, and maintain a Web site with Windows NT—including the server on the CD-ROM! It teaches the ins and outs of planning, installing, configuring, and administering a Windows NT-based Web site for an organization, and it includes detailed instructions on how to use the software on the CD-ROM to develop the Web site's content—HTML pages, CGI scripts, imagemaps, and so forth.

Price: $49.99 USA/$67.99 CDN   User Level: All Levels
ISBN: 1-57521-047-9   430 pages

Add to Your Sams.net Library Today
with the Best Books for Internet Technologies

ISBN	Quantity	Description of Item	Unit Cost	Total Cost
1-57521-007-X		Netscape 2 Unleashed	$49.99	
1-57521-041-X		The Internet Unleashed, 1996	$49.99	
1-57521-040-1		The World Wide Web Unleashed, 1996	$49.99	
0-672-30745-6		HTML and CGI Unleashed	$49.99	
1-57521-039-8		Presenting Java	$25.00	
1-57521-030-4		Teach Yourself Java in 21 Days	$39.99	
1-57521-009-6		Teach Yourself CGI Programming with Perl in a Week	$39.99	
1-57521-004-5		Teach Yourself Netscape 2 Web Publishing in a Week	$39.99	
1-57521-004-5		The Internet Business Guide, Second Edition	$25.00	
0-672-30718-9		Navigating the Internet, Third Edition	$25.00	
1-57521-064-9		Teach Yourself Web Publishing with HTML 3.0 in a Week, Second Edition	$29.99	
1-57521-005-3		Teach Yourself More Web Publishing with HTML in a Week	$29.99	
1-57521-014-2		Teach Yourself Web Publishing with HTML in 14 Days, Premier Edition	$39.99	
1-57521-072-X		Web Site Construction Kit for Windows 95	$49.99	
1-57521-047-9		Web Site Construction Kit for Windows NT	$49.99	
		Shipping and Handling: See information below.		
		TOTAL		

Shipping and Handling: $4.00 for the first book, and $1.75 for each additional book. If you need to have it NOW, we can ship product to you in 24 hours for an additional charge of approximately $18.00, and you will receive your item overnight or in two days. Overseas shipping and handling adds $2.00. Prices subject to change. Call between 9:00 a.m. and 5:00 p.m. EST for availability and pricing information on latest editions.

201 W. 103rd Street, Indianapolis, Indiana 46290

1-800-428-5331 — Orders   1-800-835-3202 — FAX   1-800-858-7674 — Customer Service

Book ISBN 1-5721-073-8

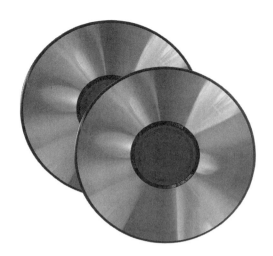

Technical Support from Macmillan

We can't help you with Java problems or software from third parties, but we can assist you if a problem arises with the CD-ROM itself.

E-mail Support: Send e-mail to support@mcp.com.

CompuServe: GO SAMS to reach the Macmillan Computer Publishing forum. Leave us a message, addressed to SYSOP. If you want the message to be private, address it to *SYSOP.

Telephone: (317) 581-3833

Fax: (317) 581-4773

Mail: Macmillan Computer Publishing
Attention: Support Department
201 West 103rd Street
Indianapolis, IN 46290-1093

Here's how to reach us on the Internet:

World Wide Web *(The Macmillan Information SuperLibrary)*
http://www.mcp.com/samsnet

Internet FTP
ftp.mcp.com (/pub/sams)

What's on the Disc

The companion CD-ROM contains the Java™ Development Kit from Sun, other programs mentioned in the book, and many useful examples.

Windows 3.1 or NT Installation Instructions:

1. Insert the CD-ROM disc into your CD-ROM drive.

2. From File Manager or Program Manager, choose Run from the File menu.

3. Type **<drive>CDSETUP** and press Enter, where **<drive>** corresponds to the drive letter of your CD-ROM. For example, if your CD-ROM is drive D:, type **D:CDSETUP** and press enter.

4. Follow the on-screen instructions in the installation program. Files will be installed to a directory named \TYJS, unless you choose a different directory during installation.

CDSETUP creates a Windows program manager group called "TY JavaScript." This group contains icons for exploring the CD-ROM.

Windows 95 Installation Instructions

1. If Windows 95 is installed on your computer and you have the AutoPlay feature enabled, the Guide to the CD-ROM program starts automatically whenever you insert the disc into your CD-ROM drive.

Macintosh Installation Instructions

1. Insert the CD-ROM disc into your CD-ROM drive.

2. When an icon for the CD appears on your desktop, open the disc by double-clicking on its icon.

3. Double-click on the icon named Guide to the CD-ROM, and follow the directions that appear.